There is a disconnect between what we say and what we do. We say we are part of Asia and want the best talent, but our behaviour says the opposite. It's the same with women and meritocracy, we say 'yes' but behaviour says the opposite.

Ann Sherry AO, Chief Executive Officer, Carnival Australia, Sydney, Australia

We are still predominantly white. There are many areas of Australia with little exposure to non-white people. The three main cities, Melbourne, Sydney and Brisbane, have 10 million people where non-Anglo tribes exist. The other 12 million Aussies have little or no exposure to non-white communities. This breeds isolation and xenophobia and increases the fear of 'the teeming masses to the North'. We do integrate very well but only in these three cities.

Bernard Salt, Partner, KPMG, Melbourne, Australia

The obstacles that make it hard for women to move up the corporate ladder are the same obstacles that make it hard for Asians to get up there too. When a senior male executive is about to take an employee to meet one of his best clients he might consider it uncomfortable and somewhat risky to take a woman or someone with an Asian background, because they are different, and therefore take a white male instead.

Diane Grady AM, Non-Executive Director, Macquarie Group, Sydney, Australia

Our government maintains stronger relationships with America than it does with Asia and until now it has been slow to recognise the importance of Asia, as has the education system. The Asian Century Report, which was done with good intent, aims to provide a strategic view on fundamental things like defence, immigration, culture and population. I think Australia is about to embark on a big change agenda to get closer to Asia and we need to get ready to follow.

Mike Smith OBE, Chief Executive Officer, Australian and New Zealand Banking Group, Melbourne, Australia

We need a whole-of-system change. This is no longer a women's issue. It's a societal issue. Two-thirds of women are now breadwinners in their households and there are no systems supporting those who have children too. We still have systems and structures that assume one partner will stay at home.

Ilana Atlas, Non-Executive Director, Coca-Cola Amatil, Sydney, Australia

Stepping Up

昂首挺进

LEAD CULTURE CHANGE FOR DIVERSITY AND GROWTH IN THE ASIAN CENTURY

'My dream is that everyone living in Australia joins the workforce believing that the opportunities are equal, their path to the top meritocratic and the door to positions of power and leadership open.

My belief is that our future prosperity rests on our ability to embrace being part of Asia and our willingness to be more gracious about celebrating the successes of others.'

Pamela Young

© First Edition 2013 Pamela Young
Published by growthcurv Pty Ltd,
PO Box 1512, Neutral Bay Junction,
Sydney, NSW 2088
AUSTRALIA

For information about the book or orders: Phone +612 99092506, Fax +612 99043969, www.growthcurv.com

Edited by Averil Moffat, Sydney Australia
Reviewed by Rod Besant, Sydney Australia
Cover design by Ed. Davad, BusinessMirror, Philippines
Typeset by Russell Jeffery, Sydney, Australia
Printed in China by Asia Pacific Offset Limited
Author photograph by Aran Anderson, Sydney Australia

Cataloguing-in-Publication entry is available from the National Library of Australia at http://catalogue.nla.gov.au/

Author: Young, Pamela
Title: *Stepping Up*: *Lead Culture Change for Diversity and Growth in The Asian Century*
Subjects:
Leadership, leading, leaders,
Diversity, gender equality, cultural diversity,
Growth, Growth in Australia, Australia-Asia relations
Culture, culture change, country culture, organisation culture, individual culture
Social change
Change management

ISBN: 978 0 9874 1200 3 (pbk)

Includes index

www.steppingupaustralia.com

To Beverley and Jack,
my greatest influencers

Dear Jim
Thank you for stepping up
Pamela L.
June 14.

Contents

Part Three: Changing Cultures

Acknowledgments

I now know why people think about writing a book more often than they actually write one. Getting started is phenomenally difficult for first timers, but the journey is also an opportunity for major personal discovery.

My thanks must first go to my mother Beverley, who unfailingly provided loving support until she passed away unexpectedly during the writing of this book and my son, Jack, whose smiling face gives me enormous inspiration and boundless joy every day.

Thanks to Rod Besant who not only agreed to review the book but who also provided above-the-call-of-friendship-duty and support at every stage of the research, writing and production phases. Similarly, thanks to Robert Milliner for reading the book in advance and providing invaluable feedback from the perspective of an experienced and respected CEO and leader with operational knowledge of both Australia and Asia.

Thanks to Bilyana Smith, Julian Canny and Natalie Filatoff for their guidance regarding the book's positioning and branding and thanks also to Stephen Balme for sharing his publishing experience and numerous helpful contacts.

Thanks to Philippa Jones and Celia Chen for preparing the *Stepping Up* title in Chinese characters, to Anne Salier and Caroline Lamb for supporting me as I juggled work and writing with child-care and elder-care, and to Marcie Richards who supported the research and analysis.

Thank you to the 100 leaders, who generously shared their time, experiences observations, insights and advice about diversity and growth in Australia and across Asia. And thank you to Nareen Young, CEO of Diversity Council Australia, Paul O'Sullivan, CEO of Optus and Cai Kjaer, Partner of Optimice for their written contributions to the background research.

Thank you to Averil Moffat, my fabulously talented and experienced editor, Russell Jeffery for laying out the book with such skill and ease, Ed Davad for the stylish cover design and Andrew Shaw for doing a final proof-read over the holidays. Finally, to all those I have not mentioned, but who listened tirelessly to hours and hours of my 'streams of consciousness' about *Stepping Up*, its content and possibilities, thank you.

Preface

Stepping Up is for leaders in business and society who are looking to increase productivity and achieve growth in the Asian Century. By building greater diversity in society and the workplace we can unlock productivity potential that is lying dormant.

Allowing both genders and people of all cultures who live in Australia to fully participate in the workplace will enable us to increase social cohesion, stimulate innovation, boost productivity, raise income levels and thereby improve individual net worth and GDP.

Realising full participation requires that everyone has the same opportunity to be appointed to positions that reflect their skills and experience, reach the level that reflects their performance and capability and be free to climb up the ladder unencumbered without bumping their heads on the glass or bamboo ceilings.

Stepping Up presents economic and social arguments for greater diversity and how the culture changes needed to achieve it are the same changes that would help to boost the growth of our industries and communities. Australia's future and the future prosperity of its people is reliant upon us keeping our nation at the forefront of Western nations and taking advantage of our proximity to, and engagement with, the fastest-growing region of the world.

Stepping Up challenges and empowers leaders to drive culture change to achieve gender and cultural diversity and enable growth. It questions our success at assimilating immigrants and supporting them to build productive careers, at welcoming home expatriates who have been away to gain valuable international experience, and at creating equitable working environments where females can develop and ascend the organisation on merit in the same way as men.

The facts are that relative to many of our global trading partners Australia is challenged by much of this. Australia needs its political leaders and leaders of business and society to collaborate, create a shared vision that will inspire the people of Australia to follow and lead us in culture change to join the more progressive societies of the world.

In this book we look at how greater diversity in society and the workplace requires culture change in the groups we belong to that shape our attitudes and behaviours. We take an in-depth look at three main cultures – country culture, organisation culture and your own culture. We also take a brief look at other cultures that impact us at home and at work such as sports clubs, communities, associations, chambers, universities, schools and places of worship.

This book raises awareness of opportunities and possibilities; provides insight into current issues through the voices of 100 leaders interviewed from across Australia and Asia; and presents readers with culture-change solutions to shift attitudes and adjust behaviours that limit our performance. The voices of the 100 leaders interviewed reflect strong consensus on many key issues and confirm the call for action. At the same time there is some disagreement amongst the leaders, which highlights the disparate nature of our society.

The scope of *Stepping Up* is broad, from leading cultural change to increasing national diversity and advancing Australia's productivity and growth in Asia. It includes discussion about things that impact these ambitions, such as the Australian culture and its values, skills shortages, gender roles and education, women on boards and quotas, multiculturalism and immigrant integration. It also discusses where we should look for leadership on diversity and the pluses and minuses of being an island nation.

Stepping Up provides readers with inspiration, knowledge and motivation to lead change in their community, company, club or clan to help make Australia a more diverse, highly productive and regionally connected country. The potential is enormous.

If you would like to be part of the nationwide community of people who are leading the way to our future, please share your thoughts, initiatives and change projects on www.steppingupaustralia.com. I would also welcome your feedback on the ideas and opinions presented in this book.

The thing the sixties did was to show us the possibilities and the responsibility that we all had. It wasn't the answer. It just gave us a glimpse of the possibility.

John Lennon, (1940-1980) English musician and singer-songwriter with The Beatles

Part One

The Power of Diversity

Part One looks at the need for action on diversity and what diversity in Australia should look like. It explores the benefits provided by greater gender equality and cultural diversity in society and the workplace, and how improved diversity could enhance relations and trade with the fast-growing Asia region.

Chapter 1 looks at the opportunities and possibilities that exist for Australian businesses and society to obtain greater workforce participation and productivity through increased diversity. Chapter 2 introduces the main themes arising from 100 research interviews with leaders from across Australia and Asia to uncover the truth about diversity and growth in Australia. Chapter 3 is a brief sojourn into my global journey discovering diversity and how I had to shift some of my childhood assumptions and biases along the way.

Chapter 1

Taking the Mantle

*'It is a curious thing, Harry, but perhaps those
who are best suited to power are those who
have never sought it. Those who, like you, have
leadership thrust upon them, and take up the
mantle because they must, and find to their own
surprise that they wear it well.'*
J.K. Rowling, Harry Potter and the Deathly Hallows

Leaders, step forward please

Stepping up is about inspiring people with meaning, motivation and the mettle to lead social change in Australia so that diversity becomes a reality in the workplace at all levels. Advancing our culture and improving diversity provides an opportunity to grow our economy and compete more effectively at home in Australia and across Asia in the Asian Century.

You might be a leader with a title and position or you might be a 'natural leader', a person without position or status but who attracts willing followers. Either way, if you have the mantle of 'leader' this book is for you and your followers. It's about achieving social change, diversity, productivity and growth.

Australia is at the crossroads on its growth curve. It has a decision to make. Resist change and face the consequences, or evolve its thinking and take the next step towards prosperity and a better future.

One way to evolve our culture – which would at the same time respond to the massive skills shortage in our economy – is to accept and include both genders and people of all cultural backgrounds equally, in both society and the workplace. This would give us access to *all* the talent and skills available already in the country and help resolve the productivity issues we face. It would also be the right thing to do.

How good would that be? By tapping into the full potential of Australia's working-age population, we could improve the productivity and performance of our businesses, industries and communities and we would also be turning our society into a fairer and more equitable place to live.

It is possible to achieve growth by accepting greater diversity in our workforce. By fully integrating immigrant workers into the workforce and allowing them to rise to the top of our organisations, our leadership teams would be more cross-culturally skilled and better at doing business in fast-growing and emerging Asian countries. If we remove the barriers that cause females to exit the workforce early we will prolong their careers and keep them actively producing in the fields they were trained for. Australia's long-term competitiveness is a reason for changing; resting on our laurels is not a clever option.

I am not alone in my thinking. *Stepping Up* brings you opinions from across Australia and Asia (largely Australian nationals living there) on these matters, which are vital to our growth and future. Here is a small sample of what is to come from the 100 leaders interviewed.

On the Australia–Asia opportunity

Leaders of Australian companies should come to China and have a look. There are a number of senior people who have never been to China in their lives. Where is the intellectual curiosity? There seems to be an indifference and intellectual arrogance.

Dr Geoff Raby, Chief Executive Officer, Geoff Raby & Associates (and former Australian Ambassador to China), Beijing, China

Australia has poor cultural diplomacy and we are being outspent by Europeans who are building soft-power relationships in the Asia region. The current generation of middle managers in Australia have a gap in their education: being able to understand the issues of Asia and knowing how to be part of the Asia region is important. It's not just about languages; it is about understanding the cultures.

Sid Myer AM, Chairman, Myer Family Company, Melbourne, Australia

Australia should have a head start over other Western countries, but it doesn't. There are a lot of German and French investors in China and they have had more time to resolve issues. There are many cultures in the European Union and people from Europe are more culturally aware when they come to China due to their experience in working across many cultures.

Joanne Wood, Chairman, Capital Eight, Shanghai, China

Sometimes we are under the illusion that because everyone in Asia speaks English that we don't need to learn Asian languages. Knowing other languages provides an entree to understanding other cultures. We are at a huge disadvantage with our Asian neighbours who speak English: we have not learned their language or made a collective effort as a nation to engage with them.

Diane Grady AM, Non-Executive Director, Macquarie Group, Sydney, Australia

Expat managers need to be careful that they don't spend all their time trying to make Asian people like us. Australians that come here tend to make the assumption that our ways are better and try and teach them how to do things 'properly'. This can be insulting to Asian people and is not the right way to approach working here.

Andrew Macintosh, Chief Executive Officer, Hanhong Private Equity, Hong Kong, China

Local people in Singapore and Hong Kong say that of all the Western foreigners in the region, the Australians are most difficult to deal with. They say Australians push the view that 'This is how it is done back home so this is how it should be down here'. This view is not appreciated by Asian locals. They say they prefer British and European expats because they find them more empathetic.

Dharma Chandran, Chief Human Resources Officer, Leighton Holdings, Sydney, Australia

On Australia's culture

There is racism in Australia like every other society on earth. It is generally directed to the most recent arrivals. The latest wave of immigrants is the group that attracts the hostility. A bias towards the Greeks and Italians that was present in the 1970s and 1980s has now gone. Now it's directed at the Iraqis and Africans who are coming here. We have never been nervous about the English or the New Zealanders who come in larger numbers because they have similar cultural origins to us.

Hugh Mackay, Social Researcher and Writer, Sydney, Australia

In the city there are some people who are passionate about diversity and are doing it, some who want to make the change but have no idea how to go about it, some who have unconscious bias; and the last group are just not interested.

Catriona Noble, Chief Executive Officer, McDonald's Australia, Sydney, Australia

It is supposed to be egalitarian here, yet there are few less egalitarian places in the world. The first thing people ask is "What school did you go to?" and "Where do you live?" so that they can categorise you.

Mike Smith OBE, Chief Executive Officer, Australian and New Zealand Banking Group, Melbourne, Australia

People go overseas to broaden themselves and broaden their skills. Australians and New Zealanders excel because they are more competitive. They are ambitious. Aussies who move overseas grow. They grow in a bigger marketplace and then they worry about coming back as it is smaller. If we want to minimise the brain drain we are facing in Australia, we have to make it easier for expats to come home – we need to support them to get back into their profession and communities.

Stephen Roberts, Chief Country Officer, Citi, Australia and New Zealand, Sydney, Australia

When people come to Australia we like them to appreciate our culture as a mark of respect and dignity. This works both ways. Here we are down at the end of the world and we need to cultivate relationships. The young Asians who come here are highly ambitious and I would like to see more people from our firm in Asia come and work in Australia; we could learn a lot from them. The growing importance of the region was illustrated at a recent financial services conference I went to where one speaker delivered in Mandarin; that was a wake-up call for all of us.

Jenny Parker, Office Managing Partner, Ernst & Young Global, Queensland, Australia

On gender diversity

If I were a chairman on an ASX board and I saw 12 men looking at me, I would be very worried as it wouldn't reflect the population. Having the right people on the board with the right skills is what is important and you have to work hard at it. The reality is that it is an old boys club and they haven't worked hard at it. The chair and the CEO should have to explain why it looks nothing like the world that they are operating in. If you had to do that for a few years it would fix itself.

Paul Waterman, President, BP Australia, Melbourne, Australia

The unfairness rattles me. The discrimination goes from the 'incredibly obvious' to the 'more subtle'. Women often get told 'We like what you do, but temperamentally you are not right for the job'. Then there was the active resistance to change. Women going on maternity leave used to be retrenched. Then male managers tried to adopt the language of change and started talking about 'including women' but they also made demeaning remarks behind their backs to protect the status quo. How long do we put up with this?

Ann Sherry AO, Chief Executive Officer, Carnival Australia, Sydney, Australia

Unless you have quotas, it is not going to happen. Quotas make you think differently. You will be motivated to allocate resources to find, train and retain the right people. You will talk more about the issues and seek to make others aware. You need to be clear that it is not just about women or gender, it is about diversity and its benefits.

Craig Drummond, Chief Executive Officer, Bank of America Merrill Lynch, Sydney, Australia

I really dislike that males are mentoring females. This so-called mentoring is really about the men getting to know the women and being prepared to say that they can do the job and 'backing them'. It's about making baby-boomer males more comfortable as they have not worked with women before. Luckily, Gen X men have more experience with women and are better with them.

Shirley In't Veld, Non-Executive Director, Asciano, Perth, Australia

Stepping Up begins with why we don't have broad diversity in our businesses and societies already and what has stopped it from occurring. Then we discuss how greater diversity can boost productivity and growth, what changes are required and how to put those changes in place.

I explore the reasons why diversity is not yet a reality in Australia, and the source of our growth challenges and opportunities, with 100 leaders from across Australia and Asia. Their insights are presented throughout this book. Australia's culture and the hidden forces that hold the status quo in place were cited as the primary reasons for many of the challenges and in the following pages I explore why this is so and how to free up our thinking to move forward. The findings from the 100 leaders are compelling. They will get you thinking about what Australia needs to do to step up and move forward.

To get forward movement and real development, Australia's culture must evolve. If we respond to external economic and market changes by making internal adjustments to our cultural assumptions, values and behaviours we can adapt to the changes as they occur. That way we keep ahead of the curve. Continuous evolution of our culture in response to the needs of society and business is the ticket to full employment and a full pay cheque.

Stepping Up seeks to draw out the inspired and enthusiastic among you to be part of the change needed to move Australia ahead. Whether you are a leader with a position title or a 'natural leader' you don't need an invitation to step up; sometimes it is okay to give yourself permission to get involved. If you believe in something enough, you can just do it.

As you read on, you might think about people you know who could be waiting for your permission to step up in your business or community. Once you identify them, find a way to get them involved.

Economic and social gains

Stepping Up is designed to support Australia's leaders to access skills and talent, improve productivity and take advantage of the growth in Asia by increasing cultural and gender diversity in Australian communities and workplaces. To achieve this we need culture change. Why? Because the economic and social consequences will have long-term effects on Australia's standing in the world. Our continued viability, growth and wealth are all compromised under the current scenario.

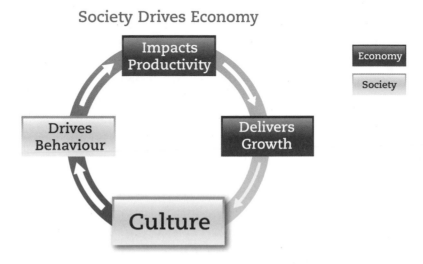

The economic argument

Skills shortages and productivity wastage cause our businesses and communities to suffer socially and financially. Likewise, our lackadaisical attitude to the rapid and radical change in the Asia region, which is due to high growth rates of most of its nations, is threatening the competitiveness of our workforce and national economy in the globalising world.

Our close alliance with the United Kingdom and America, which have been economically challenged since 2008, will have less benefit to us in the future as the centre of growth and world trade will shift to the Asia region.

During this same period Asian nations have continued to climb – albeit at a slower rate than the early 2000s. But their growth rates remain 2–3 times higher than most Western nations and that makes us uncomfortable because these new world leaders are not Western and we don't understand them so well.

By more actively engaging in the growth in Asia and by improving our own productivity through greater diversity we can begin to address the current and future economic challenges. Metaphorically speaking, we need to move closer to Asia and start to look and feel more Asian friendly.

To prepare our nation to grow both internally and across Asia, we need to unblock the cultural constraints that limit our performance. By removing the barriers to full participation and productivity of both genders and all cultures we evolve our culture, remove the waste in our society and secure our place, and reputation, in the region.

The social argument

Australia is a very traditional and conservative society and is at risk of losing sight of a strength that once made it strong – courage in adversity. Early settlers faced hardship, danger and challenge every day and what made them strong was their independence and ability to go it alone. But, as inheritors of that attitude, our self-sufficiency has also made us introspective, protective and in many ways exclusive. This is evident in the way we let people from other nations and cultures into Australia to live, but then limit their role in society until they have adjusted fully to our way of life and have earned their right to a fair go. Australia may be multicultural in terms of the nationalities that live here, but there is little cultural diversity among leaders of industry or society.

Our independence and 'go it alone' behaviour also affects our reaction to the growth in Asia – a reaction that has, to date, been slow. Other nations, both in the East and West, have been making adjustments to global shifts of power, wealth, consumer demand, market reach, knowledge, technology and language for some time, yet the Australian Government didn't release a statement about its response to the Asian opportunity until October 2012. Our lack of urgency or willingness to roll up our sleeves and get involved in Asia's development is concerning.

There is another thing that we could do better – gender equality. It took until 2010 for a female to become Prime Minister (which is 31 years after the United Kingdom, 24 years after the Philippines and Norway and 13 years after New Zealand). And the facts about the inequality of women at work, on boards, in leadership roles and in society generally are readily available. Political leadership strongly influences behaviour in our society so it is surprising there has not been more focus from that sector on the problem of gender equality.

It's time for change

The pace of change is in many cases faster elsewhere than in Australia and we could slip off the radar of our northern hemisphere allies and neighbours and become irrelevant. What are our chances of maintaining our position when we live far, far away, in a monolingual society, isolated and independent and when the advancing world is multilingual, collaborative and physically connected?

Opportunity is all around us. Perhaps it's time to employ some of the other strengths early settlers in Australia used for survival in the 1800s – adaptability, flexibility and creativity. If we did, we could make significant social change, which would lead to economic benefits as the diagram above suggests. By freeing up our thinking and visualising a more socially progressive and economically connected Australia in 2025 we would be taking the first step to joining leading nations in a new world.

Getting people of all cultures and both genders into top levels of Australian government, business and society can deliver great benefit and prosperity to everyone living in Australia, not just a protected few. It would also prepare us for demanding a leading position in Asia's growth journey.

Throughout this book I explore the relationships between cultures, performance, productivity and growth. I explore how our nation's culture influences our organisations' cultures and how that impacts business outcomes. I draw conclusions that have us looking critically at the role of government in leading social change and encouraging cultural evolution, without which people in our communities will fail to integrate fully and our local industries and businesses will struggle to reach their full potential.

I asked 100 leaders from across Australia and Asia whether they agreed with the idea that greater diversity is a major lever to our growth and whether social change through cultural evolution is the best way to enable this. Their opinions and advice are presented throughout this book.

Acceptance and inclusion boosts participation

The reason why we need greater acceptance and inclusion of both genders and all cultures in society is to improve diversity at work. Greater diversity can lead to improved workforce participation and that can boost productivity. By improving the output of local businesses, we increase Australian GDP and that can strengthen our position in the world and make us more competitive in the Asia region. When that happens everyone gains.

When businesses do well, workers earn better incomes. When incomes are up, spending increases and that keeps the economic cycle going. Also, by increasing diversity and social equality we reinvest in our dream of being an egalitarian society, a dream that sometimes seems to have been lost.

Australia has outstanding benefits – great climate, boundless natural resources, relative wealth, and accomplished people – that ought to secure our growth. We should guard against them being undermined by cultural challenges that limit the diversity of our workforce and the level of our productivity.

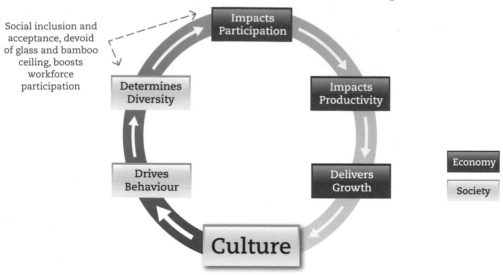

Society Drives Economy
...and Diversity Boosts Workforce Participation

High productivity is hard to maintain in developed nations like Australia that have maturing markets, rigid systems, increased competition from emerging economies, rapidly changing technology, a mobile labour force (which can and does move to other countries) and an ageing workforce and population. The key to our growth and survival must therefore be a strategy for obtaining the greatest productivity possible.

By improving gender and cultural workforce participation our productivity improves, which positively impacts our competitiveness and trading performance with other nations. This is extremely important for Australia's future because our continued growth will be determined by our ability to operate effectively in Asia, our closest neighbour and the fastest-growing region of the world.

The 21st century is increasingly being referred to as 'the Asian Century' due to the region's expected high growth rates and possible dominance of economic and geopolitical matters. In the chapters that follow I explore how Australia can take advantage of its proximity and history with the nations of Asia and how greater cultural diversity can be used to build Asia-capability and improve business performance in the region.

Full participation boosts productivity

How can greater diversity help Australia and its businesses to be fully productive and thereby reach their growth potential? The answer is twofold:

Remove the skills wastage

Firstly, greater diversity can help to eliminate the skills wastage in the Australian economy. Did you know there are people everywhere who are under-utilised due to cultural barriers and systemic constraints that often make inclusion difficult? Imagine if we could find and remove those obstructions.

Who are these people who are not fully participating? They are:

- women who would like to return to work after having children but can't find a flexible option;
- women who experience discrimination and the glass ceiling which limit how far up the career ladder they can go;
- women who become frustrated with a macho organisation culture and opt out of mainstream employment in favour of self-employment (which may or may not fully utilise their time, training or experience);
- immigrants who have come here with degree qualifications from their home country that our government won't recognise;
- non-Anglo-Saxon second and third generation Australians who experience discrimination and the bamboo ceiling, which limits how far up the career ladder they can go;
- asylum seekers who are impounded, draining GDP due to costs of housing, security, food and healthcare when they could be adding to the economy with temporary work visas that enable them to support struggling industries and communities while being processed;
- returning expatriates who, after many years overseas obtaining global experience, find it difficult to get back into the 'in' group.

Our challenge is to stimulate a shift in the assumptions that formed the values and beliefs of the Australian culture, influencing the daily behaviour of people in business and society that lead to this skills wastage. It can be changed. Nothing is impossible. The question is do we have the will to change it?

If we accept that women today are well educated and that they hold half the intellect, then as a society we need to find a way to tap into it. If productivity is an issue for Australia, then why would we leave the talent sitting at home when it could be utilised?

Stephen Roberts, Chief Country Officer, Citi, Australia and New Zealand, Sydney, Australia

The young Asians who come here are highly ambitious and I would like to see more people from our firm in Asia come and work in Australia; we could learn a lot from them.

Jenny Parker, Office Managing Partner, Ernst & Young Global, Queensland, Australia

We need a whole-of-system change. This is no longer a women's issue. It's a societal issue. Two-thirds of women are now breadwinners in their households and there are no systems supporting those who have children too. We still have systems and structures that assume one partner will stay at home.

Ilana Atlas, Non-Executive Director, Coca-Cola Amatil, Sydney, Australia

Having people from different cultures working in one company is very beneficial; it delivers skills from other countries and it gets the best out of everybody.

Gabriel Yam, Managing Partner, Arup Group, Hong Kong, China

I am comfortable explaining diversity from a productivity point of view. We have an ageing and shrinking workforce so we need everyone who is able to participate to do so. Women do well at school and university so why would we leave them out of the workforce? We need more people, we need migrants, and we need our regional neighbours.

Katie Lahey, Chief Executive Officer, Korn Ferry, Sydney, Australia

Close the gap with Asia

Secondly, greater diversity can help Australia take advantage of the growth opportunity that is available to us in the north. Our closest neighbours in Asia are opening up their thriving and fast-growing markets to other countries and foreign businesses. We can be among those who respond to their need for infrastructure development, professional, health and education services, and food and energy resources.

Australia has advantages in Asia over many other developed countries. It's geographically closer than other developed Western nations, there are existing economic and political relations and most countries have similar time zones. To be effective in the Asian region you need to be able to connect culturally and socially. Findings of the research I undertook for this book indicate that we are not there yet. However, Australia is fortunate to have very large Asian populations living in many of its cities and it could seek closer assimilation with Asian immigrants as they are well-placed to help build relationships across the region.

When people come to Australia we like them to appreciate our culture as it is a mark of respect and dignity. This works both ways.

Jenny Parker, Office Managing Partner, Ernst & Young Global, Queensland, Australia

We need our government to reinforce the importance of Australia's relationship with Asia, parents to push for Asian languages for their children in schools and business leaders to place importance on Asian languages and literacy skills in workers.

Sid Myer AM, Chairman, Myer Family Company, Melbourne, Australia

Tourists arriving in Australia are expected to increase from 6 million per annum to 25 million per annum within 10 years. Over half of the 25 million will be Chinese yet we are not planning or developing our language or cultural understanding. We adapted more to the Japanese inbound traffic in the 1980s. The Chinese will exceed New Zealanders as the top visitors and tourism revenues will become greater than the entire minerals exports.

Phil Ruthven, Chairman, IBIS World, Melbourne, Australia

Achieving greater cultural and gender diversity in business and society will prepare us to take advantage of the growth opportunities of the Asia region. Full workforce participation by people of all cultural backgrounds and both genders will increase diversity, address the skills shortage, boost productivity and close the cultural gap that limits our growth and economic performance with Asian nations.

(There are also other groups of people who are not fully employed due to bias, discrimination or system constraints and they include the disabled, aged and LGBT communities. However, this book is limited to cultural and gender diversity related opportunities only.)

Clarifying 'full participation'

'Full participation' means a person's potential relative to their level of education, skill, experience and capacity to work. Across Australia we have groups of people who are under-utilised because they are operating at levels below their education, skill, experience or capacity due to reasons that include:

- bias – conscious or unconscious;
- racial or sexual discrimination;
- a structure, system or policy;
- lack of flexibility, support or opportunity.

Others are working less than a full week or not working at all for a variety of reasons that include:

- our historical belief that you need to physically 'be' at the place of work to be working effectively;
- rigid beliefs and systems that prohibit flexible time;
- the belief that some jobs cannot be performed part-time because customers and clients want and expect access to their key contact every day.

To be free of bias or discrimination so that you can work to your 'fullest' level means:

- to be able to put yourself forward for any promotion or position regardless of gender, race, ethnicity, religion, first language or other difference;
- to be considered for promotion on the basis of merit, with transparency and without bias in the selection process or panel;
- to experience no compromise to information, opportunity or reward when working less than full-time hours and to be treated as fairly as full-time employees;
- to be afforded the same opportunity as others whether or not you are female, have children, have a non-Australian accent, are an immigrant, have coloured skin, are single, studied abroad, have been working abroad for a long period;
- to be able to apply for and expect equal rights to a position on the top team based on merit and *not* to have to fit the narrow criteria of the most prevalent homogenous groups;
- to be able to utilise training and qualifications obtained in other countries or places;
- to be recognised for your experience acquired in other countries or places.

If we have vast numbers of people who are not working to their personal capacity, then a portion of our society is disengaged and not fully utilised, which means the country and local businesses are operating below capacity and not reaching their optimum levels of productivity.

Culture: A blocker or enabler?

Culture can be both a blocker and an enabler. If your culture is not aligned with where you want to go or what you want to achieve, it can create significant resistance and frustrate progress. But when your culture is aligned with your future ambition and objectives, it can create unimaginable momentum by inspiring your people and propelling them forward.

Productivity in Australia can be increased by getting more women to remain in the career they were trained for; returning after taking maternity or other extended leave and progressing into higher positions in business. To achieve this we need to remove systemic barriers and behavioural biases. All of this requires a change in the elements of the culture that holds these constraints in place – starting with assumptions.

By valuing more highly the current and future roles of women and men in society and changing the way we socialise and educate our children – who form early notions about who they ought to be by modelling themselves on who they see – we can create workplaces and environments that encourage women to reach higher positions. To achieve this, Australians must rethink and confirm what's important for the country, its businesses and its people.

Similarly, productivity can also be increased by a greater integration of non-Anglo-Saxon populations living within Australia and their rise into business leadership and decision-making roles across industry and society. To achieve this, it will require the people in power to accept the values, beliefs and behaviours of people from different cultural backgrounds and for both parties to work together in cross-cultural teams and be more effective with our regional and global partners. Again this will require the people living in Australia to rethink and confirm what is important for our future success.

There are other commercial benefits associated with achieving higher productivity through greater diversity. They include greater contribution to the economy through more people working more hours; (who then earn) higher salaries generating more wealth; improved creativity and innovation; ability to attract more skilled labour and investment dollars; recognition from global markets of our leadership in diversity and our ability to manage social change effectively.

As agreed by a majority of the leaders interviewed, encouraging a shift in Australia's culture is key to achieving the changes we need as a nation. To achieve this, the people of Australia would have to agree on the future vision for the country; articulate its short, medium and long-term ambitions; restate what they value and adjust their assumptions that drive their behaviour. If this is to occur, people at all levels need to step up and lead.

Culture can generate attitudes and behaviour that support or reject an idea. The secret is always to be on the lookout for the direction in which it is heading. If you can identify assumptions you can generally determine which way your people are travelling, and redirecting them is a whole lot easier when you know where they have come from.

The Culture Iceberg

My work with culture started back in the mid-1980s and in the chapters below I outline the learning and observations arising from an international career specialising in strategy and culture change. I share stories from New Zealand, Singapore, the United Kingdom, across continental Europe and Australia.

Along the way I introduce a simple metaphor – the iceberg – because it expresses much about how cultures form and operate. Over the years I have used this concept in many different countries and companies and it travels across cultures.

Culture is like an Iceberg

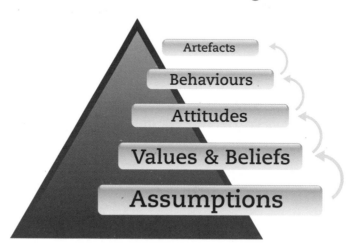

The iceberg's formation, structure and behaviour and its similarity to how cultures operate are detailed throughout Chapters 8–11 and I use it to explain the three main cultures which influence our lives:

- National Culture - how a country's culture influences the way people lead in business and behave in society and how we can influence the direction in which it is drifting;
- Individual Culture - how we behave at work and in society; why and how we modify it over time;
- Organisational Culture - why organisations' cultures differ, how they impact performance and how we align them to strategies and goals.

Each country, company and person has a unique culture that cannot be replicated. As we explore the opportunities that exist between Asian countries and Australia, we will discuss the differences between Eastern and Western cultures and how they impact our trade, foreign direct investment, tourism, immigration and relations.

The similarity between an iceberg and all three kinds of culture are fully explained below and we look at how to influence a shift in cultures so that they move in the direction we want them to go.

The Culture Circuit

A nation's culture affects the way communities, families and individuals live within it, and vice versa. People carry their assumptions, values, attitudes and behaviour preferences to work, their sports clubs, social occasions and even overseas when they travel abroad. These elements of an individual culture in turn influence the organisation culture of the clubs, communities, schools, businesses and societies to which they belong – so there is a circular motion to the effects of culture.

The bigger a cultural group, the greater its influence. Country culture and industry cultures therefore dominate organisation cultures in the same way that community and family cultures have an influence over our individual cultures. We will explore each type of culture and learn how to influence them in Part Three.

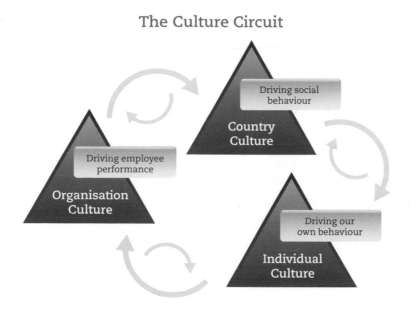

The Culture Circuit

Leadership and followship

You know that you are a natural leader when you have people following you. Friends and colleagues gather around you, they seek you out and ask your opinion and respect your advice.

Followers gravitate to people who have vision, integrity and the courage to speak their mind. These leaders don't necessarily seek the role of leadership, sometimes it just arrives. We feel safe around people who are brave because they give us a sense of taking charge and being prepared to resolve problems as they occur.

Stepping Up explores who we should expect to lead Australia's culture change and prepare our nation to achieve diversity and to take advantage of the growth in Asia. Communities and businesses in Australia have 'appointed' leaders, but it seems that they are challenged in their obligation to lead the necessary changes to achieve productivity and growth, for both have stalled. Everyone seems to be pointing the finger at everyone else, hoping someone else will address the problem.

I asked the 100 leaders interviewed who should lead this social change, how do we get people to follow and whether we can ask Australians to engage in a debate about critical issues affecting gender and cultural diversity. Critical issues like: national culture and values; gender roles at work and home; quotas for women at work; a 'melting-pot' immigrant integration policy versus our 'embracing difference' policy; and whether or not the people of Australia should expect more from their leaders.

100 leaders contribute

One hundred leaders from across Australia, Asia and further afield were interviewed to provide a basis for discussion about the issues and opportunities for Australia, its communities and businesses in the Asian Century.

The research data was acquired through intensive, qualitative semi-structured interviews averaging 2.5 hours with people aged between 35 and 70 (which included Gen X, baby boomers and post-boomers). The interviews were mostly face-to-face but some were by telephone. I recorded 16,000 lines of interview notes over 12 months.

The gender mix of the 100 leaders is 48 male to 52 female and they are of mixed ethnicity, race, and religion. The countries whose cultures they associate with, other than Australia, include New Zealand, South Africa, Kenya, Malta, England, Ireland, Italy, Greece, Poland, Germany, Norway, Russia, America, India, Sri Lanka, Malaysia, China, Hong Kong, Indonesia and Vietnam.

The people were located in 16 cities:

Adelaide	Kuala Lumpur	Singapore
Beijing	London	Sydney
Brisbane	Melbourne	Tokyo
Canberra	Oslo	Toowoomba
Ho Chi Minh	Perth	
Hong Kong	Shanghai	

And they represent 26 industries:

Accounting	Government	Publishing
Armed services	Hospitality	Public policy
Banking & finance	Insurance	Research
Consulting	Legal	Retail
Education	Manufacturing	Supply chain
Engineering	Media	Technology
Energy	Medicine	Telecommunications
Executive search	Mining & resources	Tourism
Food and beverage	Not-for-profit	

Each quote recorded in these pages has the name of the contributor being quoted, their title and company, followed by the city and country in which they live (this is not their geographic responsibility). A full list of names and a brief biography is included in Appendix I.

Approach to reading *Stepping Up*

The insights of the 100 leaders and the culture change frameworks contained in *Stepping Up* provide you with ideas to move your cultures forward by leading change. It is written with many audiences in mind because the benefits of advancing Australia's culture – achieving diversity, full participation and productivity, being able to work across Asia and securing our place in the world – are for everyone.

You can approach reading this book in several ways:

- As a business leader or member of the workforce wanting to understand economic and social issues impacting your company, career, income and economic future and to identify opportunities to engage more with Australian and Asian businesses;
- As a leader or potential leader in society – including politics and communities – looking to identify, explain and resolve economic and social issues that limit the nation and its people from realising their dreams and enjoying full and happy lives;
- As an individual who believes (or wants to believe) that Australia is capable of much more and who is willing to help lead change but is looking for clarity and understanding of the many complex issues and opportunities ahead of us.

In my experience, culture changes constantly so it is a shifting target, it involves chaos and it is rarely containable. Like the Iceberg, it's drifting; stopping it or controlling it is impossible. So you need to get comfortable with chaos, rely on your vision and trust your gut.

Down-under we have a worldwide reputation for being tenacious, outgoing and capable. So let's put that reputation into action and step up together to make this happen!

A rich collection of views

One hundred very generous leaders gave many hours of time to share their experiences, observations and advice. I would like to ask that you read their stories with an open mind and be careful not to assess their contribution as right or wrong. It helps to recognise that what we are dealing with in Australia is disparate thinking on some pretty sensitive issues and that these 100 people have participated in this project to help move conversations along by sharing their experiences.

I have selected quotes that illustrate a variety of views to demonstrate the different values held by people in our society. Opinions are polarised on many issues and you don't even need to read all the quotes to gain an understanding of how broad and varied the views are.

When you read these comments side-by-side you might be tempted to make a judgment about the person whose view is different from your own. But everyone is entitled to a view and each person's perspective will differ according to their background.

I trust you will enjoy the read and I would appreciate your feedback along the way. You can share your thoughts or ask questions at www.steppingupaustralia. com any time by either sending me a private email or joining in conversations with other interested people – leaders and followers alike.

Navigate your way

In the next chapter I set the scene by introducing the main themes arising from the interviews. Each of these is then expanded in Part 2, but before diving into them, I outline in Chapter 3 the personal journey I took to understand cultures and discover diversity. This chapter provides insight into the development of the thesis of this book.

Navigate your way

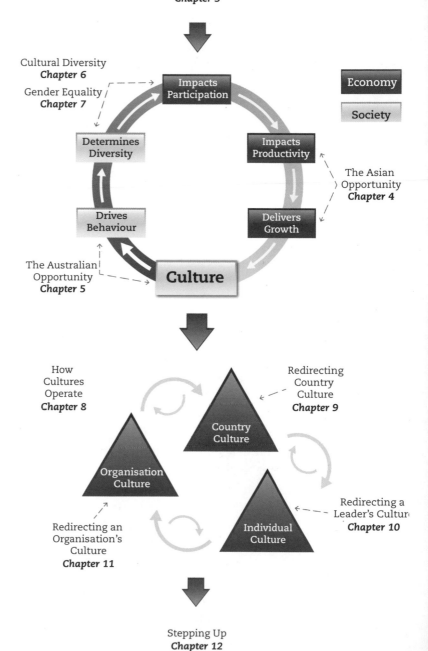

Chapter 2

Listening

A wise old owl sat on an oak;
The more he saw, the less he spoke;
The less he spoke, the more he heard;
Why aren't we like that wise old bird?
Chinese Proverb

100 leaders share their stories

When I began planning this book it seemed essential to do some listening. I wanted to test my assumptions, get a feeling for how to convey my observations to readers relevantly and be sure that my ideas about achieving greater diversity would be presented usefully.

That meant I needed to hear stories from people affected by diversity in Australia. Specifically I needed to understand their perceptions, dilemmas and challenges and to gain greater insight into some of the uniquely Australian attitudes, behaviours and norms. I began to develop a list of people to talk with and set a target of 100 interviews because that is generally thought to be the number at which research findings are statistically sound.

Now I have listened to the views and opinions of 100 leaders who are observers and influencers from 26 industries and 16 cities across Australia, Asia and further afield. Many of these generous people I needed to meet with twice. Thankfully I can say that most of the people I spoke with have a commonly held view that *it is possible* to realise greater productivity, growth and prosperity by achieving greater diversity in business and society.

The voices of the 100 leaders are presented throughout this book. There are also a number of personal stories and three company cases that illustrate how they achieved culture change to build more diverse top teams.

The 100 leaders offer opinions and advice on many topics. Some people are championing Asia–Australian relations:

Australia can only be successful if linked to the growth of Asia. Australian business, like it or not, is driven by global demand and supply. Much of the demand is coming out of Asia and we are in a good space to benefit from that. Asia is where the new markets are and where the growth is. I am struck by the lack of cultural awareness between Australia and its Asian neighbours. Our culture is still drawn from the UK and Western European countries and we still have more in common culturally with the USA than with our neighbours in Asia.

Mike Smith OBE, Chief Executive Officer, Australian and New Zealand Banking Group, Melbourne, Australia

Other people question the practices that disadvantage women:

Most organisations nowadays have women somewhere in their pipeline but for some reason they (the executives) say they are not ready. Why is that?

Uschi Schreiber, Managing Partner - Global Government & Public Sector Industry Centre, Ernst & Young Global, Sydney, Australia

I don't know how a man can walk into a boardroom with 10 others that look like him and not feel like a fraud. If you want to promote your buddy, okay, but don't then say you are all about meritocracy. How can they do that?

Paul Waterman, President. BP Australia, Melbourne, Australia

A few identify unfairness towards immigrants and non-white employees:

Racism is not necessarily noticed at school and it is not overt in the workplace. But there is definitely bias. People with accented English rarely get promotion. The arguments for not promoting them would go something like this is, 'You do not understand how the Australian culture works so therefore you wouldn't be able to do the job as well as … [another candidate].'

Dharma Chandran, Chief Human Resources Officer, Leighton Holdings, Sydney, Australia

And others identify parochial behaviours that limit foreigners and returning Australian expats from being accepted by peers and colleagues in the workplace:

We had been overseas for 17 years and when we returned we felt more foreign in our homeland than we were as Australians living in Asia or Europe. When you come back you are treated like 'a transient' and there is insufficient effort made to embrace you back into the community. It makes cultural adjustment more difficult than it needs to be. It must be much worse for experienced professionals who are not Australian.

Stephen Roberts, Chief Country Officer, Citi, Australia and New Zealand, Sydney, Australia

Australia can be a fairly closed society and international experience is often not well-rewarded. I know people with significant experience in working with global companies across many countries who have had to wait up to two years to get a job here.

Diane Grady AM, Non-Executive Director, Macquarie Group, Sydney, Australia

Key research themes

This book is heavily flavoured with the views of others. Quotes from the 100 leaders are presented in themes relating to the topic of each chapter. But to give you a sense of what is to come, here are a few quotes that I have categorised into five areas:

- Can Australia grow through Asia?
- Does Australian culture impact growth?
- Cultural diversity and the opportunities
- Gender diversity and the opportunities
- Future development of Australian society

Can Australia grow through Asia?

The first series of questions I explored with the 100 leaders were about our current and future relations with Asia, our interest in and commitment to being a more integral part of Asia, whether we were effectively engaging with Asian countries for development and trade purposes, to what extent Asian immigrants to Australia were integrated into society and how much are we tapping into the cultural insights and language abilities that Asian immigrants bring with them. Two key messages emerged:

Our role and growth potential

Some companies in Australia are struggling to grow: they are running out of runway in Australia and many industries are looking to see where they can find growth. It is obvious where they have to look. Asia is a growth market, it has greater depth than our own but it needs our know-how. We don't have to break the relationships we have, we just need to have more of them.

David Gonski AC, Chairman, Future Fund of Australia, Sydney, Australia

The idea that any country can survive on its domestic economy alone does not exist anymore.

Uschi Schreiber, Managing Partner - Global Government & Public Sector Industry Centre, Ernst & Young Global, Sydney, Australia

If your business plan or horizon is limited to Australia, then you wouldn't recognise the need for other skills in your organisation. Australian businesses need to think of themselves as a regional partner not a national participant: small and modest companies think of themselves as Australian businesses. I'd encourage them to think of themselves as a participant in a business region that includes Asia, not just Australia.

Sid Myer AM, Chairman, Myer Family Company, Melbourne, Australia

Australia may not have the viability of a major US or European multinational, but we do have impact and presence because of China's dependence on Australian resources. Until this year China's demand has been for mining and metals but it requires food and food security and is fast becoming a net importer of soy, rice, cooking oil, pork and corn. You hear stories about them buying dairy cooperatives and they are also looking at meat industries. Australia and Brazil have land with the potential for plantation and this is an opportunity for primary industry. Why are Australian businesses not in China? The opportunities are enormous and yet they are still geared towards the US markets.

Joanne Wood, Chairman, Capital Eight, Shanghai, China

Languages and cultural know-how

Learning Asian languages is a serious issue for Australia. Asian languages are important firstly for economic and commercial reasons and secondly for better integration with the region. Inbound tourists are likely to increase from the current 6 million per annum to 25 million per annum by 2020. Over half of the 25 million will be Chinese and we are not planning or developing our Asian languages or cultural understanding. The income from this tourism will become greater than our entire minerals exports and our fastest growing exports are services not goods. We need to improve our cross-cultural and language understanding to effectively export education, health and tourism to the region.

Phil Ruthven, Chairman, IBIS World, Melbourne, Australia

Australia's political leaders should explain why Chinese investment is overwhelmingly in Australia's interest, put in place some scholarships for undergraduates and properly fund cultural exchange and language programs. Considering the tax revenues we receive from China and the 138,000 Chinese students studying in Australia each year, we need to acknowledge where our interests lie. You can't deny the global numbers or how complementary our economy is with the rest of Asia.

> Dr Geoff Raby, Chief Executive Officer, Geoff Raby & Associates (and former Australian Ambassador to China), Beijing, China

We need it to become 'cool' to speak Asian languages. In 20 to 30 years from now Indonesia will be very important to Australia with over 1 billion people living right next door. We should have the debate about compulsory language, or at least encourage and incentivise foreign language learning.

> Robert Milliner, Former Chief Executive Partner, Mallesons Stephen Jaques (now King & Wood Mallesons), Sydney, Australia

Sydney is an Asian city with 400,000 Chinese people living here and yet we don't meet many of those Chinese people in the businesses I am involved in. We are wasting resources by not harnessing the talent that is here.

> Kevin McCann, Chairman, Macquarie Group, Sydney, Australia

Impact of Australia's culture on growth

The second series of questions I explored were about Australian culture and what values people identified with. I wanted to know how people felt about what they observed in their communities and workplaces and to what extent the values held today, impacted on the country's, and their own company's, ability to grow. Here is what a few people said about Australian culture, values, attitudes and behaviours:

Let's question gender roles

Having one 'stay at home' parent is such a binary concept. It is a concept that was developed 200 years ago and it no longer works for us. It really does affect Australia's productivity and participation rates of women. How do we get a more flexible work infrastructure? There are some significant decisions that require policy debate. Why are there not more people talking about this?

> Ilana Atlas, Non-Executive Director, Coca-Cola Amatil, Sydney, Australia

Australia's culture is very blokey and this has a direct impact on how organisations operate. We need societal change. It's not just males, but females perpetuate it too. It's about the roles people take on at an early age. It is perpetuated in schools and we need to look at education. We should also look at roles and domestic responsibilities at home, in the family context. We are talking about long-term change and we need urgency for change.

Dr Jacqui Abbott, Head of Flexibility and Diversity, Allens Arthur Robinson, Sydney, Australia

Having come from a very feminist background with a strong belief that women should work, I am reasonably surprised at the number of women who have children and then no longer work. I don't know the causes for that: no doubt it is largely elective. I think it is a bad example for children and, as a society, that is a disappointing trend. I think it is a good example for children to see people maintain a presence in the work environment. My mother was a teacher and worked throughout her life returning to full-time when I was nine. Having a mother who works makes you appreciate the importance of education. I explain to my children that having a career and staying in work helps you to maintain your security, it gives you a certain amount of self-esteem, it provides you a life outside the home through which you received positive reinforcement and your interests become more diverse. Children should be encouraged to do this.

Jane Owen, Partner, Middletons, Sydney, Australia

Let's change policies and systems

With regard to child care, why couldn't we provide jobs to Indonesians and other Asians who would like to come here to work? After my time with Dick Smith India, I would have loved to have brought back my maid for a couple of years to enjoy the environment. But the government would not allow me to bring her. Those of us who have lived overseas don't understand why our government won't let them in. It's an absolute shame that we don't recognise the huge benefit it would provide (to the women of Australia). People might say that going back to work might affect the kids. This is not so. My daughter said to me one day 'Mum you always worried about being late for things. That never worried us and I only ever wanted to be like you".

Debra Singh, Former General Manager, Dick Smith, Sydney, Australia

The single most important thing Australia could do (in support of gender diversity) is to free up the immigration laws to allow nannies to come and work here, but the culture will get in the way. Unions will object to bringing in people on temporary visas to do the low-skilled work.

Graham Bradley AM, Chairman, Stockland, Sydney, Australia

The thing that will sustain diversity is a cultural shift to flexible work. Acceptance that everybody will have flexible work and balance is required. If everybody is working then we need flexibility to share the load at home.

Jillian Segal AM, Non-Executive Director, National Australia Bank, Sydney, Australia

Let's give women a 'fair go'

Family is huge in our culture and fairness is extremely important to Australian people so it is ironic that they don't see the unfairness of the treatment of women.

Natalie Filatoff, Principal, Filatoff Editorial and Writing, Sydney, Australia

It's a tough gig. Women have to have a toughness to get to the top in a male environment but then they get criticised for it. They get called 'aggressive'. Women are perceived not to have experience for a job, so they don't get the job and then they don't get more experience. We have to break the cycle. Men need a different view about what talent looks like.

Neil Cockroft, Head of Diversity and Culture, King & Wood Mallesons, Sydney, Australia

Let's not tolerate bigotry

To be a member of the team in the finance industry you need to spend time in a bar. It's no good if you don't drink. It's no good if you are pregnant. It is no good if you are Muslim. As a woman you can't change it. I stopped smiling and put my head down.

Georgia (Anon), Vice President, Investment Banking, Sydney, Australia

The obstacles that make it hard for women to move up the corporate ladder are the same obstacles that make it hard for Asians to get up there too. When a senior male executive is about to take employees to meet one of his best clients he might consider it risky to take a female or Asian who the client may not appreciate, and take a white male instead.

Diane Grady AM, Non-Executive Director, Macquarie Group, Sydney, Australia

Let's catch up

Australia is behind the curve, not just in gender but in other areas of diversity. Banking in Australia is not as diverse as every other country. The banking industry in the USA has been working on diversity for 50 years. US bank trading rooms have a very diverse workforce today.

Craig Drummond, Chief Executive Officer, Bank of America Merrill Lynch, Sydney, Australia

What I saw in Australia was a segregated society: the segregation between men and women. Australians should join forces as you have it all. You have highly educated people, natural resources, world-class universities, competitive corporations – you have so much that you could have it all if your men and women joined forces.

Australia has two separate cultures living side-by-side – one for men and one for women. If you have two groups instead of one group, you can easily fall into the 'parallel society pit'. It is not in our DNA, we were not born with these values. It is cultural and results from how we socialise our people.

Arni Hole, Director General, Norwegian Royal Ministry for Children, Equity and Social Inclusion, Oslo, Norway

Many people up here [Hong Kong] think of Australians in a derogatory way. Australians don't disappoint, they deliver just the way people expect with their drunken behaviour and loutishness. When the local papers talk about Australians it doesn't denote a good image: you are friendly but you are a lad who likes to have fun.

We spend a lot of time trying to spin ourselves out of being Australian. Nobody here has time for Australian-like behaviour. There is an opportunity for Australia to make an enormous difference in Asia but the question is "how much are Australian people and businesses up for the challenge of improving the Australian brand".

Richard Mazzochi, Partner, King & Wood Mallesons, Hong Kong, China

Let's move on

We see a lot of American culture on TV and we are exposed to little else. There are many Australians who have little experience of other cultures apart from an overseas holiday. We are an accepting culture and people come here to live and fit in pretty well. We are not bad at it [integrating immigrants] but there might be room for improvement.

Jane Hemstritch, Non-Executive Director, Commonwealth Bank of Australia, Melbourne, Australia

I say to the senior leaders of my business, 'If you aspire to be on or stay in this team, you have to be good in this space (diversity). You have to be able to show me that you can do this and if you can't you won't be promoted and you will have to go work someplace else.' Diversity must be seen as paramount to all businesses in Australia in the next 10 years. This is a tough thing: changing culture is the hardest thing of all and it takes years. If you're going to be the CEO my advice is, get started and be consistent.

Paul Waterman, President. BP Australia, Melbourne, Australia

Cultural diversity and the opportunities

The third area of questions I explored related to how well we assimilated with people who arrived from other countries to live and work alongside native Australians. This included discussion about our relative performance as a multicultural society, expectations regarding integration, opportunities that arise (or could arise) from cross-cultural communities and working environments and what we hope to gain from opening our doors to immigrants in the future. Here are a few highlights:

Room for improvement

Diversity is a representation of different subgroups of people in a team. It's about building a strong team based on different capabilities with people from different origin and gender. Is Australia happy being Anglo-Saxon and male dominated?

Kathryn McLay, General Manager – Replenishment, Woolworths, Sydney, Australia

We need to adapt our environment to be inclusive. For example, if a Japanese employee fails to challenge the bosses we might say "he doesn't challenge in meetings so he is not ready for the next promotion", but what makes a good manager is different in our society from that of Japan.

Margaret Dreyer, Partner, Deloitte Touche Tohmatsu, Sydney, Australia

When politicians talk about stopping immigrants, it shows a lack of insight into the needs of corporate Australia. There's no understanding of the need to open the doors. How long do they want to keep us isolated on our island?

Kim Schmidt, Director of People and Culture, Grant Thornton, Sydney, Australia

We often talk about being a diverse country and believe that we have adopted multiculturalism. Our diversity comes from a history of migration: original settlement, Post-WWII European immigration; then immigrants from China, India, South Africa, Philippines and other parts of Asia; and asylum-seeking refugees from Africa, the Middle East and Asia more recently. Often these groups are left to resettle in their own communities and are not fully integrated into the broader community in educational, employment and broader social terms. We are more likely to employ those educated in our system and who think as we do, than a new arrival. We have made many commendable steps with respect to migration and refugees but more can be done, especially around education and employment opportunities, to assist more effective integration."

Robert Milliner, Former Chief Executive Partner, Mallesons Stephen Jaques
(now King & Wood Mallesons), Sydney, Australia

We are still predominantly white. There are many areas of Australia with little exposure to non-white people. The three main cities, Melbourne, Sydney and Brisbane, have 10 million people where non-Anglo tribes exist. The other 12 million Aussies have little or no exposure to non-white communities. This breeds isolation and xenophobia and increases the fear of 'the teeming masses to the North'. We do integrate very well but only in these three cities.

Bernard Salt, Partner, KPMG, Melbourne, Australia

If you look at [the ethnicity of] 'graduate intake' there is no bias at that level. Asians are working their way through corporate Australia but they seem to drop out by the age of 35. There are fewer Asians in the three levels below the CEO.

John Daley, Chief Executive Officer, Grattan Institute, Melbourne, Australia

We have a lot of trouble recruiting non-white Australians. They think that if they were to work in the armed services it would be like going back to the war in their home country [that they may have fled]. If we did recruit Muslims it would not be easy for them.

Cmdr Jennifer Wittwer FAHRI, Royal Australian Navy, Canberra, Australia

If being multicultural means that we need a multicultural parliament, then no, we are not multicultural.

Nigel Garrard, Managing Director, Amcor, Melbourne, Australia

After 20 years of living in Australia I can say I love the place. There is good food, friendly people and a great lifestyle. But Australia's branding is all about the Anglo-Saxon and beaches. We need to think about its positioning and the reality. Tourism advertising needs to show more cultures, not just white people. Integration here is not as good as in the UK or the USA - how many non-white TV presenters do you see on the news?

Pradeep Khanna, Chief Executive, PK Projects Management & Consultancy, Sydney, Australia

We haven't been telling people the stories. Unless we are telling stories about Australia's history, immigrants don't know where they have landed. It makes it harder for immigrants to connect. We have let the cultural side slide and it has impoverished us all. Stories embellish the culture and they help it to evolve.

Dr Julianne Schultz AM, Non-executive Director, Australian Broadcasting Corporation, Sydney, Australia

SBS conducted a survey on national attitudes towards asylum seekers. It showed 45 per cent of the population was found in some way to have anti-refugee sentiments. The general media don't help with the asylum seeker debate as it is totally one-sided. Other key multicultural issues in Australia are racism and Islamaphobia. However you have to say that Australia is in a much better state than some European countries which have declared multiculturalism dead.

> John Godfrey, Senior Commissioning Editor Documentaries, SBS Television, Sydney, Australia

The Chinese are deeply suspicious of Western practices (especially from the USA because of the trade embargoes). However Australians are seen as honest brokers. They are actively trying to grow China's business and want their country to succeed. From an Australian perspective, while that presents an opportunity, we are too inward-looking. We focus on short-term political issues and culturally we pat ourselves on the back thinking that we are a multicultural society and that we can work with people of all cultures. The reality is we are still a European Western nation and we don't have an understanding of Chinese culture or practices. We need to grasp how Asians perceive us and the first step is for Australians to better understand China, Asian languages and cultures.

> David Olsson, Partner, King & Wood Mallesons, Beijing, China

One of the most important things I discovered early in my career was that it can be confronting when you are in cultures different to your own. I have to remember "I'm not right, they're just different" and we may not agree with their values but it doesn't mean they are wrong – they are just different.

> (Anon) senior male executive in global business

Benefits of many cultures

I am not a huge fan of integration because I like difference, yet there can be more learning from people and that is very valuable.

> Natalie Filatoff, Principal, Filatoff Editorial and Writing, Sydney, Australia

When you work with teams from rich cultural backgrounds, it can only be better.

> Jenny Parker, Office Managing Partner, Ernst & Young Global, Queensland, Australia

Multiculturalism is a good thing and I'd always have people of all ethnicities on my team. Multiculturalism drives different behaviours and requires a different management response.

> Andrew Macintosh, Chief Executive Officer, Hanhong Private Equity, Hong Kong, China

Working in Asia has given me many things including exposure to much bigger projects, added responsibility, knowledge that you can't gain from university and I have become more tolerant from having exposure to people of different races, religions, cultures and styles. I have developed different styles for dealing with people and I am constantly learning.

Richard Padfield, Electrical Engineer, Arup Group, Ho Chi Minh, Vietnam

Gender diversity and the opportunities

Females make up a little over half of the population. Australian women are equal with other leading Western nations in their educational achievements yet they are dismally lagging in their participation rates in the workforce.

Why do Australia women gain high-level qualifications and then opt out of the workforce? What is it in our society or system that contributes to this behaviour? Why is the female participation rate behind so many other countries, and slipping? How does this result impact the economic performance of Australia, local businesses, cities, towns and communities? Should we be concerned? If 'yes', what could we do about it?

Here is a sample of the comments.

Current state of affairs

The way we do business in this country is like a contact sport. It is a hostile environment for women.

(Anon) Male CEO, Professional Services, Australia

I didn't know I was a female until I came to Australia. I walked into the office and they nicknamed me 'Legs'. If men call women that back home, they get sued.

(Anon) Female, Executive, Financial Services, Australia

There are a bunch of senior people who are taking gender diversity seriously. It is incredibly hard, and it is the most difficult challenge I have ever undertaken. No one has the answer and no one can crack the magic code. At this stage there is no evidence that anything works.

(Anon) Male CEO, Financial Services, Australia

Some organisations have senior male executives mentoring females and I find that quite repugnant. Why do women need mentoring and males do not? It has gone on too long that people think women need a leg up.

(Anon) Female CEO, Consumer Goods, Australia

If women aspire to be CEO they need to give 150 per cent. Being on the executive committee involves a lot of travel. You start early in the morning and have to travel 2–3 days, flat out.

(Anon) Male board member, various boards, Australia.

It worries me that some women are adopting the same bad behaviour as men. I am not opposed to quotas; to broaden the poll is important. But we need to think more creatively about how to engage people because a simple legal framework is not going to do it.

Dr Julianne Schultz AM, Non-executive Director, Australian Broadcasting Corporation, Sydney, Australia

I don't buy the argument about women on boards. It's just rubbish that there are not enough good women.

Greg Couttas, Partner, Deloitte Touche Tohmatsu, Sydney, Australia

Women aren't always the best supporters of each other. Working women are not always supportive of non-working mothers and vice versa. I'm sure there are many women who look at me and say "I don't want to work those long hours" and I appreciate it's not for everyone. It is what it is: we all have to make choices. I wonder whether the issue in Australia is that we don't provide enough flexibility to do both, i.e. to be a mum and pursue a career. Maybe more flexibility is the solution

Julie Coates, Director, BIG W, Sydney, Australia

There is a level of nervousness amongst CEOs. If they raise the expectation that certain gender targets might be obtainable then they are responsible for delivering them. If they raise expectations too high and can't deliver, then they are seriously challenged.

It is true that the most obvious areas of sexual discrimination have been identified and called. The challenge is the 'not so obvious' sexual discrimination as it is harder to identify and therefore harder to call.

Ruth Medd, Chair, Women on Boards, Sydney, Australia

Male attitudes and behaviours

People say we are a meritocracy. That's simply not true. We need to ask [male only boards and management teams] "Why do all the smart people look like you?" While they may say they are appointing more females, there is a bias towards women who are already on boards and older women. They think: "If we have one or two [token women] that will do us".

Ann Sherry AO, Chief Executive Officer, Carnival Australia, Sydney, Australia

Mateship almost got constitutionalised. It is a vehicle for the exclusion of women by men. Men are keen to promote mateship as a positive element of the Australian culture, but it's the boy's club culture in another form.

Neil Cockroft, Head of Diversity and Culture, King & Wood Mallesons, Sydney, Australia

I do not think men are anxious about the ASX changes requiring companies to report on gender. I don't think men think in generalities: I think we tend to think of 'me' and as it will take a generational change [for the impact of the ASX changes to have an effect] I don't think men feel the need to be worried.

Russell Tipper, Chief Executive Officer, Brockman Resources, Perth, Australia

Actions for consideration

I am in principle opposed to quotas as they can cause resentment and while they may result in short-term change, this may not necessarily lead to longer-term change. However, I am not saying they should be off the table permanently because we can't afford to continue wasting the talent of our population.

Diane Grady AM, Non-Executive Director, Macquarie Group, Sydney, Australia

As a society we need to change. I am in favour of quotas [regarding women on boards]: it is a systemic change that requires companies to set individual gender targets. Change has been too slow and there is plenty of material published to show that it will [continue to] be slow. All through my career I have been the first and only woman in each of the senior roles I have taken on. I look behind me and I say the change has been too slow.

Uschi Schreiber, Managing Partner - Global Government & Public Sector Industry Centre, Ernst & Young Global, Hong Kong, Australia

The important thing when you are leading a big team is not to miss any of the talent. The biggest sin is when you see leaders who aren't behaving in the right way and they turn a blind eye to it.

Paul Waterman, President. BP Australia, Melbourne, Australia

Our advice to others is not to get stuck on the business case. So much time is spent explaining the business case and outlining the war for talent etc. The better approach is to say "we are going to work on achieving gender balance and diversity because it is the right thing to do". We just stopped selling the business case. Making the message simpler and something that we could commit to was a big shift for us.

Nicola Evans, Deputy Company Secretary, BHP Billiton, Melbourne, Australia

How on earth did anyone get the idea that all the talent is in one gender? You have to challenge traditional masculinity and feminine roles. You cannot afford to lose out on the top leadership in the corporate world just because it comes in a female gender form.

> Arni Hole, Director General, Norwegian Royal Ministry for Children, Equity and Social Inclusion, Oslo, Norway

A big part of the solution is getting rid of the myths. Creating positive role models and talking about managing family and removing the structural biases against females staying at work, returning to work and climbing the ladder.

> Kathy Matsui, Managing Director & Chief Japan Strategist, Goldman Sachs, Tokyo, Japan

We have struggled to get women into our industry. We put mechanisms in place to attract them. We have partnered with Monash University to identify female engineers. To be a 'turner and fitter' requires mechanical skills that are learned and women haven't learned them yet. It is a long-term strategy to get women into the training at TAFE. Educational opportunities are not getting to women in Australia. We segregate jobs into men's jobs and women's jobs. We need to show girls that they can do anything.

> Lynley Corcoran, General Manager Human Resources, Amcor, Melbourne, Australia

There is an unconscious bias in men, in organisations and in our society. We don't foster or value diversity. Our culture is blokey and men are comfortable with it. We need to break down stereotypes and paradigms of how we think. We are not aware of how we are behaving.

> Rosemary Howard, Executive Director AGSM Executive Programs, Australian School of Business, UNSW, Sydney, Australia

Future development of Australian society

I wanted to take the opportunity to hear what others had to say about removing blockages and opening up pathways for all people living in Australia to realise their dreams: their career potential; financial independence; entrepreneurial creativity; community engagement or leadership ability; and to be fully participating in society and business. With regard to the future, I asked "If we agree that we could do better, who should lead on this?"

Many people said 'That's a good question' and 'I'll have to give that some thought'. The responses that were given to the question about who should lead on diversity are outlined in Chapter 12, Here are a couple of thoughts about what we should hope to achieve in the future:

God help us if we can't have a dialogue to openly challenge, discuss and debate the impediments and roadblocks to diversity. If we can't, then this country will wither. Change is going to come through shame and transparency or we will be struggling for generations to come.

Stephen Roberts, Chief Country Officer, Citi, Australia and New Zealand, Sydney, Australia

Parents want their children to have the best, but it seems their definition of the best is to replicate themselves. Girls should be able to fulfil their dreams and aspirations, but they feel limited by views held by people in our society. How do we change that? Is it evolution of society that we need?

Catriona Noble, Chief Executive Officer, McDonald's Australia, Sydney, Australia

I see a lot of women who are in roles like mine juggling things in ways that men don't have to juggle. Politicians talk in a way that reinforces that men are the workers and then we see advertising on television that reinforces the view that women are at home doing the washing. Children pick this up [the expected roles of men and women] through what they see and experience every day. Australia has a long way to go culturally. It is in the interactions we have every day. We have to be relentless in picking up on these things – and challenging the schools.

Annette Kimmitt, Office Managing Partner, Ernst & Young Global, Victoria, Australia

The need for skills will be an enormous issue in the future. Organisations that don't tap into all available resources will have a problem.

Dr John Harvey AO, Executive Director, IBM Australia, Sydney, Australia

Languages are part of the neural network. The study of mathematics, music and languages together provide the platform for brain development. If you take languages out of the mix it can affect a person's performance in other areas. Possessing Asian capability is more than a language however. It is an appreciation of the many things including culture and religion. It seems that languages are being dropped by students by Year 10. We need to adjust that.

Catherine Livingston AO, Chairman, Telstra, Sydney, Australia

Where to from here?

In this chapter I have introduced the main themes that arose from the 100 leader's interviews. Each of these themes is more fully explored in Part Two, which summarises the issues impacting the growth of Australia, its businesses and communities.

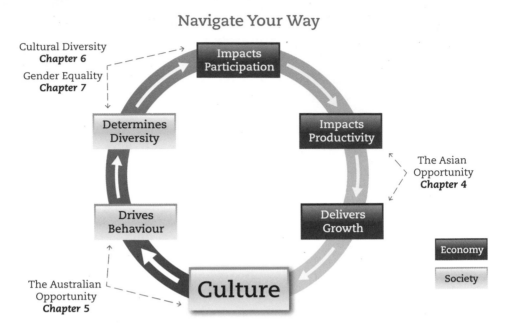

Before proceeding to Part Two to outline the issues impacting growth, I outline the journey I took to discover how cultures operate and I share my experiences living and working in more diverse cultures in Chapter 3.

I believe that a personal discovery can ignite passion and provide purpose to our lives and I hope that in sharing my story I might help others to see the possibilities ahead and to know that no obstacle is so big that we can't find a way to overcome it.

Discovering Diversity

*'The greatest discovery of all time is that
a person can change their future by merely
changing their attitude.'*

Oprah Winfrey: media proprietor, entertainer,
influencer, actress, philanthropist

Leaving home

As we journey through life, the unexpected sometimes happens, so we need to be open to change. If we grow through the changes we experience it can make us a better person and prepare us for more change.

My own journey started in the 1960s in New Zealand and it took a fortuitous turn in 1992 when I ventured across the world to discover other cultures. I wanted to understand how they impacted individuals at work, business outcomes and the economic performance of nations. Along the way I stumbled upon an unexpected gem: the power of diversity. This chapter is about that journey and my discoveries.

I have lived in three different regions of the world, as an expat executive and immigrant, to experience what it was like to live on someone else's patch. I wanted a glimpse of what it would feel like to be them. A surprising insight that sprang from this was that the patch of the world I had come from was not all that it seemed. Similarly, by standing in the shoes of others, I recognised that the childhood beliefs and perceptions I held about the regions I moved to were flawed – my assumptions were wrong.

The cultures I was exposed to as a child had shaped my view of the entire world. My perceptions of life and people in Asia, Europe and Australia were formed through the lens of New Zealand culture and the values of the country, my family, the schools I attended, the people I knew, the physical surroundings and events from my formative years. As I travelled on my journey, I had to rethink much of what I had learned.

Following repeated total immersion into the cultures of other countries I changed and grew, due to the unexpected but highly welcome influences that flowed from working and living in the diverse communities of Asia and Europe. Through this experience I now appreciate how diversity can help grow nations, businesses and societies in the 21st century – the Asian Century.

The journey begins in New Zealand, travels to Singapore, then London, across continental Europe and back down-under to Australia. I share some of the key decisions I have made at the crossroads, the lessons I have learned and a major 'aha' moment that inspired me to write this book.

Some of the major learning points included: realising that my childhood assumptions about other cultures had become part of my unconscious biases; how naïve I was about other cultures and their people before I worked abroad; what it felt like to experience racial discrimination first hand; that sexual discrimination could come from other women; and what an 'aha' moment looked like.

It is difficult to see how other cultures operate when you are in your familiar environment. But when you are new to a culture, while you are in the 'out-group' and still feeling a little 'culture shock', you can see and feel the contrasts. And as time goes by you begin to discover the magic code: the code you need to understand how to live comfortably within a different culture.

While on this journey I formed two notions about culture that are described by the Culture Iceberg and the Culture Circuit: models which were introduced in Chapter 1 and are fully explained in Part Three.

My cultural origins

I was born into a middle-class family in the 1960s in New Zealand and my cultural heritage is three-quarters Anglo-Saxon and one quarter Arabic. My family lived in New Plymouth, a small west-coast city on the North Island until I was three and then my father, Barrie, died suddenly of cardiomyopathy and my mother, Beverley, moved us back to Wellington to be near her family.

New Zealand was a stable and safe place to live. People were friendly, community minded and mostly Christian and economic conditions were pretty good. The culture there evolved on the assumptions and values of forebears of the indigenous Maori, early settlers from Great Britain and a variety of Polynesian immigrants. There were many smaller cultural groups from Europe and Asia, too, but their impact in the 1960s was minor.

My memories of early childhood are secure, warm and happy. As children our lives were filled with family and community events with people of many ethnicities. We had many Maori and Polynesian friends and we also had a large extended Lebanese family (my granddad was second-generation Lebanese). Later in my childhood my mother remarried, to a prominent criminal lawyer

Mike Bungay, whose fame and fortune changed our family culture from being 'family focused' to one that was dominated by my stepfather's career.

As children we had to listen to endless stories about his accused criminals and how their lives had gone off the rails and contrast this with his high-society friends who visited our home including politicians, judges, television celebrities, police chiefs and Maori elders. I gradually came to see that people from diverse backgrounds and experiences were driven by different values and that this impacted on their behaviour.

My brother Barrie, sister Deborah and I all finished school at 16–17 years old without finishing the final year and therefore without gaining university entrance. There was no expectation that we would do any tertiary education. The *assumption* of our family culture was that you'd get a good administration job, get married, have three children and live happily ever after. Acquiring a higher education was not a family *value* as no one had ever done that before, except my stepfather.

A few years after leaving school I did find myself in the 'nice' administration job my mother had always planned for me, but after a few years the realisation came – I needed to train for a career; to do something more interesting and useful.

Shifting assumptions

I enrolled in a Bachelor of Arts in Classics and Geography but the next year I changed both university and degree course, switching to a Bachelor of Commerce majoring in Strategy and Marketing. In the first year I was so terrified I was going to fail that I applied myself morning, noon and night and rapidly expanded my learning ability. I was astounded to find that I was no longer a C or B-grader, but was more than capable of an A grade.

This was my first real taste of the 'power of learning' and how you could excel at anything if you just tried at it. My assumptions had changed: tertiary education was an option for members of our family. I now highly valued learning and believed that anything was possible. My individual Culture Iceberg had radically and irreversibly changed.

The next year I started a Master's Degree part-time while I began my first post-university career job as Marketing Manager of a fund management company, followed a year later by a second position as Marketing Manager for an art production company. Then after leaving both companies (due to sexual advances by senior male executives) I went into a series of short-term strategy and marketing contracts.

Just two years after graduation I registered my own consulting business. No one told me I couldn't be a Strategy and Marketing Consultant at the age of 26, so I just did it.

Valuing discovery

When I established my consultancy to deliver strategy and marketing solutions to clients' growth problems, I did not initially think about organisational culture or diversity as being vital ingredients to resolving them. But I soon recognised their importance; you didn't need to be a rocket scientist to see how an organisation's culture and the behaviour of its people could either hugely help or seriously hinder the delivery of a great strategy.

When it came to selecting a Master's thesis topic I decided to explore '*How corporate culture and values impact the bottom line*'. I was intrigued by the role of culture and its power in affecting strategy implementation and I was equally fascinated with leaders who couldn't see it, or chose to ignore it. After completing the thesis I started to look at every strategic challenge through a different lens – a cultural one.

My work experience at that stage had been mostly in the services industries yet everything they taught at university in the 1980s was about products. My experience in people-related industries was building and I found I loved working with people, selling to people and the things that impacted the lives of people.

As I translated what I had learned at university into what I knew to be reality in services industries, I was pioneering and innovating. The discovery was exciting. I had uncovered something very important to services industries – the power of people and how their attitudes impacted the quality of service provided.

In the first year I built a strong client list including market leaders: Price Waterhouse (accounting), Russell McVeagh McKenzie Bartlett and Co (law), and Beca Carter Hollings and Ferner (engineering). These were my cornerstone clients, among others.

Age and *gender* were not barriers to being able to position myself as an adviser to service industries on growth issues and not being an accountant did not affect my ability to run a business. During these years my assumptions about who I was and what I could be in life changed.

By the time I was 28 I had completed two degrees, was married and became step-mum to five amazing children, learned to scuba dive and to fly single-engine planes. Within another two years, aged 30, I was speaking at international conferences and I was advising CEOs and top teams of professional firms, finance institutions and government departments. While the average age of these executives was around 45 I never once felt discriminated against due to my age or gender.

Despite all my success and busy-ness I instinctively knew that I wasn't done. It was time to prepare for a bigger journey. Without my being aware of it my individual Iceberg had morphed around me. My assumptions about life had radically changed. The values I was raised with had been challenged and my behaviour also told the story about who I had become.

Since that time I have examined corporate culture in New Zealand, Singapore and other parts of Asia, England and other parts of Europe, the USA and Australia.

It's about people not strategy

The year 1992 was a turning point. I was hungry to find the secret ingredient to achieving culture change in organisations. I had learned that it was something much deeper than a company's leadership, vision, strategy, structures or day-to-day policies and practices. The secret ingredient was hidden at the bottom of the Culture Iceberg, beneath the waterline. It was the assumptions – the lowest layer which forms and influences all the layers above – that impacts the way people respond to a leader's vision and strategic intentions.

I repeatedly observed that the key to a leader's success in implementing strategy was his or her ability to get people to buy-in to their story about where they were going. That is, it was less about the quality or appropriateness of the strategy and more about their ability to gain 'followship' (which is what I think leadership is really about).

Two challenges kept recurring. Firstly, leaders in business and society had to *stimulate passion for their vision and strategy* by demonstrating purpose and benefit to their people. Secondly, they had to *manage the internal politics, behaviours and other cultural forces* that could, and often did, work against the implementation of changes required by the plan.

The first of these was usually understood but the second, back in the early 90s, was not even recognised, let alone understood. Both of these challenges related to people, not to the market, competition, price or the quality of the product. Passion, politics and behaviour of the people are all elements representative of an organisation's culture and each element can make or break a good strategy. I wanted to learn more about the links between cultures and business performance and I felt that the New Zealand market was too small.

Experiencing a new culture in Asia

I started travelling regularly between Auckland, Sydney and Singapore developing and servicing clients in each location. My entree into Singapore was facilitated by my husband who arranged a transfer there so that we could experience what it would be like to work in Asia. I lived half-time in Singapore for the next two years; one foot in each camp. It was the best thing I ever did.

The experience opened my eyes to the role and impact of a country's culture on an economy's performance and on the organisations and people within that culture. This wonderful but tiny nation then had a population of 3.2 million including about 300,000 (10%) expatriates from almost every continent and island on the planet. Given that the country is only about 40 kilometres long and most of the expats work in and live near the city centre the concentration of foreigners is very high and you can't help but observe a 'league of nations' around you almost every day.

Costumes and status

In my first week in Singapore in 1992, as a half-time expat, there were many 'firsts'. Although I had visited the country a few times before on my way to Europe I realised that I had taken little notice of how the people lived, what they believed in, or how they behaved. This time was different. I was here to live. I viewed everything through a different lens.

My husband had flown to Singapore ahead of me and the day I arrived, he collected me at the airport wearing only suit trousers and shirt – no jacket! I soon learned that *no one* wore jackets to work in Singapore. It was just too hot. To my eyes, at first, that didn't look professional. However, it made complete sense as it was 29–31°C year-round. It had never occurred to me that such a status symbol as the tailored business suit jacket could be so easily dumped. In Singapore the jacket has no status, instead it is the three-Cs that matter: the quality of your *car*; the type of *credit card* you have and the location and size of your *condominium*.

Singapore's population comprises people from three ethnic backgrounds – Chinese, Indian and Malay – and I came to appreciate the significance of the traditional costumes that represented their ethnic background.

Language and intolerance

While we were searching for an apartment in our first weeks in Singapore, we stayed in a hotel near my husband's office in Tanjong Pagar near the docks south of the city. On my second day I went to the food market area and I noticed a sandwich bar amongst the stalls selling local dishes. It was a very hot day and I wasn't ready for hot and spicy food so I decided on a sandwich.

I waited my turn and asked "Oh hi, I don't see any wholegrain bread, do you have wholegrain bread, or perhaps a wholegrain roll, it would be great if you did, if not, I could always change to …?" The young sandwich maker simultaneously 'tutted' his teeth and huffed at me before turning to serve the Chinese-Singaporean standing beside me, leaving me to my ramblings in mid-sentence.

"What was that?" I thought, "Was that racist? Did that guy just dismiss me with a 'tutt' because I looked and sounded different? Was it because I was white or an immigrant or an annoying expat?" Whatever it was, it did not feel good. It was a very clear message and it was public. I had to wait behind the locals who 'spoke the lingo' making me feel like a misfit.

It was my first ever experience of being treated like a minority and it made me feel insignificant and out of place. I learned later that the sandwich maker probably couldn't understand my elaborate sentence but that didn't make my first-ever racist experience any less real. I now knew what Chinese people in New Zealand might feel like if subjected to impatient people or racist comment.

While Singapore's national language is English, I learned that they have localised it and they speak it in truncated sentences and they add 'Lah' to almost everything. The expats called this altered version of English, Singlish. My English was clearly not well enough adjusted to suit the Singaporean ear yet and I needed to learn it quickly. The next time I wanted a sandwich I needed to say "You have wholegrain bread, lah?" and stop and wait. Once I conquered Singlish I noticed that things went much more smoothly.

My early communication challenges were trivial everyday matters, but they affected my ability to be understood and to understand. When I meet people now who speak with accented English, I feel empathy for them and try to appreciate their difficulty in being understood and the challenges they face as they seek to understand our ways.

When I lived in New Zealand, I thought all Chinese people were the same and ran $2 shops, and that all Indian people ran green-grocery stores, because that's what many Asian immigrants to New Zealand did in the 1960s and 1970s. Now I know the truth about people from the Asian region of the world and I am thankful that I took the opportunity to go and live in Singapore where I discovered my biases.

A mini league of nations

Initially we lived in a small secluded condo along the East Coast Parkway comprising about 30 apartments which were filled mostly with expats from other Asian countries and a few Europeans who were there for a three-year posting. Our new friends were from Laos, Japan, Korea, Hong Kong, Malaysia, France, Switzerland and England.

Growing up in New Zealand we mostly thought of people from Asia as Chinese or Japanese and we never thought about them coming from other countries. We treated them all same. But I could quickly see that this was totally incorrect and ignorant. Each Asian country is as different from others as England is from France or Germany, or as America is from Mexico or Canada.

Everyone I met from a different country provided me with an opportunity to learn about their culture and how it influenced the way they interacted with people at work. Discovery became a daily occurrence and it was an experience that I would never have had in New Zealand, nor in Australia.

I began to wonder if all Western countries were ignorant and closed to difference? Did they recognise the richness that other countries and cultures have to offer? Why are people frightened of difference and the unknown? One highlight of my learning over these two years was a dinner party at the house of Laotian friends who had been living in the USA for 10 years prior to arriving in Singapore. When our charming Laotian host with an American accent delivered Italian food for dinner I felt that I was in a movie. It was surreal.

Around the table for dinner were people of seven nationalities and four religions and it was the most interesting evening full of rich chatter as we explored one another's backgrounds and origins. Everyone there was equally fascinated by the stories of the cultures of the others. It was such a memorable occasion that I recount it regularly.

That year, 1992, was the beginning of my own personal transformation and awakening. To be immersed in another country provides valuable insights about people, culture, religion, race, values and beliefs and more. You cannot pick up these treasures passing through on a three-week holiday.

Total immersion in Asia

With every flight I took back and forth between Auckland and Singapore during the years 1992–94, the contrast between the lifestyles and values of each city came into focus. I knew there was much more to discover, so I planned to make that happen.

In mid-1996 I committed to being in Singapore full-time to take the role of inaugural Executive Director with a former client, Shook Lin & Bok, a leading high-profile Singaporean law firm. The job involved developing an executive team and introducing best management practice to help the firm grow in the face of increasing competition from new entrants from the UK and USA.

Adapting to new ways

Working in the East required me to rethink and adjust many of my Western consulting and management practices. I was the only Caucasian in the firm and before long I started to appreciate the differences between the three local cultures represented there: Chinese, Indian and Malay. I had to understand, respect and work within the constraints of all three cultural norms while finding ways to gain their respect and following, without which it would be impossible to lead the change required.

I recall a number of challenging issues. Building client relationships, sales techniques and business management practices were completely different in Singapore. For a firm that wanted to develop more Western-style capabilities, to attract Western clients and compete with Western law firms, we had a lot of work to do. Before I could introduce our methods and systems, I had to understand theirs. Every technique I had used down-under had to be reconstructed to suit the local cultures and skill levels of the people.

Here is one example of an everyday challenge. In Singapore culture it is not polite for younger and junior people to speak up when older and more senior people are present. Therefore, when we had American banking clients in for a relationship-building lunch, the solicitors present would not participate in the conversation, leaving the lunch conversation to the partners and myself.

To change this I would run a session before the lunch and get each lawyer to identify the experience and knowledge that they would contribute to the client's project. Then I got agreement from each person that they would take turns to explain their own experience at the lunch. When the lunch became part of the 'business engagement process', it allowed us to circumvent the cultural protocol; we found a 'business reason' for changing the traditional behaviour. By 'presenting the firm's credentials', we reduced the cultural barriers to speaking up in front of superiors.

Feeling the cultural difference

Living in Singapore bore no similarity to the bi-culture I had grown up with in New Zealand: it seemed as though every continent, race, religion and creed was represented there. It was the most humbling and, by contrast, the most stimulating time of my career and life. Never before, or since, have I enjoyed such an explosive learning experience and this was due entirely to the diversity of cultures, people at the firm and the communities in which I lived.

By mid-1999 I had completed the planned transformation of Shook Lin & Bok and felt confident that I could leave the firm safely in the hands of the executive team I had recruited and trained. I was ready to move on to Europe for another total-immersion cultural learning experience and replaced myself with a local executive, which enabled me to depart.

Being totally immersed in the Singapore culture I could not only observe what was different, but I could *feel* what was different. The experience of living and working in an Asian culture was definitely life-changing. The contrasts were many and the memories are rich. The people there were welcoming, they shared their insights and stories, and let me peek at their lives. The country, even though tiny, had so much to offer if you were open to discovering its history, culture and hidden treasures.

Most people I know who have lived in the region have similar stories to tell and have also grown hugely from their experience. Those who live there now, who were interviewed for this book, continue to express their excitement about the current and future opportunities for growth and some even say they are unlikely to return to Australia until they retire because the work there is more interesting.

At work in cross-cultural Europe

After Singapore I made my way to London to contrast life in Europe with that of Asia. The assumptions I had taken from my childhood to Asia had been challenged and I formed new assumptions about people who were different from me. I learned to value the contributions of immigrants and foreign workers and I had become aware of the benefits of living and working in a more diverse community.

By the time I arrived in London I was feeling enthusiastic about being able to enjoy some of the things I had missed about the West and I was very much looking forward to getting back to consulting.

Integration and leadership across cultures

In London I joined Towers Perrin Tillinghast, a global management consulting and actuarial firm. I undertook assignments across continental European countries as well the United Kingdom. Some of the projects I led included the post-merger integration of Australia's Colonial Insurance bought by Winterthur Life UK owned by Zurich-based Credit Suisse; the integration of three UK-based life assurance businesses owned by Zurich Financial services (we needed to combine Allied Dunbar Assurance plc, Eagle Star Life Assurance Company Limited and Zurich Assurance plc into one business); and the organisation and strategic review of Tillinghast's own European business to discover the source of the region's growth challenges and opportunities.

The Winterthur acquisition had three different country cultures impacting the success of the integration: British, Australian and Swiss. The Zurich project was to combine and rationalise three of its existing global businesses including operations from many cultures across the world. In both cases, the CEOs were mindful of the unique qualities that people from all countries and cultures brought to the new merged entity, which was part of the value in the deal. Each party brought something to the mix. While one business might have had better products another might have more polished service delivery systems and we wanted to retain the value from each.

We used planning workshops and consultations to involve executives from all the different cultures and they brought much goodwill to the table in recognition of the fact that doing business across so many cultures was challenging and required tolerance. Europeans are used to working in multilingual and multicultural situations and while they did not always like the behavioural differences, they did respect them. There was never any doubt about the benefits that diversity would bring.

Benefits of cross-cultural skills and experience

In the Tillinghast project the priority was to assess and rank each European country's operation in terms of its culture, management practices and operational performance. We travelled each week to a different country for several months interviewing, investigating and reviewing the businesses. Some countries were more advanced and progressive than others and we were looking to identify best practice and strategies to ignite growth across the European region.

The different country cultures played an enormous part in the success and ranking of each country's operation. Yet once again, it was the ability to combine the diversity of knowledge, skills, experience and competence of individuals from across the countries and cultures that provided the biggest growth potential for this business.

These client assignments had a common feature – they all involved cross-cultural change and combined people from many different country cultures, which gave them an energy and momentum of their own. The energy arose from the need to assimilate many people from many different countries and companies – it had an element of chaos to it, which allowed us to be creative and innovative in finding solutions.

Transformational change, a different tempo

In contrast, the change projects I led for British institutions that did not involve other country cultures or people seemed to have less energy and momentum: the parameters were known. For example, I was involved in the roll-out of a transformation program at Barclay's Bank after Matt Barrett arrived from Canada to become its Group Chief Executive in late 1999. Upon arrival he commissioned McKinsey & Co to do a review of the markets and prepare a strategic plan. Then our team at Towers Perrin was asked to support the bank's executive team to roll-out the changes.

In this large iconic British bank the organisation culture was formed 300 years earlier from traditions that went way back. Long-held assumptions about the banking sector, its customers and its employees were endorsed in everything they did, said and produced. With around 70,000 employees at the time, shifting assumptions was a much bigger challenge as there was no chaos to unsettle, or unfreeze, the culture. This transformation project was not driven by a merger or cross-cultural challenge and the reasons behind the need for culture change were less obvious.

Cascading the new strategy and the culture change messages down through the levels of the organisation was more predictable and therefore had less impact. I concluded from this that cross-cultural change and unknown territory created greater opportunity to evolve cultures as they were being re-established. The chaos that came with mergers of businesses from different parts of the world was somehow helpful because the cultures were different, and that provided an opportunity to combine the best of both.

Diversity of opinion saves the day

A few years later I was leading the integration of Gerrard, a wealth management company bought by Barclays. The BBC News announced in October 2003 'Barclays and Gerrard are two complementary businesses which share the objective of offering clients a fully integrated wealth management service' and the former owner said 'We believe Barclays would be a more natural owner of the business, enabling Gerrard to fully realise its potential as well as deliver substantial benefits both to clients and employees.'

However, there was surprise on the horizon. These two organisations couldn't have been more dissimilar culturally – despite their common country cultural heritage. Other than having been influenced by the same country culture, everything else about them was widely different and their cultures had been developed on completely different assumptions – ownership models, business models, remuneration systems, markets, services, intellectual property, employees and more.

The tiny, private stockbroking firm was consumed by the enormous 300-year-old bank and a clash of culture was imminent. However, there was one unexpected nugget to behold. Just as I was expecting a walkout by professionals in Gerrard who were struggling with the bank's traditional regime, the two management teams discovered diversity of opinion wasn't all that bad.

Over some weeks and months they applied the creative thinking that sprouted from their contrast and they began to resolve their differences and agreed to look for workable solutions. It became evident that the diversity of experiences and styles – which at first appeared untenable – was the thing that gave this team a second chance.

Inclusion and tolerance in any situation can lead to huge business benefit.

Contrasting cultures across the globe

After almost five years in Europe I was able to contrast that experience with my years in Asia. The contrasts were huge and provided me with enormous learning and understanding about the differences between East and West and about the value that difference between cultures can add, including those that look very similar.

When I address audiences now, I explain how my time in Asia was more 'explosive' than my time in Europe, meaning I learned more, I grew more and I was thrilled to be experiencing the effects of broader diversity first-hand. Singapore was the height of the journey. It was stimulating, fast-paced, people were looking for change, they wanted to learn, the opportunities for business and personal growth were immense and the growth of these nations was certain. The United Kingdom by contrast felt slower, I found people were generally less hungry for change and they were quick to fall back on tradition in search of answers.

Having worked in and across so many different country cultures, it became clear how a nation's culture and its assumptions, values and behaviours shaped the culture of businesses within a country. The contrasts between two companies operating in the same market but whose parent companies were of a different country and culture, were easy to spot.

Beware of subtleties and bundling

One of the differences between Europe and Asia is that, in Singapore at least, people are more aware of the differences between Eastern and Western cultures so they are more able to anticipate how a Westerner would respond to a local cultural situation. The differences between them were recognised and accommodated. However, in the UK the differences between an English person and an antipodean working in London were less obvious and often less able to be anticipated, so there were surprises.

The differences, when they were detected, were often warmly and humorously excused and they were often described as cute idiosyncrasies that each enjoyed about the other's quirky culture. There was little allowance for how 'the subtle' difference might impact on understanding or relationships: because it was so subtle, it was deemed unimportant.

I have learned over the past 20 years that cultural 'subtleties' are *not* to be ignored. To dismiss the subtle features of anyone's culture as minor or insignificant is a serious mistake and it is in fact an insult and illustrates disrespect and ignorance.

Subtle differences between the cultures of two countries, like Australia and England, or between two companies, say after a merger between two banks, are often assumed to be 'small and insignificant' and are therefore ignored. This can be a dangerous assumption and can lead to serious misunderstanding, culture clash, other consequences and costs for relations with employees, suppliers and customers.

I have worked on merger integration assignments between organisations in New Zealand, Australia, Asia and Europe and I can confirm that many have made the mistake of ignoring the subtle – and some not-so-subtle – cultural differences and they always cost the organisation eventually. I have witnessed many de-mergers that have been caused by lack of compatibility and inability to resolve philosophical differences that are essentially cultural clashes. Cultural due-diligence prior to merger helps you avoid this from occurring.

Here's a light-hearted example from Singapore days. I recall a gondola ride to Sentosa Island from Singapore port area south of the city one weekend. We squeezed in beside a couple who were visiting from Scotland and after chatting briefly about the wonderful view below the man said 'Are you from South Africa.' "No", I replied. "Australia?" he said next. "No" I replied again. Then I offered him some help "We are from New Zealand". 'Oh, it's all the same to us!' he said, chuckling.

I'd bet money that if I had called that Scotsman an Englishman he would have quickly lost his humour. Similarly, a Japanese person mistaken for Taiwanese might not be too happy either. History and heritage are highly significant and important to people of every nationality. To brush someone's heritage off as being unimportant is usually a sign of ignorance, or worse, of racism.

We rarely make the assumption that Germans are the same as French, or that Mexicans are the same as Alaskans, yet we often treat people from two different countries in Asia as one cultural group – as 'Asians'.

In the work environment we tend to do this regularly. I have heard many leaders in Australia say 'our graduate intake is approximately 50 per cent Australian and 50 per cent Asian', bundling Chinese, Japanese, Malaysian, Korean, Vietnamese and Philippine students together as one. Are we lazy, ignorant, and arrogant or is this just a bad habit or an unconscious bias? Whatever it is, we are diminishing the uniqueness of their cultures and the contributions they have to offer.

The cultural nuggets are where the gold can be found. Understand the meaning behind the cultural nuances and you've hit the jackpot.

Returning 'home' to Australia

When I started out on the global journey in 1992, I always planned to make Sydney the final stop when I was ready to return 'home' down-under. I arrived in 2004.

I was excited about coming 'home' (Australia is just like New Zealand, I thought) and I was keen to be back in a more relaxed outdoor lifestyle like the one I had grown up in. I was looking forward to being once again within a few minutes of sandy beaches and dive locations and to be among happy people – because life was good down-under!

Well, yes, the beaches were definitely sandy and the people seemed happy. I was pleased to be 'back'. I was looking forward to engaging with a fast-paced, globally-connected progressive Australian economy, living in Australia's multicultural society with diverse communities with a 'can do' attitude and to feeling accepted back into a culture that would require little effort to understand, because it was just like New Zealand.

But to my surprise the culture did not feel so familiar and there were elements that were distinctly different. I wondered if that was because I had been gone from the region too long. Was it because Australian culture was not like New Zealand after all? Or was it because I had changed while I had been living in Asia and Europe?

Relative to where I had just come from, it should have felt more familiar but I figured the answer was the last of these three options. As I settled into Australia I discovered elements of the Australian culture that I had not noticed when I worked on client assignments here in the 1990s. I had not recognised them before because I did not live in the culture; I just popped in for a week or two at a time. You need to be 'immersed' in a culture to feel its underlying influences.

A fresh view of corporate Australia

Several aspects of corporate Australia were a surprise to me. When I arrived, the business community did not appear to be as culturally diverse as I had observed in Asia or Europe. Senior management in Australian companies was largely made up of Caucasian Australian-born males and there was a kind of *force field* around this group that separated you from it, leaving you in no doubt that it was exclusive. The homogenous group protected by this *force field* seemed to be connected by something other than corporate vision, strategic intention or professional or technical discipline. Could that be 'the old boy network'?

Australian businesses were largely national or regional and there were few globally dispersed corporations. It seemed that a much smaller proportion of the Australian workforce had experience working in another country relative to the people I came across in Asia and Europe. When I enquired about how frequently local managers were posted overseas to gain experience, I was told that not many wanted to go.

I wondered what the relatively limited cross-cultural and international experience held by Australian managers would mean for the country's competitiveness and future? Then I noticed there were fewer women amongst executive ranks, and it was rare to find coloured people at the top, either. I also wondered how the lack of diversity at the top of Australian organisations impacts on problem-solving, innovation and business performance.

The window of opportunity

When you first arrive in any new culture (country or company or club) you stand 'outside' the cultural group, metaphorically speaking, until you are acculturated into it, a process that is mostly unconscious and is learned through observation and experience. During this period you have a window of time where you notice that the attitudes and behaviours of others are different from your own. This is an important time as it's when you make your most accurate observations about the differences, before it all becomes familiar to you.

The speed at which you begin to feel comfortable in your new culture has a lot to do with the group's willingness to let 'outsiders' join in. As we heard in Chapter 2, there seems to be a view that 'outsiders' have to earn the acceptance of existing members of the cultural group. They can't just expect to 'waltz in here'; they have to take a 'lesser job' until they prove their ability and earn their stripes.

Experience elsewhere in the world is not good enough. You have to have Aussie experience. So how does this prevailing attitude towards immigrants fit with our notion of 'multiculturalism'? When we say we are 'good at multiculturalism', what do we mean?

When I think about this phenomenon, it brings to mind 'loss of productivity' and 'skills wastage'. Why would we do this: why do we make experienced people 'wait their turn'? If you were the General of an army and 10 fighter pilots more experienced than your own were loaned by an ally to help you fight your war, would you leave them on the ground studying maps to 'earn their stripes' while your lesser experienced people went out to front the enemy? Unlikely, I think, because common sense would prevail.

The risk for Australia is that if we keep skilled people from other countries out in the cold for too long they may become resentful and lose confidence, leave the country taking their skills elsewhere, or start on a new career path that is less valuable to the economy.

An 'immigrant's' view

I have been an immigrant skilled worker three times now and I recommend that everyone experience being in the 'out-group' at least once in their lives as it builds tolerance and cultural understanding. It also builds strength of character and the resilience that comes from having to adapt to changed circumstances and a new environment and from the adversity that you are sometimes confronted with along the way.

If you have never thought about the journey of an immigrant, here is an example of a few of the things they need to discover just to get settled in:

The life and times of an immigrant:
What you need to know about your new country

What resources are available;
What gender roles people play;
What success looks like;
What failure looks like;
What fun looks like;
Who will provide help if you
   need it;
How do you help others if they
   need it;
Where to go to get work;
How to get a mortgage;
How to get a local driver's license;
Which doctor to choose;
Where to go for holiday;
Where to get a deal on a car;
Where to buy a washing machine;
Which school will provide the
   best opportunity for your kids;
Which suburb will be right for
   your family;

Who are the leaders;
Who are the followers;
Who are the influencers;
How decisions get made;
How problems are resolved;
How to get recognised;
What it takes to be accepted;
How to be effective at work;
How to get socially networked;
How to get professionally
   networked;
Where the power is held;
How the power is used;
What social games people play;
What political games people play;
Who are the good guys;
Who are the bad guys;

and the list goes on and on
   and on…

This list is by no means exhaustive and while it makes sense to me – a businesswoman and Westerner – a list prepared by a female refugee from Somalia would be very different.

As you can see, a new migrant or a returning expat has a lot to cope with just to settle into regular daily life, so when they are faced with biases about their race or gender or skill level, their settling-in can become quite a challenge. If we add to their burden the need to take a 'lesser job' to 'prove themselves' to local employers before they can get a job at the same level they had before, it can be extremely challenging for them, not to mention disappointing.

Early observations

I made many initial observations when I arrived in Australia and interestingly all of them have been observed or experienced by someone I interviewed. So they were not unique to me and each of the following observations is reiterated in Part Two by someone in some way. They were:

- Australia's enormous distance from the rest of the world creates challenges and people have adopted coping behaviours to help deal with this isolation;
- the people of Australia are resourceful and self-reliant and they give the impression that they don't need anyone from outside to complete them or help them;
- the Australian culture is largely based on Anglo-Saxon values despite the wide variety of cultures, races, religions and languages spoken by people who live here;
- people from all ethnic backgrounds are welcome to live in Australia but there is an intolerance of those who fail to perfect the English language or adopt Western values and there is an expectation that they will stick to their own cultural groups;
- Australians are individualistic and competitive in nature (see Chapter 9 and link to Geert Hofstede's national culture index in Appendix II) and will give anything a go, so being sporty and outdoor-oriented helps you to fit in;
- despite the appearance that Australia is a modern society, there are still quite traditional values and beliefs held about the roles of males and females:
- there are still boundaries between the roles of women and men at work and in the home which are evident in their behaviour and language (e.g. 'mateship' is generally about men only and many daily behaviours are considered macho);
- there are very fewer executive women in corporate Australia and they are among the most highly competitive women you will find anywhere;
- the roles of women as child-carers, mothers, and home makers are protected concepts and the debate about the rights of working mothers versus stay-at-home mothers divides opinion across the country.

Prior to arriving in Australia I thought of it as a progressive country, that it valued women and accepted people from different cultural backgrounds. However some of these notions were being challenged.

Stepping back in time

I became conscious for the first time in my life that I was overstepping the boundaries set for females. I observed exclusive behaviour in social settings (such as at a cocktail party or a barbecue) and in the work environment. What I observed had not been so prominent or consistently encountered in New Zealand, Singapore or England and I was somewhat shocked to observe segregation of women from men not only because it felt weird in the 21st century but because I did not expect it in Australia.

When I asked other people who live in Australia whether this was the norm, I got very mixed responses from "Absolutely, yes" to "No, not in my group, we all mix well together." I concluded that different circumstances brought out the segregation.

I hadn't previously felt quite the same pressure when at a social gathering to go to the kitchen with the women to discuss domestics, make salads and supervise children while the men huddled around the barbecue talking sport and business. I recall several occasions when a lull in conversation fell over the sausages and steak when I dared break protocol by walking up to the men's group for a chat. I suspect from feedback I have had on this topic that the segregated behaviour I experienced occurs more with family gatherings that involve children than it does with younger, single people or childless couples.

I am not happy to have to report so late in my career – after so many committed and well-intentioned people have been working to achieve gender equality for so long – that my arrival in Australia coincided with increased exposure to sexually offensive and discriminatory remarks and innuendoes from men that seek to remind you of a woman's place.

In my first year in Australia I was at a four-year-old's birthday party. The birthday boy fell down some garden steps in front of his father who was standing there drinking a beer with other men. The father watched the child fall and called out to his wife who came running from the rear of the garden to tend to the crying child. Neither the child's father, nor any of the other men, who were all closer than the mother, moved to help the child.

Similarly it never ceases to amaze me at a dinner party with say three or four dual-career couples, how women who work equally long and hard as their partners still jump up between courses to clear the plates and help the hostess bring out the next course while the men remain seated and engaged in conversation.

I know that this does not happen in all areas of Australian society and I know there are families that enjoy more equal relationships than the ones described here. However, too often these kinds of roles are played out and I am sure everyone reading this can think of some occasions when they have been party to segregated gender behaviour that is insensitive, offensive or degrading to females.

The underlying *assumptions* of Australian society seem in some ways to be unchanged since the 1950s. Don't just take my word for it, read Part Two and hear what the 100 people interviewed say about this and you will be in no doubt that we have a situation that could benefit from a national discussion.

It's time to help with diversity

In September 2009 I attended Women on Boards' Annual Conference and was surprised by the agenda, the issues raised by women attending and the nature of the discussions. It seemed that little had changed since the late 1980s when I last attended a conference aimed at the advancement of women.

Twenty years had gone by and many well-intentioned people had worked very hard to help create a more equitable working environment for women but still the same old barriers were reported as being present. Certainly the figures still showed that the number of women in senior management and on listed company boards was woeful. I had to ask the rhetorical 'why?'

That day the keynote speaker was Arni Hole, Director General, Royal Ministry of Children, Equality and Social Inclusion from Norway who had come to share Norway's success at achieving diversity on boards. The story was so interesting that I kept in touch with her and later interviewed her for this book. The Norwegian government adopted quotas requiring 40 per cent of each gender on boards and Arni explained they got it *without destroying company value, while advancing careers and lives of both men and women*. That was encouraging to hear.

At the same conference a male ASX board director explained to the women present that they could extend their careers – they could take a few years off and come back to work after having children and 'work longer' than the men. That was not so encouraging. Women muttered under their breath that they did not want to return to work after the children left home and work until they are 70 while their husbands retired to the golf course at 55. No, this was clearly not the answer. Women wanted opportunity to combine parenting with a career.

I left Day One of the conference feeling a little disappointed that women in senior roles here seemed to be no better off than in the 1980s. I woke early on the morning of Day Two of the conference feeling guilty. My subconscious was challenging me to 'step up' and there were two questions.

The first question was an intellectual one. "If the World Economic Forum Global Gender Gap report shows other countries can enjoy greater participation of women, why could we not achieve that in Australia?" The second question was a moral one. "If you heard these issues and challenges expressed by women at conferences 20 years ago, why have you not helped?"

It took several weeks of soul searching to find and understand the reasons for my inaction. I finally had an 'aha' moment. Then I understood. I am not proud of the answer but I share it here, as it might help others to identify the things holding them back too. I was:

Too distracted – I was for many years focused on building a business, an international career and achieving goals and I didn't consider whether others were able to advance at the same rate or what barriers they may be facing. I did not notice any glass ceiling or discriminatory practices around me.

Too fearful – until a few years ago, being an advocate for gender equality was a high-risk proposition. Women who were outspoken on the subject were usually labelled 'trouble': I suppose I wanted to keep my nose clean and leave it to others.

Too selfish – I probably thought "I'm okay thanks" and that those who were struggling against a glass ceiling should be the ones to speak up and do something about it. If I could make it under my own steam, then so could other people.

Too busy – my life was so full and complete with my international career, my company, my personal life, my friends – then along came my son – that I just didn't have any time left to take on any new ventures or projects.

Ouch. As you can see it is easy to travel through two decades being driven entirely by your own goals. It wasn't until I got the 'aha' in September 2009 that I realised I could use my knowledge and experience in cultures and strategic change to contribute to achieving diversity in Australia. Then I discovered that I also had a vision for how things could be different and passion that could fuel the journey.

In 2010 the Australian Stock Exchange (ASX) Corporate Governance Council introduced changes to its *Corporate Governance Principles and Recommendations* regarding diversity of people who worked within and served on boards of ASX-listed entities. This was followed by increased activity by businesses and industry associations that were looking for solutions, ideas, training and other support to make the changes they'd need to meet the ASX's new reporting requirements.

It seemed to me that the time was right to step up and help address gender equality and I started to think about how I could do that. The more I thought about the gender challenges, the more I realised how closely linked they were to low levels of cultural diversity at the top of corporate Australia. The more I thought about cultural diversity, the more I realised that if we could achieve greater cultural diversity in the workforce, then we'd be preparing our people to be more effective operating across the Asia region which I had come to know well and where I believed much of our future growth would come from.

Greater cultural diversity and gender equality are solutions to our skills shortage and productivity issues. They would help us to grow this great country, making it more attractive to the globalising economy and mobile workforce, and to corporate investors and entrepreneurs looking for fertile ground to start a new venture. And both would help to secure a better future for our kids!

The journey ahead

When you contrast life in Australia with New Zealand, England with France, China with Japan or America with Brazil, the uniqueness of each country's culture is recognised as a function of its human history, political system, geography, power struggles, leadership profile, economic performance, religious beliefs, social order, technological advancement and so on. This cultural DNA is unique and determines a country's future and relative position to other countries in the world.

Yet while the culture of Australia is unique, it is not any more special than another. The journey of its indigenous people, the arrival of immigrants, the development of its government and legal systems, the creation of industry and markets, the establishment of local values and humour are all unique features of the culture which organises the people who live on this island continent. But other cultures are just as special and the cultural features that immigrants bring can add to the richness that is already here.

Just as a parent thinks his or her child is the most beautiful and clever, a population typically thinks that its culture is more special than others. Not true. What is true is that all cultures are unique and each has something special that can add value to the other.

Arrogantly, some people in the developed world and rich nations think that people from the developing world and poor nations have less or little to offer them. Also not true. Wealth and progressiveness is not the source of all knowledge, wisdom, innovation, creativity, motivation, vision and passion.

Likewise, intelligence and creativity are not exclusive to one particular race or gender. It is the developed world's definition of wealth (in the form of money) and progression (in the form of scientific or technological advancement) that makes those who live there believe they are superior. Less developed nations have genius, talent and skills in their populations too, they just apply it in a different way.

For countries and businesses seeking growth and opportunity, there is exponential value in having a mix of cultural backgrounds and a balance of gender in any team or community. Diversity of thought – mental ability and agility – comes from a mix of women and men, black and white, young and old, able-bodied and disabled, heterosexual and homosexual, catholic and Muslim, married and single and so on.

Stepping Up is the culmination of the learnings of my journey thus far, combined with the past 18 months of research and 250 hours of interviews about the diversity and growth of Australia. It endeavours to provide you with ideas and solutions to creating a more diverse nation. By rethinking the values we hold about the roles of men and women, the rights of foreign workers and the integration of immigrants from countries very different from our own, we are freeing up the possibility of becoming a world leader in diversity.

Clearly you would only put effort behind this if you believed diversity could deliver value. The voices and views of 100 other people on this topic are included in Part Two and beyond. I expect you'll have formed your own opinion by the time you have finished reading theirs. I remain hopeful that more and more people will agree that advancing our culture to achieving diversity is worth stepping up for.

> *You don't have to be someone special to achieve something amazing. You've just got to have a dream, believe in it and work hard. "*
>
> Jessica Watson, OAM, Australian sailor: the youngest person to sail non-stop and unassisted around the world aged 16, also 2011 Young Australian of the Year.

Part Two

The Issues Impacting Growth

Four main themes were investigated in the research interviews and these four chapters are full of the insights and wisdom provided by 100 male and female leaders from across Australia, Asia and further afield.

Chapter 4 looks at the opportunity the rapid growth of the Asia region presents to Australia. Chapter 5 explores the Australian culture and looks at the elements of the culture that the 100 leaders think will help or hinder our social development and economic progress. Chapters 6 and 7 present opinions on the current levels of cultural diversity and gender equality in Australia, they explore the costs of limited diversity and the benefits of improving it, and they include a number of personal stories from Australians who have lived through adversity.

Chapter 4

The Asian Opportunity

'Do the difficult things while they are easy and do the great things while they are small. A journey of a thousand miles must begin with a single step.'

Lao Tzu, also known as Laozi, 6th century BC. The founder of Taoism.

With the rapid growth of the emerging markets in Asia, especially China and India, it seems the current view that the 21st century will be dominated by this region of the world is an accurate one.

Since I first lived in Asia I have always been aware of the cultural richness and economic opportunity that is available to us in Australia. My narrow-minded childhood assumptions about Asian people are long gone and have been replaced with awe and respect for the many great people and nations of the Asia region that I have come to know.

For me, Singapore was the most stimulating period of my career: the pace is fast, the work is challenging, the physical environment is constantly changing, the local people are clever, the transient international populations are stimulating, the cultures and languages are diverse and the lifestyle of this major city is truly international.

People living in Australia and New Zealand are fortunate to be located so close to Asia and to have built up positive trade relations with its nations. Being a back-door neighbour has its advantages.

Look at the growth in Chinese investment: Australia has been the biggest single destination for China's foreign investment worldwide since 2006. Despite this, their investment in Australia equals only 2.5 per cent of what they spend around the world in any single year, which is about US$38 billion. That means the Chinese invest around US$95 million in Australia annually.

Until now Chinese enterprises have focused on growing their overseas investments to secure raw materials and energy. Imagine if Australia's businesses in infrastructure, agriculture, financial or other services were to grab their attention too. What if Australia could encourage them to double the annual investment from 2.5 per cent to 5 per cent? That's not such a huge leap given that China's investment into Australia has been increasing by 90 per cent year-on-year for the past five years.

According to the Foreign Investment Review Board's 2011 Report, China is Australia's 3rd largest investor (almost equal 2nd) as their US$95 million invested here equates to 8.5 per cent of all foreign investments. The US investments rank 1st (16 per cent), the UK is 2nd (8.7 per cent), Canada is 4th (8.4 per cent) and India is 5th (6.3 per cent).

While China's and India's growth rates are expected to slow a little, it will not impact their inevitable overtaking of the UK and Canada.

In addition to the investment dollars coming our way, China, India and other emerging Asian nations are relying on knowledge and technology from developed countries to help them provide much-needed products and services to their people, opening doors to Australia's exporters.

For all these good reasons it is a 'no-brainer' that Australian businesses need a clear Asia strategy, or at least a China strategy, to direct their growth.

The Economist highlights that the real GDP in China in the first decade of the 21st century averaged 10.5 per cent, while America averaged 1.6 per cent. Their best guess for the second decade is that annual GDP growth will average 7.75 per cent in China and 2.5 per cent in America. Based on this calculation China's GDP is expected to pass America's by 2018. However, *The Economist* points out that China has already overtaken America on well over half of 21 different indicators, including manufacturing output, exports and fixed investment.

A further study published in McKinsey & Company's, March 2011 *Quarterly Magazine* titled 'Urban economic clout moves East' listed the top-ranking cities in the world. It says that in 2007 only 8 Asian cities made the list but by 2025 there will be more than 20 Asian cities in the top 50 cities of the world. By that time more than half of Europe's top 50 cities, 3 American cities and one Australian city will drop off the list. It adds that 'Shanghai and Beijing will outrank Los Angeles, and Mumbai and Doha will surpass Munich and Denver'.

The 16 cities that will drop off the list by 2025 are:

- Athens, Barcelona, Denver, Detroit, Hamburg, Lille, Melbourne, Minneapolis-St Paul, Munich, Nagoya, Oslo, Rhein-Main, Rio de Janeiro, Stuttgart, Taipei, Vienna.

The 16 cities that will join the list by 2025 are all in Asia:

- Bangkok, Beijing, Chengdu, Chongqing, Delhi, Doha, Foshan, Guangzhou, Hangzhou, Mumbai, Nanjing, Shenyang, Shenzhen, Tianjin, Wuhan, Xi'an.

In *The Wealth* Report 2012 published by Citi Private Bank and Knight Frank it was noted that Asia is now home to more high-net-worth individuals with $100 million or more in disposable assets than North America. There were 18,000 centa-millionaires in Southeast Asia, China and Japan compared to 17,000 in North America in 2011. By 2016 the numbers are expected to grow to 26,000 and 21,000 respectively.

The latest figures on the expected growth in healthcare in China alone provide opportunity for Australia's healthcare providers, pharmaceutical and biotech companies as well as the professional services supporting this industry such as accountants, lawyers, financial planners and insurers. Total expenditure on healthcare was $156 billion in 2006, $357 billion in 2011 and the projection for 2020 is $1 trillion. With an average of 10 million people moving into Chinese cities annually that makes customers easy to find.

The facts and projections leave no doubt that Asia – Australia's closest neighbour – is the fastest-growing region of the world and will remain that way for several decades to come.

Asking 100 leaders about Asia

With the Asian opportunity in mind, interviews with the 100 leaders commenced with a discussion about their interest in the high-growth emerging markets of Asia and what opportunities they saw for mature markets like Australia. I wanted to gauge the level of interest and relative readiness of Australian businesses to take advantage of the changes occurring in the region around us.

Here are some of the questions I asked:

- Opportunities for business in Asia
  - To what extent do people in Australia recognise the growth in Asia and how interested are they in being part of it?
  - How well positioned is Australia as a nation, relative to its major global trading partners, to gain market share in Asia?

- Getting to know Asia
  - How important are Asian markets to our continued growth and survival as a prosperous nation?
  - Can we maintain our relative position in the world without expanding our trade with Asia?

- Australians abroad in Asia
  - What perception do people who live and work in Asian countries, hold of the Australian business people they deal with?

- How skilled are Australian managers in working across cultures relative to people from other countries?
- How culturally savvy are leaders and managers in Australian businesses?

- Asian languages and culture
  - How culturally and linguistically prepared are the people of Australia to build successful trade relations with Asian investors in Australia and how prepared are they to operate effectively offshore, doing business across Asia?
  - What does the cultural gap between Australia and Asian nations look like and what could be done to close it?

- Shaping up for success
  - How well are local businesses prepared to competitively deliver products and services to Asian countries and what advice would they give to first-timers from Australia to help them be a success in Asia?

- Australia, a world view
  - Could greater cultural diversity within the Australian workforce – especially having Asian cultures represented in senior management and on our Australian boards – strengthen international relations and performance?

- Asian people in Australia
  - How well do we embrace Asian people who come to live, work or study in Australia and are we making the most of the opportunity?

The views of the people interviewed on these topics are presented below as verbatim quotes. No interpretation. I have found over the years that the message is best conveyed in its raw form. Let's see what our 100 leaders think about our readiness to take advantage of the growth opportunities.

Opportunities for business in Asia

Learning about China

You have to understand how China works and recognise the differences in authority. You need to understand the role of the party and of the state. You have to know how to pitch yourself to Chinese businessmen, how to negotiate, the importance of outcomes, and what you have when you have a written contract and when you don't. The issue of 'face' needs to be understood to build relationships. Having a narrow commercial relationship is not enough, you have to have other relationships around that. China is a difficult place to operate in, as there is less rule of law than Western nations are used to.

> Dr Geoff Raby, Chief Executive Officer, Geoff Raby & Associates (and former Australian Ambassador to China), Beijing, China

China is fascinating. It is one of the most competitive and difficult markets in the world, but you just have to be in it. First you need to work out why you want to be in that market. Then you need to decide whether your product or service is capable of making the transition, e.g. Chinese people don't like cheese or milk products. You need to be clear about whether you are prepared to fully engage with those markets and get involved with the people – you can't do it halfway and just be 'Australian in China'.

> Robert Milliner, Former Chief Executive Partner, Mallesons Stephen Jaques (now King & Wood Mallesons), Sydney, Australia

Many Australian business leaders in China met with members of the Henry Commission regarding the 'Australia in the Asian Century' report. They pushed the need for Asian language training in schools in Australia. Teaching French, Greek, Latin and German is passé.

> Joanne Wood, Chairman, Capital Eight, Shanghai, China

Few Australian brands are making a lasting difference in China. It is a tough market and Australian companies that come here are not taking market share or making a sustainable difference. They are not thinking 'How can we make a real difference to this market?' and seem to have little vision of the opportunity. Things branded Australian are regarded as being inferior to the UK or the US.

The Chinese are going about globalisation in a very deliberate way. In each Ministry there are people who have been educated at Harvard and Oxford universities and they know what they are doing. But I don't think the Chinese are any more threatening than the Americans.

> Richard Mazzochi, Partner, King & Wood Mallesons, Hong Kong, China

We need to do more to address the Chinese tourist market correctly. At a recent address by a leader from China Tourism he said: "We don't swim and we don't sit on beaches. We are interested in authentic Australian experiences and you don't tell us where they are. You feed us terrible food and your five-star hotels are like our three-star hotels. If you want millions of Chinese tourists to come to Australia you need to sort this out."

> Ann Sherry AO, Chief Executive Officer, Carnival Australia, Sydney, Australia

There are only 3000 Australian Nationals in Beijing and 2000 of them have Chinese heritage. That's only 1000 Caucasian Australians in a city with a population the size of Australia. The number of foreigners in China is very small so visitors need to explain who they are and what their beliefs and values are.

The nature of Australia–China business has changed a lot recently. We are now seeing the next wave of investment coming from the service industries which include finance houses, banks, funds management companies, legal, architecture and engineering firms and environmental consultancies.

David Olsson, Partner, King & Wood Mallesons, Beijing, China

Getting to know Asia

Our government maintains stronger relationships with America than it does with Asia and until now it has been slow to recognise the importance of Asia, as has the education system. The 'Australia in the Asian Century' report, which was done with good intent, aims to provide a strategic view on fundamental things like defence, immigration, culture and population. I think Australia is about to embark on a big change agenda to get closer to Asia and we need to get ready to follow.

Mike Smith OBE, Chief Executive Officer, Australian and New Zealand Banking Group, Melbourne, Australia

There has been no clear government policy about Australia's engagement with Asia or what the foreign investment guidelines should be, so we might be sending the wrong messages to Asian investors. We haven't had bipartisan agreement and there has been inconsistency about what we want our position to be. We need a budgetary commitment to Asia and private enterprise could do more to push government to raise Australia's profile in the region.

We need a broader vision for Australia with regard to its role in Asia. We should be discussing what we need to do to adjust and respond to the growth needs of its nations. Everyone is trying to do it, but they don't know how. It is like the gender equality and diversity challenge; it's clear in principle but execution and change is very difficult.

Robert Milliner, Former Chief Executive Partner, Mallesons Stephen Jaques (now King & Wood Mallesons), Sydney, Australia

When you look at the world it is the more established economies that are struggling. The Asian countries started from a slightly lower position of prosperity so they have a bigger and longer runway for growth. Australia is an interesting player in Asia and is accepted by most countries. It is closely aligned in terms of time zones and weather patterns and as a developed economy knocking at the door of these untapped emerging economies there is major growth potential for everyone.

David Gonski AC, Chairman, Future Fund of Australia, Sydney, Australia

Many Australians are going to have to deal with Asia in the future. And 'dealing with Asia' does not mean making an international phone call. Building skills and capacity and thinking about yourself in a regional context is very relevant if you are an Australian business. Australian business leaders thinking about their five-year plan would be cutting themselves out of a big opportunity if they didn't consider being a regional player. You don't have to go to Asia to be dealing with Asians; you only have to go outside your front door.

Sid Myer AM, Chairman, Myer Family Company, Melbourne, Australia

Australia has no choice about whether it gets closer to Asia. The only question is 'How?' Politicians need to provide leadership and decision-making that translates to Asian strategy with a medium-term view. Australian businesses need to consider that there are 1.34 billion people living in China and just doing a big acquisition up here is not the best strategy. There are no 'quick fixes' to entering this market.

Hayden Flinn, Partner, King & Wood Mallesons, Hong Kong, China

There is a disconnect between what we say and what we do. We say we are part of Asia and want the best talent, but our behaviour says the opposite. It's the same with women and meritocracy, we say 'yes' but our behaviour says the opposite.

Ann Sherry AO, Chief Executive Officer, Carnival Australia, Sydney, Australia

Many people have lost money in Asia and Australian boards have little idea about how to do business up here. I speak out of interest in trying to make change and what you are writing about in this book is really important to Australia.

Richard Mazzochi, Partner, King & Wood Mallesons, Hong Kong, China

Australia's competitiveness as an economy relies on embracing true diversity. We might be a long way away from parts of Asia but in contrast to the USA and Europeans, Australians are comfortable working in Asia because we travel there a lot for holidays.

Uschi Schreiber, Managing Partner - Global Government & Public Sector Industry Centre, Ernst & Young Global, Hong Kong, Australia

Australia is a net exporter of talent to Asia. It is a one-way street: we don't look at who we could bring to Australia from Asia, so we could learn from them too. It's about working in multicultural teams. It's about collaborative relationships. Australian companies tend to send people up there with little thought. We should be sending those who would gain most from the development opportunity or international exposure. I think we can do better at this.

Neil Cockroft, Head of Diversity and Culture, King & Wood Mallesons, Sydney, Australia

We need to increase the number of executives and people from different cultural backgrounds, especially Asians, into management positions of Australian companies. We also need to get more Australian managers into senior positions in our Asian offices, but then bring them back before they retire to share their experience and learning with others in Australia. They have great value to offer that is often lost when they come back.

Dharma Chandran, Chief Human Resources Officer, Leighton Holdings, Sydney, Australia

You have got to go there and spend time on the ground. You need to go to Asia and build relationships. The University of NSW started with the Colombo Plan back in 1952, which offered students from Southeast Asia the opportunity to finish their degrees in Australia. There is now no country in Asia where we don't have alumni. We have tens of alumni in every main Asian city.

Professor Fred Hilmer AO, President & Vice Chancellor, University of NSW, Sydney, Australia

Australians abroad in Asia

Running an emerging markets business requires different management skills. It is your ability to acquire 'diversity of management skills' that determines whether you are successful or not. There are more and more Australian and New Zealand managers with overseas experience and who are interested in the Asian experience: you can lead a horse to water but you can't make it drink. If you don't have the interest in learning you will never be successful in Asia. When there is no interest, people fail to integrate into the Asian community.

Mike Smith OBE, Chief Executive Officer, Australian and New Zealand Banking Group, Melbourne, Australia

A lot of companies send people overseas, but when they get back there is no space for them to return to. It is only the companies that are truly global and value the experience of other cultures that encourage you to come back and let you in. Australian-based companies don't value it like global companies do.

Ann Sherry AO, Chief Executive Officer, Carnival Australia, Sydney, Australia

As an Australian you 'have to' have Asian experience. It is not a 'nice to have', it is a 'must have'. Having a holiday in Asia is not enough. Tolerance and flexibility is difficult to obtain when you are born and bred in one place.

Stephen Roberts, Chief Country Officer, Citi, Sydney, Australia

I marvelled at many things when I lived in Malaysia in the early 1990s. The first was that there was great warmth towards Australia and Australians. The second was the country's ability to get stuff done. They had remarkable ability to build infrastructure, make decisions and to implement and manage change. It was extraordinary. It was more restrictive in Australia so one couldn't help be in awe of the way in which change occurred in Asia. Today our offshore business is almost entirely in Asia.

Sid Myer AM, Chairman, Myer Family Company, Melbourne, Australia

Australians who come up to Asia can be a little arrogant: some almost lecture Asian people on how things are done in Australia. Australian managers need to send people who are successful in Australia so that they can be successful here. Don't send people with no experience of Asia, who are bold and forceful or who are looking for a cushy expat lifestyle. It's hard work and they need to be prepared for that. We tend to bring people up here who have studied Asian languages or have spent time in Asia.

Hayden Flinn, Partner, King & Wood Mallesons, Hong Kong, China

I often see board members and senior executives from Australian companies coming up to China who lack international exposure. It is difficult for them because they lack an understanding of the international business environment.

David Olsson, Partner, King & Wood Mallesons, Beijing, China

I love working in Asia, it is fantastic. I've been given the opportunity to come to a different culture, learn the language and eat their food. There are many benefits. First, the type of project that you get exposed to in Asia and the Middle East occurs once in a lifetime in Australia. In Asia they occur daily. Secondly, the opportunity for career development and promotion here is much more readily available because the projects are bigger and there are less people here with experience. Thirdly, it's a great opportunity to explore the world, meet people, have a professional job and have fun while being paid for it.

Richard Padfield, Electrical Engineer, Arup Group, Ho Chi Minh, Vietnam

If you are trying to build a business up here, you have to think beyond being Australian because you are competing internationally. If you are positioned as an Australian company, then you will be regarded as being inferior. Local people want to hear from the world's major leaders like the UK and USA firms; because we compete against them, we need to look and sound more like them. Australia needs to work on its brand and position itself better amongst the world leaders. We are trying to make that change and it's exciting. We are succeeding, but it takes a long time.

Richard Mazzochi, Partner, King & Wood Mallesons, Hong Kong, China

Australian companies need to prepare employees they are sending up here: they need to learn more about the history of the country they are coming to work in – its current issues, culture and language and try to adapt to the in-country culture before they get here. Few Australian managers have led a bi-cultural team or operated in a different culture. This can be challenging for them.

Sometimes we see Western managers working here hiring people in their own image: they just want blokes who will enjoy drinking with them after work and they tend not to hire women. One third of the people who come to Hong Kong or China from overseas don't make it as people work longer and harder here.

Andrew Macintosh, Chief Executive Officer, Hanhong Private Equity, Hong Kong, China

There can be a bias against people who lack tenure in Australia. If you've been offshore for too long you are likely to find that local managers are looking for people with local knowledge. Hiring managers are generally risk averse so they will seek out people with local experience. People who have just returned from a long period overseas often have to take a lesser job for a while to prove themselves. It is driven by conservatism and the desire to minimise the risk.

Greg Stanmore, Managing Director, Spencer Stuart, Sydney, Australia

Asian languages and culture

Speaking the language

There has been inconsistency over 25 years by both governments regarding our commitment to developing school students to engage confidently with people and languages of the Asia region. There is increasing demand by corporate Australia for cultural and language training. Managers feel their workforces are not prepared for working in the Asia region. There is a very long way to go for corporate Australia to equip itself.

Sid Myer AM, Chairman, Myer Family Company, Melbourne, Australia

Why do we still teach French and German in schools? We are still focused on London and New York. We are better off with Asian languages or Spanish. No one in the school system is looking to close the gap and if you go to schools and ask children what they know about Asian language or history they look at you blankly.

Robert Milliner, Former Chief Executive Partner, Mallesons Stephen Jaques (now King & Wood Mallesons), Sydney, Australia

Every Chinese person learns English and if Australians are really serious about engagement with China, we must take on board the need to study Chinese.

David Olsson, Partner, King & Wood Mallesons, Beijing, China

The requirement for other languages as a criterion for selecting candidates hardly ever comes up. In fact it never comes up for Australian-based jobs. Even for the expat jobs we do, we are rarely asked to find people with language experience. Australia's physical isolation means we have had no need for any other languages.

Greg Stanmore, Managing Director, Spencer Stuart, Sydney, Australia

The two most important languages for commerce and culture for Australia's growth are the languages of China (1.3 billion people) and Indonesia (240 million people – living right next door). The Indonesian language has the smallest number of words in it so it is very easy to learn. Chinese languages are harder so we need to start learning them much earlier.

Phil Ruthven, Chairman, IBIS World, Melbourne, Australia

Getting to know Asian culture

Now that Malaysia is starting to develop, the value of the expat is less than before. Malaysian education is better, our economy is stronger and the internet provides remote access to knowledge which expats used to bring. Some expats that come here are open to the different cultures and we are more open to learning from these people.

Others come only because their companies say they can advance their careers and they really don't demonstrate that they want to be here: they come for the wrong reason. Those who don't bother to understand our culture or join in our festivals do not have a good experience. The value that this person brings will diminish.

Our advice to Australian companies would be to do a cultural assessment to check a person's interest in being culturally assimilated. Technical skills are no longer a differentiator; you need to 'fit in' culturally to have value to us.

Australians may accept minorities well, but they are not good at being a minority themselves. It could be that they need to study outside their own country to develop cross-cultural awareness, understanding and skills. One-third of my team of 40 employees has studied in an Australian university so they don't respond well to being told by expats that the world revolves around all things Australian.

Christopher Lim, Senior Manager, Ernst & Young Global, Kuala Lumpur, Malaysia

My generation is still culturally engaged with Europe. In the 1980s Australians would always go to Europe. It has only been the last four to five years that Australian executives have become frequent travellers to China. Most of us don't know the political system, we couldn't name more than three provinces or tell you much about their history, art or music. Australians are culturally illiterate [regarding much of Asia] and we need to start changing that.

Kevin McCann, Chairman, Macquarie Group, Sydney, Australia

We only hire people who are culturally savvy. They either have a Chinese background or they have language skills. The market is changing very fast away from bringing in loud expats to bringing people with proven ability to operate in this environment and culture.

Richard Mazzochi, Partner, King & Wood Mallesons, Hong Kong, China

The British and Europeans have experience [through colonialism] in running multiple economies and Asian's prefer to work with people from these countries over Australia and America who have no experience in managing a colony. Australian and American executives are thought to impose their views on others. If we are to succeed in Asia we need to improve our approach to working there.

Dharma Chandran, Chief Human Resources Officer, Leighton Holdings, Sydney, Australia

Cultural differences come out as being big issues with Australians doing business in China. It is mainly to do with the fact that boards and management who come here don't understand China. They need to spend more time here and it may take another generation of people exposed to China to work their way through the ranks.

Australians have more trouble integrating than continental Europeans. Germans and French are more culturally sensitive because of their experience in cross-cultural situations. Germans are very structured like Chinese so there is a natural fit. The Italians are loved here and the Russians are also well received. When it comes to Australians, we are a long way behind the Europeans in terms of cultural appreciation. People from the USA and UK don't do better than Australians at this.

Joanne Wood, Chairman, Capital Eight, Shanghai, China

Shaping up for success

China is developing so quickly. The work is steel-intensive and Australia is benefiting enormously from iron ore and coal sales. Urban planning and architecture services are needed here and Australian firms are doing well. We have not participated in terms of manufacturing yet. We could sell more wine to China if we had the scale. Scale becomes an issue when you deal with China.

The Germans do the best here because they can provide scale and they are pouring vast amounts of money into cultural programs. The Germans take it seriously and put substantial resources into developing their relations with China.

Dr Geoff Raby, Chief Executive Officer, Geoff Raby & Associates (and former Australian Ambassador to China), Beijing, China

The sectors that can do well in Asia are many. Resources and energy are the front-runners. The agricultural sector is under done: the world is going to run short of food and we could do more to supply Asia. Many Asian countries have ageing populations and we could provide more health services. There is a big opportunity to export education and financial services, like funds management, as Asia's emerging markets move to become developed economies.

Robert Milliner, Former Chief Executive Partner, Mallesons Stephen Jaques (now King & Wood Mallesons), Sydney, Australia

Australian businesses generally come here to ask 'What can we find in China to import to Australia?' rather than 'What can we make and supply to China?' China is gradually opening the gates sector by sector as they add standards. Design and architecture companies are doing very well here off the back of their involvement in the Beijing Olympic Games. Education and training is now taking off and financial services are opening up a bit. The four Australian banks now have a presence here and there are a few small export and distribution companies from Australia. Generally the view is that Australian businesses are missing, as they don't have much of a presence on the ground here.

Joanne Wood, Chairman, Capital Eight, Shanghai, China

What we see happening in Asia is typical of an emerging economy. In the 19th century, between 1800 and 1900, Australia's average growth rate was over 8 per cent. We kept that going for over 100 years. The same has been happening in China for the past 10 years. Australia has slowed to 3.5 per cent growth per annum, as has England and other mature Western economies. Once you reach the top level, the drive and energy goes. We no longer have that, but Asia has it.

Phil Ruthven, Chairman, IBIS World, Melbourne, Australia

The changing legal economic model in China is a big opportunity for us. In the past Chinese companies have not needed nor used lawyers or accountants because business was relationship-driven. As the Chinese economy is opening up to world trade they now need external advisers to help them with international business dealings: for the first time legal and accounting services are now required and this opens up more opportunity too.

Chinese clients don't pay on an hourly basis; they pay a price for the service, which is based on the value of the service and the strength of the relationship. It is a different way of paying for the service than we use in Western nations and it becomes a testing ground for new economic models for professional service firms. This gives us an opportunity to bring different people into the business and to grow more diverse teams to facilitate innovation and aid problem-solving for our global client base.

David Olsson, Partner, King & Wood Mallesons, Beijing, China

Australia, a world view

Australia is not part of the global power base due to isolation and distance. We don't think about being more involved in the world and our role will always be as an ally. We are not big enough and we don't have the platform to lead.

Bernard Salt, Partner, KPMG, Melbourne, Australia

When you contrast our role in the world with that of China it is interesting. My experience of the Chinese is that they are more pragmatic, for example, the Chinese give aid for trade. What is wrong with that? The Chinese government supports the Kenyan government to rebuild roads and it has transformed the streets and now people are more encouraged to invest there. If we were more rational the numbers would speak for themselves and our market would attract more investment.

Ann Sherry AO, Chief Executive Officer, Carnival Australia, Sydney, Australia

It would be wonderful if Australia could get closer to the rest of the world. Our beautiful country is hanging on the bottom of the world with its mineral wealth and its delicate landscape. We could lead the work on sustainable agriculture and fit a lot more people in without damaging the land. Food and water management are areas that we could lead in. Australia should be opening its doors to so many more people but we are not willing to do that. So many Australians are afraid of things changing. We don't have much faith in our ability to run things, let alone sustain a greater population.

Natalie Filatoff, Principal, Filatoff Editorial and Writing, Sydney, Australia

Australia's self-perception is not one of arrogance but one of defensiveness. There is a lack of confidence about our ability to take a spot in the world. We are only 22 million people and we dig stuff out of the ground. There are few world-class companies on the ASX100 who don't dig stuff out of the ground. If you look at the make-up of the management and board of ASX100 companies there is little spread of age, ethnicity or gender: these boards are typically old, white men. Through greater diversity we could build confidence and take a more prominent position in the world.

Dharma Chandran, Chief Human Resources Officer, Leighton Holdings, Sydney, Australia

The world order is changing and we are seeing this gradual shift of economic power from West to East. The growth that we have seen in Asia in the last three to five years will double in the next three to five years. Our only option is to engage more with Asia, particularly with China. We feel blessed because we have economic resources that have carried us through the GFC, but we may be lulling ourselves into a false sense of security. We have three choices: we can see Asia as a customer with one-way trade; we can consider two-way trade; or we can integrate with the region and become part of it. Australia has a window of opportunity and we have to use it with all our might.

David Olsson, Partner, King & Wood Mallesons, Beijing, China

Asian people in Australia

We have many Asians studying here and then we let them go home without seeking to link them in to our society or economy. We seek education revenues rather than long-term partnerships.

David Gonski AC, Chairman, Future Fund of Australia, Sydney, Australia

There are less people coming to study in Australia for two reasons. The first is because foreign students are exposed to racism and the second is the increasing cost of being educated in Australia due to the strength of the dollar. Indian students are now going to the UK and Canada and there is less investment in the education sector in Australia.

Pradeep Khanna, Chief Executive, PK Projects Management & Consultancy, Sydney, Australia

Our CEO interviewed the young Asians in the firm and we learned that they did not see themselves having a future in the firm because there were no role models. We began to look for bias and prejudice to remove any barriers to them having long careers with us.

Greg Couttas, Partner, Deloitte Touche Tohmatsu, Sydney, Australia

Chinese people still think that Australia is a nation of Caucasian people. They know little about our country so we need to provide more information. To attract immigrants and help them to settle into life in Australia I would focus on things close to the Chinese culture, like food and shopping. They know that Australia has fresh healthy food and great seafood and we should tell them where they can go to get great Asian food and highlight that every city has got its own Chinatown.

Joanne Wood, Chairman, Capital Eight, Shanghai, China

I went to Brisbane to study in year 11 and stayed to do my degree in Australia. I am now back in Hong Kong and it feels good to work for an Australian company. They treat their people well and give them lots of training to develop themselves. I am working on a very interesting project with Frank Gehry, a world-class architect who designed the Guggenheim in Spain. The project group is a multicultural team of eight and includes three people from Hong Kong, two from the UK, two from China and one from Australia.

Australians that come to work in Hong Kong fall into two groups: those that start to learn the local culture and go to evening classes to learn Cantonese; and those that stick to the local expat groups and make little effort to learn the language. Fortunately most people from Australia are adaptive and willing to learn.

Gabriel Yam, Managing Partner, Arup Group, Hong Kong, China

2012, a year of bold plans

When I started interviewing for this book mid-2011 the opportunity for many Australian businesses to grow their business across Asia was not widely recognised. There were only a few industries and businesses that had successfully experienced working across Asia and the general opinion was that it was difficult to be successful there for many reasons, including the oscillating position by successive Australian governments. It seemed that most people looked at the opportunity for growth in Asia as being 'someone else's opportunity'.

The reality of our future growth as a nation is just dawning. During the following 18 months in which I prepared *Stepping Up*, interest peaked due to the rapid rise of Asia's standing in the world economy, the high growth rates of fast-emerging Asian nations and the global chatter about China taking over global power and position from the USA.

Just as I was close to finishing the writing of this book two reports were released:

- Asialink's 'Developing an Asia Capable Workforce' September 2012
- Labor Government's 'Australia in the Asian Century White Paper', October 2012

Both reports give us much to consider and, if implemented fully, Australia will be in a very different place in 2025. I'd like to highlight the main recommendations of these reports because, if they are to be achieved, they both require an element of social change. I will indicate how the culture change promoted in *Stepping Up* can help both Asialink and the Labor Government to achieve the ambitions outlined in their respective reports.

Asialink's 'Developing an Asia Capable Workforce'

In September 2012 Asialink at The University of Melbourne released its paper 'Developing an Asia Capable Workforce' (see Appendix II for weblink to full report). The report highlighted 11 capabilities we need to build in Australia to take advantage of the growth in Asia. They are:

Individual Capabilities
- Sophisticated knowledge of Asian markets/environments
- Extensive experience operating in Asia
- Long-term trusted Asian relationships
- Ability to adapt behaviour to Asian cultural context
- Capability to deal with government
- Useful level of language proficiency

Organisational Capabilities
- Leadership committed to an Asia-focused strategy
- Customised Asian talent management
- Customised offering/value proposition based on customer insights
- Tailored organisational design with tendency to local autonomy
- Supportive processes to share Asian learnings

The report then summarises a 4-part strategy needed to bring these changes about. The strategies are:

- Advocate broadly the case for developing an Asia capable workforce;
- Accelerate the development of Asia focused strategies with Australian businesses taking the lead;
- Invest in developing Asia capability throughout the Australian workforce;
- More effectively educate Australia's future workforce for the Asian Century.

The Asialink Task Force identified many important steps in the report. They advise that we need to take these steps to be a credible player in the Asian market and to ensure a prosperous future for Australia and its people. If

Australia could build these 11 capabilities it would be preparing the Australian workforce very well for developing relations with and doing business in Asia, not to mention the expansive careers Australians could enjoy across the region.

However, there is a hitch. Implementation of the four strategies to achieve the capabilities is subject to the forces at the bottom of the Australian culture. These forces – the underlying 'assumptions' upon which the country's culture is formed and which influence the values and behaviours of Australians – can be an obstacle. These assumptions can create resistance to change if the people of Australia do not embrace the things we seek to change.

The capabilities listed by Asialink are necessary for our future and can bring about the changes sought, but they will only bring about changes to the top layers of the Australian Culture Iceberg, which on their own might not be sustainable.

If we take the changes and developments the Asialink report promotes and put them into the 'Iceberg' below, we can see that knowledge, experience, relationships, adaptability, capability, languages, leadership, commitment and talent management are all *behaviours that we hope to develop* in our people; and customised offerings/value proposition, organisational design and processes are all *artefacts that we hope to build* to support the performance of the people.

For these artefacts and behavioural changes to be effective and sustainable, there must be changes to the assumptions, values and attitudes of Australian culture at the lower levels. These changes need to be led by government, and supported by business and society.

Asialink's recommendations can help evolve the top layers of Australia's Culture Iceberg

When a culture is initially formed, the bottom layers come first. They form and influence the top layers (see Chapter 8) and they dominate the evolution of a culture as it drifts over time. Top layers can influence lower layers by reinforcing their existence; however, making adjustments to top layers only will rarely produce sustainable culture change if the assumptions below are not aligned as they can work against your planned intentions.

The changes recommended by Asialink's report, if implemented alone, could be undermined by assumptions, beliefs and attitudes held by Australians about the Asia region, Asian people, the value of languages, the role of Australia in the region, where the investment dollars should go, and whether they want to share their island equally with Asian immigrants.

Could these be the assumptions of our country culture relative to Asia?

- 'Asian development efforts are only ever partially successful';
- or 'Asian excitement is short lived';
- or 'Australia can manage alone';
- or 'Australia and Asia are like polite neighbours who meet at the street party but don't wish to invite each other into their homes'.

If these kinds of assumptions do exist at the bottom of our culture, then Asialink's recommendations will certainly be compromised. We need government leaders and leaders of society and business to embed assumptions that will aid our growth in Asia not hinder it.

Labor Government's 'Australia in the Asian Century White Paper'

The second report was released 28 October 2012 by the Labor government outlining 25 objectives to build Australia's competence and performance across Asia to 2025. It lists these 25 objectives under 5 core strategies:

- A productive and resilient Australian economy;
- Building capabilities;
- Operating in and connecting with growing Asian markets;
- Building sustainable security in the region;
- Deeper and broader relationships.

The foreword by Prime Minister Julia Gillard advised that:

> This White Paper is a plan to build on our strengths and shape our future. It details how, by 2025, Australia can be a winner in this Asian century by becoming more prosperous, more resilient, and sharing the new opportunities. It calls on all of us to play our part in becoming a more Asia-literate and Asia capable nation.

The Executive Summary says:

> Within only a few years, Asia will not only be the world's largest producer of goods and services, it will also be the world's largest consumer of them. It is already the most populous region in the world. In the future, it will also be home to the majority of the world's middle class.
>
> Success in the Asian century requires a whole-of-Australia effort, with businesses, unions, communities and governments being partners in a transformation as profound as any that have defined Australia throughout our history.
>
> It is in the interests of all Australians – and therefore in the national interest – to develop the capabilities and connections that Australia will need, so that we can contribute to, and learn from, the region, and take full advantage of these opportunities.

The 25 objectives are stated in this report as *targets* for the nation to achieve by 2025. The government's ambition as expressed in this report is to help Australia become a more prosperous and resilient Australia, which means to be 'part of the Asian region and open to the world'.

The report's 25 objectives are exciting. However, like the Asialink report, *Australia in the Asian Century* also focuses on the elements at the top of the Australian Culture Iceberg. In order to assure effective implementation and sustainable change, the government will need to identify the assumptions and values of the Australian culture that will aid or inhibit the achievement of these objectives.

To assist in understanding I have listed the report's 25 objectives in the table below and identified where they sit on the Culture Iceberg. (A link to the full report is in Appendix II). The 25 objectives are mostly expressed as *artefacts that need to be put in place or behaviours we expect to result* from the structural or systemic changes.

There is no argument that these 25 objectives are all necessary to keep Australia growing, maintaining its competitive position and building a strong economy to take it through to 2025. However, if we only do these things without changing the assumptions people hold, then we are operating in the Band-Aid Zone of our culture's evolutionary pathway. These developments will only produce sustainable outcomes if the lower levels of the Australian Culture Iceberg – assumptions, values and attitudes – are aligned and supportive of the evolution we seek: that is, we move the Australian culture to The Redirection Zone (Chapters 8–11).

'Australia in the Asian Century White Paper'

25 Objectives outlined for 2025	Culture Iceberg Layer (explained in Chapter 8)
Skills and Education	
1 All Australians will have the opportunity to acquire the <u>skills</u> and <u>education</u> they need to participate fully in a strong economy and a fairer society. Australia's school <u>systems</u> will be in the top five schooling systems in the world and our universities and training systems will be among the world's best.	Education systems = artefacts Skills = behaviours Education policy = value
Innovation	
2 Australia will have an <u>innovation system</u>, in the top 10 globally, that supports excellence and dynamism in business with a creative <u>problem-solving</u> culture that enhances our evolving areas of strength and attracts top researchers, companies and global partnerships.	Innovation system = artefacts Problem-solving = behaviour
Infrastructure	
3 Australia will implement a <u>systematic national framework</u> for developing, financing and maintaining nationally significant infrastructure that will assist governments and the private sector to plan and prioritise infrastructure needs at least 20 years ahead.	National framework = artefact
4 Australia's <u>communications infrastructure and markets</u> will be world leading and support the rapid exchange and spread of ideas and commerce in the Asian region.	Communications infrastructure and markets = artefacts
Tax System	
5 Australia's <u>tax and transfer system</u> will be efficient and fair, encouraging continued investment in the capital base and <u>greater participation in the workforce</u>, while delivering sustainable revenues to support economic growth by meeting public and social needs.	Tax and transfer system = artefact Greater participation in the workforce = behaviour
Regulatory reform	
6 Australia will be among the most <u>efficiently regulated</u> places in the world, in the top five globally, reducing business costs by billions of dollars a year.	Efficiently regulated = artefact
Environmental sustainability	
7 The Australian economy and our environmental <u>assets</u> will be managed sustainably to ensure the wellbeing of future generations of Australians	Asset management = artefact
Macroeconomic and financial frameworks	
8 Australia's <u>macroeconomic and financial frameworks</u> will remain among the worlds best through this period of change.	Macroeconomic and financial frameworks = artefacts
Building Capabilities	
9 Australia's <u>school system</u> will be in the top five schooling systems in the world, <u>delivering excellent outcomes</u> for all students of all backgrounds, and systematically improving performance over time.	School system = artefact Delivering excellent outcomes = behaviours
10 Every Australian student will have significant <u>exposure to studies</u> of Asia across the curriculum to <u>increase their cultural knowledge and skills</u> and enable them to be active in the region.	Exposure to studies = artefact Increase their cultural knowledge and skills = behaviour
11 All Australian students will have the opportunity, and be encouraged, to undertake a <u>continuous course of study in an Asian language</u> throughout their years of schooling. All students will have access to at least one priority Asian language; these will be Chinese (Mandarin), Hindi, Indonesian and Japanese.	Continuous course of study in Asian language = artefact and behaviour

12 Australia will remain among the world's best for <u>research and teaching in universities</u>, delivering excellent outcomes for a larger number of Australian students, attracting the best academics and students from around the world and strengthening links between Australia and the region.	Research and teaching in universities = artefact and behaviour
13 Australia will have <u>vocational education and training systems</u> that are among the world's best, <u>building capability in the region</u> and supporting a highly skilled Australian workforce able to continuously develop its capabilities.	Vocational education and training systems = artefact Building capability in the region = behaviour

Asia capable leaders, workplaces and institutions

14 Decision makers in Australian businesses, parliaments, national institutions (including the Australian Public Service and national cultural institutions) and advisory forums across the community will have <u>deeper knowledge and expertise</u> of countries in our region and have a <u>greater capacity to integrate domestic and international issues</u>.	Deeper knowledge and expertise (intellectual property) = artefact/behaviour Greater capacity to integrate domestic and international issues (intellectual property) = artefact/behaviour

Adaptability

15 Australian communities and regions will benefit from <u>structural changes</u> in the economy and seize the new opportunities emerging in the Asian century.	Economic structural changes = artefact

Social foundations

16 Australia will be a <u>higher skill, higher wage</u> economy with a fair, multicultural and cohesive society and a growing population, and all Australians will be able to benefit from, and participate in, Australia's growing prosperity and engagement in Asia.	Higher skill, higher wage economy = artefact Engagement in Asia = behaviour

Operating in and connecting with growing Asian markets

17 Australia's businesses will be recognised globally for their excellence and <u>ability to operate successfully in Asian markets</u>. Australian businesses will <u>offer high-value goods and services</u> as they link into regional and global value chains. Small and medium-sized enterprises will be integrated into Asian markets.	Offer high-value goods and services = artefact Ability to operate successfully in Asian markets = behaviour
18 The Australian economy <u>will be more open and integrated with Asia</u>, the flow of goods, services, capital, ideas and people will be easier, and Australian businesses and investors will have greater access to opportunities in Asia.	Be more open and integrated = behaviour

Australia's agriculture and food sector

19 Australia's <u>agriculture and food production system</u> will be globally competitive, with productive and sustainable agriculture and food businesses.	Agriculture and food production system = artefact

Building sustainable security in the region

20 <u>Australian policies</u> will contribute to Asia's development as a region of sustainable security in which <u>habits of cooperation</u> is the norm.	Australian policies = artefact Habits of cooperation = behaviour
21 The region will be more sustainable and human security will be strengthened with the <u>development of resilient markets</u> for basic needs such as energy, food and water.	Development of resilient markets = artefact

Deeper and broader relationships

22 Australia will have the necessary <u>capabilities</u> to promote Australian interests and maintain Australia's influence. Australia's <u>diplomatic network</u> will have a larger footprint across Asia.	Capabilities = artefact Diplomatic network = artefact
23 Australia will have stronger and more <u>comprehensive relationships</u> with countries across the region, especially with key regional nations –China, India, Indonesia, Japan and South Korea.	Comprehensive relationships = behaviours
24 Australia will have <u>deeper and broader people-to-people links</u> with Asian nations, across the entire community	Deeper and broader people-to-people links = behaviours
25 Australia will have <u>stronger, deeper and broader cultural</u> links with Asian nations.	Stronger, deeper and broader cultural links - behaviours

Successful implementation of both Asialink's recommendations and the government's 25-point plan will rest entirely on whether or not we identify and adjust the assumptions upon which Australia's current culture has been based.

Fast change requires a shift in assumptions and a 'jolt' to the culture's foundations. Without a shift in assumptions the changes we seek for Australia will take several generations to achieve.

Key messages about Asia

There was not a single person interviewed who did not agree that the growth in Asia presented a significant opportunity for Australia, but few keenly embraced the idea personally. The opportunity was generally thought to be for other people, other sectors.

About half of the 100 leaders were passionate about the need for the Australian government and local business leaders to do more to prepare the Australian workforce to take advantage of the Asian opportunity. They expressed frustration at the lack of consistency and clarity of policy that, if present, could make a huge difference to the take-up and success of Australians doing business in Asia.

Australians living and working in Asia are very enthusiastic about the potential and they seem highly charged by the working environment and challenges they are surrounded by. However, they express a degree of disappointment and even frustration at the lack of preparedness of a high proportion of Australian expats who are transferred to Asia for career advancement purposes.

Australia's isolation and lack of physical border with neighbouring nations was referred to frequently as a reason for poor language skills and cross-cultural understanding. These are limitations but they are by no means barriers to doing things differently in the future. A commitment to closer economic relations with Asia and investment in languages in schools and in facilitating the movement of labour in both directions could change things immeasurably.

Let's act on the issues

From the following summary of the issues raised by the 100 leaders we can begin to consider the steps we need to take.

- The Asian opportunity for Australian businesses is real and big:
  - We are not taking advantage of our historical ties or close proximity to Asia;
  - Asian nations welcome Western technology and experience;

- Australia has been arguing about which countries to align with and there is a high level of anxiety that we will be taken over from the north;
- Parts of Asia are said to be more sophisticated and more developed than Australia and we can learn from them: yet there are reports of Australians arriving in Asia with an arrogant attitude that 'our way is better';
- It is difficult for Australian businesses operating in Asia as each country has a different legal system and statutory requirement: better to focus on a few;
- Australians have to think beyond being Australian when doing business in Asia as it is a truly international market space.

- Australians are comfortable in Asia but can be arrogant and might not fit in:
  - There is an increasing number of Australian and New Zealend managers with experience in Asia and that provides competitive advantage;
  - The Australian expats sent by their companies to develop careers should be only those curious about the host country's culture and values to ensure they have a good experience and add value to the local operation;
  - Technical skills are less sought after due to the internet providing access to knowledge: Asian businesses are now looking for leadership and management skills;
  - The Asian view of the Australian Brand is not entirely positive (drinking and larrikin-like behaviour): we should think about rebranding and repositioning;
  - Australian expats in Asia have great difficulty getting 'back in' to a top job here and are told to 'take a lesser job' to prove the experience they acquired.

- We really must learn Asian languages and build Asian cultural competence:
  - Chinese people will be our major immigrants, investors, foreign students and tourists and we have little Chinese language ability or cultural understanding;
  - Australians tend to holiday in Europe and America before China and other parts of Asia, especially the northern nations;
  - As an Australian manager you now 'have to have' Asian experience and understand how to do business in Asia and with Asian people;

- We think that because Asians speak English there is no need for us to learn Chinese, this is a myopic view and will limit our growth in the region;
- China appears to be least understood and Australian management and boards who go there are criticised for their lack of cultural understanding.

- Big trade opportunities exist but we need to be more focused and hungry:
  - Asia started its growth journey recently: it is entering 'consumerism' and will have 8 per cent growth rate for several decades so we need to be involved;
  - Opportunities for Australia to export to Asia increases as its emerging nations become more developed: they need education, financial services etc;
  - Government funding still goes to Europe-centric projects more than Asian ones and we need to try to change that;
  - Australians travel to Asia more than Europeans and Americans so the few who are working in Asia are more comfortable there and have an advantage;
  - Australia seems to lack hunger, know-how and confidence for doing business in Asia;
  - Australian companies tend to import from China rather than export to it, and those who do export rarely offer innovative products. Scale is also a problem.

- Australia's role in the world is limited by its vision, government policy, isolation and poor diversity:
  - The Australia government still looks to the United Kingdom and America for political alliances: it should be building stronger relations in Asia as that is where our future trade and growth will come from;
  - There has been inconsistency regarding government policy on Asia for years, although reviews are underway to change this;
  - Without bipartisan political leadership we limit our ability to get a sustainable growth strategy for Asia;
  - Our isolation and distance make it hard for us to participate in global leadership matters and Australia is too small to lead;
  - Leading Australian businesses could get more involved in political debates and influence our role in the world, and greater cultural diversity on our boards would provide greater understanding of global issues.

- We could do better for Asians living in Australia:
  - The Chinese are expected to be our top visitor group by the end of this decade and we have no strategy to prepare our people or local business for that;
  - Australia is a net-exporter to Asia and we are missing the opportunity to get Asian talent to our skills-short industries and businesses;
  - We have few Asian people in senior management and board positions of Australian companies and we need to look to increase their participation;
  - We don't seek to integrate or keep Asian students studying here so they go home and take their learning with them;
  - Foreign students are subject to high fees and racist attitudes so Asians are looking to Europe more than Australia for education.

If Ann Sherry's view that 'there is a disconnect between what we say and what we do' is accurate, then we need to closely examine the assumptions of Australia's culture and local business cultures to see what is holding us back. To talk-the-talk but fail to walk-the-walk is a phenomenon well known to business and political watchers all over the world. Saying that you believe in something that just never comes true is a sign of weakness that is transparent to others. If Australia is fooling itself, it is unlikely to be fooling the onlookers; especially onlookers from Asia who we may need to rely on in the very near future.

There are so many questions to answer. Can Australia afford to ignore the views and voices of our leaders who want to see greater involvement in Asia? Can we take the risk that European nations prepare their people faster and smarter than Australia can, or is willing to? Have we thought through the consequences of remaining monolingual in a globalising economy where our major business partners are multilingual and have significantly broader cultural experiences than people born and bred in Australia? Are we prepared to ignore the opportunity to teach our people Asian languages and Asian history, culture, music and art, which would help increase their tolerance and ability to work successfully with and live alongside people from Asian backgrounds?

Let's become Asia-literate

In 2006 the British Council commissioned a study called *English Next 2006* to look into the future of the English language. The author David Graddol concluded that monoglot English graduates face a bleak economic future as qualified multilingual youngsters from other countries are proving to have a competitive advantage over their British counterparts in global companies and organisations.

The report highlighted that the lack of students fluent in a foreign language in both Britain and the United States will eventually weaken the competitiveness of both countries. I expect this assessment applies equally to all English speaking nations that have poor take-up of foreign language learning.

The report brims with reasons why our children should learn Chinese, such as:

- Because of the current boom in the Chinese economy, greater knowledge and broader experience may give them significant advantages in the globalised workplace of tomorrow;
- In a world where everybody speaks English, being a native English speaker does not carry much weight, however the ability to speak several languages could prove to be extremely advantageous and kids who learn Chinese will put themselves at the top of the multilingual list;
- Today, nearly 1.4 billion people speak Chinese – nearly three times the number of English speakers;
- The advantages of learning Chinese, or any other language, provides an edge in geopolitics or economic competition;
- The dominance of the English language on the internet is declining and other languages are now proliferating;
- Mandarin and Spanish are challenging English in some territories for educational resources and policy attention;
- The competitive advantage which English has historically provided its acquirers (personally, organisationally, and nationally) will ebb away as English becomes a near-universal basic skill, making the need to maintain the advantage by moving beyond English will be felt more acutely;
- When kids learn to speak Chinese they benefit from an expanded cultural awareness. Language is a look into another culture. One doesn't need to be proficient in Chinese languages in order to do business in China. But the exposure and the motivation to show that one understands and respects the Chinese culture is really half the battle won;
- Young people wanting to take on challenging global leadership roles must possess a deep understanding of and appreciation for other cultures, economies, history and languages.

The report concludes: 'With the rapid globalisation and the economic rise of China, our educational systems have a responsibility to prepare children for the demands of their future. The question is when, not whether, the schools are going to adjust.'

English Next 2006 is now several years old and illustrates how far Australia is behind in its thinking on this topic. Could it be time for our government to step-up to the platform on this very important topic and make a strategic decision, and possibly some long-term investment?

Let's embrace Asia and be part of it

We know from past experience, and we hear from the 100 leaders throughout this book, that some people just don't value change, or Asia, or Asian people, or immigrants, or expats, or the knowledge you gain when you work offshore. For example, we hear below that expats who go away to work overseas find it impossible to get back in at the same level and that hiring managers say they need to 'take a lesser job' to prove themselves; so why would people put their hands up to go away when this is the prospect of their return?

Stepping Up is full of compelling examples that suggest we need to get to the bottom of the Australian culture to effectively build an Asia capable workforce to do more business in the region. Implementation of the changes recommend by Asialink and the government's White Paper would serve to adjust only top layers of our national Culture Iceberg and this leaves us in The Band-Aid Zone as described by The Culture Zones detailed in Part Three.

These Zones, which relate to our state of cultural evolution, illustrate that Australia is currently somewhere between The Comfort Zone and the Band-Aid Zone. You'll need to read Part Three to fully appreciate how the Culture Iceberg and The Culture Zones can work to support your business change initiatives and to know how to move into the place we need to be: the Redirection Zone.

No doubt: we need to act now

The signs are all around us. The pace of change is rapid and there is no doubt where the future growth is coming from. If we choose to walk blindly or with blinkers on it's pretty clear that bigger and hungrier economies will beat us in the fight for market share in Asia.

Australia is not immune to being negatively affected by the rapid growth in Asia. If Australia fails to respond quickly we could lose out economically and politically now and in the future.

Our political leaders have been slow to step up on Asia or invest in building Australia's Asian capability. If Australia were a company, its medium-term existence would certainly be at risk. The recent reviews are welcomed but we need political leaders to lead change with conviction, to advance our position in the Asia region ahead of more distant economies.

Similarly, too few Australian businesses operate extensively offshore. Local industry and business needs to build Asia capability urgently and pursue the Asian opportunities more aggressively, putting pressure on government to support them, or we could still be talking about this 10 years from now.

I believe we need to move on developing much greater capability to perform economically across the region now. We need to address the fear, remove the blockages and empower all Australians to be actively engaged in the region's growth. By closing the cultural gap we have with Asia, we substantially reduce the impact of the physical gap.

To do this, we absolutely must address the resistance to getting closer to Asia and get excited about being part of its growth. We also need to encourage Australia's culture to evolve, get national agreement about what we want Australia to stand for, where we want to be in 10 years and how we will get there.

The prospects are very exciting and as the younger generations have been raised closely with many cultures in Australia, including those of Asia, I expect that they will be keen to follow your lead.

Chapter 5

The Australian Opportunity

'Myths are fine when they inspire, but what if they actually weaken us by blinding us to the truth about ourselves?'

Hugh Mackay in *Advance Australia...Where?*, Social Researcher and Writer, Sydney, Australia

A large part of Australia's readiness to take advantage of the opportunity in Asia and Australia is a function of its culture. Similarly, its ability to embrace greater diversity is also directly linked to its values and beliefs.

So to write a book about how to achieve diversity, it's important to obtain a clear understanding of the elements of Australia's culture and one of the best ways to identify the elements is by asking the people who live in that culture. While the research sample for this book is narrow (mostly urban Australian leaders engaged in the corporate sector, as well as business leaders in Asia who are from, or do business with, Australia) their views are highly relevant as they represent the group that needs to help lead the change to enable diversity.

The things that are valued in a culture are the things that get attention. Beliefs that a population holds firm are those driving attitudes. Attitudes that a population has towards people and things invokes a response from people outside the population. And behaviours exhibited by a population are a reflection of its attitudes, beliefs and values. Behaviours are the 'tell-tale' sign of the other elements of a culture that are not necessarily immediately evident.

All countries are afforded the same wonderful opportunity to use the positive and strong elements of their culture to achieve their internal goals and they can also use their culture to develop international relationships. Most countries and cultures are known for their distinct and memorable behaviours – otherwise known as traditions or customs – that people from inside and outside the culture observe.

For example, a well-known American custom is the celebration of Thanksgiving in November each year in remembrance of the early settlers giving thanks for a successful harvest that would see them through the harsh winter months; a New Zealand custom is indigenous people performing the Haka (traditional Maori war dance) at official ceremonies and major events; the Japanese are known for their Tea Ceremonies and they even have training courses to teach people how to conduct the ceremony properly; the Irish tradition of celebrating St Patrick's Day by wearing green costume is celebrated by people all over the world whether Irish or not; and Hindus in India wear the Tilak, a red mark of blessing or greeting placed on the forehead between the brows which is considered to be the seat of wisdom and mental focus.

Australia's customs and traditions

It is always interesting to see how a country promotes its customs and traditions. If you Google 'Australian Customs and Traditions' it delivers websites that reference jackaroos (cowboys), larrikins (hoodlums), mateship and the barbecue – or barby (which has become a widely popular method of cooking food in Australia and involves 'prawns on the barby' for special occasions). All of which leave you with the impression that it is a very relaxed society.

This statement was taken from an official government website:

> 'Australia's diverse culture and lifestyle reflect its liberal democratic traditions and values, geographic closeness to the Asia–Pacific region and the social and cultural influences of the millions of migrants who have settled in Australia since World War II. Australia is a product of a unique blend of established traditions and new influences.'

However, the customs or traditions are not detailed in the website this was taken from. What is listed instead are shared values and a statement about Australia's egalitarian society. These are said to be:

Shared values

At the same time, everyone is expected to uphold the principles and shared values that support Australia's way of life. These include:

- *respect for equal worth, dignity and freedom of the individual*
- *freedom of speech and association*
- *freedom of religion and a secular government*
- *support for parliamentary democracy and the rule of law*
- *equality under the law*

- *equality of men and women*
- *equality of opportunity*
- *peacefulness*
- *a spirit of egalitarianism that embraces tolerance, mutual respect, and compassion for those in need. Australia also holds firmly to the belief that no one should be disadvantaged on the basis of their country of birth, cultural heritage, language, gender or religious belief.*

An egalitarian society

In most practical ways, Australia is an egalitarian society. This does not mean that everyone is the same or that everybody has equal wealth or property.

But it does mean that there are no formal or entrenched class distinctions in Australian society, as there are in some other countries. It also means that with hard work and commitment, people without high-level connections or influential patrons can realise their ambitions.

I suspect some people might want to contest the list of values based on current experiences: the disparities between the roles of women and their pay levels questions 'equality of men and women' and the private education system questions 'equality of opportunity'. The idea that 'no one should be disadvantaged on the basis of their country of birth, cultural heritage, language, gender or religious belief' is admirable but let's see whether our 100 leaders interviewed think we are actually living this.

While egalitarianism can be argued many ways, it is true that senior management of most listed and private companies are predominantly white males and when it comes to boards they are also heavily populated with white males of an advanced age suggesting that tenure might carry more weight than meritocracy, and that the 'old boy network' might also be favouring its own. So the statement 'people without high-level connections or influential patrons can realise their ambitions' is also questionable.

One custom of the Australian culture that I did find described in as much detail as the Japanese Tea Ceremony is the *Acknowledgment of Country and Traditional Owners*: a ceremony made at the start of official gatherings or special occasions. It is performed as a mark of respect for Aboriginal protocol and most locals and visitors would have experienced this custom at some time.

Compared with other countries, Australia's customs and traditions, things that are distinctly and uniquely Australian, are much less about tradition and more about attitude and lifestyle. Due to the huge numbers of immigrants since the mid-1940s and the borrowing of custom and traditions from other cultures, it seems that Australia might have missed an opportunity to maintain old, or develop new, formal customs and traditions, things that convey history and values of previous generations and leaders of days gone by.

Without direction cultures can drift

Cultures of young countries, like young companies and young people, are still forming and there is a much greater chance of influencing the shape and direction of a young culture than an old one. But there are challenges. For countries like Australia, for which the dominant European culture dates back only as far as 1788 and where the origins of the people are varied, there are too few common stories, traditions and behaviours among the current generations for the culture to have matured. People from different backgrounds don't always have empathy for one another and leaders from one group can jostle to maintain the values that are important to his/her group, while not paying sufficient attention to the values of another group.

I believe we are capable of advancing our culture faster than people give us credit for. Waiting for culture to evolve over time in a nation that is made up of immigrants from all over the world is a high-risk strategy. Like icebergs, cultures drift and they can end up where the current takes them. Australia's opportunity is to guide its culture to a place that is helpful to its notion of the future, but that requires it to have a clear image of what the future will hold.

Hugh Mackay has this comment to make on what people say are Australia's values: "Three of our favourite 'national values' sound suspiciously as if they were borrowed from the French Republic's *liberte, egalite, fraternite*, though they are generally presented in reverse order as Australia's own: mateship, egalitarianism and the 'fair go.'" I included these three 'favourite' values in my questions to most of the people interviewed and many offered their opinions, which are recorded below.

By the time you get to the end of this book, I will have discussed more about the values and behaviours that would help Australia to build greater diversity for greater productivity; how we can build them into day-to-day living; and who we should look to for leadership.

Exploring Australian culture

Let's review what the 100 leaders thought about the questions I put to them. Here is a sample of the questions:

- What is fabulous about Australian culture that Australians should be proud of?
  - What do Australian's most admire about the culture?
  - What elements of our culture do we want to pass to the next generation?
  - What is unique and serves us well internationally?

- What elements of Australian culture do you question...and why?
  - Are there any things that you are embarrassed about?
  - What should we not pass down to the next generation?
  - In what ways are we 'blind to ourselves'?

- What are the core values of Australian culture?
  - What things in our society and the way we live do we value most?
  - What espoused Australian values do you think are actually not true and should be challenged?

- What attitudes do people hold?
  - What attitudes are prevalent in our society that you think are positive?
  - What attitudes are prevalent in our society that you think are negative?
  - What attitudes do you think Australians should hold that would be helpful to achieving diversity and growth?

- What behaviours do you see that explain Australian culture?
  - What behaviours do you see that give the world a good impression?
  - What behaviours do you see that give the world a poor impression?
  - How can we change these behaviours?

- What cultural challenges would you like to see addressed?
  - What is our cultural Achilles heel?
  - What are our biggest challenges and why?
  - Are Australians ready for cultural change?

What's fabulous about Australian culture?

As I meet other CEOs and customers I notice there is a huge 'can-do' attitude in this country. Australia is very pioneering and it serves the country well. We have had a big group of Australian managers do very well in the USA and other places. They are adaptable and they work hard. There are a number of success stories.

Paul Waterman, President, BP Australia, Melbourne, Australia

With regard to multiculturalism we do extremely well and in part that is because we live well here. If we were a poor or small nation and had an influx of people from different cultures we might not be so friendly if we thought we couldn't provide for our families and we might resent people taking our jobs. As a wealthy and big country, there is lots of opportunity for everyone and we are a great country to migrate to. I don't think they [immigrants] should be fully integrated as the differences [they bring] are the things that enrich this country.

Natalie Filatoff, Principal, Filatoff Editorial and Writing, Sydney, Australia

It annoys me when we get beaten up. I think we are good at multiculturalism: it's not just about the different types of restaurants. You can see it in sports, the arts and music. You just need to look at the surnames of the people who are doing well.

Sid Myer AM, Chairman, Myer Family Company, Melbourne, Australia

We need to remember Australia is a young multicultural society, not an old one.

Nigel Garrard, Managing Director, Amcor, Melbourne, Australia

I think Australia does pretty well at multiculturalism. Sydney and Melbourne are more like Hong Kong these days. There is a mix of Asian-born and Australian-born people and in government we are starting to see more Asian faces. I don't think we are too bad if you look around the corporate world. Australia is educating 138,000 Asian students a year and most of them will probably go back to their home country, engage in business and in 15 years it will be helpful to have these alumni in senior positions in the corporate world across the region.

Dr Geoff Raby, Chief Executive Officer, Geoff Raby & Associates (and former Australian Ambassador to China), Beijing, China

If you look at our campus you can see that the Australian culture is now changing: close to 25 per cent of the students originate from 120 countries. When you look at the students you can't tell who is an Australian national and who is a foreign student because both groups are very culturally diverse. They study, play sport and do work experience in industry together. There's no obvious cultural gap at any level – from the first year students to the PhD students.

Professor Fred Hilmer AO, President & Vice Chancellor, University of NSW, Sydney, Australia

It is important that immigrants pass on their heritage to their children through stories. It has been a very enriching thing for my son to hear where his grandparents came from [Russia and Japan]. They tell him the reasons why they left their homelands and what their hopes were when they came to this country. I don't think we tell enough stories about how Australia came together, who the immigrants were, where they came from and why they came. It is important that we share the stories with others outside of our families too: it is these stories that will unite Australians.

Natalie Filatoff, Principal, Filatoff Editorial and Writing, Sydney, Australia

What's not so fabulous?

We need to start with an 'aha' about how closed we are as a society. Boards have to understand that what they are doing isn't sustainable. Most men on public company boards grew up when women stayed at home and cultural diversity was something they got when they went on holiday. Their life experience is quite narrow.

It also goes beyond boards. Everything we do here is about limiting access to the good stuff. Those in power have a systematic way of cutting people out. Anywhere that you can make a reasonable amount of money is a closed shop; it's to protect the supply side. If you are a doctor from another part of the world, you have to do another few years to be able to work at your level here. If you are an engineer, you might be able to get a job if you graduated from a university in a Western country or perhaps southern Asia. We say that we give people living here all the same rights, but we are locking people out. We have no one holding up the mirror.

Ann Sherry AO, Chief Executive Officer, Carnival Australia, Sydney, Australia

The recent sexual harassment cases in Australia remind us that something is wrong with the Australian culture. We continue to behave as we did in the 1970s. Men still don't get it. There is no respect.

Richard Mazzochi, Partner, King & Wood Mallesons, Hong Kong, China

When I came to Australia I expected to meet a society that was discussing issues relating to gender diversity. I expected to hear that it was valued and it meant something. I expected to see the newspapers reflecting the issues and to read that the politicians are chatting about it. I expected to see courage to discuss it, but it wasn't there. I felt I met a conservative society, not a modern one. Australians don't discuss diversity and gender equality like we do in Norway.

The topic is not in your frontal lobe. You need to have a frontal attack on the masculinity stereotypes in Australia. The stereotypes are deeply rooted in Australian society and you lack family policies [to support women who want careers as well as children]. If you don't get gender equality into the frontal lobe you won't get the other types of diversity coming along either. You need to analyse the whole complex structure: Australia needs to modernise itself.

Arni Hole, Director General, Norwegian Royal Ministry for Children, Equity and Social Inclusion, Oslo, Norway

Sydney people pride themselves as living in a global city. The truth is we are a long way from the action and we like it that way. People don't like the idea of the Singapore Stock Exchange buying the ASX: while they say they can see the advantages, they don't agree with signature companies being owned by foreigners.

There is a sense that immigrants should have to start at the bottom and that it is somehow good for them. They can't just wander in here and expect a job, they have to work their way up. They should take what they can get and work their way into the system. "Prove yourself! We won't make it easy!" This attitude leads to an erosion of skills. It's a blind prejudice.

Hugh Mackay, Social Researcher and Writer, Sydney, Australia

If men on boards have the power, why would they give it up? If they love having the space to themselves, why would they share it? Chairmen seem to keep hiring people who look and sound like them. That said, people do come along who are seriously good and they are smart enough to know that they need the talent of everyone.

Ilana Atlas, Non-Executive Director, Coca-Cola Amatil, Sydney, Australia

The risk of failure is greater for women because the media here are harder on women than they are on men when they stumble.

Julie Coates, Director, BIG W, Sydney, Australia

It's been called a blokey culture and I think that this is kind of true. When you're in a social situation there is definitely segregation [between the men and women]. The result is you get exclusion.

Paul Waterman, President, BP Australia, Melbourne, Australia

Multiculturalism is an excuse for indifference. It is still pale, stale and male. We have not integrated vertically (maybe horizontally).

Neil Cockroft, Head of Diversity and Culture, King & Wood Mallesons, Sydney, Australia

As soon as those 'clubby' discussions start they are naturally exclusive for most women.

Jane Owen, Partner, Middletons, Sydney, Australia

Some of my clients haven't got the cultural 'aha' yet. They are still adjusting to the gender diversity challenges and many of them are not concerned by the ASX guidelines. Some are ignoring the guidelines and will wait for the 'if not, why not' question to come from the regulators.

Margaret Dreyer, Partner, Deloitte Touche Tohmatsu, Sydney, Australia

We have a very macho culture, therefore it is culturally difficult, but we are open to change if it is voluntary. It is okay if it is encouraged and led, not pushed.

Jillian Segal AM, Non-Executive Director, National Australia Bank, Sydney, Australia

I had the benefit of working once where culture and gender diversity were the norm. It was pure joy working across cultures and learning constantly from the others; they brought so many other dimensions to the table. That was in the UK and when I came back to Australia it felt like a white monoculture here.

Annette Kimmitt, Office Managing Partner, Ernst & Young Global, Victoria, Australia

There is inherent racism in Australia. It is a hangover from the 'White Australia Policy' of the early 1900s. Australia was frightened of anything different. Even today there is intolerance of heavily accented English and of people who have different behaviours. The culture and values debate is starting. On the one hand there is increased social pressure to have more babies and at the same time women are asking for space in the workforce. Our inadequate childcare systems make it hard for more women to build careers and a higher divorce rate leads to greater need for, and appetite for, women to work.

Katy McDonald, Director of Human Resources, Minter Ellison, Sydney, Australia

I don't think men really know what diversity means and why they have to do it. Years ago when women started going back to work after having their children, many men would think "she is doing it for me: to be a more stimulating companion for me". Men didn't realise that she didn't go back to the workforce to entertain them or to be a more stimulating dinner companion. Men are threatened by women who want to build careers.

Hugh Mackay, Social Researcher and Writer, Sydney, Australia

In Australia in the 1980s and 90s we were keen to learn from different people and there was a push to bring in other cultures and value the difference they brought with them. However the current cultural diversity situation is heart-breaking: I can't remember the last time I heard a conversation about 'languages'.

> Dr Julianne Schultz AM, Non-executive Director, Australian Broadcasting Corporation, Sydney, Australia

Despite broad diversity at all lower levels of our university, it's different at the top end. Our boardroom directors are much older and mostly male: we are rooted in our old habits. We have put in targets to get more diversity in level five but we have a way to go. The older people in society will not change quickly so it is up to us all to help influence that change.

> Professor Fred Hilmer AO, President & Vice Chancellor, University of NSW, Sydney, Australia

Casual racism is more noticeable here. Attitudes to ethnic groups are expressed in everyday discussion. Some towns, on the face of it, look multicultural but they are actually quite segregated. There is a general alienisation of the Muslim community and young white Australians think Muslim men are not embracing the values. The Cronulla riots are evidence of that but thankfully it has got better since then. There is concern about radicalisation of the young Muslim Australians: they are seen as the enemy. Australia is at a crossroads and this could become problematic if we don't do anything about it.

> John Godfrey, Senior Commissioning Editor Documentaries, SBS Television, Sydney, Australia

An egalitarian society won't handle a second class of people. Yet in the past 25 years the rich have got richer and the poor have got poorer.

> James MacKenzie, Chairman, Mirvac, Melbourne, Australia

The way in which languages and literacy have been treated in the school system is a sorry state of affairs. Recently the trends have gone south. There is some awareness in government that learning languages is important, but when it comes to winning votes, this topic doesn't count and the funds stop flowing.

> Sid Myer AM, Chairman, Myer Family Company, Melbourne, Australia

There are pockets of progress being seen now because of the ASX governance changes. Many companies are just beginning to look at the issues, especially those industries where few women employees exist. No one is doing a stellar job at gender balancing.

> Ruth Medd, Chair, Women on Boards, Sydney, Australia

We have a very conservative culture. We still accept racist comments and are allowed to make them. We continue to take 'boys only' sports to the office (like golf and rugby). Our excessive drinking is nothing to be proud of. We still have schools that educate girls and boys separately; it's not a good idea but it's ingrained in our culture.

There is a lot of 'dark' in corporate Australia because we are measured on short-term profitability and billable hours. Managers select people who fit in and look like themselves; the risk is reduced if you don't have people with different viewpoints. The many cultures we have in Australia are not reflected at top levels: they are all Anglo-Saxon at the top.

Kerry Jukes, Consultant, Chief Executive Women, Sydney, Australia

'Father and son' sleep-outs and 'dads-only' school fundraising dinners set values that we take with us. Unconscious bias starts here; you are not born with it. It comes from the home, school and social environment in which we were raised. It becomes so embedded that we don't see it. Don't blame the kids: blame the schools, parents, teachers and the religious infrastructure. When the kids in Australia today get jobs, how will they deal with the unconscious bias that they have taken from their upbringing?

Stephen Roberts, Chief Country Officer, Citi, Sydney, Australia

What are Australia's core values?

The good values we see here are family, safety and work ethic. People in Australia like to work but they want work–life balance, this has become an important value. Democracy is important: Australians don't like politicians much but they'll put up with them.

Mike Smith OBE, Chief Executive Officer, Australian and New Zealand Banking Group, Melbourne, Australia

We need to ask what the core Australian values are and how much we expect people who come to live here to change [to adopt Australia's values]. I believe in a 'fair go' – this is special. Egalitarianism, this is real. I'm not sure about mateship, it suggests 'pack mentality' and it is not special to Australia.

Jane Hemstritch, Non-Executive Director, Commonwealth Bank of Australia, Melbourne, Australia

We value 'a fair go'. There is a lot of pride in Australia but we're not sure how to embrace other cultures, and there is an element of racism.

We are not valuing the Asian opportunity. We should have a debate about compulsory language or if we are unable to make it compulsory, then we should at least encourage and incentivise language learning. People who say "Yes, we are Asia-ready" are deflecting the issue. Australian business readiness [to operate in Asia] is really poor. How many Australian companies have experience in Asia and can understand the cultural nuances and speak the language? Competitive advantage is to be smart, to plan and strategise. The simple fact is that we are relying on our natural resources and falling behind other countries when it comes to Asia.

Robert Milliner, Former Chief Executive Partner, Mallesons Stephen Jaques (now King & Wood Mallesons), Sydney, Australia

I think the man in the street would regard mateship as 'going out with the boys and drinking too much'. It is a drinking culture and people in Australia regard that as an important element of their culture.

Hayden Flinn, Partner, King & Wood Mallesons, Hong Kong, China

If you asked people at a barbecue whether mateship, egalitarianism and 'a fair go' were Australia's core values they might say 'yes'. But mateship only applies so long as you look like me. And egalitarianism fits so long as you are in my group. It doesn't mean we are all bad, there are many good people. At Arup we recognise that sometimes we don't live our values very well and we need to revisit them from time to time.

Dr Robert Care AM, Chair UK, Middle East and Africa Region, Arup Group, London, United Kingdom

The things we should value are equality, inclusiveness and enjoying the differences in people that live here. How do we turn those things into something we seek out, rather than tolerate? As a society we are not valuing learning languages enough; yet you get an understanding of different cultures by learning languages so it is very important.

Uschi Schreiber, Managing Partner - Global Government & Public Sector Industry Centre, Ernst & Young Global, Hong Kong, Australia

I'm not sure what it is to be Australian now. I don't see mateship or 'a fair go' as being our values. And the way we deal with the boat people is breeding suspicion into our society when we should be trusting people from other places.

Peter Bailey, Chief Executive Officer, Arup Group, Sydney, Australia

We don't seem to take the big 'nation-building' decisions any more. Are we too comfortable? Have we got lazy?

Matt Tomaszewski, Director-Writer, Triton Media, Sydney, Australia

Most Australians play sport, which makes ours a participatory culture. When you are cast in a sporting environment at school, mateship builds through the sporting culture and that unfortunately leads to exclusions [of women]. I can see how it has happened. It will require a generational shift to fix it.

Stephen Roberts, Chief Country Officer, Citi, Sydney, Australia

What attitudes do people hold?

I never used to see racist attitudes, but I have become more aware of them over the last 10 years. I am not home in Australia very often so I don't know what has caused it. Perhaps it's the level of immigrants from Asia? People used to worry about the Japanese coming in the 1980s, then the Koreans, now it's the Chinese. I hear attitudes about the boat people and there is a religious bias against Islamic people and their faith.

Joanne Wood, Chairman, Capital Eight, Shanghai, China

People's attitudes to diversity are complex. Australia is not a melting pot like the US. Americans are proud to be American. They will tell you that they are Italian-American. When you ask people here about their heritage they just say 'Australian' and don't mention any other cultural heritage.

Paul Waterman, President, BP Australia, Melbourne, Australia

Before I started work 30 years ago it was expected that women would not be working by 30 years of age but they would be at home with children. Amazingly the general community still expect that today.

Kathryn Fagg, Former President - Corporate Development, Linfox Australia, Melbourne, Australia

Our attitude against Islam is the new big bias. We are not comfortable with anyone who practices a religion that we don't understand. We don't look at the skills of the people in detention centres and when they come out of detention they are either mad or bad. It's not consistent: we never demonise people who overstay their short-term visas.

Ann Sherry AO, Chief Executive Officer, Carnival Australia, Sydney, Australia

Australia is an 'immediate results' culture. The short-term attitude is a hindrance: it is the biggest obstacle in any business. There are no long-term plans and we are not good at investing in our future. In engineering there is huge value attached to design work as it is very important to deliver the ongoing benefit.

Peter Bailey, Chief Executive Officer, Arup Group, Sydney, Australia

The market in Australia is small so there might be only four 'right' people for a job. When hiring, you need to be careful that unconscious bias doesn't interfere with your decision. To avoid attitudes impacting on our decisions, we have enforced broader participation in the hiring process. People coming here go through 15 interviews to get a senior appointment. That helps to ensure buy-in from many different parts of the company and a range of people. As a country we haven't done a great job [regarding females, race, religion, or other minorities] and we have to do a better job.

Craig Drummond, Chief Executive Officer, Bank of America Merrill Lynch, Sydney, Australia

The big issue for us is our fear of foreigners and the boats. Australia's island mentality is behind this. The important thing about 'Go Back to Where you Came From' (an SBS documentary on refugees arriving by boat from Asia), was that it provided a voice that was missing from the debate – it humanised the debate. Many Australians say "Turn back the boats, we don't want boat people" and I don't think this is right. We are signatories to the UN refugee charter and like other signatories we should allow them to stay.

John Godfrey, Senior Commissioning Editor Documentaries, SBS Television, Sydney, Australia

People define 'the best company' as the one that makes the most money. Our society lives by this view too. It is a sign of increasing national affluence. When I was a kid most houses had a TV, stereo and a bike. That was all. Now kids have all that plus scooters, skateboards, roller blades, computers, game boys, Xbox's – everything imaginable! We don't necessarily have a huge amount of money, but our kids have so much that we don't know what to buy them at Christmas. People just seem to want more and more. We live in a lovely street but we only know three neighbours because we drive into our garage and the gates close behind us. Community life has gone: as a society we are just too busy.

Matt Tomaszewski, Director-Writer, Triton Media, Sydney, Australia

It's a very small and competitive market and people can't just waltz in here and expect to get recognition. They have to earn that.

(Anon) CEO of a global business (an immigrant to Australia)

Hiring managers are risk averse. They are less interested in overseas skills; they want local knowledge. This attitude is driven by conservatism and short-termism. Returning expats or foreign nationals often end up taking a lesser job for a while to prove themselves. It requires different leadership to see people with overseas experience as an opportunity, not a risk.

Greg Stanmore, Managing Director, Spencer Stuart, Sydney, Australia

What do our behaviours convey?

There is more attention given to diversity here in Australia than in New Zealand. It's fashionable to talk about diversity here; it's a matter of the times. It's deeper than a flirtation and Australians seem to be reflecting on serious questions and searching more robustly for national culture and icons.

Rob McLeod, Chief Executive Officer, Ernst & Young Global, Sydney, Australia

Last year I went to a dinner with other school mothers. The other four women were stay-at-home mums and they were talking about how to keep the shirts white, how to clean the school hats and which days were better for grocery shopping. I had not thought through what it was like to be a housewife instead of a businesswoman. Surely there must be some way to support women who want to work flexibly to balance out their day. This cannot be a very satisfying existence.

Jane Owen, Partner, Middletons, Sydney, Australia

It's a male dominated society. Women take the line of least resistance. They go off and find a different way to survive: they start their own businesses.

Natalie Filatoff, Principal, Filatoff Editorial and Writing, Sydney, Australia

There is a fairly duplicitous attitude in our society. I understand that guys want to be together, but is it necessary that they go out drinking all the time? If one of those guys said "I hate doing this – spending half my wages at the pub every Friday night, because it makes me feel miserable" that would be a really good thing. There is a level of tolerance of poor morals in our society, which is not great.

Matt Tomaszewski, Director-Writer, Triton Media, Sydney, Australia

We have a 'Fortress Australia' set of values and a collective society. Our desire for egalitarianism means that we don't let true entrepreneurs flourish – unlike Silicon Valley, which was built on the American psyche of entrepreneurialism. We are a halfway house.

Greg Stanmore, Managing Director, Spencer Stuart, Sydney, Australia

Until recently the people of Sydney enjoyed many women in political positions including the Prime Minister, the State Premier, the Governor General and many more high-ranking women. People talk about it all the time because it is unusual and is now noticed. But this won't necessarily last. As they are replaced it is more likely that men will get back in. Both the New South Wales and Queensland premiers are now men and the next Prime Minister is likely to be a bloke too.

Hugh Mackay, Social Researcher and Writer, Sydney, Australia

When I lived overseas people talked about Australia as a sexist place. I didn't agree. But when I came back 17 years later I could see it. There are a lot of men drinking a lot of beers and the ladies tend to gravitate to the kitchen. How did that happen? This doesn't help women in the workplace.

Stephen Roberts, Chief Country Officer, Citi, Sydney, Australia

What cultural challenges need addressing?

If the future is bright and people have good incomes they feel more confident and then they procreate. It doesn't matter if you are a developed or developing economy, the benefits of closing the gender gap are phenomenal. You are not maximising the growth potential of your country if women are not participating in the workforce or if their career progression is capped halfway up the ladder. Women make most of the spending decisions in households so it makes good sense to have them involved in the decision-making in industry too.

We train all these women and then at a certain point they walk out. It makes no economic sense to lose your talent pool. We need to inject the entire organisation with the mindset that this is imperative to the bottom-line. The world is becoming more global, clients are more global and they are not going to do business with all white male teams.

Kathy Matsui, Managing Director & Chief Japan Strategist, Goldman Sachs, Tokyo, Japan

While there may be hundreds of years of resources to mine, it is a little more difficult to see where else Australia is going to thrive. People here are pretty 'can-do' but what will be Australia's future competitive advantage? The desire for higher wages makes industries outside of resources much less competitive. In the USA many industries have had to restructure to alter their wage structure. Australia needs to find new growth opportunities.

Paul Waterman, President, BP Australia, Melbourne, Australia

We are a population-short country and we need skills and talent wherever it is. Talent doesn't get distributed racially. What are our local businesses missing if they only have white faces? I think our short-term focus hurts Asia development. A CEO's tenure is now so short that it is dysfunctional. Three to five years is just not enough to develop relations with Asian countries. If all this stuff is getting under the radar then we are clearly ready for debate about diversity.

Professor Fred Hilmer AO, President & Vice Chancellor, University of NSW, Sydney, Australia

You have to show that you care about your cultural capital. Our cultural capital is our diversity and tolerance. You need to understand the role of your culture in your life or you can't understand the culture of others. It's not just about going to the gallery it is also about how I behave with people around me. The Chinese are not shy of the word culture; it does not make them feel self-conscious. In Australia when you talk about culture they think you are arty-farty. Culture is about deciding what part of the past you are going to put out there in the future.

David Kelly, Research Director, China Policy, Beijing, China

The stories we tell are important. What does a good mother look like? What does it mean to be a stay-at-home-mum? Should women be able to do both? I hear guilt from the women who work. We need to raise awareness of these challenges and share the success stories.

Tristan Landers, former Executive General Manager, Corporate Sustainability, Commonwealth Bank of Australia, Sydney, Australia

We need a discussion about Asian languages in primary school. Why do we wait until high school? The education system here is a closed shop and it is disconnected from the society that we live in. There is a lot of stuff we teach in schools that is boring and irrelevant and most of what we teach doesn't lead to jobs. The absence of maths and science limits kids' opportunity for jobs. It's not that difficult to change but it needs leadership. Giving parents more control in schools is one option.

The teacher registration system here is antiquated: you can only teach the subject matter of your primary degree, which is very limiting. We should be prepared to follow examples of success from overseas. The Education Minister in the State of New York recruited people from industry, gave them a three-month teacher-training course and then put them into schools to teach. The results were encouraging. The system in Australia frustrates people trying to retrain. The world is changing but the way we teach doesn't.

Ann Sherry AO, Chief Executive Officer, Carnival Australia, Sydney, Australia

Key messages about Australian culture

Recognising that issues exist is the first step to any change program. Taking action to address the issues is the next step. Hugh Mackay, Bernard Salt, SBS, the ABC and others have been writing and talking about the cultural challenges facing Australia on a regular basis for the past decade or two and this would suggest that there has been some recognition by some pockets of society that there are issues to be addressed. The frustrations expressed by the 100 leaders in their interviews suggests that too little has been achieved to address these issues.

Let's summarise the main elements of Australian culture mentioned by the 100 leaders that can help or hinder progress. As you review these, you might think about what these mean for you and your business or local community and how you might help to lead change:

- Australia's population comprising predominantly immigrants from Europe, Asia and the Pacific has produced a *multicultural society* that enjoys a mix of cultures and customs from many places;
- *Integration* has not been a major feature as many immigrants live in segregated areas but most of these communities *live in relative harmony* with their neighbours;
- The *can-do, hard-working* attitude was praised on the one hand but the increasing desire of younger generations for *work–life balance* was also noted as a real challenge facing managers today;
- The affluence of our society was thought to be leading to *self-indulgence and selfish behaviours* yet it was also noted that this affluence exists only in some pockets of society;
- We need to be more aware that our actions are being *observed by our kids* and they are forming *unconscious biases* from our values and behaviour and these will present challenges for them in the workplace when they grow up;
- *Egalitarianism* received mixed reaction with some leaders believing that it does exist while others dismiss it as a reality of life in Australia, reminding us that not everyone gets access to high-level education or has the right connections to get behind the *force field* at the top of organisations;
- Workplace measures of *leadership and management capabilities* are historically based on the attributes of Caucasian males, which can be a disadvantage to females and people from other races and ethnic backgrounds;

- *Mateship* was generally considered something useful to and valued by males only: it was linked to sports, considered clubby and it is thought to be a mechanism used to exclude women;
- '*A Fair Go*' idea and the *can-do* attitude are said to be strong elements of the Australian culture and examples were given where people have benefited personally. But there is a counter view that while anyone 'can' give anything a go, the lack of egalitarianism means that people do *not start out on a level playing field* and therefore some have major advantages over others due to cultural background, life experiences and circumstance;
- Concerns were raised about the *brain drain* and whether Australia could maintain its growth if the talent could not be attracted back. But then we also heard about the parochialism which acted like a *force field* resisting their re-entry into the workforce when they returned and some people believe they should '*prove themselves*' and not expect to walk into a job at the same level they were at elsewhere;
- Many people spoke of the blokey, clubby, *macho and male-oriented* culture which was likened to life in the 1950s, 60s and 70s and which was recognised as being a barrier to obtaining *full participation of women* in the workforce and shows a lack of respect (or possible fear held) by one gender of the other;
- People spoke of the *power retained by men at the top* and the closed society which prohibits people from getting into the 'in-group' and how *the systems marginalise and exclude people*, including preventing women from climbing the ladder; immigrants from working at the same level here as they did in their own country; and even limiting Australian-born white men who did not go to the right school (as in most countries, breaking into the aristocracy when you were born a commoner can be quite a challenge);
- We heard frequent references to *racism* and anxiety over *Asians and Muslims* and people practising religions that we don't understand;
- There is a consistent belief amongst leaders that *achieving full-participation of women at work is an economic necessity* and that by removing the barriers that cause them to leave the workforces will increase productivity and prosperity.

Let's clarify helpful future values

All cultures – whether the culture of a nation, a business or a school – have helpful and not-so-helpful elements. The thing we need to be honest about is which elements of Australian culture help and which hinder the country's progress and growth and its relations with its regional trading partners. The points made above suggest there are many issues that we need leadership on and the first and foremost of these is the need to agree on the desirable elements of the future culture of Australia.

If we remain 'blind to ourselves' we run the risk of our culture getting further away from where we want and need it to be (see Chapter 8 for how cultures drift). The more it differs from how we really want it to be, the harder it is for the country, its industries and businesses to achieve their ambitions.

The 100 leaders have identified issues that are critical to Australia achieving diversity, productivity and growth. We need national discussion on these issues and we need it now. How do we go about leading a national conversation about Australian culture? The challenge is similar to driving a change program across a national or global organisation: suggestions for where the leadership can be found and ideas for driving a social change program are included in Chapter 12.

Let's show boys and girls how it should be

A personal disappointment for me is in the school system and how it creates stereotyped gender roles for our children. I recall before my son Jack started school aged five years and three months he had a friendship group that was half boys and half girls. All his friends had been made at kindergarten, sports groups and play groups. By the end of the first term of his first year at school he had 'learned' through the local school's day-to-day teaching and classroom practices that boys should play separately from girls. He also learned the colours that boys wore and started to reject the clothing items in his wardrobe that did not fit the stereotype. This very radical change in behaviour occurred in just 10 weeks.

Two to three years later he reported that the class teacher (a female and a new graduate) enjoyed regular tea-parties and cheer-leader chanting activities with the girls at break times, expressly excluding the boys. She offered no similar activity for the boys. The segregation and exclusion sent the boys a strong message that they were not as important to her: I know this from overhearing a discussion between my son and two friends in the back of my car one day.

Two years on again, at a different school, I was at my son's annual school musical. Two of the items on the program were listed as being 'by the school choir'. However when we got to them I was surprised to see that the girls and boys had been separated. The boys got up first and performed a rap dance wearing a variety of flat-caps turned backward, and then the girls got up in neat-layered rows and performed something resembling a lullaby from the early 20th century. The contrast could not have been more striking.

The music department had previously found that getting boys to join the choir was difficult so, to increase its appeal, they offered them the opportunity to do a song that included a little rap dancing. It worked, the boys joined, but in the process the girls were segregated and because the girls' recital was so gentle by comparison it signalled different behavioural expectations. I know the school did not intend this to be the outcome: the intention was to encourage boys to join in an activity they had been socialised to think was 'not for boys'. Yet in the process they may have sent the wrong message to the girls. Next year I hope the girls and boys will do a rap dance together.

Biases and discriminations within the school system and modelled by teachers can have long-lasting effects on children who observe the behaviour and take away messages. Whether intended or unintended, behaviours deliver a message about who and what is valued.

These are just a few examples of dozens, if not hundreds, of observations I have made where children have been segregated and treated differently. This is the beginning of Australian children learning that males and females are to be treated differently in Australian society because they are valued differently and this learned behaviour then ends up in the workplace.

As Stephen Roberts, CEO of Citi says above, "*When the kids in Australia today get jobs, how will they deal with the unconscious bias that they have taken from their upbringing?*" When Stephen contemplates how to get gender balance in his leadership team at Citi Group, he knows that the values and behaviours of his employees were established at school and that the task of changing their values as adults in the workforce is a very big challenge indeed.

Sadly, it doesn't stop at schools. Anachronistic men's only events, activities and clubs still prevail in our society. They should have died out with the advent of the women getting the vote in Australia in 1902 but they are firmly entrenched in Australian society. Even sadder (and I can only presume it was out of a need to have comparable clubs to support women as they were excluded from men's clubs) women have now started up their own exclusive clubs.

We have the likes of Chief Executive Women and the Lyceum Club providing exclusive (restricted) entry and support for senior women in the same way as the Athenaeum Club was set up to provide an exclusive club for senior males (although they do now occasionally permit a few females). In the same way the 'old boy's network' formed hundreds of years ago, the 'old girl's network' is also forming now, presumably to counteract the effects of the exclusion.

What is most interesting is that membership to the women's clubs is based on the same model as the men's clubs – invitation only. Senior women of corporate Australia have missed the opportunity to take the high ground and illustrate how antiquated and pompous the 'invitation only' concept is. In a world where women are demanding meritocracy regarding selection for executive jobs and positions on boards, it would have been more supportive of their argument had women taken the opportunity to illustrate how meritocracy works. Times are constantly changing and cultural evolution is definitely an option for these clubs.

Our society is full of signals that send messages to each gender that they need to do things apart and need to be treated differently. We still have 'Girl Guides' for girls and 'Scouts' for boys. Why? We have the 'Women's Dinner' for the school mothers to do their fundraising and a separate 'Men's Dinner' for the fathers to do theirs. Why? Are we really as progressive and forward thinking as we would like the world to think? When are we going to recognise that we need to adapt our society constantly to reflect the changes in the world about us?

In addition to the separate institutions for each gender, there is ongoing variance in the behaviour levelled at females and males. Boys' sports receive much greater funding than girls sports. Boys schools find fundraising easier than girls schools. Male-only sports get most of the sports coverage in newspapers and on television.

What will it take to initiate change to the things that are hindering progress? What assumptions, values, attitudes and behaviours need to be features of the Australian culture if we are to shift the elements of the Australian culture that are keeping us from achieving our aspirations?

Why is our society intent on acculturating our children in the 21st century – the Asian Century – with values that prevailed in Queen Victoria's time? How can we ever expect to build a diverse workforce where both genders and people of all cultures get a fair go?

Let's find people who are willing to lead

While there are lots of environmental and systemic factors that influence the assumptions and values that we form, I believe that the single most influential factor is the human response to our challenges – the way in which our leaders signal what is important through their behaviour.

Catriona Noble, CEO of McDonald's summed up the situation facing Australians when she said "*In the city there are some leaders who are passionate about diversity and are doing it; some who want to make the change but have no idea how to go about it; and some who have unconscious bias – and the last group are just not interested.*"

We learn through the behaviour of others – especially those who are the leaders of our cultures. In a country culture it is the Prime Minister who we expect to lead, in a business it is the CEO, in a town it is the Mayor, in a school it is the principal and in a religion it is the head of the church, mosque, synagogue etc.

We need to encourage leaders across Australia to consider the cultural challenges that restrict people in our society from: having full careers that allow them to reach their potential; having a say in the way things are run; being able to access opportunities and living life in an egalitarian way.

In a young country that has been built through immigration and which has cultural contributions from many different places, we need clear and consistent leadership to steer our culture as it evolves and give direction to our everyday and long-term decisions.

Has the admired Australian cultural attitude of 'she'll be right mate' dampened our instinct to leap out of bed each morning wanting to resolve the cultural challenges that are holding us back? Or is this a 'catch-22' situation where there is a problem for which the only solution is denied by a circumstance inherent in the problem?

Chapter 6

Cultural Diversity

'If you talk to a man in a language he understands, that goes to his head. If you talk to him in his language, that goes to his heart.'

Nelson Mandela, former anti-apartheid activist and
President of South Africa 1994-99

Cultural diversity is as important as gender diversity for a few of the 100 leaders but for the rest it did not appear to be a current priority. Even when I probed for understanding of the national issues with those who signalled cultural diversity was not an issue in their company, I found the conversation still came to an end rather quickly. This was unexpected for a country that prides itself on being multicultural.

Those in Australia, who have worked in other regions of the world will probably agree that the senior ranks of corporate Australia are a little underweight in terms of cultural diversity by comparison. They will also be aware of the limitations of having a group that represents only one or two of the many possible views when analysing the problems and making the decisions. There are generally opportunity costs associated with such limitations; important information, skills and experience are missing from the table. If only one cultural group is represented, how will other groups who are members of the organisation, customer base or community feel about their decisions?

Often we find that our strengths can at times also lead to weaknesses and having reviewed the interview notes I feel that we are not 'out of the woods' yet. There is no argument that Australia is one of the most multicultural societies of the world; many nationalities live here. But whether they are allowed to participate fully and equally in the economy and share in the good life, is questionable. Social stability is important, but so is being able to tap into all the skills and resources at our disposal.

First in, first served

I wanted to know why cultural diversity is not a high priority of business leaders of Australia and why in some cases it is completely absent from their radar. How can it not matter, given that since 1945, when the population was just 7 million, a further 7 million migrants (including almost 700,000 refugees) have settled here?

Of the 22.7 million people living in Australia today, 27 per cent (6 million) are first-generation Australians (people living in Australia who were born overseas) and 20 per cent (4.5 million) are second-generation Australians (people born in Australia with at least one parent born overseas). The rest were born as third- or fourth-generation (or more).

The top ten countries of migrants in descending order are: the UK, New Zealand, China, India, Vietnam, Italy, Philippines, South Africa, Malaysia and Germany. I am sure there are individuals among them who are visionaries and aspiring leaders and who might want to be involved in leading and shaping the country or local industry. Most populations can be described on a standard bell-shaped curve and if you assessed the skills, talents and capabilities of the people living in Australia the outliers are unlikely to come from just one cultural background.

Australians are proud of the fact that the country is multicultural, yet there seems to be a tension between letting people from other countries into Australia and allowing them to fully participate in economic, social and political leadership. The tension is most obvious between immigrants who look or sound like those who were 'first in', Anglo-Saxon settlers of the 1700s and 1800s, and those who don't.

Immigrants from the United Kingdom and New Zealand who have English as their first language and are also Caucasian seem to have fewer concerns about settling in, compared to Asian or African people who don't have English as their first language and whose cultures are substantially different. In my experience even Germans and South Africans, whilst also Caucasian, can experience some challenges getting accepted in Australia if they arrive with heavily accented English (which is their second language).

Whilst Australia has a global reputation for having grown through a large immigrant population since WWII, it is also well known that the indigenous people have not always been treated equally, that the power base is still largely controlled by people from Anglo-Saxon backgrounds (Australia's earliest migrants' cultural origin) and that more recent immigrants from Asia, Middle East and Africa live in cultural clusters, are not fully integrated and face occasional racial unrest.

With the rise of China and the phenomenal growth of the whole Asian region expected throughout this decade, Europe and America will become less important trading partners and we will come to rely more heavily on Asia for both imports and exports. The sooner we open all the doors to our society to non-Anglo-Saxon people and encourage their social integration and full economic participation, the more quickly we will prepare a broader section of our workforce to operate across national borders.

Some sectors, certain conditions

Over the past 2–3 decades business leaders of some industries have started to recognise the economic benefits of having culturally diverse customer service staff to serve culturally diverse customers in meeting their everyday needs. This particularly applies to basic needs such as education, health, food, postal services, transportation and banking. However, where the economic need has been less obvious there has been less blending of the cultures.

Cultural diversity is also evident in sectors that rely on the labour of immigrants. People who are skilled are sought after to address labour shortages, and those who are unskilled and prepared to work for lower wages and in less attractive conditions are also highly prized.

Making allowances for immigrants to work in 'some sectors' under 'certain conditions' suggests there is tolerance but only within acceptable parameters.

This is not cultural diversity at its best. Australia could do better, if it chooses to. For example, the government could be more open to recognising the foreign training, experience and qualifications of skilled workers. Every time I get into a taxi I ask the driver where he or she is from and what they did in their home country. I am no longer surprised, because I hear it so often, that they have a trade or professional qualifications and experience that they can't use in Australia.

Here's a short story that illustrates what I mean about how Australia limits access to skills and thereby minimises its productivity and GDP. Recently I interviewed a number of Mandarin teachers to run an after-school language class for my son and half a dozen of his friends who were keen to learn an Asian language.

I was told by three of the four Mandarin teachers I interviewed that they were unable to teach in schools in Australia as the government did not recognise their degree or teaching qualifications. One of three explained she was told that she would need to complete a two-year Masters degree in order to gain an Australian teaching certificate. As a new immigrant her need to earn an income was greater than her freedom to indulge in further study, so she was forced to start her own business offering private lessons to individuals like me.

Language-learning chronically undervalued

The reason I started to look for a private Mandarin class for my son was that his school offered only Spanish in junior school: Asian languages were not offered until high school. I asked why there was only one language offered in the junior school and I was advised:

- The National Curriculum allows only *one* hour of language tuition per week for primary classes;
- Spanish is easier to learn as its closer to English and with only one hour each week the children are more likely to develop some level of competency (Mandarin requires a massive 2600 hours to reach 'fluency' whereas languages related to English, like French and Spanish, take only 600 hours to reach the same level).

One hour per week of language tuition in primary schools in Australia, for children who are at their peak age for learning and absorbing languages, tones and accents, is woeful and the loss of opportunity, wasteful.

Why is language learning so chronically undervalued? It could be ignorance, complacency, fear, low priority, lack of interest or budget, or any number of other reasons or a combination of many. But whatever the reasons, our future economic survival relies on someone stepping up on this and leading the charge to drive change.

Our children will be severely disadvantaged in the multilingual world of multicultural societies that are forming across the globe, where English is becoming the norm (and will no longer be the advantage). The advantage for globally mobile employees in the future will be multilingualism.

Learning foreign languages to advance the nation's people is a priority elsewhere:

- in China the official line is that English is taught in Grade 3 except for bi-lingual schools which teach it from Grade 1. In most schools the children get one class each weekday and are offered additional tuition opportunities after school and at weekends should they wish to pay extra for it;
- 21 of the 31 European countries require students to study another language for at least nine years;
- the European Parliament has spoken out in favour of every pupil learning not one, but two, foreign languages citing multilingualism as one of the region's great potentials;
- in Switzerland it is compulsory for children to learn two foreign languages from the age of eight and they do 3–4 hours per week;

- in Norway, Malta and Luxembourg they start language learning as early as six;
- in German-speaking parts of Belgium and Spain they start at the age of three;
- in contrast, in Great Britain students only come into contact with another language at the age of 11 and in the USA students start learning a language at age 14.

You can see that multilingual nations are multilingual for a reason – they believe in the benefit that language and cultural learning can deliver to their people and they invest in it.

As we know from our understanding of business and culture, the things that are *valued* are the things that get done. If Australia valued the cultures and languages of its immigrants and neighbours, particularly those neighbours upon whom it might rely for its future trade and growth, it would invest in that by supporting the introduction of more cultural and language learning in primary schools.

Australia stands to gain strategic advantage by appreciating and valuing the opportunities its Asian neighbours can offer. Language professors of world-renowned universities are in general agreement that children ideally should be introduced to foreign languages as early as the age of three and, if not then, in primary school. Also, a child's first foreign language *should be one that they are likely to hear being spoken in their own country*.

After Italian and Greek, Chinese languages are the next most popularly spoken in Australia and this group is growing annually with the increasing number of immigrants from China. So there is a much higher chance that Australian children would find a Chinese-speaking person in their school, local store or community before they would find one who speaks Spanish.

By the time a Chinese language is offered to children in Year 7 in Australia, native speakers are already at a major advantage over those for whom English is their first and only language. We end up with a significant disparity between the two cultural groups rather than bringing them together.

If your inner voice rebels against the notion that an Asian language would be of value to your child, then consider who they might be mixing with when they get to work. As we now know, the numbers of Asian immigrants, students and foreign investors are rising rapidly each year and the likelihood that your grandchildren are going to be Eurasian increases annually.

Language learning leads to greater cultural understanding. Cultural understanding leads to greater integration in society and diversity at work. Diversity at work delivers different experiences and skills which, when applied to problems, can lead to more innovative solutions.

Break through behavioural barriers

One HR executive in Australia told me that they take in 50/50 Australian and Asian graduates each year and the business has a mix of cultures. However, his managers had a tendency to go to the 'white faces' among their staff for more complex problems as they believed the connection and understanding was better. The suggestion was that the Asian employees didn't communicate so well and that they couldn't think outside the square. It was therefore safer to delegate the job to a Caucasian: even a Caucasian immigrant with an accent was preferred over an Asian one.

When I reflected on my experience as the only Caucasian person in an all-Asian law firm in Singapore, I could understand the situation. Initially I had empathy and recognised the challenge. But then I remembered some of the ways that I approached the difference in our styles. It took some time but I did it by explaining and demonstrating to my newly hired Asian management team how Western practices in operations, human resources, business development, administration, communications and IT worked and highlighted the benefits to them.

Next I helped them to understand why I *valued* these different practices, that they would help the lawyers deliver the service quality that the firm's clients expected and that they would be rewarded when we achieved our goals. All of the team were degree-qualified and they were hired by me to help drive the change, so they were selected for this task. After about 12 months this new team became more confident in their ability and began to adapt more quickly to changes as they were introduced. They grew into a very well functioning, highly respected and successful team of managers and change agents.

In addition to these new functional managers at the law firm, there was another group that adapted really quickly too: the younger lawyers who had studied in a Western university in the UK or the USA. These people already had exposure to different ways of working and, having returned to their 'homeland', they could see how some Western ways could 'add to' the local practices to build a stronger international firm. So Asians who have studied in Australian universities prior to taking up jobs here should also be able to adapt faster if guided and invited to do so.

Western behaviours obviously do not come naturally to people raised in Asia, the Middle East or Africa, and vice versa. However, human behaviour is learned, you just have to want to learn it. To deepen the understanding of your new learned behaviours you need to understand the assumptions and values of the culture.

When you are a Western manager in Asia you soon learn by observation when to bow your head, not to pass your business card with one hand, to order the meat, fish and chicken dishes at the start of a dinner and leave the rice until last, to take a gift in a red packet when you visit a local family in their home and many more local behaviours and customs. Similarly, Asian people who come to live in Australia soon learn that it is okay to speak up in a meeting and that challenging the boss on something that is vital to the business is not only acceptable but also admired. But Asian people won't necessarily know to do these things unless you say it is okay, illustrate how it is done and make space for them to grow into this new behaviour.

When you are working with people from different cultural backgrounds it takes time to develop a sense of mutual understanding, trust and respect. It also requires consideration, good communication and strong leadership. The rewards are intrinsic as well as extrinsic so it is well worth the effort.

Anyone from any background or level of education is capable of becoming culturally savvy and improving their cross-cultural understanding. As Mike Smith, CEO, ANZ Bank said in Chapter 4, you have to be interested in learning and have a curiosity about the cultures of other people. Exposure with interest, leads to understanding and that leads to tolerance and then appreciation.

If you are born and bred in Australia and have never lived or worked in a foreign country, then perhaps you could consider the possibility of an overseas posting sometime soon. If you are an Anglo-Saxon executive in Australia who came from another country, try to reflect on your arrival as an immigrant and remember how it felt for you. If you are Asian and find the Western methods of communicating and decision-making confusing, odd or illogical, ask someone to explain why we do what we do and seek understanding about what is expected of you.

Cultural diversity in Australia

Some of the 100 leaders interviewed were already working in a culturally diverse environment or were currently engaged in looking for ways to build greater cultural diversity. Their views are recorded below and are divided into three areas:

- Observations of others:
  - What was it like for your parents when they arrived?
  - Can you describe what it felt like when you arrived in Australia?
  - What are the cultural differences you noticed most?

- Attitudes of Australians:
  - How important is cultural diversity for Australian business and society?
  - What should we seek to achieve and how?
  - What does cultural diversity look like in your cultural groups?

- Traps and tips:
    - What do you think we need to do better?
    - What has worked for your cultural groups that others could follow?
    - How can we get people to care more?

In the section below I have identified the cultural heritage and location of the person being quoted so you can appreciate their perspective a little more.

Observations of others

I came from America and now live and work in Australia.

When I first arrived in Melbourne I saw many Asians walking the streets and I thought it was a really diverse place. But people said to me "It's actually not that diverse, they are just here to study and then they leave." Walking about the office here does not feel as culturally diverse compared to other countries I have worked in.

Talking about diversity in Australia is complex. In the USA people know diversity is a discussion about ethnicity, gender, sexual preference etc. The way people think about ethnicity here is less obvious. There is a big Greek population here but people won't acknowledge it. The Aboriginal situation is complicated and everyone knows about their plight but the solution is unclear. There is a real polarity and it is like an open sore.

The immigration conversations are a bit weird because everyone here is an immigrant. When you talk about 'opening-up' immigration to others, it's not well received and doesn't make you friends. The 'boat people' have even become an electioneering lever.

The quality of life here is fantastic and so people are protective of it. Australians don't want a huge population and smog. There is fear that it could be overrun with people if it is not managed. Australians just don't seem to want people coming in.

Paul Waterman, President, BP Australia, Melbourne, Australia

I am a third-generation Australian with Greek heritage and I live and work in WA, Australia.

Throughout all school days people called me a foreigner, yet I am Australian. We are slightly racist here but once Australians get to know people from other cultures, it gets better. It is much more multicultural now than when I was growing up, although I am on the Ports Board in Perth and most of the Port's staff is Anglo-Saxon. It's not a conscious thing it's just the make-up of the workforce at the Port.

Marie Malaxos, GM Production and Development, Buru Energy, Perth, Australia

I am a second-generation Australian with Polish heritage and I live and work in Australia.

My father came from Poland after World War II and if Australia had closed its borders then, where would I be? It's not that people *want* to leave their home; who wants to do that? There are compelling reasons why people are forced to find a safer place to live.

I worked on Channel 7's *Border Security* television show a few years ago and I didn't like what I saw: the racist side of Australia upset me. We were filming at the airport and the Customs people were okay to deal with, but there were staff in other departments who tried to hide their racism, but failed. An African refugee family arrived one day dressed in old clothes from a charity bin, they had no money or home to go to and they said, "Can you believe the government pays for these people to come here? I bet they don't even speak English."

The television series *Go Back to Where you Came From* by SBS Television shows the scab of Australia that needs to be exposed. It is an agenda that needs to be pushed. These racist people are not always where you think they are. It's the rough edge of 'the lucky country'.

Matt Tomaszewski, Director-Writer, Triton Media, Sydney, Australia

I am from Hong Kong: I studied in Australia but now live and work back in Hong Kong.

It is always interesting to work with people from different cultures. Having people from different cultures working in one company is very beneficial; it delivers skills from other countries and it gets the best out of everybody. I work with Australians in Hong Kong and they are adaptive. I also work with mainland Chinese who bring different views and come to Hong Kong to learn new skills and grow their career so they are enthusiastic.

If individuals are not willing to be integrated it is difficult. When I went to Brisbane to study in Year 11, I found the first few months difficult. In a class of 30 there was a group that I learned not to approach; you can only take a relationship as far as they will let you. But I adapted to the ways of the high school and enjoyed my time there. It was noticeably better at university because it was more culturally diverse, but there were still a few students who blocked out people from different cultures because of the fear of the unknown. The same happens in Hong Kong: many local people don't go out to mix with people from other cultures as they feel they are a threat to them in some way.

Gabriel Yam, Managing Partner, Arup Group, Hong Kong, China

I am an Australian-born Chinese from Perth, Australia: currently on transfer to Hong Kong.

The transition to Hong Kong was easy because there was no language barrier for me as I have a Chinese background. I understand some of the cultural differences here: for example I know about the religious holidays and Chinese festivals.

Life here is so different to what you have been used to in Australia; you have to have an open mind. I moved from a three-bedroom house and driving to work in Perth, to a tiny flat and using public transport in Hong Kong. If you don't embrace the lifestyle changes it can get you down. There are ups and downs so you have to be willing to change; you'd be naive to think that life is going to be the same.

Regarding work, I expected it to feel the same at Arup Hong Kong as it was at Arup Western Australia; but it feels like two different companies. The office culture is different because the countries are so different and Hong Kong has 1500 employees whereas there were only 120 in WA. The working hours in Hong Kong are longer and there are more deadlines, which brings stress. It's a very competitive environment and everyone works harder and longer than in Australia. I am surviving by learning better time management. So far I love it and I am valuing the experience very much.

Sally Wong, Engineer, Arup Group, Hong Kong, China

I am Australian and live and work in Australia

In our commitment to achieving cultural diversity we try to represent the local people (our customers and communities) by matching the nationality of our employees to them. We hired people from at least 10 nationalities from the last recruitment intake and we partner with local businesses to build affinity with them.

We have a new paper plant that runs at 1.6km per minute and requires highly skilled workers, which we have found from Finland, Germany, Austria, South Africa and Canada. We also have labour from Fiji, Vietnam, Sri Lanka and many more countries. Everyone goes through a five-day induction program and two three-day culture appreciation workshops to help them assimilate through better understanding of both the Australian and Amcor cultures.

Lynley Corcoran, General Manager Human Resources, Amcor, Melbourne, Australia

I am Australian and live and work in Australia

We have cultural diversity because of our global footprint. BHP is in so many countries that we have so many different nationalities working for us. We know that we can put together an expat team but we also know that we must have local hires on the team too.

Nicola Evans, Deputy Company Secretary, BHP Billiton, Melbourne, Australia

I am Australian and live and work in Australia

Arup has a strong corporate culture that translates well across the Western world. Where we see the strain is in understanding our Asian immigrants. Assimilating Asian employees into our Australian businesses can be a challenge. We do not have Asian people at the top of our firm in Australia, yet we do have Asians leading our Asian businesses. Unconscious bias plays a role here as we tend to want our leaders to look like Australian leaders.

Peter Bailey, Chief Executive Officer, Arup Group, Sydney, Australia

I am from the UK: I joined Arup in Sydney and now work for them in Vietnam

Asian people are reserved in the way they work and they expect to be led by their line managers. Trying to get them to do something 'outside the box' or to be proactive can be quite a challenge: it is something you have to work at. Australian workers on the other hand are forward-thinking and 'out there', so managing different cultures in the team is a skill you need to develop.

Richard Padfield, Electrical Engineer, Arup Group, Ho Chi Minh, Vietnam

I am Australian and live and work in Australia

I work for a global company now. The difference is profound. I can access talent from all over the world and I have men and women on my leadership team from Asia and Europe. Carnival Australia has achieved 20 per cent growth for the past five years compared to 5 per cent in the rest of the tourism industry and I believe we are getting this growth because we have a more diverse team which means we have people who bring different ideas and fresh thinking to our challenges. The global team makes a difference.

Ann Sherry AO, Chief Executive Officer, Carnival Australia, Sydney, Australia

I am Australian and I live and work in Australia.

I first recognised the importance of the disparity between the Anglo-Saxon culture and one that is very different from what we know in my early career. I went to Groote Eylandt, an island off the North East of Australia, to negotiate with the Aboriginal community over a project we had going on up there. I had to sit under a tree to talk with the community elders rather than an office. Initially it felt odd but then I realised that was their way and I learned to engage with them using their customs, not mine. Understanding their cultural traditions better helped me to understand what was important to them in the business relationship.

Russell Tipper, Chief Executive Officer, Brockman Resources, Perth, Australia

Attitudes of Australians

I came from India and live and work in Australia.

There are a lot of people starting their journey [as new immigrants] so it can be challenging for them. We need to understand that there is no right or wrong way and just acknowledge the differences and make an effort to bridge the cultural gap.

> Pradeep Khanna, Chief Executive, PK Projects Management & Consultancy, Sydney, Australia

I am Australian and live and work in Australia

I worry about the more recent refugees to Australia. I work with schools in western parts of Sydney where many immigrants live and I don't think that we are going to create the right opportunities for them to get to university. This will limit their ability to integrate more broadly across society.

Expecting immigrants to outperform Australian-born students whose first language is English is unreasonable and the older they are when they arrive in Australia, the less chance they have at perfecting their English before they have to compete for a university place. If they arrive in year nine and their English is not good enough they are unlikely to get top grades in Years 11 and 12. If they arrive at 18 with little or no English and enter the workforce they will most likely end up driving taxis when they could be quite capable of training for a technical or professional career, if the language was not a barrier.

The university system is biased towards private school students because the entrance criterion is based solely on grades, so immigrants are very unlikely to get in. There is little discussion about whether Australians would be prepared to give immigrants more support so that they could get a better job, be a bigger contributor to the workforce and GDP and be more socially integrated and participate in shaping Australia's future.

At the other end of the spectrum the elite and highly educated immigrants end up in selective schools which are now becoming 'Asianised'. These schools choose kids who are doing well academically and don't assess them on other important criteria.

> Robert Milliner, Former Chief Executive Partner, Mallesons Stephen Jaques (now King & Wood Mallesons), Sydney, Australia

I am Australian with Ukrainian heritage and I live and work in Australia

Few Australian leaders know how to manage other cultures. They don't understand the behaviours and norms of their workforce too well. We are a country made up of many cultures but I'm not sure that we are embracing them.

> Alec Bashinsky, National Partner People & Performance, Deloitte Touche Tohmatsu, Sydney, Australia

I came from the UK and now live and work in Australia.

Cultural diversity is at a low level in Australia. It gets more 'white' as you go up the ladder and that's mainly because you get white men hiring and promoting in their own image. Given the Asianisation of the Australian workforce we need to look deeper into this. Some of the businesses I have worked with in Australia are very Anglo-Saxon in their composition. Cultural diversity is not only about understanding each other's culture better, it is about working in cross-cultural teams. Our failure to achieve vertical integration means that we limit our GDP.

Neil Cockroft, Head of Diversity and Culture, King & Wood Mallesons, Sydney, Australia

I am Australian with Greek heritage: I live and work in Australia

One of the findings that came from a survey we did with non-executive directors was that they believed they needed 'skills' diversity on their boards, not necessarily gender or cultural diversity. They also commented that the reason they didn't have many Asians on their boards was that they would have to travel to board meetings. Getting cultural diversity on boards is more of a challenge than gender diversity.

We currently have a strategy to address the lack of non-white partners in our firm. We identified that young Asians in our firm did not see Asian role models above them and therefore did not plan a long-term future here. As we admit more partners from diverse cultural backgrounds, we hope they will become role models for these young people.

Greg Couttas, Partner, Deloitte Touche Tohmatsu, Sydney, Australia

I am Australian with Maltese heritage: I live and work in Australia

Ernst & Young made a conscious decision some time ago to address cultural diversity. We approached it in a series of steps. An early initiative was to provide an inclusive environment for indigenous employees and another was to maximise the opportunity for Asian graduates. Then we developed a Japanese business group in response to the significant amount of Japanese investment into Victoria. By having people with Japanese language skills in the group we have been able to access work in that segment of the market.

Annette Kimmitt, Office Managing Partner, Ernst & Young Global, Victoria, Australia

I am a British-born Australian and I live and work in Australia.

In some companies there is a noticeably different ethnic composition in the under 35 group. Asians are working their way through corporate Australia and if you look at the graduate intake there is no bias at that level. But by and large they drop out before reaching management. Whether there is a bamboo-ceiling or not I don't know, as we have no hard data, but it would make sense for us to start taking some notice.

John Daley, Chief Executive Officer, Grattan Institute, Melbourne, Australia

I am Australian and live and work in Hong Kong.

I don't think anyone has tried to change our [Australians'] attitude towards Asians. If we can have a 'Be Tidy' campaign then why can't we have a 'Think Positively about Asia' campaign? To shift mind-sets in Australia about Asia there needs to be leadership and corporate governance changes.

Richard Mazzochi, Partner, King & Wood Mallesons, Hong Kong, China

I am Australian and live and work in Australia

We have a multicultural society in terms of people who live here, but when you look at parliament and senior business leaders, there are so few non-white people there. We should care that people would be confronted by this.

Rachel Slade, General Manager, Westpac Group, Sydney, Australia

I am Australian and live and work in Australia

There seem to be few Chinese or black faces in legal and banking. Yet the opposite is true of medicine; there are many Asians who are doctors and dentists. It seems that first-generation parents are channelling their second-generation children towards certain careers, which they believe are more appropriate for some reason and this affects diversity in the pipeline.

Katy McDonald, Director of Human Resources, Minter Ellison, Sydney, Australia

I am Australian and I live and work in Australia.

Most of the immigrants in Western Australia are Caucasian. There are a few North Africans and Asians but they are not coming in the same numbers as people from South Africa, England or New Zealand. Our media has a lot to do with a lack of cultural diversity because as soon as there is a problem they report the nationality, i.e. the person's cultural heritage is part of the descriptor used in the news report. They always say 'it is an Asian', but they never say 'it was a Caucasian'. They just highlight when a problem is presumed to be caused by a person who is different from the rest of us. Our attitudes show the truth.

Russell Tipper, Chief Executive Officer, Brockman Resources, Perth, Australia

I came from America and now live and work in Australia.

Why don't we transfer employees internationally more often? It's because of the culture challenge, the cost and the lack of people wanting to move to another country. We have a fantastic global mobility program which supports the few people who do want to move – typically they are people who have a spouse with an overseas opportunity and they want to join them, or they just want to go to another country to live for a while. We have absolutely got to find a way to be more mobile and to think about transferring skills internationally.

Lynn Kraus, Managing Partner Sydney, Ernst & Young Global, Sydney, Australia

I am a New Zealand-born Australian with Dutch-French heritage: I live and work in Australia

I don't know why we don't have many non-white people at the top of our organisations. If you look at the number of Indians and other Asians walking around our universities in Western Australia, there should be no reason for it. It is not a conscious thing, so perhaps Australian society's acceptance of Asian and Muslim people is still evolving. The effects of the 'White Australian policy' are still evident. In the 1960s we treated Italians and Greeks poorly and called them wogs but now they are integrated and well accepted. It's a time thing. People need time to get used to others being part of the tribe.

Shirley In't Veld, Non-Executive Director, Asciano, Perth, Australia

Traps and tips

I am Australian and I live and work in the United Kingdom.

When you look up, you see what is there. If it doesn't look like it should, you have to change the leadership so that it looks like the business you want to be.

Dr Robert Care AM, Chair UK, Middle East and Africa Region, Arup Group, London, United Kingdom

I am Australian and live and work in Australia

You need to get data on your employee's cultural background to understand your demographic profile. The data tells you everything: it tells you where you need to be and what your organisation needs to look like. We ascertained that 32 per cent of IBM Australia's population identify mostly with a culture outside of Australia and two-thirds of that group is from Asia.

We now have an Asian Diversity Network and we ask them what they need and what we can do to support them. They recognise that workplace behaviours are different here and they have asked for assistance in understanding business communication and to help build confidence to speak up and participate more in meetings.

Robert Orth, Director Human Resources ANZ, IBM Australia, Sydney, Australia

I came from South Africa and I now live and work in Australia.

You need to treat cultural diversity separately from gender diversity so that you don't get an average performance. You mustn't blur the boundaries. Gender must remain gender and culture must remain culture. If the KPIs are blurred, how will you know if you have achieved? Addressing cultural diversity is slow as everything has to be invented.

Margaret Dreyer, Partner, Deloitte Touche Tohmatsu , Sydney, Australia

I am Australian and I live in Australia and work across Australia, Singapore and the UK

We have 1500 staff in Australia and around 200 of them are on 457 Visas: that is 13 per cent of our staff. Many are from the United Kingdom but we also have people from East Asia, Singapore, Europe and the USA. We also take in 40-60 people each year of which a large proportion are 2nd and 3rd generation immigrants and they are still strongly influenced by their heritage, so we have 'celebrating diversity days' in each office to increase understanding and acceptance. The cultural diversity starts to drop off at mid-levels.

Diversity of thought is the big thing! We find that people who have cross-cultural working experience bring different ideas and better solutions. A lot of our projects are large-scale and we bring people from all over the world to work on them: that way we get access to the large project experience from people elsewhere.

Diana Cross, Australasia Human Resources Leader, Arup Group, Melbourne, Australia

I am Australian and I live in China

Our upbringing in Australia prepared us to work with people from across cultures. My Chinese friends here don't understand why we work closely with all Chinese people – people of all different origins. The discrimination that people experience in China is not because of their gender, it's because of their place. They call people from the country 'migrants' and they are not considered equal. Attitudes to cultural diversity here are much more challenging than in Australia.

Philippa Jones, Managing Director, China Policy, Beijing, China

Integration or 'embracing difference'?

The official view is that 'integrationist' policies are not effective as a means of managing cultural diversity and that we should move away from trying to create a 'melting pot'. Instead we are being encouraged to 'embrace and celebrate cultural difference', which is thought to be a better solution for Australia.

Many of the 100 leaders interviewed noted Australia's stated preference was *not to integrate* immigrant cultures but to recognise their difference and they contrasted this with the American melting-pot style of multiculturalism. However, they also talked about the success of the melting pot and how in America, immigrants of all generations proudly state that they are an American-Italian or an American-Japanese. Their confidence to be both American and acknowledge themselves as Italian or Japanese as well, seemed be very well known and admired. Americans are very proud people and from what you see from the outside, the melting pot seems to have worked well for them.

When I asked about which was better for Australia, there was less certainty. As Paul Waterman shared with us above, his experience is that Australians are less comfortable saying what their cultural heritage is and instead have a tendency to say 'I am Australian' and look uncomfortable if they are pushed to identify where their olive, brown or yellow complexion comes from. Why is that? Is it because they are concerned about racism, or is it because they want to separate from their cultural heritage rather than be proud of it for some reason?

When I asked people about their take on Australia's level of success at multiculturalism, the most common theme was about food and restaurants. People commented how few Thai restaurants there were in the main cities in the 1970s and how there are now several in almost every suburb. I started to gain the impression that 'to love their food' was being offered as proof of the Australian people's 'acceptance of their difference'.

Since the First Fleet arrived in 1788, all 22.7 million Australians, except about half a million indigenous people, can trace their origins to an ancestor who has at some point arrived by boat or plane as an immigrant. As we noted in Chapter 5 it takes more than a couple of hundred years for a new country culture to mature and Australia is still looking for that single identity that all Australians can connect with.

I worry that if Australia continues to say that it should 'value the difference' instead of 'integrate the group members' that this might be another of those covert methods Ann Sherry, CEO, Carnival Corporation talked about – is this just another mechanism for blocking people out: marginalising the subgroups and keeping the control of business for the minority group at the top?

In my experience working with organisations that have stalled growth, cultural problems are nearly always part of the problem. Some of the causes of the cultural (usually described as behavioural) problems are: lack of clear leadership and common vision or goals; powerful and conflicting subcultures; and lack of proper post-merger cultural integration creating tensions and misunderstandings. All of these can create internal inefficiency, raise costs, and ignite conflict and disharmony.

Also, in many cases where I have seen a lack of cultural integration following a company merger or acquisition, it nearly always coincides with tension between subcultures and generates inefficiencies, which have been known to result in a de-merger down the track.

I believe what we are seeing in Australia regarding the lack of immigrant integration has the same risks and costs. Like a poorly integrated acquired company, a country can suffer from the same reaction to a lack of acceptance of the new arrivals. If the country doesn't have strong leadership and a clear vision that both the old and new residents accept and are prepared to follow, confusion can arise. If we don't have agreement about a set of common goals and be prepared to work together in harmony it is likely to result in misunderstanding, lack of unity and disharmony.

Food-for-thought? Is it time to revisit our assumptions about 'melting pot and integration' (more objective) versus 'embracing and celebrating cultural difference' (more subjective) and should we also check our motivations and ensure we are not avoiding giving up something that we could do without?

Embracing cultural difference is *of course* what we all want, but if that subjective notion allows us to avoid providing full and equitable access to jobs and positions to immigrants 'until they have proven they deserve it' then it could be a bit like settling for the ASX's 'naming and shaming strategy' to solve the gender imbalance when we really need quotas.

Two encouraging personal stories

As I talked with people when researching these topics I heard some amazing stories and I asked several of them to share their personal stories and experiences of cultural and gender diversity in Australia. Below are two cultural diversity experiences that illustrate how lucky we are – those of us who have never experienced adversity.

Laura Wong – Vietnamese refugee

The first story is by Laura Wong who is a senior women-in-operations in the manufacturing sector. She arrived in Australia as a child refugee by boat. She shares how she and her family made a new life in Australia and explains how her determination to succeed has been rewarded despite the odds being against her at the start (an immigrant whose first language was not English and a female).

This amazing woman focused on making her brave parents proud by building a strong career, which has provided her with the means to a good life in Australia. She now enjoys Aussie lifestyle and family time with her husband and two children. From refugee beginnings, Laura is now a senior manager in one of Australia's leading manufacturing companies.

Laura's story

I came from Vietnam in 1975 as a result of the war in Vietnam. My dad was a senior officer in the police force working for the South Vietnam government. We were forced to leave our homeland due to the risk that my dad would be killed by the Viet Cong when they invaded South Vietnam in 1975.

We escaped from Vietnam via a cargo boat. Half way on the trip for survival it was announced that the boat we came out on had a hole in it and our journey was very challenging and life threatening. We were fortunate to be rescued by a British army boat and were taken to a concentration camp in Hong Kong for six months until we were able to apply for residency in Australia. Back home my parents were very wealthy and we had maids and drivers. We lost everything and arrived here with nothing.

We had to start over again and both mum and dad worked in a factory to make ends meet. Dad worked for Victa Mowers and mum worked at Kirby Refrigeration as a labourer. Life was hard compared to Vietnam. They worked extremely long hours so the next generation could have a good start. There was very little money, so we never had any of the luxuries or things like normal kids have in Australia – even school camps weren't an option.

We were the first Vietnamese to arrive in this country so all our friends were Australian. Everyone made us feel comfortable and we were never teased about our nationality. Life was tough growing up, especially watching my parents work so hard and some days they would cry when they reflected on what they had lost. They also had feelings of guilt and inadequacy as they felt they weren't providing for the children. This made me more determined to work hard to make a good life for ourselves as well as make my parents proud as they gave up so much.

As first-generation Australians, my sister, brother and I had to succeed. I studied a Bachelor of Business and started at Amcor as an assistant accountant 17 years ago. The early days in Amcor were very male-dominated and the males, mostly Australian natives, ran the place. It was very difficult to climb the corporate ladder in Amcor if you were female, or Asian. You have to work hard to be recognised and I had to fight for every role and justify why I should get the role.

I recollect when I applied for a job as a commercial manager for the New South Wales cartons plant around 13 years ago I didn't even receive a proper interview as the General Manager at the time spent a large part of the interview on the phone. And then I was told that I couldn't get the role because I didn't have grey hair.

Most females at Amcor are in a functional role and there are few females in General Management or plant manager roles. The factory floor is 90 per cent male. I think it's really tough for females to work in a male-dominated environment as some feel they need to be one of the boys. My personal feelings are that you don't need to be one of the boys, just be yourself.

The early stage of my career was tough with very limited opportunities and it got to a stage when I decided to look for another job and I resigned. Suddenly they valued me, changes occurred and they gave me a company car and new opportunities. Amcor has changed over the last six years: there is high focus on diversity, and talent council reviews and they really focus on developing talent in the business. They are now much more open and I wouldn't be here if it was not for them.

I was fortunate six years ago to have a new Divisional General Manager of the cartons business, David Berry who mentored me. He gave me the opportunity to run the New South Wales cartons business. I was totally opposite to what people expected, that is, I was not your typical Caucasian male. It was no longer an issue being Asian or young or female.

When people meet me now they say "Oh, you're running three sites?" and they can't believe that it is actually a female and they usually expect a Caucasian. I have built the reputation in my career to be good at what I do and I'm respected for my ability, not my race or gender.

When you look at Amcor people they are very multinational and if we don't understand their cultures, how do we move forward? It is a struggle in manufacturing but I love it. I love going down to the factory floor and talking to people. We have all different cultures working in our business including people from China, Lebanon, Vietnam, Sri Lanka, Italy, Greece and India.

Our recruitment philosophy is to get the best skills for the job, and these people happened to be the best skilled and most suitable for the role.

Being a woman in manufacturing is very satisfying. You get to see what you are making and producing. You can see the machines running and the products coming out the end. You interact with customers and then you see your products on supermarket shelves. And when you buy the box that you made with the food in it, you feel good.

Over the last six years with the changes made by the senior leaders of Amcor I have found that it's much easier to progress up in Amcor. They are focused on people's ability with bi-yearly talent council and performance reviews. Individuals are promoted based on their merits and I have been fortunate to be offered three different roles over the last six years.

Laura Wong, General Manager Specialities, Amcor, Sydney, Australia

Dr Charlie Teo, AM – world-leading neurosurgeon

Charlie Teo is a leading Australian neurosurgeon who graduated from the University of New South Wales before heading off to complete a fellowship in the USA. In the 10 years he spent in America he gained a world-wide reputation for pioneering minimally invasive brain surgery that has proven to extend the lives of cancer sufferers and many others. He returned to Australia in 1999 and established The Centre for Minimally Invasive Neurosurgery and

The Cure for Life Foundation. When I read his Australia Day 2012 finalist's speech I wondered how could this accomplished man have had such a difficult start to life and then still be able to achieve so much? I wanted to hear more.

Charlie's story

My parents arrived in Australia from China in the early 1950s. Both my parents were Buddhists and they came here to pursue careers in the medical profession. When I was 12 my parents divorced but my mother found the money to get me through the prestigious Scots College in the Eastern suburbs of Sydney.

Racism and bullying

My memories of Scots College are mixed. I was a minority; there were very few non-Caucasians there. The bullying was rampant and anyone who was a minority was verbally, and sometimes physically, abused by other kids. I remember one boy was kicked in the back so viciously that it was actually broken. Because it happened so frequently, invariably some teachers would turn a blind eye to the victimisation. Strangely, we considered the bullying as some kind of ritual. As if it was there to mould character.

There was no public debate on racism in those days (1970s) but there was plenty of it at my school. Many of my friends were the marginalised ones; the coloured boys, the immigrants, the short boys, the fat boys and all the boys who looked different from the mostly white kids who were doing the bullying. It's amazing how adversity builds strength and how the bullying and my management of it moulded my character over the years.

I don't know what I would advise boys going to the schools today. I feel that part of the reason I have achieved so much in my life is due to the strength of character that arose through this adversity. What I do know is that it would be better if the adversity we faced as children came from some other challenge in life other than racism.

There was little improvement when I went to the University of New South Wales. I expected the Asian students would provide me with some sense of belonging. But because I was Australian and not Asian we had very little in common. I did not speak any Asian language, understand Asian cultures and I had not even had a Chinese girlfriend. So yet again I had a small clique of marginalised but special friends. However, once I went to Basser College I did feel part of the group and had a really good experience.

There wasn't a single day that I didn't experience some racism; in almost every public place I went there was some racist remark made by some ignorant guy. I had a Caucasian Australian girlfriend with blonde hair and every time I went out with her someone would make a remark to her about going out with a Chinese man. But by the time I had reached dating age I also had my black-belt in karate which I applied not irregularly and once to the largest of eight guys who decided to have a go one night outside the Roundhouse at the University of New South Wales.

When I started my internship at the hospital the overt became covert! When you are wearing a white coat and the lives of your patients are in your hands, the discrimination is not so obvious but it is just below the surface. I recall as an intern being told on several occasions that patients had requested 'a white doctor please'.

I then lived for 10 years in America, which was a completely different experience. There was not a single occasion when I encountered any racist discrimination. The disparity was so amazing I found it hard to believe. I am not sure of the reason. America is a meritocracy. You are promoted and accepted according to your merit. Americans see Chinese people as possessing high intelligence, to be high-achieving and ambitious. And Chinese people usually hold a good position in society and are revered for their success. I experienced this on many occasions. It was reverse racism.

The force field and tall poppy
Australians pride themselves as being egalitarian; they say no one should feel they are better than others. Yet when you try to excel in your field, whatever race, some people like to pull you down. It's the tall poppy syndrome.

When I returned to Australia in 1999 I was faced with a different kind of discrimination: professional jealousy. I excelled in the USA and got a big name for myself. I travelled the world speaking at medical conferences and I pioneered a minimally invasive neurosurgery technique for people suffering from brain tumours.

Some neurosurgeons found my success in the USA a little confronting and were not happy with my return to Australia. They initially declined my entry to the Society and made it difficult for me to gain recognition as a medical professional. After a television interview in May 2007 about my use of key-hole surgery for removing brain tumours the president of the Neurosurgical Society of Australasia published a statement in The Australian implying that I was a 'self-promoter' and that I was not considered a pioneer as the program had insinuated.

Since then some in my profession regularly seek to damage my reputation and discredit my techniques. Despite this, patients come from all corners of the world and, thanks to the minimally invasive techniques and my fantastic team, many of them experience longer lives with less complications and better outcomes. In addition, doctors from hospitals all around the world still come to my practice in Sydney to learn about the technique. Unfortunately only one Australian-based doctor has taken up this opportunity.

Dr Charlie Teo AM, Director, Centre for Minimally Invasive Neurosurgery, Sydney, Australia

Learning from others

Laura's story left me feeling energised and hopeful. She broke through barriers that many of us allow to stand in our way. She and her family arrived with nothing, yet a decade later she was preparing to go to university and start her climb up the ladder of corporate Australia. Incredible!

If Laura, a female refugee from Asia, can achieve tertiary qualifications and rise to senior management in a manufacturing environment that is traditionally male-oriented, then there is potential for any woman in Australia to realise her dreams.

Charlie's story is widely known across Australia due to his 'celebrity doctor' status and from becoming a finalist in the Australian of the Year Award 2012. He believes that the racism he was exposed to as a child no longer exists, that Australia is now a much more tolerant society and he is proud that his home country has moved on.

I asked him if he thinks there are still some strains of racism here, but that perhaps he is now protected from it because of his professional success, celebrity status and high standing in the community. He replied 'I hope not'... but I continue to wonder. I have no doubt that Charlie's view that it is better in Australia now than the 1970s and 80s is correct, but I suspect from what the 100 leaders have said, that there are still Asian or non-Caucasian people at our schools and in our communities who see it or are subjected to it.

Apart from racism there is still awkwardness amongst Caucasian people who have not had exposure to Asian people. I completely understand this as I was one of those people before I first lived in Asia in 1992, but I am surprised 20 years later in multicultural Sydney to find the situation still exists.

Key messages about cultural diversity

Let's summarise the things highlighted above that we ought to consider as we work towards building a more diverse society and workplace to boost productivity.

- How do we address the 'First in, first served' syndrome to make it easier for immigrants of non-English speaking backgrounds to feel at home in Australia more quickly, to be more readily accepted and to help them get work in the fields they are trained for at a level which reflects their experience?
- How do we change the systems that reject the qualifications and training that immigrants bring with them and break the 'Some sectors, certain conditions' trend which limits the opportunities of people migrating to Australia?

- How do we achieve a 'U-turn' in the current thinking of the people in the Australian education system who are responsible for: policy-setting regarding foreign language learning; the national curriculum; and public spending on language-learning and cultural appreciation?
- How do we encourage greater tolerance in local managers who have little exposure to working in other cultures and therefore lack cross-cultural experience, to help close the divide between people of different nationalities in the workplace and in society?
- Why do we close our borders to asylum seekers when we could give them temporary work visas while their request for permanent entry is being processed and send them to regions that have serious labour or skill shortages?
- How can we encourage more Australians to go offshore for a period to gain cross-cultural experience and knowledge of foreign markets and to build international business connections to strengthen our competitive advantage? How can we secure their re-entry to the job market after three, five or ten years away so that they can get back in at the level that they are skilled for without having to 'wait' or 'prove themselves' all over again?
- Why have we allowed the bamboo ceiling to emerge and how do we remove it? How do we get the same mixed cultural profile that we have among the under-35s in the over-35/senior ranks where important decisions about Australia's future are made.? How do we ensure we have mixed culture role models for our younger people to learn from?
- How do we speed up the process of raising awareness about the need for and benefits of cultural diversity and get it onto the radars of more leaders? And how do we reflect the multicultural population in our society in the senior ranks of business and industry?
- Is 'embracing diversity' good enough? Does it protect us from our tendency to want to limit exposure of new immigrants to 'the good life' for their first decade or two in our great country, i.e. until they prove themselves? Are we avoiding giving up something? Why is the good that comes from the American-style 'melting pot' not good enough for Australians?

Let's 'live' the cultures of others

The cultures of people from another region of the world are not likely to make sense to you if you have never been there, lived there or spent meaningful time with people who live or have lived there. But being open-minded and curious really helps.

If a person in your community or company had recently arrived from, say, Ghana, imagine what you might discover about their culture if you exercised your curiosity. You might ask: 'What is it like to live in Ghana? Who is in power there? What do the people value? What religions do they practise? What are the national foods? What are your traditions and customs? What are the main languages? Why did you leave? Why did you choose Australia? How did it feel when you arrived? What can I do to help you settle in? How can I learn more about your culture?'

Everyone's culture is unique and special. Being curious about the culture of others can lead to some amazing discoveries. Being curious enough to ask questions is a good start, but fully appreciating the uniqueness of a culture doesn't come until you 'live it'. A holiday to a foreign location won't do it. Reading a book or watching a movie about another country won't do it. A delicious Italian dinner on Melbourne's famous Lygon Street (known for its international cuisine) won't do it. And even a day trip to Little Asia in Cabramatta west of Sydney won't do it.

There's only one way to fully appreciate a culture different from your own and that is to 'live it'. If you don't get the opportunity to transfer with your company you can go under your own steam. There is nothing stopping you from buying a plane ticket to a country that you are curious about (subject to getting a visa), finding somewhere to live, getting some work to pay your bills and then enjoying the discovery of everything around you.

To fully appreciate the values and beliefs or gain enlightenment from someone else's culture you need to be immersed within its forces (see Chapter 8). The closest thing most of us come to in experiencing the forces of a culture is when we have moved schools or jobs. When things look and feel very different, we notice that attitudes and behaviours of the people are different too. When you move to another country you also feel the change. In fact, a short time after you start living in a different country you unconsciously begin to absorb its values and behaviours. The absorption of cultures is not always a conscious thing, often it just happens – like when you pick up the accent of the people around you.

Let's allow immigrants to fully integrate

If we can improve our understanding of global cultures by obtaining jobs overseas and living in another country for a period of time, then we can also improve our understanding of the cultures that immigrants bring to this great country by getting closer to them and allowing them to integrate more fully into our society.

If we keep the recent immigrants in their cultural clusters and don't encourage social integration, then how can we ever hope to understand one another? If we don't allow them to 'live it' (live the Australian way of life amongst Australians) when they come to Australia, and if we don't allow them to integrate more fully into our society where they can perfect their English, how can they ever achieve high enough grades to gain entrance to tertiary education qualifications? If new immigrants don't get equal access to higher education and we continue to allow the metaphorical bamboo ceiling (like the glass ceiling) to operate in corporate Australia, then we severely limit our ability to build culturally diverse organisations, with culturally diverse executives and boards that reflect our multicultural society.

When you can't 'live it'; you can only observe it. People interviewed in Asia advised Australians moving to Asian countries for work to be prepared to 'live it' when they get there. They say that you need to mix with some local people, learn a little of their language and share in their traditions and customs in order to have a good experience and be valued by the locals. Similarly, we need to allow our immigrants and foreign workers the same opportunity in Australia. If we don't let them integrate, will they have a good experience?

Let's remove the 'waiting' time

I think we need to challenge the notion that people arriving in Australia to work should have to 'wait' to have their skills and experienced recognised. When I went to Singapore they didn't make me wait. When I went to the United Kingdom they didn't make me wait. So why do we do that in Australia? Why do we make immigrants wait while they prove their capabilities?

One CEO told me that it was because Australia is a small market and there wasn't enough space. Yet markets are supposed to be contestable places where competition reigns free to allow supply and demand to find the best price. Right?

If we are 'protecting' our market from invasion by new arrivals and if we are putting on blinkers to the value that they bring until we no longer notice their difference, how is that affecting the quality and competitiveness of the Australian marketplace? Does it affect the economy? Is that kind of market place going to attract much-needed talent – whether it be foreign or returning Australian expats – to the Australian workforce?

If we make people who bring experience from thriving careers in other countries 'wait' until they have proven themselves, what is happening to the value that they bring? Where is it going? What happens to their sense of pride and self-worth in the meantime? What happens to immigrants who do not have English as a first language who are highly qualified in their own country and are told that they cannot use their talents and skills here? Where do they go? What do they do instead? Drive taxis?

I have heard many reasons why immigrants and returning expats should wait – why they need to 'earn' their place and why foreigners shouldn't come without perfect English. For those with an enquiring optimistic mind it wouldn't take long to find a counter-argument for each and every limitation. I know that there are security issues and those relating to health and safety, but with the large portion of population that is underproductive due to constraints facing females and people from culturally diverse backgrounds in Australia, it would be my preference to look for solutions rather than create barriers.

Australia is an extraordinary country with endless opportunities and talented people, which is why so many others want to live here. It has enormous potential that we cannot access with the current low levels of growth and small population size. Population growth, and accessing the full participation of people who have untapped skills, are vital to ensuring Australia's prosperity.

It is important that we don't hand over a poorly performing and ill-equipped country to the next generation. The world around us is increasingly adaptable, accessible to everyone, technologically driven, multicultural, multilingual and the workforces are mobile. Through greater cultural diversity at home and more effective and swift integration of immigrants, we can prepare our people for our growth across Asia.

Let's check ourselves for bias

> *'I don't mind if they come to live in Australia, but it's not right if they don't learn to speak our language'*
> Anonymous – A small business owner from Sydney.

Not far from this small business is a very popular bakery where early morning commuters stop for breakfast and trades-people call by throughout the day for snacks and lunches. The proprietor is from Cambodia and he has lived in Australia for 14 years with his wife and two daughters. He always has a welcoming smile on his face, his food is delicious and fresh, his prices are competitive and he works long hours to meet the demands of the locals in this well-to-do suburb. He is a valued member of our society – says the foot traffic going in and out of his store – yet according to his neighbour he probably shouldn't have been let in to Australia as his English isn't 'good enough'.

I chuckle at him as he is giving me $1.20 change from a $5 note saying "One million twenty change for you". I reply smiling "That's one dollar twenty, I think" and he blushes again and chuckles back. He has *never* miscounted the money or short-changed me in the seven years I have been buying from his store. He knows how to count and calculate perfectly well, it's just that he mixes up his nouns occasionally.

When I recall the times people in Asia misunderstood my English and how I was 'tutted' at and ignored in a Singapore sandwich bar for my poor accent, I can empathise with this man. He is here to make a living for his family as a retailer in Australia, he performs a great community service and yet is criticised because his English is not perfect.

It's an adverse situation. When immigrants bring industry and add to Australia's economy, what is it that motivates us to make their lives harder? What do we gain from this behaviour? Is the intolerance of people in our society whose first language is not English tolerable?

It is very challenging being an immigrant. And it is weird that as a nation built from a steady flow of immigrants we still lack tolerance of the latest arrivals.

> *My mother said I must always be intolerant of ignorance*
> *but understanding of illiteracy. That some people, unable*
> *to go to school, were more educated and more intelligent*
> *than college professors.*

Maya Angelou, born 1928, author, playwright and poet; Civil Rights activist; colleague of Martin Luther King. She recited her poem 'On the Pulse of Morning' at President Bill Clinton's inauguration in 1993.

Chapter 7

Gender Equality

Talk does not cook rice
Chinese Proverb

I prefer to use the term *gender equality* rather than gender diversity as it focuses the mind and better describes the need for gender balancing in our society, the workplace and at home. As the population approximates 50/50 male/female, then opportunities for equal access to employment, health, wealth, leisure, social connection and all other major indicators of quality of life should also be 50/50.

Hope is not a method

When I attended the *Women on Boards* conference in 2009, which made me sit up and take notice of the lack of progress on gender equality in Australia (discussed in Chapter 3), I asked myself "Is the lack of progress due to inaction or have we just been hoping for change but not doing enough to effect it? Or if there has been action, why is there so little progress?"

One of the things I have always believed is that you shouldn't rely on hope to get things done. I believe if you want something you have to go and get it, ask someone else to deliver it to you or at the very least initiate some actions that might bring about what you seek.

What surprised me was that women at the conference were still talking about the same things as 20 years ago: the glass ceiling; the lack of affordable child care; the paucity of role models for women at work; the fear among men of the changing role of women; how that might affect them; the bias in managerial decision-making; the difficulty getting back into work after raising children; the power of the old-boy-network and how it excluded women; the lack of support some women show to other women and … the list went on and on.

I wondered at the sense of it all. As I believe a problem is just an obstacle to be overcome – I decided to give it some serious thought.

Women in corporate Australia

The 2012 Australian Census 'Women in Leadership' report reveals the following:

- A decade of negligible change for females in executive ranks;
- There are only 7 female CEOs in the ASX200 (up from 6 in 2010) and 12 in the ASX500;
- Women hold 9.7 per cent of executive management positions in the ASX200 (up from 8.0 per cent in 2010) and 9.2 per cent in ASX500;
- Women hold 12.3 per cent of directorships in ASX200 but only 9.2 per cent in the ASX500;
- 39.4 per cent of ASX200 companies have at least one female in the executive (up from 38.1% in 2010) and the remaining 60.6 per cent of ASX200 companies have no female in the executive and 63.1 per cent of ASX500 companies have no females in the executive;
- Women hold 6.0 per cent in line management and 22.0 per cent support positions in ASX200 (and 6.2 and 22.5 per cent in ASX500).

How could it be that after the efforts of many leaders in business and society throughout the 1980s, 1990s and early 2000s the situation remains largely unchanged? Why is it that behaviours of people in organisations have not changed despite the vision, leadership and sponsorship of many well-intentioned CEOs over the past two decades?

Why is it that women who are equally or better educated than men are not reaching the senior ranks of business in Australia? Why are they still banging their heads on the 'glass ceiling' – the inevitable, unseen and intangible, impenetrable layer that blocks the lift to the top?

Norway leads the way

Arni Hole, Director General, Norwegian Royal Ministry for Children, Equity and Social Inclusion offered a reason at that conference in 2009 for which she was the keynote speaker. She said "The reason Australia is behind other leading western nations with regard to gender diversity is because it is not on your radar. It needs to be in your frontal lobe and you need to be prepared to discuss it and do something about it."

Arni has been actively involved in achieving a major turnaround for women in Norway, which resulted from legislation changes that required companies to appoint 40 per cent of the under-represented gender to their boards. The law affecting state-owned and inter-municipal companies went into force by January 2004, with a two-year period of transition and the law affecting around 500 public listed companies was enforced in 2006, with most complying by July 2008.

Female representation on Norwegian boards hiked from 7 per cent in 2003 to 39 per cent in 2008. Incredible progress! There was no 'hope' involved. They took action to move the needle: Norway introduced new laws to change century-old behaviours. The new laws served to shift an assumption of Norwegian culture that 'boards were the reserve of males', to a new assumption 'that some places would be reserved for high-achieving females'.

Two years after Arni came to Australia I interviewed her for this book and she said "When I came to Australia in 2009 I expected to meet a society that was discussing issues relating to gender diversity. I expected to hear that it was valued and meant something and to read in the newspapers that politicians are chatting about it to illustrate their courage to do something about it. I did not see this: instead I felt I met a conservative society, not a modern one that discusses issues affecting its people and industry."

I asked the 100 leaders interviewed whether Australia should follow Norway's example and legislate quotas. Their responses are recorded below.

I explain in Chapter 9 how Norway's actions redirected its Culture Iceberg and irreversibly impacted the assumptions and values that drive behaviour in that country.

Women on boards by industry

Cai Kjaer, partner of Optimice, has been analysing Thomson Reuter data for all of the 2000+ ASX-listed companies and the associated 12,500 board positions and he compared the gender distribution of board positions across industries (see the table below).

The top three industries with the highest proportion of board positions occupied by women are insurance, containers and packaging and banks. At the bottom are capital goods, metals and mining and paper and forest products.

Cai says, "The available number of board positions per sector is vastly different, making comparison less meaningful. For instance, metals and mining has 4348 board positions with 309 occupied by women which equals 7.11 per cent, whereas insurance has 109 positions occupied by 21 women which puts there percentage up to 19.27."

If metals and mining can find the women, why can they not be found in other sectors too?

Note: The following table presents raw data extracted from Thomson Reuters on 14 Nov 2012. Board positions for ASX-listed companies where either the GICS code isn't applicable, and/or where the classification is pending, have been omitted. Thus, a total of 138 board positions are not included in the table.

Women on boards by industry

GICS Industry Classification	# Board Positions Women	# Board Positions Men	Total #	% Board Positions Women	% Board Positions Men
Insurance	21	88	109	19.27%	80.73%
Containers & Packaging	5	21	26	19.23%	80.77%
Banks	24	104	128	18.75%	81.25%
Consumer Durables & Apparel	27	123	150	18.00%	82.00%
Consumer Services	53	242	295	17.97%	82.03%
Household & Personal Products	3	14	17	17.65%	82.35%
Food & Staples Retailing	7	33	40	17.50%	82.50%
Construction Materials	13	64	77	16.88%	83.12%
Real Estate Investment Trusts	44	237	281	15.66%	84.34%
Retailing	41	238	279	14.70%	85.30%
Transportation	33	206	239	13.81%	86.19%
Materials	4	26	30	13.33%	86.67%
Media	34	230	264	12.88%	87.12%
Real Estate	48	346	394	12.18%	87.82%
Semiconductors & Semiconductor Equipment	3	22	25	12.00%	88.00%
Pharmaceuticals & Biotechnology	47	349	396	11.87%	88.13%
Chemicals	9	68	77	11.69%	88.31%
Diversified Financials	98	765	863	11.36%	88.64%
Telecommunication Services	22	172	194	11.34%	88.66%
Health Care Equipment & Services	43	358	401	10.72%	89.28%
Commercial Services & Supplies	41	376	417	9.83%	90.17%
Software & Services	41	378	419	9.79%	90.21%
Automobiles & Components	6	57	63	9.52%	90.48%
Utilities	22	217	239	9.21%	90.79%
Food, Beverage & Tobacco	24	246	270	8.89%	91.11%
Technology, Hardware & Equipment	15	156	171	8.77%	91.23%
Energy	130	1,400	1,530	8.50%	91.50%
Capital Goods	62	681	743	8.34%	91.66%
Metals & Mining	309	4,039	4,348	7.11%	92.89%
Paper & Forest Products	-	21	21	0.00%	100%
Grand Total	**1,229**	**11,277**	**12,506**	**9.83%**	**90.17%**

Women in the arts, education and government

An Archibald Prize finalist drew my attention to the gender profile of the finalists. In the table below you will see that for a 12-year period the number of female finalists and winners was significantly less than men.

It is a curious thing – why would males be better at art than females? Are there any physiological or psychological reasons why males might produce better artworks? When I asked my friend why 70–80 per cent of the short-listed finalists were males and why 80 per cent of the time men won this prestigious prize over females, it was suggested that:

- While the artworks are shown to the judges anonymously, everyone knows the individual styles of the artists and can guess whose work it is;
- Maybe the criteria used to assess the artworks are based on features that are more prominent on a man's work over a female's work;
- Perhaps the judges are using features of past winning works – influencing their judgement.

Archibald Prize Finalists

	2012	2011	2010	2009	2008	2007	2006	2005	2004	2003	2002	2001
Total Number of Finalists	41	41	34	39	40	41	36	36	40	41	31	31
Male Finalists	29	29	27	27	32	31	25	30	32	31	22	21
Female Finalists	12	12	7	12	8	10	11	6	8	10	9	10
Female % of Finalists	29.0%	29.0%	20.6%	30.8%	20.0%	24.4%	30.6%	16.7%	20.0%	24.4%	29.0%	32.3%
Gender of Winner	Male	Male	Male	Male	Female	Male	Male	Male	Male	Male	Female	Male

Source: *www.thearchibaldprize.com.au*

Perhaps this excerpt taken from the Archibald Prize website provides a hint? Maybe old 1930s assumptions about a female's role in society and her ability to produce great works of art remain uncontested in the art world. See what you make of this highly quoted statement from Max Meldrum who in 1938 was an Archibald finalist the same year that Nora Heysen won the Prize:

'If I were a woman, I would certainly prefer raising a healthy family to a career in art. Women are more closely attached to the physical things of life. They are not to blame. They cannot help it and to expect them to do some things equally as well as men is sheer lunacy.'

Max Meldrum

We have come a long way – or have we? The following chart shows the EOWA Women in Leadership Census of 2008 and 2010. The change in two years is negligible. Not only are there few women on boards, but the percentage of university Vice Chancellors has dropped from 21.1 per cent to 17.9 per cent. Women in Federal Parliament have increased from 29.6 per cent to 30.1 per cent over two years – that's almost as good a 'no change'. I think it is fair to say progress had been very poor up until the ASX changed its guidelines in 2010 and fear that continued 'no change' will lead to quotas, has driven the increase of women on boards from 8–13 per cent. It's amazing what a little accountability and transparency can do.

Status of women in the workplace

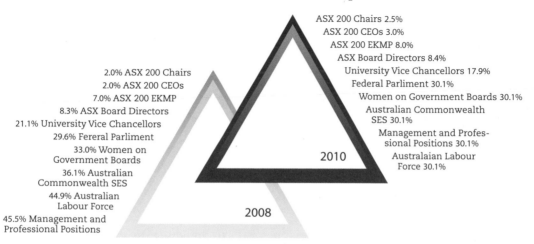

ASX 200 Chairs 2.5%
ASX 200 CEOs 3.0%
ASX 200 EKMP 8.0%
ASX Board Directors 8.4%
University Vice Chancellors 17.9%
Federal Parliment 30.1%
Women on Government Boards 30.1%
Australian Commonwealth SES 30.1%
Management and Professional Positions 30.1%
Australaian Labour Force 30.1%

2010

2.0% ASX 200 Chairs
2.0% ASX 200 CEOs
7.0% ASX 200 EKMP
8.3% ASX Board Directors
21.1% University Vice Chancellors
29.6% Fereral Parliment
33.0% Women on Government Boards
36.1% Australian Commonwealth SES
44.9% Australian Labour Force
45.5% Management and Professional Positions

2008

Australia's relative position on gender

You are probably familiar with Australia's ranking in the World Economic Forum Global Gender Gap's (WEFGGG) Annual Report (a link is provided in Appendix II). If not, here is a brief summary of the report and its main findings.

Since 2006 the WEF has been tracking gender-based disparities across 135 countries, which represent 93 per cent of the world's population. The report measures the size of the gender inequality gap across four key areas (see below) and each country receives an overall *ranking* in relation to the other countries and a ranking in each of the four key areas. In addition, each country receives an overall *Index score* which considers performance based on each of the indicators.

Index score

Index scores are available for each of the four key areas based on performance, independent of the performance of other countries. Scores can be interpreted as the proportion of the gender gap that has been closed, with 0.00 indicating that 0 per cent of the gender gap has been closed (inequality) and 1.00 indicating that 100 per cent of the gender gap has been closed (equality).

Australia's overall Index score improved slightly from 0.7271 in 2010 to 0.7291 in 2011. Australia has experienced a modest improvement since the first Gender Gap Report was released, with its score experiencing a 1.8 per cent improvement on its 2006 score. Scores given to each of the four key indicators in 2011 were:

Educational attainment scored 1.00   (High achievement)
Health and survival scored 0.9738   (High achievement)
Economic participation and   (Room for improvement)
  opportunity scored 0.7565
Political empowerment 0.1861   (Underperforming)

Australian women proudly scored equal first with other nations for educational achievement but a little less praiseworthy is the score for economic (workforce) participation. I hesitate to comment on the score of 0.1861 for political empowerment as this is a little too sad. Where are all the educated women going and why are they not helping to govern this great country? There was serious under-performing in all three indicators for this category:

Women in parliament –   score 0.33 (25% women)
Women in ministerial positions –   score 0.30 (23% women)
Years with female head of state –   score 0.02 (one year)

These figures show there is much work to be done to get equal female representation in industry and even more to be done in governing the country. But let's look at the overall ranking against the 135 countries.

Ranking

Although Australia has seen a small but steady increase in its *Index score* over the six years, its overall *ranking* comparative to other countries has been steadily declining. This indicates that Australia is showing slight improvement across the board on gender equality but is failing to see improvements at the same rate as other countries. As a consequence its overall ranking relative to the other nations has slipped steadily from 15th place in 2006 to 23rd place in 2011.

The countries doing better than Australia from 1st place in descending order are: Iceland, Norway, Finland, Sweden, (who have been consistently in one of the top four places since 2006), Ireland, New Zealand, Denmark and Philippines (who have been oscillating between 5th and 10th place since 2006) Lesotho and Switzerland (who have risen from 43rd and 26th respectively) followed by Germany, Spain, Belgium, South Africa, Netherlands, United Kingdom, United

States, Canada, Latvia, Cuba, Trinidad and Tobago and the Bahamas in 22nd place.

While Australian women rank equal first with other countries for educational attainment, we have a long way to go to correct the tendency for women to opt out of the workforce despite their efforts to become so highly educated.

More women, better performance

In the past few years there have been many reports published by media, market watchers, research companies and consulting firms about the impact of having more females on boards, in management and in the workforce. You don't have to go far to find them or to read the proof that a more balanced gender mix in problem-solving and decision-making teams produces a better result.

In July 2012 a Credit Suisse Research Institute Report showed that women on boards improved company performance by 26 per cent.

The report highlighted:

'Companies with women on their boards performed better in challenging markets than those with all-male boards in a study suggesting that mixing genders may temper risky investment moves and increase return on equity.

Shares of companies with a market capitalisation of more than $10 billion and with women board members outperformed comparable businesses with all-male boards by 26 per cent worldwide over a period of six years, according to a report by the Credit Suisse Research Institute, created in 2008 to analyse trends expected to affect global markets.

The number of women in boardrooms has increased since the end of 2005 as countries such as Norway instituted quotas and companies including Facebook Inc. (FB) added female directors after drawing criticism for a lack of gender diversity. The research, which includes data from 2360 companies, shows a greater correlation between stock performance and the presence of women on the board after the financial crisis started four years ago.

Net income growth for companies with women on their boards has averaged 14 per cent over the past six years, compared with 10 per cent for those with no female director, according to the Credit Suisse study, which examined all the companies in the MSCI ACWI Index. (MXWD) The net-debt-to-equity ratio at companies with at least one female director was 48 per cent, compared with 50 per cent at all-male boards, and the study showed a faster reduction in debt at businesses with women on the board as the financial crisis and global economic slowdown unfolded.'

100 leaders' gender perspectives

The subject of gender equality was most passionately commented on in the research interviews for this book. In fact in many interviews it dominated the time. This is quite possibly because of the increased focus on gender in corporate Australia since the ASX changes were announced mid 2010 and the heightened media coverage over the past few years. The content gathered is therefore much richer and broader and the information has been presented under the following headings:

What do you think about women on boards?
- How satisfied are you with the rate of progress?
- How accurate is the argument that Australia has too few good/ experienced women for board-level roles?
- What would you like to see done differently?

What do you think about having quotas?
- Do you think Australia should implement quotas, and why?
- How can they benefit women, Australia and business?
- How can they harm women, Australia and business?

How well are women supporting each other to achieve gender equality?
- Why do women not see that other women need their help?
- What does it mean when a women turns her back on another woman?
- Is it possible to climb the ladder and still be supportive of other women?

What's happening with gender roles, mentoring and education?
- What changes are you seeing in society regarding gender roles and how are the changes impacting women, and men?
- What kind of mentoring should we offer and what do we expect of mentors?
- Are we doing enough to educate children about roles at work and home?

What does gender bias look like?
- What biases have you experienced in your career?
- What forms of bias are most prevalent?
- What would you like to see done to address the bias?

What issues do we need to address?
- How aware is Australian society of the issues affecting diversity and growth?

- Are businesses doing enough to get gender equality?
- What would you like to see from our leaders to address issues?

What opportunities do we need to consider?
- What could we do better to help women build careers?
- How can we increase the pace of change for women?
- What are we not seeing?

What strategies have you employed?
- What has worked?
- What has not worked?
- What strategies can we not do without?

What advice do you have for others?
- Can you share your experiences?
- Are there any shortcuts that others should know about?

What do you think about women on boards?

Women on Boards (WOB) wanted to see ASX200 companies achieve 25 per cent women on their boards by the end of 2012. The numbers climbed from 8.7 per cent in 2010 to 14.5 per cent in August 2012 which is a step forward but too slow. When you look at the ASX201–300 the situation is even worse with only 7.6 per cent in January 2012.

About 30 per cent of the ASX200 still have no women. Many say 'the women aren't available' yet others are finding them. Of the 110 women appointed in 2011 to the ASX200 boards, half of these were not members of an ASX board previously, which shows that you can find good women capable of stepping up. Companies without women need to look more widely.

Ruth Medd, Chair, Women on Boards, Sydney, Australia

It is different once you move into a non-executive director role: you are less tolerant of bad behaviour. I recall reading a survey about women on boards and they found that male board members said women on boards are too disruptive and they get too much into the detail.

When I first got onto a board, I knew I was being appointed because I was a woman so I had to prove that I was a valuable contributor in order to pave the way for other women. There were some males who were definitely negative about women on boards. Fortunately it has changed dramatically in 10 years.

Catherine Livingston AO, Chairman, Telstra, Sydney, Australia

One of the reasons the number of women appointed to public boards has skyrocketed is because of the AICD mentoring program (where male board members mentor females aspiring to get onto a board). In typical Aussie male style some directors became somewhat competitive in getting their mentees placed onto boards. I guess this is one way to get change.

> Diane Grady AM, Non-Executive Director, Macquarie Group, Sydney, Australia

While women on boards are a minority they will adapt to survive. If you get a woman on the board and she doesn't have a say – if her views don't count – then she won't be able influence change. Women need to know that there is a reason why they are there: they need to start by challenging decisions. We also need to be careful that we don't end up like Norway with a few women having most of the directorships. What we need is a higher number of women having directorships to get impact.

> Margaret Dreyer, Partner, Deloitte Touche Tohmatsu , Sydney, Australia

The ASX changes have been met with mixed reception. Some boards will use the guidelines to introduce change, for the others it will still be 'tokenism' that gets the women there. I accept that this might continue to be the way for some women to get in. But within 12–18 months there will be a groundswell of women on boards. What I think is much more important now is women in the C-suite. Women need to be in decision-making roles because once they are in the CEO's position they can impact change.

> Katie Lahey, Chief Executive Officer, Korn Ferry, Sydney, Australia

They say that can't find great women for boards but they are only looking for lawyers and accountants. They need to look more broadly for other skills that will help their companies meet the growth challenges they face.

> Dr Julianne Schultz AM, Non-executive Director, Australian Broadcasting Corporation, Sydney, Australia

There are 1200 ASX200 directors and there is a healthy debate about quotas versus guidelines. The new ASX guidelines about gender requirements have been well received because they are guidelines and not legislation. Directors and chairmen of ASX companies are very supportive, but they want to know how to do it [achieve gender diversity].

> Amanda Mostyn, Executive General Manager, People & Development, ASX Group, Sydney, Australia

They put people on their boards who won't rock the boat. So even though they say let's embrace diversity, they don't put it into practice. I say "None are so blind as those who will not see."

> Marie Malaxos, GM Production and Development, Buru Energy, Perth, Australia

I do understand people's concerns about targets and that it might interfere with meritocracy but this could also be self-serving, unhelpful and ill-informed. The empirical evidence is to the contrary. If you change the platform you open up opportunities for everyone. When it comes to talent there's no gender divide. We need the change and I'm determined to see change.

John Denton, Chief Executive Officer, Corrs Chambers Westgarth, Melbourne, Australia

There has just not been enough progress of women on boards. Thirteen per cent is still wildly under-represented. My concern is, what does this say about the effectiveness of our boards? Three-quarters of our economy is spent on the consumer and one-quarter is on investment capital. As women drive most of the consumer spending they should be represented on the boards. Currently boards are characterised by short-termism and panic. Women would bring a different temperament to a board and would add the consistency and stability that is missing.

Phil Ruthven, Chairman, IBIS World, Melbourne, Australia

What do you think about having quotas?

We heard the same excuses from our people in Norway that you are hearing from people in Australia about quotas: that women who are not ready might get over-promoted. To be elected to a board you need to be nominated by an election committee. The general assembly would not nominate a person who is not ready to be elected to a board. It's not a job that you need to compete for. To be elected to a company board you need to be nominated. This is a democracy and it has nothing to do with being less qualified. Switzerland, Germany and other European countries are now considering quotas because of our success.

Arni Hole, Director General, Norwegian Royal Ministry for Children, Equity and Social Inclusion, Oslo, Norway

I have gone from not believing in quotas, to thinking that we might have to follow the more progressive nations. There are still many major companies that have no senior women. There is something in the Australian culture that prevents us from being aggressive on targets. The ASX guidelines were introduced to get all businesses to set targets yet I hear people saying they are not going to set targets because they don't want to be locked in, in case they can't make it. If there is no burning platform why would people change?

Kim Schmidt, Director of People and Culture, Grant Thornton, Sydney, Australia

I like targets: we aspire for half our emerging population to be female and for the leadership team to be 50 per cent female too. Goals are really important and that's a very different thing from having a quota. Quotas are corrosive and they put the burden of fixing the problem on women. What happens when you get a fantastically qualified woman on a board and people say cynically that it's just because of the quota? It puts the burden on the woman to carry it off. I like transparency and I like targets. Quotas are an invitation not to embrace gender diversity.

Paul Waterman, President, BP Australia, Melbourne, Australia

The Norwegians did it with quotas. They felt that if they left it to an organic process it would have taken 100 years. To move the needle you need to force it faster. You need punishment and punitive treatment to those who will not play the game. I am evolved in my thinking on the topic because societies change very slowly.

Kathy Matsui, Managing Director & Chief Japan Strategist, Goldman Sachs, Tokyo, Japan

The debate about quotas is a substitute for action. The number of women on boards is just not enough and we need women in management too. Let's just do it. We can argue endlessly.

Uschi Schreiber, Managing Partner - Global Government & Public Sector Industry Centre, Ernst & Young Global, Hong Kong, Australia

I am sceptical about how many people are doing something about it. How many are doing 'just enough' so they are being seen to comply. Naming and shaming will drive people to comply. I don't think quotas will move the figures. What we have to do is grow the pot.

Giam Swiegers, Chief Executive Officer, Deloitte Touche Tohmatsu, Sydney, Australia

How well are women supporting gender equality?

I have always found extremely successful businesswomen very scary. They would ignore me at conferences and turn their back on me. When I was at Alcoa I spent some time with women executives in our USA operations and they were far more supportive. When I travelled to China, Malaysia, Indonesia and Vietnam I was dealing with prime ministers and other dignitaries and they never made me feel odd because I was a woman. Maybe we need to evolve a bit further: this competition between senior women is a uniquely Australian thing.

Shirley In't Veld, Non-Executive Director, Asciano, Perth, Australia

Some women at the top are criticised for being too tough. To get up there they often have to take on certain behaviours to compete against men and these are not always considered attractive in a female. Often women who get to the top behave the way they do unconsciously.

Diane Grady AM, Non-Executive Director, Macquarie Group, Sydney, Australia

Corporate women climb the ladder and it's very competitive. It is okay to compete with men and women, but in Norway we have long-term solidarity between women. You can have solidarity and be an individual at the same time. You need solidarity among women to help each other because that's what men do, they have the old boy network.

Arni Hole, Director General, Norwegian Royal Ministry for Children, Equity and Social Inclusion, Oslo, Norway

I don't believe that women consciously resist helping other women; it is that they don't see the problem. There are women who get to the top without bumping up against the glass ceiling because they didn't encounter any blockages themselves.

Kim Schmidt, Director of People and Culture, Grant Thornton, Sydney, Australia

Women can sometimes be poor supporters of other women. Perhaps we should expect women's organisations to be more rigorous in finding ways to get their women members to support other women.

Jillian Segal AM, Non-Executive Director, National Australia Bank, Sydney, Australia

Is it a sign of weakness if you are a woman and you lean down and pull other women up?

Paul Waterman, President, BP Australia, Melbourne, Australia

A lot of women who are in top positions almost don't want other women up there with them because it makes them look better. That's what worries me about what we are doing; are we going to have more competition between women? We have to be careful that we don't create an 'old girls network'.

Marie Malaxos, GM Production and Development, Buru Energy, Perth, Australia

Since moving into this new role I have had some difficulty getting support from other senior women in the Navy. I have been road-blocked by them because they think everything is the same for everyone. They have reached the top despite being married and having children and they don't see that other women who take time out [to have a family] are in any way disadvantaged. They are unwilling to consider that not everyone is like them.

Cmdr Jennifer Wittwer FAHRI, Royal Australian Navy, Canberra, Australia

What about gender roles, mentoring and education?

Research shows that girls do better in single-sex schools. This is true if you define 'better' as academic results. If great marks are the key to the future then that would be relevant. However I am not convinced that females who go through single-sex girls' schools know how to relate to men as friends and colleagues, and the same is true for men who go to boys schools. Could our focus on single-sex education be contributing to the challenges we see in the workplace?

Diane Grady AM, Non-Executive Director, Macquarie Group, Sydney, Australia

When I think about it now, I'd rather my son had gone to a co-ed school rather than a single-sex boys' school. I realised when he got to university that there are many aspects to schooling. One is social development and a lot of social growth includes both boys and girls. It is part of life and learning about effective social interaction between both genders might be better to have sooner than later. I know it creates challenges by generalising this way, but I now believe that children would have a better education in a co-ed environment. It would possibly prepare them better for entering the workplace.

Stephen Roberts, Chief Country Officer, Citi, Sydney, Australia

I look at my daughters (now young adults) and they have confidence that they can do anything. They are not daunted by the work environment they are entering. Their generation has mostly had working mothers and know what it's like to consider starting a family mid-career. They also know it is mentally and physically demanding and to get through every 24 hours balancing work and family is a task of Herculean proportions.

Catherine Livingston AO, Chairman, Telstra, Sydney, Australia

Women carry a larger share of the home responsibility. They have to deal with society questioning whether you are a good mother if you are a working mother and they have to deal with their own upbringing [and question values passed down by parents of a different generation]. Women who are concerned about other women need to be mentors. It is incredibly demanding to be a mentor.

Men also need support through this process. Some are coping fine with women taking on bigger careers and others are not so fine. Some men feel that the jobs are now going to women and they feel discriminated against. Men are being pressured to share the domestics at home and to be more involved with child-minding by working wives. We need to have broader discussion and offer support for both genders.

Jillian Segal AM, Non-Executive Director, National Australia Bank, Sydney, Australia

Most of us live in an environment where there is a yin and yan. We have to look at the man's role in the gender diversity education process, for there is an unintended consequence to the changes we are trying to make. We need to talk about what men have to do differently now, so that boys know what their future roles are.

As women step up to take their place in society we are seeing increased feelings of underachievement and suicide amongst men. This is about men's inability to manage the social change and they are passing the insecurity down to the next generation. We need to better define the nature of men's and women's roles for the future. They were not so neatly divided up a couple of generations ago. I watch men who take on child care and increased domestic duties struggle to explain their new role to their peers. Very few men speak up about it. To be a stay-at-home dad is not an easy role and there is much we can learn from the husbands of successful women.

Ann Sherry AO, Chief Executive Officer, Carnival Australia, Sydney, Australia

We need to educate young girls that they can do anything and that manufacturing is not a dirty place to work. That means we have to promote non-traditional careers and educational opportunities right across Australia and the broader community. Amcor advertised that it was running an evening information session for women to tell them about careers in our paper mills and several mothers called to ask if they could bring their daughters. That was very encouraging and the session went extremely well.

Lynley Corcoran, General Manager Human Resources, Amcor, Melbourne, Australia

We need to see change in our consumer advertising which continues to reinforce the notion that women are the only people in the household who do the washing. How often do you see a washing-powder advertisement showing a husband being challenged by getting the football shorts or nappies clean? And then there's media. You can turn 12 pages of the *Australian Financial Review* before you will see a picture of a woman and it is likely to be an advertisement of an attractive long-legged woman with a big smile carrying shopping bags.

All the wrong messages are still going out and it is building up in our children's DNA through what they see and experience every day. We need clearer messages in the schools about future gender roles too.

Annette Kimmitt, Office Managing Partner, Ernst & Young Global, Victoria, Australia

With regard to the preschool child-care shortage in Australia, this is limited by our resistance to allowing an underclass to coexist by admitting immigrant labour pools of people who wish to work as nannies. Australia's minimum wage laws prohibit cheap child care, not to mention the firmly held value within our society that *mothers* should look after their children.

Early childhood education makes an enormous difference to long-term learning: it is believed to improve educational outcomes, so there is more we need to do here. It's not just preschool child care that we need to examine but after-school care. Few schools offer sufficient after-school care services. In addition to the lack of support during the school term, parents also have to cover 16 weeks of holiday per year. When you ask your employer if you can work 38 weeks only, they put it in the 'too hard' basket.

John Daley, Chief Executive Officer, Grattan Institute, Melbourne, Australia

In professional firms it is not just the partners who have to grow into this new world with more senior career women, but the clients need to adapt too. They need to get used to the fact that women might not be available five days a week, learn to be flexible and adapt to the new ways of working. They need to plan their requirements around a flexible three-day week. Instead of asking for a male partner to ensure they get 100 per cent attention, clients should think through how they can use technology to access women when they are not in the office.

David Gonski AC, Chairman, Future Fund of Australia, Sydney, Australia

Men have enormous pressures on them to be the breadwinners. If a wife decides she wants to go back to work the man might think that she is saying "You're not doing well enough honey so I'll help you." At Arup we wanted our male employees to know it is okay for them to work flexibly as well as the women, so we promoted new polices for both genders and we had both men and women take up the opportunity. After a while some of them started returning to full-time because there were some systems that we had not thought to change, which they perceived as being inequitable to part-timers. We are working with male and female staff to modify and improve these systems to make flexible working a real alternative.

Peter Bailey, Chief Executive Officer, Arup Group, Sydney, Australia

Our business community in Australia is aged, white and male. It's a culture that men are comfortable with. Women do things differently and they play a bigger role than men. But women don't have the same toolkit, so they have to be better than men. Females don't plan careers in the same way as males. It would help men at work if they better understood a woman's career path and the priorities.

Rosemary Howard, Executive Director AGSM Executive Programs, Australian School of Business, UNSW, Sydney, Australia

It is pretty egalitarian in the television industry, but people tend to get streamed into stereotypical gender roles. The young guys are asked to go to the sheds and collect boxes and do the heavy lifting for the crew; they tend to get the more hands-on jobs. When the young women come in, they are often given a production assistant's role. Over time the women end up as production managers: they hold the purse strings and manage the budgets. This is partly because of where they started but it is also because it's a better career for women raising kids. There's a lot of travel required in the filming side of TV production.

Matt Tomaszewski, Director-Writer, Triton Media, Sydney, Australia

In 2009 a group of women leaders from the manufacturing sector started Women in Manufacturing – it is now a national organisation and has broadened to include women-in-operations. One of our roles is to lobby Government and the education sector to change the way girls are socialised at school. Both parents and girls need to be made aware of the opportunities that manufacturing offers females and we need to challenge their thinking about careers in engineering.

Lisa Eccleston, Group General Manager Human Resources, Amcor, Melbourne, Australia

Recent surveys show that women still do more work in the home than men and if you weigh up a woman's paid and unpaid work they are both about the same amount of time in the week (50/50). This means that for every hour females spends at their paid job, they work the same number of hours around the home.It is the male baby boomers, and older, that have the problem. Gen X and younger men are sharers. Even blokes who need prompting do help. They may need prompting, but they are willing to share the load when asked.

The average family in Australia is spending $33,000 on outsourcing (e.g. house cleaning, dog walking, lawn mowing, food shopping). For the first time in history the money spent on outsourcing is greater than the money spent on retail. Outsourcing helps to regain lives, reduces pressure and stops the fighting.

Phil Ruthven, Chairman, IBIS World, Melbourne, Australia

The roles of women and men are still so different. Males think they have to be the breadwinner and too many think 'It is okay for my wife to go back to work but only if it works for me i.e. everything else in our life must still tick along and the housework must not be neglected'.

I don't think we really do anything to support women in relation to gender equality and if we really want it, we have to take action to get us there. The government has to address the problem of child care and not allow the costs to suck up all the earnings. Women want to go back to work, they have a brain and they want to use it to feel fulfilled.

Debra Singh, former General Manager, Dick Smith, Sydney, Australia

In China we are living in a culture with very little diversity. To us, Australia looks like a very good example of diversity. We see more female law graduates than males coming out of Australian universities. Is that not a good measure?

Philippa Jones, Managing Director, China Policy, Beijing, China

What does gender bias look like?

Times have certainly changed in the last decade, but when I was hired in the 1970s to be a journalist for the Australian Financial Review, the editor at the time hired me in a pub, drunkenly, saying you can have the job because 'blokes will tell girls anything' and women were also cheaper. Within a short period of time after that, about half the staff of the AFR were women. It was great that they hired us all, but this was not reflected in the paper. Women were never on the front page, only the men. It is still very much like this today. Many women journalists work at the AFR but there is still a paucity of businesswomen profiled or whose comments are sought for publication.

Dr Julianne Schultz AM, Non-executive Director, Australian Broadcasting Corporation, Sydney, Australia

It's a tough gig. Women have to have a toughness to get to the top in a male environment but then they get criticised for it. They get called 'aggressive'. Women are perceived not to have experience for a job, so they don't get the job and then they don't get more experience. We have to break the cycle. Men need a different view about what talent looks like.

Neil Cockroft, Head of Diversity and Culture, King & Wood Mallesons, Sydney, Australia

When the kids were at school my wife was the Chair of the Council at our daughter's girls-only school and was involved with fundraising there. She always found it more difficult raising money for her school, than it was at my son's boys-only school. The fathers were readily giving their money to the boys' schools, but they were not so generous when it came to the girls' schools. How do we amputate this kind of behaviour? What does it convey to our kids?

Bias starts somewhere, you are not born with it. Don't blame the kids, blame the schools, the parents and the religious infrastructure.

Stephen Roberts, Chief Country Officer, Citi, Sydney, Australia

The problems are deeply rooted in our history. Women were considered the weaker sex for so long that we have some deeply seated attitudes to change. While we are seeing more women in the workforce, it's going to take a lot longer to see women in leadership. There is bias around what a leader looks like; the traits that we used to model leadership are typically male traits. When women emulate the man's style of leadership, it either works for them or it doesn't.

Katy McDonald, Director of Human Resources, Minter Ellison, Sydney, Australia

Our male bosses still don't get how it feels to be a woman in the Navy. They don't understand the isolation or the need for mentoring. When I went to sea as a young woman there were only two females on the ship and the other woman was several ranks below me so we could not be friends [socialising between ranks is difficult].

Our change started in late 2008 when the Navy launched a cultural reform and changed its structure and leadership. The Admiral, our CEO, is leading from the top and he began by creating the role of Navy Women's Strategic Adviser and had it report directly to his position to illustrate the importance of diversity to Navy. Our key strategies include culture and systems change to support gender balancing and we are looking at more flexible options for career-path planning.

Cmdr Jennifer Wittwer FAHRI, Royal Australian Navy, Canberra, Australia

I didn't experience the bias until I had twins. I only noticed it when people started asking how I was going to cope with three kids in less than 15 months. I could feel their anxiety about how I would work and have children too. Even though my husband was at home as the full-time carer, it was apparently still an issue for them.

Angela Tatlis, Managing Director, Invoke Performance, Melbourne, Australia

When I returned to Australia from Hong Kong I was told several times by recruiters that their clients were looking for females to fill their group HR positions and that this was driven by the ASX changes to meet gender targets. While I fully understood the need for CEOs to get better gender balance into their executive teams, we need to be careful that the bias doesn't go the other way.

Dharma Chandran, Chief Human Resources Officer, Leighton Holdings, Sydney, Australia

I don't join women-only groups and I won't speak to women-only audiences because it feels hypocritical to have female-only functions. I have had people trying to get me to apply for Telstra Businesswoman of the Year, but I find this notion repugnant.

Shirley In't Veld, Non-Executive Director, Asciano, Perth, Australia

One day back in the USA we were recruiting for a new Director of Marketing and I realised were we only looking at males for the role. Then we asked 'Why wouldn't we promote a woman to this role? And then we did. She had a different style from the males; she was quieter and she didn't beat her chest or drink lots of beer on a Friday night. So we could have missed her. But we put her through the process and appointed her as the best candidate and she did an outstanding job.

Paul Waterman, President, BP Australia, Melbourne, Australia

What issues do we need to address?

Current Issue - Pace

25 years ago I started to look into why women were not in senior positions, appearing in the media, winning writers awards, and not being nominated for Australian honours. I am tired of hearing only from male opinion leaders in the corporate world. Twenty-five years on; little has changed.

Carol Schwartz AM, Non-executive Director, Stockland, Melbourne, Australia

Current Issue – Getting beyond the basics

Programs designed to 'fix' women are not helpful. Too much time is being spent on the hygiene issues like pay equity, child-minding, flexibility and mentoring. While these things are necessary you can get tied up with 'initiatives' when you really need to look at the culture. Senior women need to speak up about behaviours that they see which need addressing.

Tristan Landers, former Executive General Manager, Corporate Sustainability, Commonwealth Bank of Australia, Sydney, Australia

Current Issue – Don't interfere with motherhood

Motherhood is a sacred cow. It's taboo. It is precious and wrapped up in political correctness. No one talks about 'motherhood' because it is a tough conversation. You can't tamper with the concept socially, and at work some women feel they can't mention their kids.

Edyta Torpy, Oceania Diversity & Inclusiveness leader, Ernst & Young Global, Sydney, Australia

Current Issue – Recruiters' bias towards men

The wake-up call for me was when I realised that we needed to tell our recruiters that the way they were doing things was not acceptable. We had to have a deep conversation and ask them why they were not identifying women for the short list. Once we started to ask 'Why not?', we got a step change and women started to appear on short lists. The lesson for me was the power of the question. It is not to be underestimated. You need to ask 'Why do we do it this way?' and then you get to have a different conversation.

Paul Waterman, President, BP Australia, Melbourne, Australia

Current Issue – Childless senior women as role models

Many of the most successful women in high-level positions don't have children. They have adopted a male model and behaviours to survive. It would be really good if this didn't need to be the case. Young women look up and think that's the preferred option.

Neil Cockroft, Head of Diversity and Culture, King & Wood Mallesons, Sydney, Australia

Current Issue – Keeping women in non-traditional sectors

It is very challenging keeping women in an engineering career long enough to have them rise to the top. At the lower levels we are lucky to have up to 20 per cent of female staff and then we lose them when they get married. The work is dirty, it can be dangerous and the hours are long. Females work on engineering solutions in a different way from men and it would be great to have a few more women as they balance out the management group. We need to work harder at finding ways of keeping them engaged.

Gabriel Yam, Managing Partner, Arup Group, Hong Kong, China

Current Issue - Flexibility

We can't expect women to be superwomen and hold down two full-time roles – one at work and one at home. It is incumbent upon leaders in the workforce to meet the conditions of employment as flexibly as we can. At ANZ there are a lot of front-line roles that can be done part-time. Our people can start late and leave early which allows them to drop off and pick up children and they can work from home in the evening. For these arrangements to work you need a high sense of trust. Output is far more important than hours in the office. I don't care about the hours, only the quality.

Mike Smith OBE, Chief Executive Officer, Australian and New Zealand Banking Group, Melbourne, Australia

Current Issue – Biasing effect in tertiary education

Gender is an issue in Australian universities. Many lecturers are female, yet most professors are male. It's not so much sexist behaviour but you have to have five A-Star publications to get promoted to professor and women who take career breaks often find this difficult to achieve. It's an industry norm that has to be addressed as there's got to be an opportunity cost to not using 50 per cent of the talent.

Professor Alec Cameron, Deputy Vice-Chancellor (Education), University of Western Australia, Perth, Australia

Current Issue – Women's careers less important

Even the converts [the so-called female supporters] have a small reservation about how women can manage at work when the kids come into the picture because women seem to be the ones who take the time off when the children get sick [rarely the man]. There is a general assumption that when the chips are down the male is the breadwinner and that his career cannot be derailed, whereas the woman's career can.

Hugh Mackay, Social Researcher and Writer, Sydney, Australia

Current Issue – Encouraging females to stay longer

Fifty-five to sixty per cent of law graduates recruited into local firms are female and academically they are as good as, or better than, the males. Yet in just a few years 40 per cent of them are lost to in-house counsel jobs, overseas positions or to other local firms. Most firms have unconscious bias and flexibility programs in spades to try to shift attitudes. But it's still a challenge for them.

Kevin McCann, Chairman, Macquarie Group, Sydney, Australia

What opportunities are there to consider?

Current Opportunity – Female managers in services are good

Women are making better managers than men especially in service industries and service industries are now 70 per cent of the economy. Women have a more involving style of management than men and this is helpful at the executive level when you are doing things in groups. This is less important when you get to the CEO level, as you often have to stand alone on a decision.

Phil Ruthven, Chairman, IBIS World, Melbourne, Australia

Current Opportunity - Females can excel in non-traditional sectors

I did a mathematics degree at university and knew that I did not want to end up teaching so I sought some advice about other careers. Engineering was suggested and sounded interesting and like a great opportunity. There were not many women doing it in those days, but now there are many more females doing engineering, geoscience, geology and geophysics in Western Australian universities. People often say "Wow, it's unusual to find a woman in that job." But I can be tough if I need to be; and in this industry you can get walked over if you can't hold your own.

Marie Malaxos, GM Production and Development, Buru Energy, Perth, Australia

Current Opportunity – Chairmen and managers now challenging recruiters to check for bias

In the past 12 months there has been a genuine attempt to hire females particularly at board level. Some chairmen are now challenging whether we are looking broadly and fairly enough at both genders and we are noticing that both women and men genuinely want work–life balance.

Greg Stanmore, Managing Director, Spencer Stuart, Sydney, Australia

Current Opportunity – Influencing men

One thing that helps us today is that many male leaders and managers now have 18-year-old daughters who are influencing them.

Jane Hemstritch, Non-Executive Director, Commonwealth Bank of Australia, Melbourne, Australia

What strategies have you employed?

Strategy – Encourage men and women to work together

Women have been talking to themselves about diversity issues for too long. Nowadays I try to only address audiences that have at least 50 per cent men: unless men and women work together change is not going to happen.

Diane Grady AM, Non-Executive Director, Macquarie Group, Sydney, Australia

Strategy – Exchanging genders and cultures

We have targets in place but the local market is tight. Finding senior women in banking in Australia is very challenging. We need to think laterally and think of hiring younger women. To help achieve diversity we think about moving people around the world. We recently did a swap of a mid-30s male from Perth to London and got back a mid-30s female from London to Perth. Immediately that changed the dynamics of the team in Perth as females bring different skills. For us, global movement of staff is an important part of the solution.

Craig Drummond, Chief Executive Officer, Bank of America Merrill Lynch, Sydney, Australia

Strategy – Educate and demonstrate diversity values to keep skills

Our driver to increase the focus on women came from the need to access more skills. The IBM population is a very diverse group and it is our role to shape and change attitudes and views of the people who come to work here. We help them to understand and accept the need for women, disabled, aged and other less populous groups. When people accept the need for diversity, their attitudes and behaviours change.

John Harvey AO, Executive Director, IBM Australia, Sydney, Australia

Strategy - *Women provide a solution to skills shortage*

To solve our skills shortage problem, we are looking at ways to encourage girls and women into our industry. We have partnered with TAFE and are looking at supporting women into their programs. We are also sponsoring them into internships.

Lynley Corcoran, General Manager Human Resources, Amcor, Melbourne, Australia

Strategy – *Flexibility for males and females*

For women the issue of flexibility is paramount. We know that women's careers are nonlinear and at some point they are likely to prefer flexible work (including part-time, job share or an individualised working schedule). Seventy-eight per cent of IBM Australia staff does some work away from the office, which may include making calls from home or attending an off-site meeting. It's not uncommon to hear dogs barking on a sales call. At IBM, where or how you have the meeting does not matter. It's about results and outcomes.

Megan Dalla-Camina, Director of Strategy, IBM Australia, Sydney, Australia

Strategy – *Link diversity to KPIs and rewards*

Accountability makes a difference. We now have accountability for managers and that changes the way they operate. I am being watched by my manager and he is being watched by his manager. Those things [measures] mean a lot to people in our business. My compensation is now at risk if I do not achieve the required diversity targets. Our diversity numbers in banking in Australia are lower than the rest of the world and they are significantly below the USA numbers so we are focused on addressing this.

Craig Drummond, Chief Executive Officer, Bank of America Merrill Lynch, Sydney, Australia

Strategy – *Get 'top team' to own diversity*

When I came to run BP in Australia I looked at the figures over the previous five years and the numbers were flat-lined. The representation of women as a percentage of our workforce was unchanged. I said to the team 'Whatever we are doing it is not working.' They suggested sending someone out to hire a diversity manager to address the issues. I looked at my team and said 'But what can you do differently to get a different result?' We talked about it, the penny dropped, they stepped up into the space and started to take actions that made a difference.

We focussed on three areas: leadership intensity, flexible working and performance management. We still have a long way to go, but we are making inroads on changing the leadership culture as people understand that to be a top-level leader at BP Australia, they must be able to create and lead a diverse, inclusive team.

Paul Waterman, President, BP Australia, Melbourne, Australia

Strategy – Kindergarten, early child care and parental leave

We know from our research in Norway that paid parental leave for fathers gives them security. By keeping their jobs safe they know they can come back afterwards. The three things that we put in place, which changed the role of men and women for us were: kindergarten; early child care; and parental leave. Without these three things you can't achieve gender balance.

> Arni Hole, Director General, Norwegian Royal Ministry for Children, Equity and Social Inclusion, Oslo, Norway

Strategy – Diversity as a system, not an activity

We treat diversity like safety – it's important and it must take priority. We track things like how many females on the recruiting panels and how many are selected. We examine flexibility and have started to put it in place in various parts of our business (but a paper mill runs on 12 hours shifts so this make it challenging for us).

> Lisa Eccleston, Group General Manager Human Resources, Amcor, Melbourne, Australia

What advice do you have for others?

Advice – It's not about gender, it's about skills

When people say "Men don't want to give up the power", I advise that women should focus on doing a good job and work in a merit-based system. I think the gender discussion was yesterday's discussion. We have women in all roles in the companies I am associated with. The biggest challenge now is getting the skills. I know the mining companies are looking for skills in any gender.

> (Anon) Male CEO and board member, Australia

Advice – The business case

The best way to promote any change is to demonstrate the need by presenting a good argument. The key arguments are: why would you restrict yourself to half the talent pool; why would you not have people who represent your customer base; did you know that women are known to handle machinery with more care and the equipment lasts longer?

> Jane Hemstritch, Non-Executive Director, Commonwealth Bank of Australia, Melbourne, Australia

Advice – Keep in touch with mothers on leave

Organisations that stay in touch with the women who go on maternity leave are the best at getting them back. By including them in events and allowing them to keep their emails open, they managed to keep close contact. Women returning from maternity leave have to be realistic and be prepared to go back in at the appropriate level. If their former staff members have risen above their post, they should be proud of them.

Jane Hemstritch, Non-Executive Director, Commonwealth Bank of Australia, Melbourne, Australia

Advice – Ensure gender-balanced teams

People don't tend to focus on the importance of gender diversity enough. A while back a bid team was put together comprising six men. When we noticed what we had done we changed it and put in three women to work with three men making it 50/50. It is important that we put the right people in the right roles and that people understand that not all talent is in one gender.

Greg Couttas, Partner, Deloitte Touche Tohmatsu, Sydney, Australia

Advice – Stay connected and involved

It is not realistic for women to take two years off to have children and expect to be able to easily pick up where they left off if they don't keep their hand in, in some way. Women should make more effort to stay connected with the organisation while they are away. Better still they should try to work a few days a week and to keep their maternity leave short. The idea that 'you are not a good mother unless you're a stay-at-home full time mother', is incorrect.

Diane Grady AM, Non-Executive Director, Macquarie Group, Sydney, Australia

Advice – Open our minds, and doors, to home help

When I raise the need for child-care assistance with government they don't appreciate the need or importance. The people who drafted the immigration rules were probably men and they are out-dated. There are people who would want to work as helpers in the Region and I have no idea why the government would not open the doors to let them in to provide support to women who want careers. In Asia everybody has that kind of help. In Australia the perception is that it is indulgent to have a helper. One of my junior executives pays $4400 per month in child care after tax so that he and his wife can both pursue careers.

During the years in which my family and I lived in Asia we had helpers and they became part of the family. Their wages went to their families in their home country to educate their children. We have definitely changed the lives of the people in that community. Everyone benefits.

Mike Smith OBE, Chief Executive Officer, Australian and New Zealand Banking Group, Melbourne, Australia

Three stories: discrimination, sexual advances and bullying

During the interviews I heard many stories of poor behaviour affecting women and I asked three women to tell their stories. The first is Jane Owen, a senior partner at Middleton's law firm who shares one of her experiences as a young lawyer and highlights the need for her profession to keep looking for barriers, and rejecting discrimination, that limit the careers of female lawyers and staff.

The other two are women in their mid-30s whose stories I am sharing anonymously to avoid them facing repercussions for having spoken out. They are mid-career and it could impact on their continued climb if they say who they are. In these stories they are fictitiously called Georgia and Rachel. Both these outstanding young women have endured many years of unacceptable behaviour and it shocked me to think that this still goes on in the 21st century.

'How Little Times Have Changed' – by Jane Owen, Partner, Middletons

I started in my profession in 1990 and was overwhelmed by the impression that you need to be seen to be working very long hours. You needed to be there at 9 pm because merit was linked to time in the office.

But that wasn't the worst of the behaviours I noticed as a young lawyer. The other disturbing pattern was the predatory approach of senior men towards women professionals. For example, two years and nine months into my career I was leaving my firm to study a master's degree at the University of London. One of the partners I had worked for took me to lunch on my last day. I was 26 and he was mid 40s and married with a large number of children [more than five]. He looked across the table at me and said "Jane, your leaving the firm has ruined my aspirations of taking you away and shagging all weekend".

What? I didn't get it. What makes a middle-aged man old enough to be your dad, think that an attractive, 26-year-old, single woman would be receptive to such an unexpected and unwelcome advance? After quickly changing the subject I had to suffer through the remainder of the lunch. It was painful.

In 1996, at the age of 29, I became a partner and as you are less likely to be a victim of predatory behaviour by partners when you are one yourself, I did not fall prey to the same behaviour. However, many other women still had to learn avoidance and coping strategies. Sadly it creates a situation where young women need to avoid being alone with senior male colleagues or partners after hours. You also avoid drinking too much and you learn to be cautious at social events. As a junior lawyer you were fair game and this limits your chance of a fair career progression. You can't stop people falling in love if they meet at work, but extramarital relationships and predatory behaviour do still exist and need to be addressed.

It is a 'lose–lose' situation for a young female lawyer to be put in this situation. Whether you engage or don't engage with the person making the advances there is always an unhappy outcome. If you accept his advances, then when the relationship is at an end it leaves you in a compromised situation. If you reject his advances, then you are the subject of unconscious bias going forward. There should be serious consequences for any partners guilty of chastisement.

In my role now as a senior woman partner I take any issues of inappropriate behaviour to the board. I am pleased to say it has become less common and boards act on any notice of indiscretions in the proper manner. However, the fact that it does still exist from time to time means that we have more work to do as a profession.

There is another form of discriminatory behaviour that I have witnessed a number of times throughout my career and that is covert undermining of women to keep them out of the partnership.

In one of the firms that I joined mid-career, I started as a non-equity partner. It was explained that in a short time, given satisfactory performance, I would be offered an equity partnership. When it came to the meeting I was told 'they didn't feel comfortable with me'. I pressed them for a more detailed explanation but it was not forthcoming.

I was perplexed. The decision was clearly not based on merit as I had met all the fee targets and client development expectations required of me in the period concerned. As I looked at the group of men who were responsible for the decision I realised that as I was the only female partner in the entire group, they were simply uncomfortable with people who didn't look like them.

We need to keep talking to men and women in our profession to challenge the paradigms that make it so difficult for women to succeed in this industry.

Jane Owen, Partner, Middletons, Sydney, Australia

'Opting-Out' – by Georgia (a fictitious name), 35-year old, highly talented and successful, investment banker

I grew up in regional Australia on a farm. When I was 13, my parents moved from primary production into grain marketing. I used to help in the office and sometimes when traders called I was the only one there to answer the phone. While they detected I was young, they assumed I was a university student. I just played along. As a consequence, I developed at this early age a little knowledge and skill in business and client relations.

Underpaid and overworked

After finishing school I decided to take a gap year and I landed my first job as the junior in a funds management marketing team and was paid $18,500 pa.

I explained to them that I was only going to stay one year because I was then going to university. They convinced me to stay on and offered to pay my university fees, so I studied part-time and stayed in the firm for four years. While I was extremely grateful to have my studies paid for, I felt I wasn't getting remunerated fairly, based on discussions with male colleagues and mentors in the firm. One of them was paid a salary that was four times greater than mine: he was the same age and didn't have a degree yet either. This was my first experience of how males were treated differently from females.

After completing my degree I joined a global accounting firm as a graduate in the transaction services division. I wanted to get into a graduate program with a 'same age' peer group to get better training. Everything went well until I took a transfer to another division in the firm and was so devastated by the experience that I left the firm and never looked back.

Sexism at its worst

The transfer looked good on paper but it was the worst career move I ever made. The men in the team talked about 'tits' and 'arse' all day long and they were so disrespectful towards women that I immediately knew I had made a wrong decision.

There were two women in this team of 10 and the other women seemed to accept the behaviour. There was blatant perving and I was hardly ever included in the deal discussions and they clearly didn't value me as a team member. I didn't know why they hired me and I was in complete isolation, very unhappy and my learning hit a wall.

But it got worse. These men went drinking at lunchtime regularly and openly discussed visits to lap-dancing bars after leaving me in the office taking phone messages for them while they were out. This was 2005 not 1975! I left the firm six months later. I had serious thoughts about leaving professional services but was headhunted by two investment banks subsequently and I expected things to be far more professional. Fortunately each move was good for my career but as I climbed the ladder the number of female peers and role models decreased dramatically, which became a concern.

Predatory men

In all six firms that I worked for in my banking career, men 'hit on' me. The approaches always came from senior, married men who did not expect that I would be surprised about, or would rebuff, their sexual advances. On one occasion I was overtly asked to become a mistress over lunch and I had thought I was there to have a discussion about him becoming my mentor!

In the first two cases, there was an overtly sexual company culture, but later I recognised that there was a pattern across the whole sector, at least in Australia. Male bosses however, were attracted to their young, intelligent and capable female employees and they behaved as if it was their right to seek extra-curricular relations. I have mentored quite a number of young women in financial services and more than half have admitted to sleeping with their boss or another MD-level man. Most regret it completely.

Why does this happen? I believe the leadership group is either involved in, or turning a blind eye to, this behaviour and young female employees know that it is 'taboo' to speak out about it, as it is most definitely a career-stopper.

Toxic culture

I started to feel sick about being part of the firm's graduate recruiting team: I could not look these young women in the eye at the interviews and tell them that they were going to have a glittering career. What I wanted to say, honestly, was:

'To work in the finance sector you needed to spend time in a bar, be prepared to fraternise with members of the team and never complain about anything. It was no good if you didn't drink. It was no good if you were pregnant or might be soon. It was no good if you were Muslim. And it was no good if you were too 'opinionated' or 'aggressive' of course. You either had to accept it and play-the-game or stay under the radar, which of course is the worst thing you can do from a rapport-building and promotion perspective.'

Once I hit 30, I figured out how to be a woman in business and how successful my feminine approach and attributes could be as a leader, an adviser and at the negotiation table. Can I distil it into a checklist now? Probably not, but I can say that taking time to 'feel my way' through situations rather than being left-brain about everything has really worked for me!

No change

While I had always focussed on mentoring younger women and leading diversity discussions and so on, it was still an uphill battle to get more women into the game and to help them build careers that recognised the effort they put it. In the 15 years I had been in the finance sector I felt nothing had improved for women. No one was listening.

The current generation of young men is different, but that can quickly change. They come out of university with open minds and behave equitably towards their female peers, but once they join the finance sector they start to model the behaviour of the men who they are supposed to follow. Within 12 months they have observed and adopted the behaviours they see above and have formed the necessary power relationships to get their first promotional opportunity or bonus. It is a sad situation.

Opting-out to get a life

I had a very successful career in finance, earned big money, developed an amazing network and have the luxury of many choices in my life. However, the stellar career came at a large personal cost.

A few years ago I chose to leave the industry and resurrect my life. I wanted a more fulfilling and balanced existence in roles where I would not have to behave like a man to receive respect, recognition and reward. So I did what thousands of Australian women do, I opted-out of employment in banking and started my own business. I now consult to owners of small businesses to help them redirect their efforts towards having a whole life, not just a successful business.

I'm now happy, loved, healthy, still financially viable and I look five years younger than five years ago! When I reflect now on my career in the finance sector and life in general, I think what a huge challenge Australia has ahead.

Women are just not perceived as being as important as men in Australian culture. We all know we're not supposed to say that, but it's true. Catch-up is a hard game to play, especially without a cheer squad.

Georgia (Anon), Executive, Investment Adviser, Sydney, Australia

'Bully Bosses and More' - Rachel (a fictitious name) is a highly skilled, 35-year-old multi-lingual, lawyer

I studied law between 1998 and 2001 and achieved top grades and I worked part-time in a small law practice while I studied. Upon completion I took up a clerkship in one of the top city law firms of Australia. In no time at all it became very stressful. In my first few weeks I was asked to draft documents without proper briefing or guidelines and they were returned to me with a lot of red-penned marks, crossings and notations. There was no debrief given or development discussion about what they wanted me to do differently.

Whilst in this firm I had two women bosses and one male boss. The male boss was polite and respectful and I really enjoyed working with him. The two female associates were nightmares. One of them got to where she was by doing it tough and she wanted everyone else to experience the same.

I asked to be moved to a different department and my first boss on rotation there was a woman and she took delight in stripping people down. The second boss on rotation was a man and he cornered me in the lift one day and asked me if I'd be interested in having an affair with him. He was married with children and his affairs were well known in the firm. It seems he had become so comfortable with his affairs being public knowledge that he felt he had licence to approach anyone. Not only was I insulted but I realised my career there was over and began to look for another job.

When I got to my new firm in 2005 I decided that culturally the legal profession was not for me and I started to think about moving out of the industry. In the meantime, I was promoted to senior associate and I knew the next step was going to be an offer of partnership. But upon reflection I decided I didn't want that – I had no role models, I didn't enjoy the culture, I was expected to work ridiculous hours which limited my chances of succeeding at a relationship and the ethics and values did not fit with mine. So I moved on.

I switched to working in a management consulting firm where I have been for one year. I took a massive pay cut to start a new career in a less competitive sector that is not so male-dominated and it has been worth it. The culture at my new firm is people oriented, the work is extremely interesting, the leaders and managers are respectful and the career prospects much more promising.

Rachel (Anon), former lawyer in banking and legal industries, Sydney, Australia

Need for men to respect women

Too many women I talk with have memories of sexual discrimination or some kind of bias levelled at them because of their gender. I really did think that lunchtime visits to laptop bars and being propositioned at work by senior males looking for a fling went out 20 years ago.

I am either naïve or have just been too busy to notice that it is still going on. I was alarmed and disappointed to hear Georgia's and Rachel's stories. That middle-aged married men with children are still propositioning junior professionals while senior management continues to turn a blind eye to it, is just appalling. I know I shouldn't have been so stunned at this news as there have been a number of harassment cases in the courts in recent years. But to hear the detailed personal accounts from these two young, intelligent and very capable women, whose careers and lives have been interrupted and stalled because of predatory behaviour, macho cultures, bullying bosses, discrimination and bias, was really disheartening.

Both these women are outstanding and talented and after working hard to get their degrees and contributing more than a decade climbing the ladder it is shameful that they both feel their dreams of being at the top of their profession are just an illusion and that the personal cost of continuing in those careers are just way too high.

The biggest disappointment is our apathy. Leaders, managers, employees and board members of these organisations, must know the behaviour exists and their lack of attention endorses it. We need more CEOs to set a good example and to take tough action against those who are unable to act respectfully to women.

Key messages about gender diversity from 100 leaders

Regarding women on boards:
- Progress has been too slow getting women onto boards and people are tired of hearing the excuses;
- Women who get onto boards need to be more courageous and influence change;
- The performance of all-male boards must be limited by the lack of skills that women and people from different backgrounds bring;
- Most women who are on boards are lawyers and accountants and this narrow search criteria continues to exclude women from other careers;
- We need to hear less 'talk-the-talk' and see more 'walk-the-walk';
- Boards look nothing like the world we operate in and Chairs should have to explain this to shareholders.

Regarding having quotas for women on boards:
- People are divided on the issue of quotas however there seems to be a rising acceptance that this is a likely outcome due to the incredibly slow pace of change and those who are in favour feel strongly that it needs to happen now;
- Norway heard the same 'excuses' as offered by people in Australia about the danger of quotas; their experience is that decision makers did not vote people onto boards who are not ready;
- One view is that quotas are corrosive and they put the burden of fixing the problem on women;
- Several people believe you need quotas to force change to move the needle.

Regarding the level of support that senior women give to other women:
- Too few senior women champion other women and they may not realise there is a need for it; some just don't know others need a hand to break through the barriers;
- Some Queen Bees exist and they don't like to share their space at the top; they pull up the ladder when they get to the top to keep other females out; fewer females means you are the star and there is less competition;

- Extremely successful business women can be tough on other women; some women find them scary as they can be unfriendly to other females; and they can be slow to offer help to other females if they didn't get any help themselves;
- Some think it's worse in Australia than other countries.

Regarding gender roles, mentoring and education:
- There is a view that boys and girls who go to single-sex schools might not relate so well to the opposite sex in the future and perhaps this is contributing to the challenges we see in the workplace;
- Mentoring and reverse-mentoring is considered helpful; men and women who are concerned about gender equality/women should be mentors;
- There are unintended consequences of these changes on men and we need to talk more about changes to men's roles too and how we can support these changes;
- We need to promote non-traditional careers and educational opportunities for girls and women across Australia;
- Advertisers need to gender-balance their ads; politicians and legislators need to change their language and recognise two-thirds of women do paid work; media need to seek comment from both genders equally.

Regarding gender bias
- It can be incredibly obvious or subtle: women can be highly skilled for a job but then they are told they 'don't fit the culture';
- Women are expected to be tough to get top jobs, but then are criticised for their behaviour;
- Boys schools get more generously funding by parents; the message to girls is they are less valued;
- Getting promoted to executive jobs requires women to score highly on leadership criteria based on male behaviours as the existing dominant group;
- Too few businesswomen are profiled in business pages, males still dominate the newspapers – even on topics that are exclusively women's issues!
- People still think that if you have children your work performance will be compromised;
- Some males are being told by recruiters that their clients are looking for females for roles, excluding men from the shortlist.

The issues to address are:
- unacceptably slow pace;
- child care during school holidays;
- getting beyond the basics to change culture;
- motherhood being a sacred cow;
- recruiters' bias towards men;
- female role models in top positions are often childless;
- keeping women in non-traditional sectors;
- complacency and comfort;
- mentoring women is thought to be an exercise in comforting men;
- lack of flexibility in most workplaces;
- biasing effect in tertiary education;
- women's careers less important;
- how to encourage females to stay longer;
- need for lower cost nanny labour force to boost productivity.

The opportunities to consider are:
- female managers perform very well in service industries, which are growing;
- highlight female role models that are now in international careers;
- highlight the females who are excelling in non-traditional sectors;
- hiring managers are now asking recruiters to check for bias;
- allowing low-cost Asian nannies temporary work visas;
- Gen Y daughters are now educating their Gen X and baby-boomer dads.

The strategies others have employed are:
- Males mentoring women;
- Inter-country exchanging of different gender/culture employees;
- Educate and demonstrate diversity values;
- Development programs to support the rise of females;
- Flexibility for males and females;
- Link diversity to KPIs and rewards;
- Getting the top team to own diversity;
- Kindergarten, early child care and parental leave;
- Women sought to solve skills shortages.
- Demonstrate the need for change by presenting a good argument;
- Keep in touch with mothers on maternity leave;
- Be flexible to attract mothers back;
- Ensure gender-balanced teams;

- Get the CEO to actively and publicly show support;
- Chip away at small steps; Rome wasn't built in a day;
- Include the men; it is a business issue;
- Back yourself;
- Stay connected and involved;
- Accessibility to child-care support enables women to work.

The views shared by the 100 leaders have left us with much to think about. In many cases the arguments are polarised but there is not always a natural gender divide. While people argue for and against quotas there are males and females at both ends of the spectrum. It's clear there are many unresolved issues and even more conversations to be had.

Why so little change?

After all these years why has there been so little change? There are many reasons, but here are some that are highlighted by the findings of this report for you to consider:

- Turning a blind eye: Society continues to accept men behaving badly
- Self-interest: Anxiety over job security and position power
- Fear of failure: Psychological safety is low
- The comfort zone: Early stage culture needs to be evolved
- The band-aid zone: When you are tinkering with only the top of culture

Turning a blind eye

Leaders of Australian businesses who continue to turn a blind eye to lecherous behaviour, harassment and bullying, which create hostile environments for female employees, need to take a long enquiring look in the mirror. Turning a blind eye is not acceptable. Ask yourselves how you'd like people to treat your daughters when they enter the workforce. What action would you take if your daughter was a victim?

If you are not female, Asian, Muslim, a foreign worker, new immigrant or white male who does not value the 'boys club', you possibly don't know what discrimination feels like. However, most of you will have witnessed some of the challenges outlined above. If you know instinctively that the comments made by the 100 leaders and the stories shared by these 3 women are true, but you have not done anything to rid your organisation of such behaviour, then you might be 'turning a blind eye'.

As a leader you have been passed the mantle to lead those behind you to achieve ambitions and goals. You can only do this effectively if you address the gender challenge and the waste that comes with the loss of mid-30s females who opt out of their careers. In the 21st century, it's not sensible to accept that 'women leave mid-career': instead we should be looking for ways to change our organisations to make them equitable and enjoyable places for women to work in a flexible way.

Self-interest and anxiety over job security

The leaders I refer to here as turning a blind eye are not just males. Women leaders are 'staying mum' on the topic too. I asked one of our most senior women leaders to read the three cases presented above and comment on the significance and impact that this reality is having on our ability to achieve gender diversity and she declined. She indicated that it was 'not appropriate given her role' and suggested that it might have a negative impact (presumably on her company, or perhaps on herself).

In my optimism I hoped the opposite were true: one would expect that her employees, clients, stakeholders and communities would be proud of her leadership and direction on this important issue. Instead, she appeared concerned that she might be judged for interfering or that speaking up on such a sensitive matter could in some way impair her reputation of that of her organisation.

I'd have thought that we could expect high-profile and highly-paid women, who have been granted both position and power to lead a nation-wide business, to be a spokesperson on issues relating to workforce participation and productivity. I would also expect them to speak out about people who face discrimination or who feel there are major roadblocks to a meritocratic succession. What do you expect? Do you expect them to lead change and should we be sympathetic to them when they fall shy of the task out of fear of being criticised by male colleagues?

Male leaders have been protecting their positions and watching the backs of their peers since your great-great-grandmother was a baby, so it is unfair of me to single out a female leader. However just as men in our society look out for one another, so should women support other women and use their position power to call for action and lead on it.

Fear of failure: low psychological safety

Over many years I have met a lot of well-intentioned male leaders who are genuine in their attempt to change their work environments to ensure equity and opportunity for all by leading from the top. Many have invested in personal development and coaching and have sought advice to achieve understanding that would help make them better leaders to meet the challenges of their time.

Every time I have been involved in leading change that requires leaders to adopt new behaviours I have noticed that there is one condition that must exist for them to try a new way of doing things. There must be psychological safety. No one wants to set themselves up for failure and most of us like to think that we are pretty good at what we do. So when we are asked to do something new or differently, we are not always eager to try in case we fail. In addition, if we don't know how, we are less likely to give it a go. We are all human and, males and females alike, sometimes we need clear instructions about what needs to be done, why it's a better way and how to do it. In any change situation I always begin by providing knowledge and systems to support the new behaviour sought. First, I explain the change, then demonstrate it and then let them practise. If you ask someone to try a new way of doing things without the knowledge and support, they can feel anxious about entering an unknown situation. However, once they have had a practise, they feel safe that they won't fail. Lack of psychological safety is a key cause of resistance to change.

The comfort zone: culture must evolve

One of the reasons why there has been little change for women in many organisations is that the assumptions and values of its culture have not evolved to a point where gender diversity is appreciated and desired. The changes we need start in country culture, then an individual's culture and then we can expect change in an organisation's culture.

The change can only happen with leaders who are enlightened about the need for diversity, who are open to change and want to lead their people to evolve. When you are in the comfort zone you are harbouring old values and you are reluctant to let them go because they worked so well for you in the past and you are not thinking about new values that might better meet the needs of your people today. Part Three shows how you can evolve all your cultures to help speed up the pace of change to achieve gender balance.

The band-aid zone: tinkering with culture

Some organisation cultures are evolving but many are stuck in the band-aid zone. This is where you are tinkering with HR interventions at the top of the cultures – introducing new artefacts to shift behaviours - and are constantly being surprised as to why your interventions stall when you take your foot off the gas.

Long term sustainable change requires a more concerted effort to remove the old assumptions at the bottom of the culture that hold old unhelpful attitudes and behaviours in place. The reason I call this the band-aid zone is that the solution is rarely permanent: it merely serves to cover up the festering sore below until the band-aid loses its grip and falls off.

Let's rethink gender roles and games

Samantha (a fictitious name but a real person) is an early-40s highly experienced businesswoman, well known to people in corporate Australia and globally for her work. She is an opinion leader on many topics and regularly receives recognition for her many initiatives.

In a recent conversation she told me that she pays $30 per hour for home help but doesn't tell her husband as he would not approve. The helper comes in while they are both at work. Why does she do this? Firstly, because he would not appreciate 'why' she needed help: even though she is a working mother he thinks that she can still manage the housework and home administration in her spare time. Secondly, he would not approve of her spending $30 an hour on something he considers menial and unskilled. Thirdly, she knows it would lead to a disagreement and predicts it would be unlikely to get his understanding on the subject.

She is not alone in this. Women the world over have learned to keep things to themselves for a quiet life. However, it seems from the interview findings that many women in Australia are frustrated and unhappy with the situation: they talk about it and complain about it and sadly many are also exhausted from trying to change it. So they stop trying to change it.

I have heard some amazing stories from husbands who share the load at home with their working wives but we also know that many working women are still doing the majority of the housework and home administration. While there is increasing participation of women at work, there is still a need in many households to increase the role of men at home to ensure work–life balance for each partner.

Why is it that some women prefer to keep quiet? Much of human behaviour is learned: just as some females learn to avoid conflict and others accept the role society has prescribed, a male's beliefs about a woman's role at home or at work are also learned. The conditioning starts the minute we are born and continues daily throughout our lives.

To change behaviours we need to be exposed to new situations, conditions and learning. However, that is proving to be a bigger challenge for corporate Australia than imagined. Why? Because the beliefs and behaviours are embedded in our society and to change behaviours at work we need to change them in society.

How to change the roles you play

One thing that would help males and females wanting to break through the patterns of behaviour described by Samantha's story above would be to read *Games People Play*, a book on human psychology by Eric Byrne. It's an easy read, interesting and very helpful. It was a 1964 best-seller with over five million copies sold and it is still relevant today.

Eric Byrne introduced 'transactional analysis' which is a way of interpreting interactions between people. He describes three roles that people play out in their daily interactions as the Parent, the Adult and the Child. He illustrates how negative behaviours we see in everyday life are explained by switching or confusing these roles.

The boss who talks to staff in the tone of a controlling 'parent' will often engender a 'childlike' reaction that might look like obedience or excuses or even a tantrum. None of these behaviours are helpful in business so the parent-like boss is limiting his or her ability to get the best from his people.

A husband who plays 'parent' with his wife similarly will engender a 'childlike' reaction from her. Husbands who control the household finances and expect their wives to be responsible for all the chores are limiting the opportunity to have an equal, respectful 'adult-to-adult' relationship.

Games People Play by Eric Byrne is still available and will only take a few hours to read and get the idea. Improving interactions you have with people at work, at home and in life in general is worth it. See the link for this book on www.steppingupaustralia.com

Quicken the pace with mixed-gender teams

First, we need to recognise that gender balancing is best served by a mixed-gender effort. Female and male leaders need to show the people of Australia that they respect one another's skills and talents sufficiently to work together on this.

Women don't want men to fix things for them. They don't want them to 'fall on their sword' either. Mutual respect, a transparent agenda and an open dialogue with a gender-balanced task force of equally skilled individuals who share a common vision and goals about the future will bring about the fastest change and the most fruitful results.

A while back I was having a morning coffee with a non-executive director who sits on several ASX100 boards. I asked him "Why are we getting males to mentor women and why are we building all-male task forces to lead the charge on gender diversity?" He replied "Well, if the system that is failing was built by men then it should be fixed by men." When I offered that perhaps a better solution might be to get the best of both genders together he replied "But where would you find as many experienced women as the men who are doing this work? There are just not enough women with CEO or board experience."

I tried to contain my look of disbelief and then enquired "When you got your first CEO role and your first board position, you didn't fail. So why would you expect a female who has also had a successful 25–30 year career comprising say 6, 8 or 10 promotions to fail at the last post?"

The best relationships are those where there is mutual respect, shared power and effective two-way communication. Whether the relationship is a political alliance between two countries or a relationship between two people, the same qualities tend to exist. Australia's future relies on its ability to *bust the bias*.

The elephant in the room

Leaders who continue to say that their culture is supportive of females, their policies and systems are equitable and that equal career opportunities exist for women as for men – while their company's gender statistics are at odds with these claims – might need to confront the elephant in the room. If you can't walk-the-talk then you need to watch what you say.

Are females actually perceived to be 'less important' and are we just very clever at camouflaging it? Are we paying lip-service to the idea that women should have careers and participate in running the country and big business? Are we just letting enough women through so that it will give the impression that females are considered equal while we covertly reinforce barriers to keep their number from swelling too high?

Some leaders interviewed believe that the introduction of quotas is needed to put an end to the talk; to turn women on boards into a reality; and to quash the myths that there are few women suitable for board positions and those women who lack experience might fail at their last promotion.

Until October 2012 we saw little overt leadership on addressing gender equality from our first female Prime Minister, Julia Gillard and while there are a number of senior females on boards and in CEO positions who have been vocal about issues relating to gender equality, the pace of change is just too slow and the impact underwhelming. More courage, leadership and commitment to a 'step' change is required.

The elephant in the room is definitely there and I felt its presence when I started talking with people about the idea of writing this book. I got very clear signals and some overt comments that it is 'not the done thing', that to discuss the rights and roles of women in public was too controversial. A few people at the start of the interviews – both males and females – presented me with immediate arguments about why women 'are okay' as if to shut the conversation down. I got the feeling that some women were trying to justify why they had accepted 'their place' in society. I even had five people tell me that writing this book 'was brave'. Interestingly, these people were all female.

I tentatively pursued discussions and over the year that I conducted the 100 interviews I found that people became less concerned and more willing to speak frankly. I assumed this was because the ASX changes had forced the discussions to occur inside organisations and there was increased frequency of media coverage, public debate and business events with 'gender equality' at the top of their agendas. This illustrates that the more we talk about it, the more familiar we get with the issues, the less scary they become.

Need for cultural change

The behaviours we have read about in Part Two spring from the country and communities in which we were raised, the families we were born to, the schools we attended and the education levels we each have attained. As we take these values into the organisations in which we work, we shape the values there too. As we select employment opportunities we seek out companies that have similar values and behaviours to our own. All of this indicates our desire to live within the cultures we know and which make us feel comfortable.

To change the status of women in the workplace is going to require a shift in the assumptions that people who live in Australia hold about the rights and roles of each gender at work, in society and at home.

Without a shift in assumptions there will be no corresponding shift in behaviours and another decade will go by. If we can shift behaviours in society, these will lead to a shift in behaviours in the workplace. Long-term sustainable gender equality requires a permanent shift in the foundations of our culture from which behaviours flow. Part Three presents a method for bringing about these changes and shares some cases studies of three companies that have done that.

One big question we need to consider along the way is 'Who will we expect (and allow) to step-up to lead this *bias busting* and *force field* removing drive to achieve gender equality?'

Beyond delusions and myths are courage and pride

Australian's have history in acts of bravery and pioneering and they know what it takes to step-up and lead the charge. They have proven they have mettle in war, tenacity as Olympic champions, boldness as politicians, nerves of steel when faced with bushfires, cyclones and floods… and yet when it comes to facing the challenges of balancing the roles and livelihood of gender in society, the brave become silenced and the daring lose their way.

Why is gender equality not a priority? How can we believe that our economic success to date comes from sufficiently rigorous foundations that we are guaranteed sustained performance in the face of skills shortages and productivity challenges, not to mention the underlying frustration and tension between those who believe women need to be given a 'fair go' and those who do not?

We need to find more male and female leaders with the courage to speak out and demand change in people around them who are resisting or blocking gender equality. At the same time we need those in control of the *force field* to let go and allow skilled women to rise to the top on merit.

We are capable of forming a vision for an Australia in 2025 that has adjusted to allow highly capable women to share in the running of the country and companies and in doing so, we can set a path towards being a progressive and nimble nation that commands the attention of those around us.

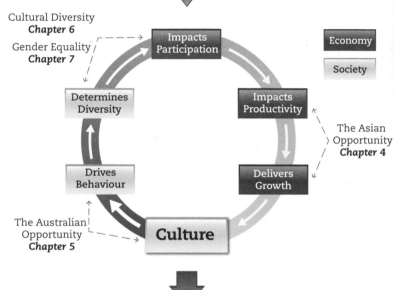

PART 1

WHAT
The power
of diversity

Taking the Mantle
Chapter 1

Listening
Chapter 2

Discovering Diversity
Chapter 3

PART 2

WHY
The issues
impacting
growth

Cultural Diversity
Chapter 6

Gender Equality
Chapter 7

Impacts
Participation

Economy

Society

Determines
Diversity

Impacts
Productivity

The Asian
Opportunity
Chapter 4

Drives
Behaviour

Delivers
Growth

The Australian
Opportunity
Chapter 5

Culture

PART 3

HOW
Changing
cultures

How
Cultures
Operate
Chapter 8

Redirecting
Country
Culture
Chapter 9

Country
Culture

Organisation
Culture

PART 4

WHO
Leaders
and
society

Redirecting a
Leader's Cultur
Chapter 10

Individual
Culture

Redirecting an
Organisation's
Culture
Chapter 11

Stepping Up
Chapter 12

Part Three

Changing Cultures

Some of the amazing qualities of Australia that made it successful over the past 200 years are now creating challenges for the country and its people. Part Three outlines how cultures operate and how to change them.

It explores country cultures, individual cultures and organisation cultures and how evolving our thinking can support businesses and society to make greater diversity a reality. Chapters 8–11 are brimming with helpful concepts, models, tips, examples and new language that will help you to adjust any of the cultures you belong to that are holding you, or your business or local community, back. Chapter 10 includes three personal stories which illustrate how the roles of men have changed and Chapter 11 has three company case studies detailing their culture change and diversity successes.

Chapter 8

How Cultures Operate

What a man believes may be ascertained,
not from his creed, but from the assumptions on
which he habitually acts.

George Bernard Shaw, (1856-1950) Irish playwright and
co-founder of the London School of Economics

It's remarkable that 100 years before corporate culture was observed and defined an Irish playwright, George Bernard Shaw, identified the foundation of our beliefs and behaviours as assumptions. In this chapter we get to the bottom of the 'Culture Iceberg' to understand how cultures operate; a precursor to being able to change our attitudes and behaviours.

In 1990 Edgar Schein, an American Psychologist at the Sloan School of Management in Massachusetts, wrote a paper called *Organisational Culture*, which set out to define and analyse 'culture' as it is used in the field of organisation psychology. He wrote 'The concept of organisational culture has received attention in recent years both from academics and practitioners' and this reminds us just how new the study of organisational culture is.

Since the 18th century the word culture has been used to describe the process of cultivation or improvement of agriculture and horticulture. During the 20th century culture was used to describe the betterment of individuals and the refinement of national aspirations or ideals. It has only been in the past 20 years or so that we have applied the word 'culture' to describe the elements that give rise to organisation behaviours. Now 'changing culture' is slowly becoming recognised as a viable and credible component of strategies for improving business performance and stimulating growth.

When I completed my thesis in 1988 on *How Cultures and Values Impact the Bottom Line* I was, like Schein, searching for answers about the connection between human behaviours and business performance. In the intervening years, much has been learned. *Stepping Up's* secondary title indicates that you will discover how to '*Lead culture change for diversity and growth in the Asian Century*' and that's what Parts Three and Four are designed to do.

Throughout Part Three you will hear the words 'cultures, assumptions, values and behaviours' a lot. These words have been devalued in the past 20 years as organisational culture was initially thought to be the domain of the human resources department and has frequently been referred to as 'the soft stuff'. The words culture and values have been mistakenly thought to relate solely to human behaviour and whether or not people are happy and working productively together. Big mistake!

The culture of your country, organisation or community club can make or break your ability to realise profit. Culture influences every business decision you make: it influences which companies you acquire, which technology you use, which markets you operate in and which investors you attract.

As a 21st century leader, who hopes to be successful in this fast-paced Asian Century, you need to take culture seriously, recognise it as critical component of your growth and performance and get comfortable with leading culture change.

In this chapter we will look at:

- Defining culture: How assumptions dominate
- The elusiveness of culture: Why is it so difficult to grasp
- A leader's challenge: Conquering the 'hard stuff'
- The Culture Iceberg: How cultures operate
- Culture blind spots: The traps of changing culture
- The Culture Circuit: How different cultures impact you and vice versa
- Culture zones: Identifying how far your culture has evolved
- Behaviours are learned: How to unlearn them
- Sustaining change: Making diversity stick

As you can see, this chapter is about culture change, which we need if we are to boost diversity in Australia and in its businesses and society. I am going to break away from the diversity discussion for a moment (for this chapter) to introduce you to my favourite tools, which you can use to lead culture change. We need to gain a good appreciation of how cultures operate, before we can start to think about the best way to change them to achieve diversity.

The concepts, models and elements of a culture described here will help you to appreciate and analyse any cultures you belong to that you think need evolving and redirection. If you are familiar with how cultures operate you can skip this chapter and go straight to Chapter 9 – Country Culture, Chapter 10 – Individual Culture or Chapter 11 – Organisation Culture, whichever interest you most.

Alternatively, if you are familiar with how cultures operate, but would like to refresh your thinking as you consider the challenges you face, then perhaps a quick read of this chapter might be a good idea.

You cannot survive as a leader or be an effective leader in the 21st century, the Asian Century, if you don't know how to stimulate and manage the evolution of a culture or feel comfortable with continuous change. The pace of social, economic, technological and environmental change is so rapid that you need to be able to reinvent yourself, your organisation and your products and services constantly. This reinvention is not just about R&D, innovation, market segmentation, differentiation and positioning: every renewal requires a shift and realignment of the culture that drives the attitudes, behaviour and performance of your people.

The use of language is an important part of getting traction in a change program and you will find, throughout this chapter, lots of new language that you can use to help explain how cultures operate. Language helps to give meaning to concepts that are elusive and it can be used to bond people from different subcultures.

> *We never look beyond our assumptions and what's worse, we have given up trying to meet others; we just meet ourselves."*
>
> Muriel Barbery – born (Morocco) 1969, French novelist and professor of philosophy

Culture Iceberg

Defining culture

It generally helps to start a conversation about culture by defining it. We know that culture relates to the way people act, which indicates what is important to them. However, here are a few of other interesting features of culture that we need to understand in order to know how to change it:

- Organisational culture is the term used to describe the pattern of *shared mental assumptions* about how a group solves its problems.
- These assumptions are *learned by the group members* as they adapt to what is going on externally and as they seek to integrate internally.
- They are the *'taken-for-granted'* things that are accepted by the group as being true without needing proof. They are so accepted that they become *unconscious, unchallenged and unseen.*
- These assumptions are known to work well so the group comes to *rely on them* – they are conditions that will always exist and are extremely hard to change.
- Assumptions are taught to new members of the culture as *the correct way to be* (to perceive, think and feel about things going on in relation to the problems).
- Assumptions are the *sole driver behind the values, beliefs, attitudes and behaviours that* emerge as a consequence of those assumptions and become known collectively as culture.

What is an assumption?

The most important word in this definition is, of course, *assumptions*. They govern and influence the development of every other aspect of a group's functioning. They are unconscious and they guide human expression. When we talk about assumptions, we generally talk about 'the way things are done around here'. That is, how managers make purchase decisions in one business might be very different from how they make them in another business, and the reason for the difference is usually something to do with the underlying assumptions that have been shaped over many years.

For example, as an IT director in a professional firm partnership, you probably have to pass your recommendations for a computer upgrade to the Managing Partner to take to the next partners' meeting for discussion and approval. Because that's where capital expenditure decisions are made. Yet in a national transportation business, the cap-ex budget decisions might devolve to the CFO or even to you as the IT Director, and 'the way you do things around here' could be very different.

These differences are a function of the assumptions of founders, current leaders, the industry norms and the economic times. If you are the IT manager at the transportation company and you move to an accounting firm, you'll notice a very different 'way' of doing things which immediately signals the assumption, values and behaviours of the firm's culture. If you like the new 'way', all well and good. If you don't, then you'll experience discomfort and perhaps even culture shock.

People naturally form communities or groups to enable action through which they seek development, expression and recognition. They use these groups to fulfil their needs and desires. In forming the groups, a hierarchy develops. Most often groups are formed with intention and purpose, like a real-estate company, a tennis club or a radio station. Sometimes they form organically as a consequence of proximity, as in reality TV shows like 'Big Brother', or when volunteers find themselves thrust together unexpectedly after a natural disaster and have to quickly sort out who will lead and who will follow. In these cases the group struggles to form boundaries around behaviours, to sort out leaders from followers, to agree what is valued and what is not.

Assumptions form problem-solving patterns

No matter how a group comes together, within a short time a culture begins to form and mental patterns (of problem-solving and decision-making) are established. The group members come to rely on these patterns as a way of sorting things out; the patterns guide the way they think, feel and act. These patterns become the culture. New members observe it and adopt it.

Let's consider for a moment how the founders of a community or group that was consciously formed, went about establishing their culture. Think of Australia in the late 1700s when the First Fleet arrived to set up camp. What early messages did they communicate about how the group would function?

Think of Steve Jobs, Stephen Wozniak and friends who created Apple computer in Job's parents' garage in California in the mid-1970s. What early ideals did they have about establishing a creative and free-spirited culture to foster innovation? Innovation is certainly highly valued at Apple – more so than most companies I can think of.

What about BHP and Billiton when they were established in Broken Hill in 1855 and on Billiton Island, Indonesia in 1860: what unconscious assumptions influenced their early decisions about the values that would drive their businesses? The assumptions of both businesses must have been similar to make it possible to merge the cultures of these two huge organisations 140 or so years later.

Assumptions lie beneath and influence the formation of the values and beliefs that the group holds, and the attitudes and behaviours that arise as an expression of those values and beliefs. Each group's assumptions are based on the cultures of its founder, industry, purpose and environment.

Assumptions underpin the culture hierarchy but the power brokers who created them need to be open to allowing them to evolve with time. The first step is identifying what the assumptions are. This can be a challenge as they are unconscious and hidden in most cultures.

Good and bad organisation cultures

Good cultures feel energising and productive to be in. The people are happy, positive, future-thinking, co-operative and all pulling in the same direction. Good cultures are usually more adaptable and gently respond to evolutionary shifts without experiencing too much resistance. The assumptions of good cultures are aligned to the stated direction of the business and everyone knows how they are expected to behave to get to the desired outcomes.

Bad cultures are the opposite of all that. They drain you of energy as you are fighting off internal competition, dealing with unhealthy politics and silos, squabbling for resources, stomping up and down to get attention for your division from corporate leaders and you generally feel that few people are pulling in the same direction. The assumptions of bad cultures usually favour and serve a select group and are not well aligned to the strategic direction of the business.

Back in the 1980s, many leaders used to think that creating internal competition was an effective way of getting the best performance from their people. But over the past two decades there has been a switch to a more highly collaborative environment, consultative management styles and employee involvement in decision-making, recognising that this fosters greater trust and loyalty and thereby greater motivation and performance.

Here are a couple of thoughts about culture from our 100 Leaders:

Exposure to different cultures creates a more rounded and different you.
Russell Tipper, Chief Executive Officer, Brockman Resources, Perth, Australia

One way to merge people from different [country] cultures is to have people [some of them] in the government and parliament so they feel represented.
Philip Iskandar, Engineer, Arup Group, Singapore

We have had [gender] discrimination for over 200 years in Australia so a little bias the other way is okay.
Dr Robert Care AM, Chair UK, Middle East and Africa Region, Arup Group, London, United Kingdom

Some people think that because they went to Bali for a holiday they have developed an appreciation of Asian cultures.
Marie Malaxos, GM Production and Development, Buru Energy, Perth, Australia

Mateship almost got constitutionalised. It is a vehicle for the exclusion of women by men. Men are keen to promote mateship as a positive element of the Australian culture, but it's the boys club culture in another form and it goes back to power for men.
Neil Cockroft, Head of Diversity, King & Wood Mallesons, Sydney, Australia

Let's not dwell a moment longer. Let's move on to understand how cultures operate so that we can work at solving some of our cultural challenges and get diversity happening.

> *While you judge me by my outward appearance, I am silently doing the same to you, even though there's a ninety per cent chance that in both cases our assumptions are wrong."*

Richelle E. Goodrich – born 1968, American children's author

Elusive culture

Have you ever had the feeling that there is something eluding you when you are trying to fathom your company or country culture? Just when you think you have it all worked out, something happens and people's reaction surprises you. It's a slippery thing, culture, it's never constant. But that's what makes it so interesting: it really keeps you on your toes.

Some of the reasons why culture is elusive are:

- much of it is invisible and it evolves around us without us noticing;
- it's changing constantly so we are never too sure what we are dealing with;
- it is a concept so it cannot be held, boxed or quantified;
- it is arguable: you can debate values, attitude and behaviour endlessly;
- it is highly deceptive and it can, on its own, manipulate behaviours of people within its group membership without anyone's conscious involvement;
- people who are aware of its existence, power and sources, can use it to manipulate others for their own desired outcomes.

Culture is about people. It is about the way they interact and behave and it is formed, largely, by the people who hold power (official and unofficial). It's formed to create order for the people in that culture and to influence what they think and how they behave.

It is also about strategy structure and systems; these *artefacts* must be aligned with your business ambitions to make the culture work for you. Variance across your business – vertically or horizontally – can create subcultures, which always have the potential to increase your culture's elusiveness by multiplying the challenges you face.

Elusive as they may be, behaviours in your culture can be anticipated and predicted if you can identify the hidden assumptions that lie at the bottom and align them to match your ambitions. If you can eliminate unhelpful assumptions and replace them with assumptions that will produce the behaviour you seek, you can influence and direct your evolving culture as it drifts along.

Changing culture is the 'hard stuff'

The prevailing message from the 100 leaders, as presented in Part Two, is that Australia can do better and Australians deserve better. They did not conceal the cultural limitations of the society in which we live. They shared their concerns honestly and expressed their frustrations, putting forward suggestions and opportunities for change.

The secondary message is a call for help: the 100 leaders want more people – and especially those in government – to cooperate, agree on the future and remove the obstacles to Australia's growth. Many leaders have been trying to build greater diversity for many years but find that hidden forces working against them quietly and unwittingly erode their efforts.

100 leaders highlight the issues

The 100 leaders said the resistance to change that they see in the attitudes and behaviours of people is widespread across people in Australian society, government and business. They gave examples of the kinds of restricting attitudes and behaviours they observe around them including: the roles and abilities of females at work; the roles of men at home; the rights of immigrants to get appropriate jobs; the need for language learning to equip our future workforce; the integration of cultures within our communities so that they may also be better integrated at work; and the hurdles for women to get on boards and into senior management.

The beliefs, attitudes and behaviours that limit progress on these very important unresolved issues are embedded in the Australian culture and they are controlled by the assumptions that lie at the foundations of culture. These aspects of Australian culture in turn affect the culture of Australian businesses.

To build a diverse and productive workforce that can operate effectively within Australia and with our nearest and fastest-growing Asian trade partners, our 100 leaders say that Australia needs to evolve its culture. To do this we need a better understanding of the assumptions that give rise to the values people hold and the attitudes and behaviours they exhibit.

Leaders everywhere can help

If you are a leader in any of the cultures you belong to (business, local community, school, synagogue or sports club) you can help influence these changes by initiating conversations that raise awareness. It is in your interest to help align values and behaviours with the outcomes you seek. Because cultures affect each other (as people move between them) a shift in attitudes in any one of your cultures can influence a shift in another: so your opportunity to participate in the change our 100 leaders are asking for is now.

If you are an employer you have the biggest opportunity of all. About 11.5 million Australians are employed in paid work. Everyone you employ has the ability to influence your culture positively and negatively. If some of the people you employ hold the restricting attitudes we have heard about and bring them to work each day, they can influence the same thinking in others. The more people you employ who hold values that are not helpful to your organisation's goals the harder it is to keep your organisation culture on track.

And then there are those who don't work – the other 11.5 million people. They consist mainly of family elders, non-working parents and children. Society has a role in influencing elders and parents whose stories shape, and often control, family cultures. If we could work with leaders in society to help adjust the attitudes of Australians to support greater diversity this would reduce the amount of culture change business leaders would need to do with employees who bring their attitudes with them.

Sustaining change is hard

Many people call culture the 'soft stuff'. They tend to think that matters relating to 'human behaviour' in organisations are less tangible, rigorous or quantifiable than operations or financial management. They therefore consider it less vital or valuable to the business. But attitudes to this 'soft stuff' are changing. One of the 100 leaders interviewed had learned the truth during his 10-year experience of trying to achieve gender equality. He said:

It is incredibly hard. It is the most difficult challenge I have ever undertaken. No one has the answers and no one can crack the magic code.

People say mentoring is important; then you hear mentoring is a waste of time. You put programs in place to support the development; then you get women who make it incredibly hard for males and they beat them up when they don't like the language they use to explain it.

I have watched other male CEOs put initiatives in place to get gender equality over the past 10 years and when they make a mistake, they get beaten up – then they give up and walk away.

Anonymous CEO

Delivering gender balance can be a more challenging task than improving volumes, margins or market share. It is indeed the *hard stuff*. Listed companies in Australia are now required to report on gender and some are saying that are reluctant to put targets in place as they are unsure how they are going to achieve them. Unlisted companies have choice about whether they build a diverse workforce or not.

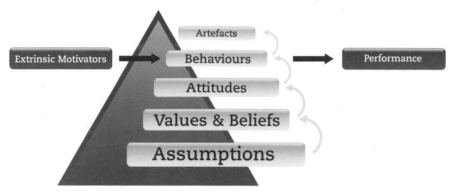

Line managers who still think behavioural issues are the *soft stuff* are being naive. As the CEO implied above, changing culture is the *hardest stuff* of all. Changing behaviours cannot be delegated to the HR division to 'fix' because HR interventions at the top of the culture cannot alone shift assumptions. But CEO's can take tough strategic decisions that are counter to old assumptions, thereby eliminating them and replacing them with new ones.

The only way to change behaviours of a culture to achieve diversity and improve organisational outcomes is for the CEO and other executive leaders to drive it and live the changes themselves. The power brokers have proprietorial responsibility for the assumptions and until they live they change, the *hard stuff* is not done.

The Culture Iceberg

The similarities between organisation culture and an iceberg are numerous, so the iceberg is a great metaphor. Let's take a look at those similarities.

Imagine an iceberg drifting in the ocean. It's an enormous, icy mass that effortlessly and soundlessly fills the horizon leaving you in awe of its unexpected presence. You know it is there, you can see it, but fully appreciating its reality is out of your reach.

So what do icebergs and cultures have in common?

Both have large, awesome structures

Icebergs are enormous structures and they have been around for up to 10,000 years. Most form along the west coast of Greenland where vast glaciers drift slowly toward the sea. Great blocks of ice break away, a process known as calving, and these blocks, or icebergs, drift in the ocean's currents. They provide temporary shelter for living creatures and they carry deep inside their layers the remnants of creatures of days gone by. It seems inconceivable that we might be able to change or direct them: they find their natural resting place and we accept that.

Cultures are remarkably similar. They too are large powerful structures imposing their will on people around them, providing shelter and a place for us to be together. We rarely see them form, yet they appear around us when we are not looking and they command our attention.

Both structures are triangular and unique

When we are asked to draw an iceberg we typically depict it wider at the bottom and coming to a peak at the top. But each is in every way unique. Icebergs form in response to their surroundings leaving us little ability to influence their shape.

Cultures are also unique and form with the greatest mass at the bottom. People see only the part 'above the waterline' and they remain oblivious to the volume, shape or power of what lies below. Like an iceberg, a culture morphs in response to environmental conditions, changing shape as it drifts along and being pushed about by the wind until it arrives in a different place.

Both hide their foundations

Only a tiny portion of an iceberg sits above the water: 90 per cent of its mass is hidden beneath the waterline, which is where the phrase 'tip of the iceberg' comes from. You need to go to some trouble to see what is under the water. The submerged part, which is rock-hard ice, directs where the visible part ends up. The power is in the hidden, unknown region.

The power of culture is also in the hidden region: it lies in the assumptions at the bottom of the organisation iceberg. When you want to effect a positive change to one or more layers of culture, you have to get to the hidden area. This is no small task.

The power of the assumptions is so strong it can work against you and create tension – just as when the wind blows an iceberg in one direction while the current is flowing in another. Because the foundation (the part beneath the waterline) is a bigger mass than that above it, the current wins; this is exactly what happens with your organisation culture or country culture icebergs. The assumptions that lie at the bottom – the large, powerful, unconscious and invisible force – controls the directional flow of all the visible layers of your culture iceberg. So, if you are trying to change the culture of your business, club, town or mosque sometimes you will find that old assumptions at the foundation of your culture are at odds with the new thinking you are trying to introduce.

Assumptions are below the surface: hidden, unseen and unconscious

Both feign stillness and silence

Icebergs are so quiet you can't hear them and they drift so slowly you can't see them moving. It can take 2–3 years for an iceberg calving from a Greenland glacier to drift 3000 nautical kilometres to Newfoundland. The iceberg's direction of drift is irregular, affected by wind and currents, and the journey can take 2–3 times that of the straight path.

Cultures are always drifting too. They drift so slowly that it's difficult to find evidence of their movement and they are so quiet that you can't hear them shifting positions but, over time, they always end up some place else. We must therefore pay attention to where our culture is drifting as we can't guarantee it is going to end up where we want it to be and, due to its sheer size and weight, trying to redirect an organisational culture is a gigantic task.

Both have unexpected, dramatic occurrences

Icebergs change size and shape and occasionally, unexpectedly and dramatically, small pieces shear away changing their structure and impacting the surroundings. Icebergs melt slowly as they travel and they can become unstable and subject to collision, breaking up or rolling without notice.

Cultures melt, roll and break up too. An organisation's internal conflicts, pressures and stresses are representative of a vulnerable culture that is undergoing what is usually an unexpected change. Most managers can remember a time when they have had to deal with a squabble between departments (conflicting subcultures), poor morale and low productivity (unclear assumptions, values or beliefs to work with), disharmony between two merged businesses (lack of post-merger cultural integration and shared assumptions) or increasing staff turnover (lack of inspiring and motivating behaviour by leaders).

Culture Iceberg layers

Layers defined	Examples
Artefacts	
Artefacts are the physical and visible things that the leaders put in place to help the group members know how to behave – how to respond to daily tasks, problems and challenges. Artefacts represent the assumptions, values and attitudes that lie below. Organisation structure charts and position descriptions	Organisation structure charts and position descriptions - Policy statements, employment contracts, reward systems - Language used, names given to products and activities, jargon and tone - Choice of office, factory or shop position, layout, design, branding - Artwork, style and quality of promotional materials, uniforms - Gifts, sponsorships and prizes
Behaviours	
Behaviours describe the way things get done. The learned behaviour or mannerisms of the group members are exhibited as habits, rituals, rites and norms such as:	- The expected codes of behaviour - Common practices that help to regulate daily activities and install order - Ceremonies or repeated acts that become part of daily life - The manner in which seniors and elders are treated - The way members greet each other and respond in a crisis, or not - The way the members show respect, or not - The way the members play together, or not
Attitudes	
Attitudes are the first of the layers that is more visible and more easily understood. They are 'thoughts' that describe a group's viewpoint and the position it takes on matters of relevance and importance. These could be observed as:	- A stance - A posture - A thought or feeling - An outlook - Boldness or reservedness - Compliance or defiance - Arrogance or insolence
Values	
Values are a set of principles or beliefs that set the standards and morals for group members and often include:	- The standard you aspire to reach - The way you want to treat each other - The way you want to be perceived by others - The meaning you give to things of importance - The significance or weight that you put behind something - The things of importance to the group that require attention
Assumptions	
Assumptions lie deep at the bottom of the culture and form the foundation for all other layers. They are unconscious, rarely expressed and are usually taken for granted. They are so deeply entrenched in the organisation's psyche that they are incredibly difficult to identify or change: they first need to be discovered, consciously recognised and understood. They are often described as:	- A mind-set: which dates back to previous founders and leaders - Philosophy: a school of thought that indicates the truth, how things ought to be, which has a causal relationship with the way people act - Organisational script: the unwritten chorus whose music plays in the corridors without acknowledgment but which is absorbed unconsciously by group members who pass through

Glaciers form on land over thousands of years. Each snowfall accumulates on top of the last, the layers of snow are compressed and anything lying on top of one layer – such as a dead animal – is compressed within the layers. The lower layers are more dense and solid than the top and these characteristics hold true for the iceberg when it breaks away from the glacier.

The layers in an organisation Culture Iceberg also form slowly over many years. The lower layers are impacted year on year by the top layers, which by their very existence reinforce and ratify the truth that lies beneath – the truth that is almost unimaginable in terms of its size, power and density. This foundation layer of culture – the assumptions – is an enigma: mysterious and difficult to understand.

The table opposite defines each layer and gives examples of the things you can look for when analysing your cultures.

Getting to the bottom layers is key

People often ask, 'Why is it that some organisations' culture-change programs succeed, when other organisations' programs fail?'

Generally those that succeed shift long-held assumptions hidden below the metaphoric waterline and 'jolt' the belief systems of employees to the point that they recognise things have changed and there is no return. Leaders don't always consciously set out to shift an assumption, sometimes it is their conviction to change the way things get done and courage to see it through that delivers the 'jolt'. These situations are increasing in frequency as frustration pushes CEOs to try more revolutionary measures to get the changes they seek. There are three company case studies in Chapter 11 that illustrate how this can be done.

With 20 years experience in dealing with organisation culture and culture change, people are now realising that resistance to change is less likely to be tolerated and leaders are getting better at identifying it and calling it. Hard work is really needed when the resistors are protected by the old assumptions. Trying to entice resistors into following your lead by adjusting vision, values and artefacts will not by itself produce sustainable culture change. Assumptions control cultures so you have to change your culture from the bottom up, although you can adjust the top layers at the same time to reinforce the changes you seek. Unless you change assumptions, you won't get rid of the resistance permanently.

Language in culture

People in a cultural group create their own language. It is a very important aspect of culture and is part of the glue that makes people feel part of the gang.

It can also be used to exclude members who don't fit or who are not part of the group. Here are some country examples you will be familiar with:

- In Australia people say, "She'll be right, mate!"
- In New Zealand people say, "It'll be ok, eh?"
- In Singapore people say, "You be good, lah!"
- In England people say, "There's nothing to worry about, yeah?"

In organisations we can use language to help us understand the culture. Organisations that highly value their people often use the 'family' metaphor and language. They also talk a lot about flexible time, work–life balance and teams and they organise buddies for new members, social clubs, weekend picnics and offer day-care facilities.

Companies that use the older style military-oriented language such as 'Let's beat the opposition', 'We will fight to take market share' or 'Success through product dominance' usually drive their people hard and often set up internal competition to eliminate relaxed behaviour.

Position titles signal what is valued by different cultures, who is important and where their focus is. Once bank tellers were called 'tellers', today the frontline staff are called Customer Service Managers or Client Services Consultants. Receptionists in hospitals used to be called just that, now they are called Patient Services. Phone operators at universities used to be called operators now they are Student Services. Instead of functional labels people now have titles that indicate they are there to provide service. These changes suggest we value the needs of customers more and believe in their rights to choose alternative providers.

All kinds of labels have changed, not just job titles. Technical Training Programs have become Personal Development Programs. We don't talk of a Pay Slip anymore; it's a Rewards and Benefits Scheme. The HR department is now the People and Culture division. The Sales Team is now the Client Service Team. The Complaints Department is now the Customer Satisfaction Team.

Culture groups also use language to convey their values in other ways too. Schools and sports clubs have anthems to convey their purpose, the army and the police have codes of conduct that convey their regulatory nature, religions and hospitals have principles that convey their care standards, and factories and mine sites have safety standards and dress codes that convey their desire for zero injuries.

Organisations can use language to signal change. New job titles, division names, codes of practice, product and brands, programs and policies and just about anything can be renamed to signal a shift in assumptions or different values and a new way of operating.

Culture blind spots

Over the years I have identified four major 'blinds spots', traps that are hard to see. Generally people don't know they exist or that they are impacting their culture in some way. Because they are 'blind' spots, people don't know to look for them.

The four blind spots are:

- The power of assumptions (internal)
- Changing only the visible layers (internal)
- Recognising and respecting subcultures (internal)
- The impact of other cultures (external)

If you proceed with culture change without recognising your blind spots your interventions will always be at risk of sabotage by these internal and external forces. Identifying and addressing issues related to blind spots is the key to achieving sustainable culture change and sustainable diversity.

1st blind spot: The power of assumptions

When most people talk about culture they usually think about attitudes and behaviour. That's because these are things that everyone can see. Yet assumptions, which are hidden, are absolutely essential to your understanding of culture change. They are the foundations of all the other elements of culture.

Understanding culture helps us to understand what is occurring. When we understand what is occurring, we are in a better position to change things that are not working. If we don't know that assumptions exist, or what they are, and if we don't bother to understand them, then we don't have a chance of changing the other elements *permanently*.

Assumptions are the bedrock of any culture. On the rare occasion that I have seen some awareness of the existence of assumptions there is often a tendency to ignore them. It can be confronting to unearth them and even more challenging to try to change them. They are powerful and hold the status quo. People who gain advantage from the status quo, who have been in the culture the longest, are least likely to support you tampering with them.

In families this is often the grandparents, in communities it might be the older members who sit on the local Council's committees, in companies it could be the people on the board or the founders who are resisting giving way to younger managers, in schools it might be the older longer-term professionals without a leadership portfolio and in sports clubs it is the members who use the social club as a home away from home.

People with tenure in a culture, rely more heavily on the assumptions of that culture to keep things constant. Often when you try to change them you get resistance. Unearthing assumptions takes willpower and changing them takes confidence and courage.

2nd blind spot: Changing only the visible layers

Unfortunately, most efforts to change culture in organisations start with the parts of the culture that you can see; that is the things at the top of the Culture Iceberg such as artefacts and behaviours. Why 'unfortunate'? Because these interventions, alone, will not produce sustainable, permanent change.

People start by changing artefacts and trying to encourage a shift in behaviours; these things are visible, better understood and easiest to get at. Most often the human resource and internal communications teams are charged with responsibility for building programs to make this happen. But such initiatives – leadership development, skills training, mentoring programs – are addressing *symptoms* not *causes* of poor diversity. If you address only the symptoms, the causes (mostly assumptions) will live on and the problems will recur. Unless you identify the assumptions that drive the behaviour, you are putting a Band-Aid on a sore.

'Fixing women' through leadership and mentoring initiatives, or with pay equity and flexible work practices, will not adjust a macho culture. It won't uncover unconscious bias in decision-making (by other leaders) or deep-seated beliefs that male clients prefer to work with hard-working type-A males who are available 24x7 either.

Similarly, providing training programs for Asian graduates to help them improve their communication skills in meetings is not going to shift deep-seated anxieties some managers may hold about the narrow range of skills Asian employees are thought to have.

Many industries in Australia are experiencing skills shortage, and after examining their employee mix they have realised that it is male-heavy and possibly narrow in its blend of cultures. So they start to change HR policies (artefact), ask recruiters to send more women on the shortlist (artefact, behaviours), upgrade the facilities to accommodate both genders and more cultures (artefact), train managers to be more equitable in their supervision and development of all genders and cultures (artefact, behaviours). None of these actions gets to the causes at bottom of the culture that create the environment you need to change.

If organisational leaders want a sustainable change in their culture to attract a broader workforce, they must change assumptions that led them to the situation in the first place. If the assumption is 'No matter what, women don't survive in dirty industries', then you need to prove the assumption wrong. You need to make 'Women are successful executives in dirty industries' a reality.

3rd blind spot: Recognising and respecting subcultures

When two or more icebergs drift into the same path, the inevitable happens. They collide without warning, make a thunderous noise and create turbulence in the ocean around them. So, too, can subcultures collide and cause disruption.

In company situations, subcultures are sometimes highly visible and recognised; other times they are not. Failing to acknowledge their existence or respect their difference is sometimes born out of ignorance (leaders don't notice) and at other times arrogance (leaders don't care). But, whatever the case, they will not go away. Instead, the risk that they will cause disruption or tension between groups, and thereby undermine the achievement of company goals, increases with the degree of variance between them.

When you contrast industries – say, mining, manufacturing, retail and tourism which have different origins, codes of practice, channels, asset requirements and skills used – the underlying assumptions of each industry culture differs hugely and these impact what values and beliefs are adopted and how behavioural norms form. The degree to which these industries are able to attract and retain women or Asians and nurture them to senior management will depend on whether they feel they are valued, treated equally and given opportunity to rise to the top on merit.

Recognising and respecting the unique qualities of another group's culture is the secret to avoiding unhappiness and pain. I have observed in post-merger integration that most pain comes from unexpected challenges arising from the differences between cultures. For those companies merging or taking over another that operates across many global markets, there is the added complication of dealing with multiple country cultures at the same time.

Not all subculture clashes originate from a merger. There are frequently differences in assumptions, values, attitudes and behaviours between functional departments and operational units or between branches in different cities or states. The key to effectively working together requires that both parties work to understand the assumptions of the other and in doing so they will begin to appreciate what is important to one another.

Almost every organisation I have worked with has had a subcultural challenge that undermined the implementation of a strategic initiative. Some of the biggest challenges have been observed when one company acquires another: for examples: an accounting firm buying a niche consultancy; a recruiter buying an IT outsourcing company; a general insurer buying a life company; a bank buying an independent financial advisory business; a newspaper company buying a magazine business; and an engineering firm buying an environmental consultancy. When you have disparate companies in your group, be aware of the challenges that the sub cultures can create, overtly and covertly.

4th blind spot: The impact of other cultures

Cultures do not stand alone, they impact one another as people move between them. Surrounding cultures are brought into your organisation every day as employees walk in the door carrying the assumptions and values they have acquired from other cultures – their family, sports clubs, community groups or place of worship. Some of these other cultures will have values that fit with your organisation culture but others may not, causing the individual some challenges as they seek to fit in to your culture.

In businesses, managers often specify, as part of the recruitment process, experience or background they think the new recruit should have. These specifications are a way of finding people who will 'fit in' to the prevailing culture. In addition, the psychometric testing that organisations use to help select people for jobs is another mechanism hiring managers use to try to identify the people who will 'fit in' the best.

According to AIM National Survey 2010, companies in Australia with greater than $10 million turnover have an average staff turnover of 15.5 per cent. Most companies spend a great deal of time trying to get their people to understand their culture and to comply with their values and code of conduct. Yet if they lose 15 per cent of them every year, consider the impact – effort and cost – of having to acculturate the newly hired employee population every year.

The time and cost of acculturation increases as your employee numbers rise and the more disbursed they are geographically, the harder it is to influence them. That is a very big and expensive task.

Staff Turnover

Total employees	New employees to acculturate each year (based on an average of 15 per cent turnover)
100	15
4,000	600
22,000	3,300
55,000	8,250

Board members and executives presumably know the financial costs of staff turnover. But have they thought about the external influences that new people bring in when hired, requiring ongoing investment in training, development, mentoring and culture changes programs?

The bigger the organisation the more interested executives should be in trying to impact social change, to align cultures and values held in society with those they need to operate a progressive business. If we can influence greater diversity in society we'd have fewer problems with diversity at work. Over time that would help to reduce the costs of staff turnover, orientation and culture change for businesses.

When I asked one CEO whose business spanned all seven states "Would your organisation get behind a national campaign to shift some of the values that are blocking you from achieving diversity?" he replied, "Why would I do that, I am only interested in my people". He missed the point, but if he had understood the 4th blind spot he might have been persuaded of the merits of his company influencing the values in society.

Few organisations factor in the effects of having so many new people bringing in different cultural influences or the costs of acculturation. Even fewer leaders recognise the need to use their influence to bring about the culture changes in society, that would help them to build positive cultures in their own business and which would foster diversity.

Absorbing other cultures

Becoming 'acculturated' into a new culture is like inhaling pollen in the early spring. It is unseen, unconscious and on most occasions there is no recognisable effect. Just as we don't know what pollens have been breathed into our system unless we happen to be allergic, we also don't know when our behaviour has adjusted to 'fit in' to the norms of a new culture. The adjustment occurs slowly and unconsciously – unless the values and attitudes of the new culture are vastly different from our own and we find ourselves in 'culture shock'. In this case we will be more conscious of the difference and choose to make the adjustment to 'fit-in' or if it doesn't suit us we may choose to leave the cultural group and look for another that fits better.

Let's take a look at the example in the diagram below. Here is an average Australian adult male who is, say, 28 years old and lives in Brisbane. He works in a bank, is second-generation Italian and is studying part time at Griffith University. He belongs to the university football club and to the local church. He is influenced by all of these cultural groups' assumptions, values and attitudes: Australia, Brisbane, Griffith University, GMAFC, the Italian community, and the Roman Catholic Church.

Imagine how the number of influencing cultures will expand when he marries an Australian-born Malaysian woman from his church who is an engineer. How many other cultural groups will be in his sphere? It could expand to include the Malaysian community, various schools, children's sports clubs, his wife's industry culture and more.

Every time anyone joins your culture they bring with them the assumptions, values and attitudes they have adopted from elsewhere. These might be aligned, or not, with those of your cultural group.

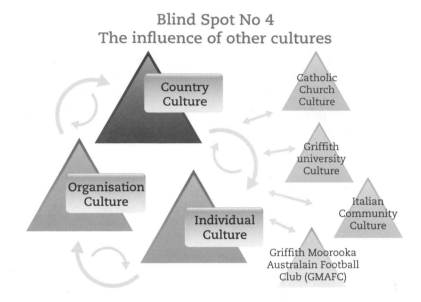

Blind Spot No 4
The influence of other cultures

When it comes to gender and cultural diversity, we are now observing increased pressure on all groups to be more tolerant and accepting of difference. Yet it's interesting that while we might have fourth-generation Australians showing intolerance of people of different cultural backgrounds who *don't* upset our existence (they live peacefully in nearby suburbs), we also have high levels of tolerance of Anglo-Saxon people who do upset our existence (creating organisational conflict and resisting change).

These are just some of the 'other' cultural groups to which we belong:

- Country culture – the country we are raised in strongly impacts who we are and what we believe, the assumptions and values of that country are firmly embedded in us, our family and communities around us.
- Family culture – the family we were born into is the most dominant of all our cultures and it forms the foundations that we carry with us through life – along with the impacts of early experiences and observations.
- Individual culture – as we grow up and travel through life we adopt assumptions and values that influence the beliefs, attitudes and behaviours we exhibit.
- Organisation culture – all organisations that we belong to, now or in the past, will have an impact on our culture and vice versa.
- Religious culture – religious beliefs, rites or rituals are often indoctrinated into our daily lives.
- Sports culture – a big part of the Australian national psyche – but also the individual pursuits we take on will have an influence who we become.

- Industry culture – as we train in a trade or profession we take on the cultural norms of that industry and we are often drawn to industries that have values that fit with our own personal values.
- City, suburb and community cultures – the town and communities we were brought up in shape who we become. If we were born in a farming community we are likely to hold different assumptions from people raised in cities.

Blind spots cause delay

These blind spots are some of the reasons why changing culture to achieve diversity takes so long. We fail to recognise that assumptions exist; we rely on changes made to the top layers of culture only for too long; the task is initially delegated to HR and receives little support from business managers, and insufficient CEO sponsorship, at the start; we don't fully appreciate the impact other cultures have on our employees; we underestimate the power of the subcultures and our efforts towards effecting change are evolutionary, when they more often need to be revolutionary.

This is why culture change can take 3, 5 or even 10 years. The learning curve has been slow. As highlighted above, the study of organisation culture is a relatively recent occurrence. With increased knowledge and experience, companies will be able to make faster progress. The more expansive the learning the faster the culture change initiatives in your business will take effect.

The Culture Circuit

The Culture Circuit is about you. You have a role in every culture you belong to and vice versa. Like an electrical 'circuit', a special type of network that has a closed loop giving a return path for the current, the Culture Circuit is also a closed loop which influences and is influenced by each component in the circuit.

Individuals in the circuit

The diagram below shows us how central individuals are to the Culture Circuit. Individuals make up the employee groups that form organisations and they also make up societies that form countries. So if we are unhappy with the culture of the organisation or country to which we belong we might be part of the problem. First we can look inward for a solution, to see if there are changes we could make, and then outwardly we can seek opportunities to influence change in others.

Leaders are the ones who usually step up to take on the role of driving change but if you are not currently a leader you could think about whether you want to be one. Everyone in a culture contributes to it and can take the opportunity to help drive change within it. To reach your potential, it helps if several of your group cultures are travelling in the same direction and are aligned.

The Culture Circuit
Elements are reinforced in each culture

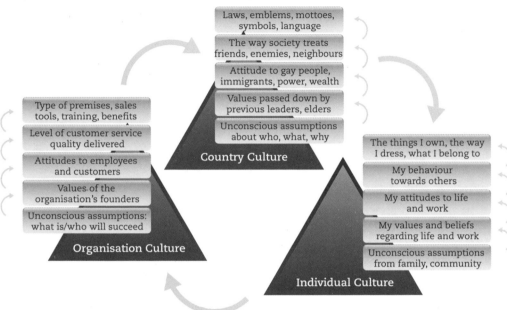

The diagram above also illustrates how assumptions, values and attitudes flow around a circuit from one culture to another. Our attitudes to life and work and our behaviours toward other people go with us to our place of work and in doing so we impact the culture of the organisations we work with.

Every one of us contributes to the values and belief systems of our various cultural groups and therefore we have a right to ask others to consider changes if we think them necessary. Any one of us can take responsibility to lead the group to a better future. Or we can take a back seat, fold our arms, and wait for others to do it.

Whether we like it or not, we are all living and working within a Culture Circuit. When we complain about things that don't work to our satisfaction, we ought to draw up our own Culture Circuit to view the groups we belong to and ask which ones have limiting assumptions. Next we could ask 'How can I help to adjust them?' Everyone has choice about whether to stay within a cultural group or not; everyone has the choice to move to a different group or step up to lead change in any groups that need to evolve.

'The price of greatness is responsibility.'

Winston Churchill on leadership

Fit in or opt out

Blind spot No. 4 (above) highlighted how we move between cultures and that there are many of them. Our values and behaviours travel with us when we join clubs, schools, communities and places of worship and the influence goes both ways.

As a member of any cultural group, we perpetuate its reality if we accept the assumptions and adopt the behaviour of the group or, if we feel it is not producing the best outcomes for the group, we can seek to influence a change, that is, help it to evolve.

We generally comply with the current cultural norms of the groups we join. But if the values of the new group don't fit well with our own we have several choices: we can opt-out (leave and find another group); try to fit-in, say nothing, but do little to support the values (passive aggressive); actively resist; or seek to lead others in the group to adopt new values and behaviours (lead change).

Leaders in business or community have a duty to lead change if there are elements of the culture that are inhibiting progress. It is possible to change a culture in a short period of time if that change is desired and driven: it does not require a new generation to make the change. But it does require leaders who are prepared to contribute to change and to start by changing themselves. To take up a new value, or belief or behaviour usually requires that we let go of something old, or acknowledge that there is a better way of moving ahead.

To bring about change in the world in which we live, we need to be part of the change. When we are constantly reinventing ourselves we are better placed to help others make adjustments too. The most successful leaders are those who always find something else to learn.

'There is nothing noble in being superior to your fellow man; true nobility is being superior to your former self'.

Ernest Hemingway on self-improvement

Culture Zones

Zones are indicators of how far, or how fast, a culture – country, organisation, sports club – has evolved. Zones help us to identify what stage our culture is up to and this guides us in our forward journey.

Cultures need to evolve to the third Zone to thrive. The three Zones are: the Comfort Zone; the Band-Aid Zone; and the Redirection Zone.

The Comfort Zone

Organisation cultures that are not going anywhere are characterised by the word 'comfortable'. They may be described as fat, happy and lazy, or arrogant and resting on their laurels, or unaware of their lack of progress.

When I first started working with organisation cultures in the late 1980s, 'comfortable' regularly topped the list of words offered by employees when describing life at the company being surveyed. Thankfully in the past two decades it is much less frequent for obvious reasons: the pace of technological development is faster, competition is fiercer and economies are more turbulent.

You just need to think about the changes that have occurred to be reminded that nothing is constant. Black and white television gave way to colour, books are slowly giving way to iPads and Kindles, local community youth clubs have given way to online social media, facsimiles have given way to scanning and email, telephone calls are under threat from Skype calls. If you are in a 'comfortable' workplace you should be worried.

'It is not the strongest of the species that survives, nor the most intelligent that survives.
It is the one that is the most adaptable to change. '
Charles Darwin on evolution

Continuous change and adaptation is as critical to the viability and survival of your organisation, sports club or government department as it is to the orangutans in Borneo who face extinction due to habitat destruction. Organisations that are still in the 'Comfort Zone' in this day and age are at great risk of decline. Also, if you are not meeting the needs of the people in your cultural group, they either take a walk (look for others groups to join) or, if they do stay, they exist passively and resist helping you to meet your ambitions.

The Comfort Zone:
No Culture Change Occurring

Artefacts

Behaviours

Attitudes

Values & Beliefs

Assumptions

The Band-Aid Zone

If you have been trying to introduce changes to your culture that just won't stick, then you are probably in the Band-Aid Zone. If you feel that you are taking two steps forward and then one step back, there may be hidden forces at the bottom of your Culture Iceberg working against your initiatives. To be in the Band-Aid Zone on your journey, means you are experiencing blind spot No 2.

For much of the past decade leading businesses have been developing their cultures to attract scarce labour resources; retain customers in an increasingly competitive and service-oriented world; and encourage the support and commitment of all stakeholders. However, much of the development has been in the top layers only: improved artefacts that foster employee engagement, investor relations, customer loyalty; and programs such as mentoring, leadership development, skills training, orientation and buddy systems that are designed to shift behaviour and attitudes.

There have also been changes to structures, systems and policies to create more fluid and flexible organisations like cutting middle management, decentralising operations and other strategies to increase efficiency and communications.

The Band-Aid Zone:
Changing top layers only

Knowing that people are important and that having the right organisation culture is key to obtaining their best performance is the beginning of a positive culture-change program. And when you introduce changes to the top, visible, layers of your culture you will see some shift in attitudes and behaviours. But I have heard leaders say "If you take your foot off the pedal, the old behaviours return". The reason is usually that their new initiatives are being undermined by old assumptions that are lying at the bottom of the culture. The changes made to the top layer are not permanent or sustainable until you change the assumptions that direct them.

Sometimes you can see old assumptions at work very clearly when a new boss arrives and brings new assumptions and values from a previous company or different experience. She begins to roll out the way she wants things done and people who have been in the company for a long time, and who have come to rely on the old assumptions, respond with "That's not the way we do it here, this is what works for us!" The new boss is conscious that they are resisting change and has two choices – bend to their will to obtain their cooperation (and thereby reinforce the old assumptions) or insist on change being accepted and 'jolt' the culture so that everyone knows that times have changed and there is no going back.

Like a Band-Aid, changes to the top layers of the culture merely cover, hide and (sometimes) address the symptoms that become evident. Like a Band-Aid, these quick fixes eventually lose their stickiness and fall off, exposing what lies beneath. The Band-Aid Zone is an interim state and to achieve sustainable diversity, to build an organisation fit for regional growth and ready to respond to the increasingly multicultural world, Australian businesses need to move into The Redirection Zone where old assumptions are challenged and more revolutionary culture change can occur.

The Redirection Zone

Long-lasting sustainable culture change requires a shift in assumptions. A shifting of assumptions feels like a 'jolt' because it is a fundamental shift of the foundations upon which everything else was built. People notice. It usually involves a revolutionary shift and can cause some discomfort to those who have come to rely on the old assumptions. It therefore requires courage and commitment on the part of the leadership team. But for that to occur there must first be understanding and belief in the way cultures operate.

A 'jolt' to the assumptions is nearly always associated with a highly significant change in artefacts and behaviours; this change to the visual layers reinforces the revolutionary adjustment to the unseen and unconscious ways of doing things. (You will read in Chapter 11 how leading companies shifted old assumptions and developed new ones with very clear undisputable actions that signalled the value of women in previously male-dominated environments. Things changed immeasurably and permanently.)

The Redirection Zone is where you need to be. Ironically, you need to get comfortable with being uncomfortable. Change is a constant and unavoidable thing in corporate life today. Get used to adaptation and you get used to being at the forefront of your market. The more groups in your Culture Circuit you influence to become comfortable with adapting to change, the more progressive Australia will be and the more nimble its people.

The Redirection Zone:
Where assumptions get jolted

Moving through the zones

Cultures have to pass through all three zones to effect a major change. The journey can be evolutionary or revolutionary or a mixture of both. Culture change does take time but those companies that are used to continuous change can effect a change much faster as they usually face less resistance. They know how it feels and are not frightened of the turbulence – in fact they revel in it.

Cultures unused to change can take a very long time getting beyond resistance and there can be frustration along the way. Often leaders of these companies feel beleaguered and give up the role before seeing the benefits of their endurance. Later leaders who arrive when resistance has been worn down, making their change-leading journey less onerous, often get the glory.

As a leader of change you first need to identify which zone your culture is in. Then you need to identify how far you have to travel to get to the Redirection Zone. It can be done in a few years, or decades depending on:

- Whether you accurately assess your starting position and the distance you need to travel;
- Whether your organisation is used to change and ready for change or not;
- The size of your cultural group membership and how wide its geographic spread;
- The age of the culture and how embedded the assumptions, value and beliefs are;
- The external economic conditions (are they drivers for change?);
- Your own culture's performance – socially and economically (is there a burning platform?);
- Whether you choose an evolutionary or revolutionary change strategy;

- Whether you are prepared to 'unfreeze' your culture by giving it a 'jolt';
- How resistant the assumptions, are to change;
- The level of investment you make;
- How committed you are to driving it through when the going gets tough.

An evolutionary, guided 'culture redirection' process is generally all most organisations need, unless they have issues that need addressing urgently. Then a revolutionary process is more effective at getting necessary results in a short time frame. Most of all it takes courage, vision, belief and a strong top-team aligned to the vision and commitment to see it through.

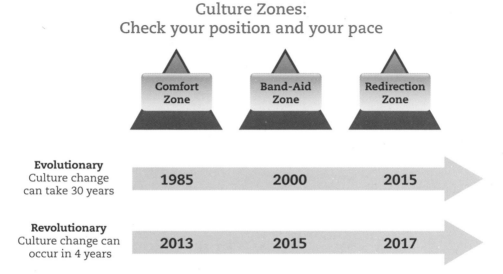

Culture Zones:
Check your position and your pace

How to unlearn behaviours

Ivan Pavlov was a famous Russian physiologist at St Petersburg University who won the Nobel Prize for physiology in 1904 for his advancements in the study of behaviour modification and classical conditioning.

Pavlov became famous in the West in 1901 when he released the findings of an experiment in which he examined the rate of salivation in dogs and discovered the 'conditioned reflex'. The idea of 'conditioning' as an automatic form of learning became known as the 'Pavlov's Dogs' phenomenon.

Pavlov presented the dogs with food in consecutive sequences and then rang a bell. Each time the food was presented the dogs would salivate. They later came to associate the ringing of the bell with salivation. Next Pavlov would ring the bell but offer no food, and the dogs would still salivate. This became known as the stimulus-response effect and has since been used to modify behaviour in both animals and humans.

Stimulus response occurs daily

I shared this story with my son Jack recently as he stood at the kitchen counter watching me carve a hot roast leg of lamb saying "Mum that looks so good my mouth is filling up with water". I chuckled and explained 'Pavlov's Dogs' and the stimulus-response effect to him; how he saw juicy hot roast meat, smelt its fabulous aroma and salivated.

We know from our own experiences that after a few occurrences, we smell the meat cooking, but not necessarily see it, and yet we still salivate. I think everyone can recall walking in the front door of their mother's house and upon smelling their favourite food, want to taste it immediately. That's the stimulus-response effect in action.

We don't always appreciate how simply we learn our behaviour from life's experiences; every behavioural response we have ever learned has an explanation and can be modified.

Here are some examples:

- Babies learn from their first day in the world how to get attention, they cry when they are hungry;
- Dogs learn how to get attention when left outside in the cold, they bark at the back door;
- Children in kindergarten learn how to get the teacher's attention, they put their hand up;
- Prisoners learn not to touch the boundary fence as it is electric;
- Cows learn not to touch the boundary fence as it is electric;
- Employees learn how to get a pay rise or promotion; they focus on delivering the agreed outcomes;
- Bosses learn how to motivate an employee to work longer hours; they offer them something they seek – like a new car, overseas trip, pay rise or bigger office;
- Two people in a relationship learn what makes the other person angry or withdrawn, and they try to avoid doing it again.

All of this helps us to understand how cultures form.

Positive versus negative stimulus

There are times when a positive stimulus alone will produce a good result, but there are other times when you need both positive and negative together. I repeatedly hear people in organisations say "We tried getting our people to do that but it didn't work". So I ask "Have you identified the right stimulus that will invoke the behavioural response that you seek?"

Most organisations I have worked with choose to start with positive stimulus as they worry that a sanction might create a negative atmosphere or seem too tough. In my experience, while most leaders start their culture-change programs with the positive stimulus, they discover that it's only partially effective. That's because all change meets with some resistance. The people who are willing to make an effort to work together to resolve differences respond positively, but those who are not tend to sit back and leave the work to others, appearing passive, while they are actually covertly undermining the changes put in place.

The most effective stimulus-response culture-change method in a group situation is to apply <u>both</u> positive and negative stimuli at the same time. People then have to make a choice – to cooperate or not. They cannot sit back being passive-aggressive and hope not to be spotted. If you do not employ negative stimuli at the same time, the naysayers can hide in your organisation and cost you in every way.

At least 80 per cent of the organisations I have worked with have some proportion of people who resist the proposed changes in a passive-aggressive way. This drains the company of energy and slows the change process down.

As the definition for culture says above, the behaviour of people in a culture is learned:

'...*assumptions are learned by the group members as they adapt to what is going on externally and as they seek to integrate internally....*'

We know that assumptions are the ultimate driver of behaviours in any cultural group and these will dominate. We also know that all cultures drift, so they can be guided – or modified. The challenge is two-fold. First we have to adjust the assumptions upon which all behaviour is based, and then motivate a relearning of the behaviour using the right stimulus. The secret is to select stimulus-response that will reinforce the shift you seek in your assumptions.

If there is no 'outcome' for poor behaviour you are unlikely to motivate 100 per cent good behaviour. You need to align your stimulus-response strategies with your efforts to shift assumptions so that everyone is aligned to your culture and supporting your ambitions to reach targets and objectives.

Shifting behaviour in any culture and relearning how to respond to a situation is entirely possible. You just need to be serious about getting the change and have the courage to put the sanctions in place. The older the culture, the more firmly entrenched the assumptions. The more people in the culture group, the bigger the challenge. However, no culture is immune to change; they are just resistant and require more effort to redirect.

Sustaining change: Making diversity stick

Having explored cultures and how they work, we can now get back to the topic of diversity.

Purging cultures of out-dated assumptions is absolutely critical to achieving sustainable culture change that will allow diversity and growth to prevail. This does not necessarily mean you need to purge your company of the people who created them or who guard them, but it does mean you will have to encourage them to let go of the old assumptions and support the culture change.

Australia has great potential to be a world leader in many things. But at this stage the facts suggest that cultural diversity is not one of them. Being a multicultural society does not naturally create cultural diversity in the workplace, nor does it protect Australia from having elements of racism or sexism penetrate its society.

Similarly, the levels of participation of Australian women in the workplace are relatively low by world standards. Our boards and executive teams are grossly under-represented by women and our socialisation of girls in schools and communities has not been adjusted sufficiently to create gender balance across industries. We have not yet dispelled the belief that 'mothers ought to be full-time stay-at-home parents' or that 'women can opt out of the workforce' mid-career.

Changing culture in society is a precondition to permanently changing culture in the workplace. That is, sustaining the changes you introduce to workplace culture, to achieve diversity and growth, requires change in Australia's culture. Everyone can help.

The next three chapters look at how you can initiate conversations about assumptions and values in three of the most important cultures in your Culture Circuit: your country culture, your individual culture and your organisation culture. You can choose to read these in any order; however I have presented them in the way they form – country culture comes first, it then influences the formation of your individual culture as you adopt the values of your country, family and community, then finally you take these into the organisations that you establish or join.

You may wish to go straight to Chapter 10 and read about how to change your own individual assumptions and values, or to Chapter 11 for examples of how organisations have done it. You can always come back later to read about how to influence a shift in your country's culture.

Chapter 9

Redirecting your Country Culture

'If you live in a community and bring your children up in that community, if you keep taking and taking, it's just like a big water tank. If you take everything out and you don't put anything back in, it's going to be empty. But if you keep putting something back… that tank will keep on being topped up, and when you die your children will benefit.'

Eddie Quong,1925–81, second-generation Australian, former baker and Chinese community leader in Darwin

Achieving cultural diversity and gender equality to boost productivity in corporate Australia requires a conscious shift in Australian values to shift the attitudes and behaviours the 100 leaders have described. That means cultural change.

There are many amazing qualities of Australia's Culture to be proud of, but there are also elements which some people are critical of and want changed.

Many of the 100 leaders interviewed expressed frustration at the dilemma Australia faces. How can we have so much to celebrate and yet have such poor diversity in the workplace, which is affecting our productivity? In this chapter I will shed some light on how some elements of Australian culture are limiting its progress and what we can do to change them. We will discuss:

- How country culture dominates the Culture Circuit;
- How strong characters can impact country cultures;
- How Norway shifted the assumptions of its culture;
- How country cultures form and operate;
- The challenging elements of Australian culture;
- How outside influences impact performance;
- An example of Australia's Culture Iceberg (based on the 100 leaders' views);
- How we each contribute to change

The impact of country culture on the Culture Circuit

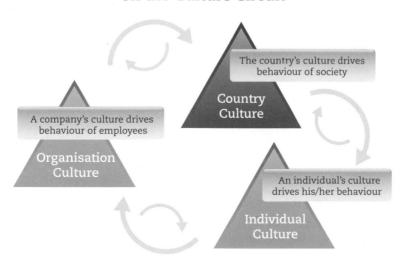

The country's culture drives behaviour of society

Country Culture

A company's culture drives behaviour of employees

Organisation Culture

An individual's culture drives his/her behaviour

Individual Culture

Country culture dominates

Of all the cultures in the Culture Circuit the one that impacts most on who we are and how we live our lives is our country culture. It precedes everything and it shapes everything and everyone who lives on this land.

As a business owner, political leader, town mayor, rugby club CEO, or school principal your ability to create a unique organisation culture is limited by the assumptions, values and beliefs of the Australian culture, which direct the behaviour of the people who live in the nation. That is, you are limited by the beliefs they hold, their vision for Australia and whether they have a desire to make it bigger and better, or not.

'I can't tell my people that our organisation's inability to deliver gender equality is due to our country's culture; that will just give them an alibi for inaction and to blame someone or something else.'

Anon, CEO Australia, global business

This statement was made by a chief executive who is exasperated at his efforts to stop the outflow of women from his organisation. He described having made great progress, increasing the numbers of senior women for a year or two, but then suddenly and without warning or apparent reason the numbers of senior women started to fall again.

I explained the two-way flow of influence between cultures in the Culture Circuit. Even if you have comprehensive programs for sponsoring females to the top of the organisation, there are still several major challenges you need to check, starting with the blind spots (detailed in Chapter 8). Look for assumptions that are undermining your effort; be careful not to use Band-Aids but to change lower layers of your iceberg as well as those at the top; recognise and respect subcultures; and look for impacts that flow from other cultures in the Culture Circuit – especially the impact of country culture.

Influence flows both ways

Remember, the higher your staff turnover, the more people you have to 'acculturate' each year. The secret to long-term 'sustainable' change in your organisation is to get a shift in the values of Australia's country culture. If we can influence the values people hold before they walk into our organisations, the less work we have to do to change our organisation culture year on year to keep it from slipping back (of course this assumes we have identified and addressed the blind spots and the laggards who undermine our good work).

The good news is that the influence of the cultures in the Culture Circuit flow both ways, which means you get to influence the Australian country culture through your leadership. You get the opportunity every day to convey your vision for a bigger and better future for Australia to the people in your sphere of influence (at work, at home, at the tennis club, at business clubs etc).

The country culture to which you belong influences you, your individual culture and the culture of all the other organisations and groups in your Culture Circuit.

Ethnic origin secondary

As the dominant culture in the Culture Circuit, Australian culture will dominate other country cultures that are introduced through immigration; European, New Zealand, Asian, African and Middle Eastern cultures are all secondary to and are reduced by the Australian country culture.

If you are a fourth-, third- or even second-generation Australian (i.e. born in Australia), it is unlikely that your ethnic heritage – whether it is British, Vietnamese, Italian, or Brazilian – will dominate. Most people will associate more with the culture of the country they have been raised in than the one their parents came from.

As a second- or third-generation Italian you may have been called Giuliani or Isabella, eat lasagne and ossobuco at home, and celebrate Italy's national holidays – but the chances are you will feel a more comfortable cultural fit in Australia than when you go to Italy to visit relatives.

Country culture dominates
over religion and ethnic cultures

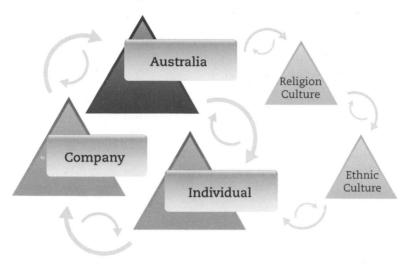

I asked the 100 leaders interviewed which country they associated with firstly and secondarily and this point was confirmed: the majority said they associated with Australian cultural first and the culture of their ethnic background second.

Our country's culture determines the behavioural norms of the society in which we live. As we grow up we observe the behaviours of people around us and adopt them as our own. These unique behaviours are recognisable to outsiders as being distinctly 'Australian behaviours' and are used to differentiate between us (as we heard in Chapter 4 from people living in Asia). The same goes for the other layers beneath behaviour on the Culture Iceberg. We observe them, adopt them and use them to help us solve problems and make decisions throughout life.

When the kids in Australia today enter the workforce, how will they deal with the unconscious bias that they have taken from their childhood?
Stephen Roberts, Chief Country Officer, Citi, Sydney, Australia

As the Culture Circuit shows, country culture influences the formation of our own individual culture. There are of course other influences on an individual's behaviour, which is covered in the next chapter, but country culture is the dominant player. When you travel abroad, you can identify a stranger's culture by their mannerisms, attitudes, behaviours, dress, language and accent. It is the features of our country culture that we each exhibit in the same way that makes it possible for others to guess our country of origin.

Strong characters can impact country cultures

As you can see from the arrows in the diagram above, it is possible for the individual culture of high-profile, influential or charismatic people to flow-back to impact on a country culture too. This requires much more effort to effect, but it does happen.

The individual culture of strong characters have been known to impact the beliefs of people in the same cultural group and those outside of it watching on – some positively and some negatively (depending on your point of view). High profile individuals whose beliefs and behaviours have impacted on others include: Nelson Mandela, Mahatma Ghandi, Mother Teresa, Winston Churchill, Margaret Thatcher, John F Kennedy, Germaine Greer, Aung San Suu Kyi, Oprah Winfrey, Barak Obama and many more.

In the same way as courageous leaders can make tough decisions that 'jolt' their company's Culture Iceberg, so too can our political leaders make tough decisions that shift assumptions and behaviours of our country culture that can impact organisation culture overnight.

You might say that the Labor Government of Australia did this with the introduction of the Carbon Tax which shifted the assumption that 'big industrial players who pollute the environment can get away with it' to 'now they can't'. The Carbon Tax (a country-culture artefact) also shifted what big industrial players are investing in (an organisation-culture value) and the relationships between

The impact of the Carbon Tax

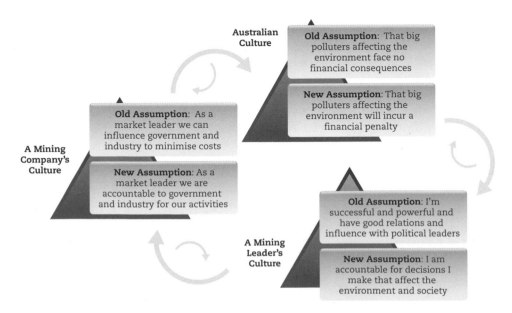

government and business leaders has changed as a consequence (behaviours of both cultures). The Australian government introduced a Carbon Tax to shift the underlying assumptions of big polluters in order to influence a corresponding shift in their attitudes and behaviours. The diagram below shows how this works. This phenomenon works across all aspects of business and society and the flow of influence can be seen running both ways. Just as big mining magnates tried through their wealth and influence to effect a shift in Australia's country culture by opposing the Carbon Tax, so have business leaders tried to stall the introduction of quotas for women on boards with scaremongering strategies about the likely downsides of promoting females to top jobs. If our political leaders do implement quotas (artefact) this, too, will change our country culture and force a change to organisation cultures because very different business behaviours will be needed to meet the legislated changes.

Norway shifts assumptions

The Norwegians did it. They 'jolted' the assumptions of their country culture by establishing quotas. This systemic change (a new artefact) enforced the behaviour change they had been unable to effect any other way. By making the new behaviours of Norway's country culture compulsory, the Norwegian Parliament radically changed the underlying assumption that 'women are not suitable for board positions', to 'women are capable of holding board positions' overnight.

This radical change 'jolted' the foundations of the country culture permanently and it also had a flow-on effect. It changed the individual culture of Norwegian people and the organisational culture of Norwegian companies too. The changes 'dominoed' around the Culture Circuit and resulted in improved and sustainable diversity on Norwegian boards. The changed attitudes and behaviours of individuals and organisations are unlikely to be reversed while the law remains in place.

The link to the full story is listed in Appendix II but essentially the Norwegian Parliament in 2003 introduced a legal requirement for at least 40 per cent of the seats on boards to be filled by the under-represented gender. This legal proposition called for the regulation of the 500 PLCs in Norway as well as all of the wholly state-owned and inter-municipal companies.

The plan was to make sure that both genders were represented on the boards of companies that either have a broad spread of shares or are publicly owned. They wanted to make sure that boardrooms should cease to be a male preserve. The law affecting the PLCs was enforced on 1 January 2006 and by July 2008 the proportion of female board members had risen to 39 per cent (up from 7 per cent in 2003).

The speed with which the change took place is unprecedented. By implementing the quotas and making compliance compulsory (a change to the artefacts) they enforced a change in the way government institutions and listed companies operated (shifting organisational values, beliefs, attitudes and behaviours) and by installing penalties for non-compliance (a negative stimulus) they achieved a cultural revolution.

The Norwegian government shifted its country culture assumptions and 'jolted' the culture forward to arrive at a place that they predicted would take 100 years if left to evolutionary means.

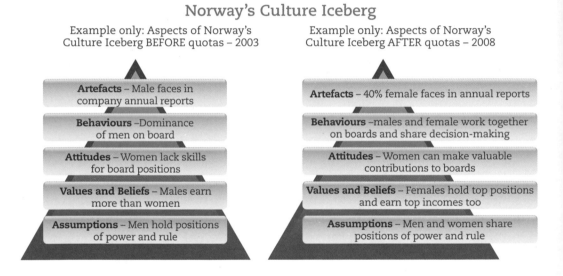

Norway's Culture Iceberg

Example only: Aspects of Norway's Culture Iceberg BEFORE quotas – 2003

Example only: Aspects of Norway's Culture Iceberg AFTER quotas – 2008

Artefacts – Male faces in company annual reports

Behaviours –Dominance of men on board

Attitudes – Women lack skills for board positions

Values and Beliefs – Males earn more than women

Assumptions – Men hold positions of power and rule

Artefacts – 40% female faces in annual reports

Behaviours –males and female work together on boards and share decision-making

Attitudes – Women can make valuable contributions to boards

Values and Beliefs – Females hold top positions and earn top incomes too

Assumptions – Men and women share positions of power and rule

How country cultures form and operate

The culture of a country extends back as far as its civilisation can be traced and it evolves with every significant change – country borders revised, independent states established, modern legal systems adopted, languages dying out, natural disasters occurring and military dictatorships overthrown. Every day country cultures face some degree of evolutionary change.

There are old and new cultures, which we affectionately call the Old World (Africa, Asia and Europe) and the New World (discovered from the 15th century onwards and referring particularly to the Americas).

The recorded history of America and Australia is merely a few hundred years old compared with countries in Africa, Europe and Asia where civilised societies formed thousands of years earlier. When we are considering the culture of a country, we need to consider the influences on its people over time. The early settlers of Australia arrived principally from the United Kingdom and life was very different from what they had known before.

As the culture definition says in Chapter 8, culture forms as people in the group respond and 'adapt to external situations' and as they 'seek to integrate internally' the assumptions upon which they base their behaviours are established. How the people of Australia responded to situations they faced in 1800, 1900 and 2000 have influenced the current-day culture: the values and behaviours of Australians today.

While early settlers in Australia brought with them British laws, traditions and values they soon developed their own local culture based on what they found here and their response to the external environment.

Since January 1788 when the First Fleet arrived, immigrant Australians have been influencing the assumptions, values, attitude and behaviours of the culture here. At the start the people were mainly from European nations and had white skin tones, but then people of other races and nationalities began to arrive. The artefacts we see around the main cities, rural areas and coastal towns tell stories of the early arrivals, their heritage, the industry they established and their way of life.

Australia's culture includes the way people think, what they understand about the world they live in, the knowledge base they share, the outlook and shared goals they have and the patterns of behaviour they exhibit.

History provides cultural understanding

To understand culture, we look at its history. The history determines the assumptions; the hidden and unconscious mind of the nation. The assumptions of the indigenous people of Australia are based on tens of thousands of years of history, but the assumptions brought by European immigrants who arrived from the 18th century onwards have formed much of the foundations of present-day Australian culture.

The history of modern-day Australia is so short that we can still see the influence of early settlers in the way people behave today. The British rule, the lives of the free and not-so-free settlers, the gold rush, the mining boom, taming the rugged land, surviving the outback, developing industries, establishing laws and states and parliament and so on.

As Europeans arrived by boat in the 18th and 19th centuries, they had to quickly learn how to deal with the forested land, the vast distances, the hot climate, the dusty soils, the creatures they had not encountered before and much more that was new. They also had to cope with being so far away from their homeland.

These experiences shaped attitudes that have been passed down to Australians today. The people developed resilience, independence and survival skills and they have a strength of character and humour that is evident in their daily interactions.

Each local area is influence by its climate, industry, economic prosperity, local leadership, religion, immigrants, the good times, the bad times and more. Each state of Australia has its own local subculture and each town yet another.

Australia's 'Country Culture': Evolving since 1788

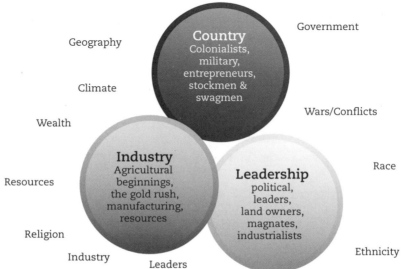

The diagram above shows some of the many factors impacting the formation of our country culture. The history of the nation is important. The type of leaders it has had affects the culture because their individual values influence what gets attention, how they lead and where they lead the people. The industries that arise from the land and environment and the economic outcomes influence how people live their lives. Physical neighbours' cultures impact one another but Australia does not have to worry about that, its culture is quarantined.

Traumas and events shape culture too

There are upsides and downsides to Australia being an island nation. The upside is that Australia has no adjoining neighbour to cause disputes over land or natural resources; it is better protected from invasion and illegal immigrants; it can control the spread of disease and guard against the arrival of plant and animal pests; and it can manage its own affairs unencumbered. The downside is isolation.

To appreciate how the past 225 years have impacted the attitudes of modern-day Australians we need to trace the historical journey of the people and identify the things that have been imprinted on the Australian psyche. It also helps to contrast the relatively safe and secure island existence of the Australian people to those who live in countries that have long-running battles with bordering neighbours or who have endured repeated famine, flooding, earthquake, war, plagues and other traumas. The traumas and scars of each country's experience are imprinted on its cultural memory.

Think about how the assumptions, values, beliefs and behaviours of the following cultures would have been impacted as a result of what they have experienced in their history:

- Countries that have endured years of ongoing conflict:
  - The Israeli–Palestinian conflict over borders, security, control of Jerusalem and more;
  - The people of the Congo after two major wars which between 1996 and 2003 and in the five years following the aftermath saw 5.4 million people killed;
  - The many years of Russian assault on the Afghan people followed by the past decade of tyrannical rule by the Taliban

- Countries that have recently endured a devastating single catastrophic event:
  - The Americans after the twin towers collapsed in New York on September 2001 (known better as 9/11);
  - The Japanese after the earthquake of April 2011 off the coast caused a tsunami that devastated towns and caused a number of nuclear accidents reviving memories of the devastation of Hiroshima in 1945;
  - The Norwegians after the shooting rampage of Anders Breivik on an Island outside Oslo in July 2011 killing 84 young people.

These events shaped the values and attitudes of the people who live in these cultures. Some will have formed beliefs about their ability to trust certain groups of people; some will have formed unconscious biases about those who did wrong by them; and some will be harbouring fears. What new attitudes and behaviours might they have taken on to protect their families and communities in the future? What artefacts would you expect to see representing their history and their values if you travelled to their countries?

Following is an example of how the overnight change to America's country culture assumptions could have impacted the layers of the iceberg above.

Example only: Aspects of America's Culture
Iceberg BEFORE 9/11

Example only: Aspects of America's Culture
Iceberg AFTER 9/11

Artefacts – Twin Towers on the skyline; relaxed airport security; Pentagon unscathed

Artefacts – 9/11 Memorial: North and South Pools; rigid and inconvenient airport security; Pentagon repaired

Behaviours – People walk freely around cities, people feel safe travelling internally; people trust others; Muslims welcome

Behaviours – People walk cautiously around cities, people less safe travelling internally; people suspicious of Muslims

Attitudes – We can live freely in our country; we protect our people and provide a safe place to live; our leadership

Attitudes – Resentment towards Arab/Muslim people; concern over freedom; vulnerability about being attacked; some people in the world resent US dominance

Values and Beliefs – Independence, liberty, justice, equality and patriotism

Values and Beliefs – National security, liberty, justice, equality and patriotism

Assumptions – Our national security is watertight due to our great world dominance, military strength and physical isolation from trouble spots

Assumptions – Terrorists threaten US national security; world dominance can fuel hatred, military strength may not protect us; trouble can find us on our own land

Australia's isolation quarantines culture

Australia is far away from any other nation, it provides an incredibly safe place for its people to live and has few catastrophic events other than natural disasters. There are few security issues on the border and, with plenty of space for the tiny population, there is little squabbling over resources.

The distance and isolation has in the past been considered a good thing as it quarantines us from the troubles of the world. The weather is kind, the land supportive and the oceans productive. What more could we ask for?

Well, as you will know by now there is much more we could ask for. But before discussing that, let's take a brief look at the work of Geert Hofstede, which you might find interesting if you haven't seen it before. It is relevant to much of the discussion regarding diversity; immigrant integration; whether having different cultures at senior management level is important; whether we should invest in learning Asian languages; and how can we develop our Asian trade relations.

Behavioural drivers of culture

When I lived in Singapore, I repeatedly heard local people say "Australians and New Zealanders are a lot like Americans". What they meant by that was 'Australians and New Zealanders are more independent, immediate and self-projecting than us'. These comments are an expression of how Asian people see people from our three nations: they observe that we are similar in our behaviours, and very different from Asians.

Eastern cultures are more inclusive and group-oriented than most Western cultures and Professor Geert Hofstede, a former Dutch researcher, compiled what he called *National Cultural Dimensions* and the table below shows that Western nations score very differently from Eastern nations.

Table A: Geert Hofstede's National Cultural Dimensions: Scores for Western and Eastern nations

	Power -Distance	Individualism vs Collectivism	Masculinity vs Femininity	Uncertainty Avoidance	Long-term vs Short-term Orientation
Western Nations					
Australia	36	90	61	51	31
New Zealand	22	79	58	49	30
United Kingdom	35	89	66	35	25
America	40	91	62	46	29
Canada	3	80	52	48	23
Eastern Nations					
China	80	20	66	30	118
Singapore	74	20	48	8	48
Japan	54	46	95	92	80
Hong Kong	68	25	57	29	96
India	77	48	56	40	61
Philippines	94	32	64	44	19

As you can see from Table A, Western nations score very differently from Eastern nations. Contrasting Australia with our biggest trading partner China, there are some notable differences. Working from left to right in Table A above:

- Chinese people have a far higher acceptance of hierarchical order in which everybody has a place (80) than Australian people who strive to equalise the distribution of power and demand (36);
- Australia is a far more individualistic society (90) than China which is a more collective society (20);
- Both countries Australia (61) and China (66) have a slight preference for achievement, heroism, assertiveness, competitiveness and material reward for success;
- Australians (51) are neither uncomfortable with uncertainty nor do they want to control the future – they are both relaxed and not adverse to taking risks, yet in Chinese society (30) adherence to laws and rules may be flexible to suit the actual situation and pragmatism is a fact of life;
- Chinese people take an incredibly long-term view of things (118), which is related to the teachings of Confucius and indicates that persistence and perseverance are normal, whereas Australia by contrast (31) is a short-term oriented culture focused on traditions, fulfilling social obligations and quarterly profit and loss reports.

Table B: Geert Hofstede's National Cultural Dimensions: Description of dimensions

Power- Distance : how a society handles inequalities of power among people:	
High scores	people accept a hierarchical order in which everybody has a place
Low scores	people strive to equalise the distribution of power and demand
Individualism versus Collectivism	
High scores	people have a preference for a loosely-knit social framework - individuals are expected to take care of themselves and their immediate families only (they talk about 'I')
Low scores	people have a preference for a tightly-knit social framework - individuals expect their relatives or members of an in-group to look after them in exchange for unquestioning loyalty (they talk about 'we')
Masculinity versus Femininity	
High scores	people have a preference in society for achievement, heroism, assertiveness and material reward for success. Society at large is more competitive
Low scores	people have a preference for cooperation, modesty, caring for the weak and quality of life. Society at large is more consensus-oriented
Uncertainty Avoidance	
High scores	uncomfortable with uncertainty about the future, uncomfortable with ambiguity, intolerant of unorthodox behaviour and ideas...wants to control the future
Low scores	societies maintain a more relaxed attitude in which practice counts more than principles...can cope with an uncertain future, happy to let it happen
Long-term versus Short-term Orientation	
High scores	Societies with a short-term orientation, strong concern for establishing the absolute truth, normative in their thinking, exhibit great respect for traditions, small propensity to save for the future, and a focus on achieving quick results.
Low scores	In societies with a long-term orientation, people believe that truth depends very much on situation, context and time, they adapt traditions to changed conditions, have a strong propensity to save and invest, thriftiness, and perseverance in achieving results.

The differences between these two groups of nations gives you a sense of the challenges that people who live and work in diverse businesses and societies face every day. Imagine how valuable this knowledge is for executives responsible for operations between Australia and China or some other Asian nation. Similarly, people living in multicultural Australia would benefit from appreciating the different cultural backgrounds of the people they mix with at school, work and in their local neighbourhoods.

All Western nations that hope to participate in and benefit from the growth in Asia will have to develop an appreciation for Asian cultures. Australia has little current advantage over other nations apart from proximity – but it could develop advantage by encouraging Asians who live in Australia to take a bigger role and involving them in regional business strategic planning. By removing the bamboo ceiling and sponsoring them to rise to the top of our organisations and boards there would be a positive impact on our future in the region.

Advantages of living diversely

People who live in countries that are physically connected by a common border to one or more other countries – such as Thailand, France and Chile – learn about these differences because they live alongside each other. They gain appreciation and understanding of how the cultures of their neighbours might influence their attitudes, behaviours, needs, wants and desires. That gives them great advantage economically, politically and socially.

For example, economically it helps them in their trade relations and negotiations; politically it can help them with local and regional security and environmental issues; and socially it can help to preserve harmony and build cross-cultural relations as their mobile workforces drift across borders.

The majority of countries in the world enjoy these advantages because the majority of countries are connected. Of the seven continents of the world (excluding Antarctica which is mostly uninhabitable) Australia is the only one that is made up of only one nation. Asia, Africa, North America, South America, and Europe all have dozens of nations neighbouring one another.

Of the island nations that exist some are conveniently located next to a continent or other major nation, such as Japan, Greenland, Great Britain and Cuba, and others are very far away from anyone, such as Australia and New Zealand. Our isolation (distance) and our lack of neighbours (aloneness) have had their toll on our competitive advantage. Have we been resting on our laurels too long? Are we expecting 'the good life' to continue without our being more prepared to build businesses that can operate effectively with other cultures?

Is being a monoglot (a person who speaks only one language) an advantage in this mobilising, global, technology-enabled and multicultural world? When 'being able to speak English' was an advantage, perhaps being an English-speaking monoglot was a good thing. But now that English is widely spoken by people in most major markets of the world, our previous advantage has diminished.

It's likely that nations that allow their next generation to remain monoglot will find this a great disadvantage in the 21st century. If we wish to be involved in the growth in Asia and hope to maintain a world-class education system that prepares future generations for careers outside Australia, we need to be at least bilingual or at best, multilingual. The general view is that Australia needs to expand its regional trade to sustain growth and prosperity and to participate more fully and effectively, so we are going to need more language skills.

If we cannot pull Australia closer physically to Asia, Africa or America, then how do we overcome the economic, political and social disadvantages of not having physical neighbours or having the cross-cultural understanding and experience of countries that do share common borders with neighbouring countries? There are several massive untapped opportunities that would increase our understanding of other cultures and equip our society and workforce with the added knowledge, skills and talents we need. These include:

- Getting closer to and learning more from immigrants to Australia can reduce anxiety and embarrassment about being isolated and without neighbours and it would increase tolerance and reduce racism;
- By mastering other languages we can increase our desire and confidence to travel and work in other nations that are different culturally from Australia, and we can learn a great deal about cultures when learning languages;
- By encouraging greater integration of immigrants we would have a more diverse leadership in business and society which would help us in global transactions and regional expansion of business;
- By showing greater appreciation for and acceptance of all cultures that exist within Australia we would build stronger relations with the country of their origin.

Living diversely has only upsides. It will not interfere with the qualities we love about living in Australia: the weather and beaches will still be here; the humour, arts, music and culture that is uniquely Australian will still be here; the prawns on the barby will still be here; and the Melbourne Cup, the Bledisloe Cup and the Australian Open will all still be here. It will however result in a much more diverse group of people sharing in leading the country, its industries and its societies than is presently the case.

If we allow Australia to become multilingual as well as being multicultural – by learning Asian languages and interacting with Asian immigrants in 'their' language, not English – we would be opening Australia to realise its enormous potential. The more we allowed this to occur, the more comfortable we would become living and working across other cultures.

Challenging elements of Australian culture

There are four key elements of life down-under that challenge the Australian culture and the people who live here, making it difficult for our society and businesses to grow and prosper.

They are:

- Being far-far-away – the well-known 'tyranny of distance' situation;
- Inward-looking island culture – no neighbours, no need, no care;
- Lack of cross-cultural experience – little empathy or interest;
- Anglo-Saxons rule the multicultural nation – an oxymoron?

These challenges may not sound new, but because it is vital that we act to address them and unblock the pathways to a better future, I have included them here.

Being far-far-away

Of the G20 countries of the world, Australia is probably the most isolated. The travel time to all other major nations is significant and even though our Asian trading partners are mostly on the same or similar time zone (0–2 hours' time difference) it still takes seven (Singapore) to twelve hours (India) to reach most of them by air.

When you live in any city in Europe or Asia you can fly to many other leading nations in one, two or three hours. When you live in Australia it's a very different story. There is no quick access to the largest economies of the world, which are mostly located on continents far from Australia – North America, South America (Brazil), Europe and China. Our remoteness and distance has had an impact on Australian culture.

More recently, I'd say Australians have taken to the idea that our geographical remoteness is an asset as it distances us from the world's trouble spots, especially regarding terrorism and even economics. So the 'tyranny of distance' is now thought to work in our favour. To some extent, our absurd obsession with border protection (fuelled by fear-mongering policies on both sides) is a symbol of our wish to stay remote and isolated.

Hugh Mackay, Social Researcher and Writer, Sydney, Australia

Australians have a tremendous ability to travel the world, they are well-received and people admire their personality. They do that between 25 and 28 and then they go back to Australia, and that's the end of it for most people. Australia's isolation is its disadvantage and it is paying a price. People there fear the unknown and avoid change. Smart people look to change policies but that isn't happening. Australians have a perception of being important on the world stage, and occasionally they are with their sporting achievements, but in reality Australia is a small player and far away.

Richard Mazzochi, Partner, King & Wood Mallesons, Hong Kong, China

Why do we have racism in Australia? It's because of the isolation, not poor education or social or economic policies. It is because we have no immediate neighbours bordering us. If you live in Europe you see people from other countries every day. They cross your borders bringing their language, culture and food, infiltrating your culture and society to the point that you need to make adjustments. You learn tolerance and to live together.

I had racist thoughts about the Vietnamese when they first came to Australia. There was a bad Vietnamese element for a while and people judged all Asians as 'bad': my mum and I experienced increased racial discrimination towards us during this time. It wasn't until I went to visit Vietnam as an adult that I saw what a gentle race they are and changed my view of them.

Racism is born out of ignorance. Once I was exposed to these different cultures I realised how foolish I had been. You don't resolve racism by legislation. You need to have a personal experience living in other people's cultures.

Dr Charlie Teo AM, Director, The Centre for Minimally Invasive Neurosurgery, Sydney, Australia

The tyranny of distance is unhelpful. Even within a global firm, shifting an employee to Australia is like shifting them to Antarctica. The interaction and movement of people in Europe is so much easier than in Australia.

Craig Drummond, Chief Executive Officer, Bank of America Merrill Lynch, Sydney, Australia

As a nation we have the features of and behave similarly to a remote rural town: access is difficult; travel costs are higher; people think twice about visiting us; we have to ship everything in from far-far-away which puts up our import costs; our exports are less competitive as they too have high transport costs attached to them; we behave parochially towards others; and there is less pressure on us to evolve our culture as there are no immediate neighbours for us to compare ourselves with.

As we know, our strengths, when overdeveloped, can lead to weaknesses. In response to Australia being so isolated and alone, the culture has adapted certain behaviours: we have developed independence, resilience and survival skills (our strengths) but according to some of the 100 leaders interviewed, this has created a sense of arrogance and a view that we don't need the help of others nations or people (our weaknesses).

Australia has been accused of developing an over-enthusiastic sense of self. Its leaders must be honest about the country's capabilities and needs if it is to compete effectively. When people express their frustrations about the limitations of Australia, its growth potential and its place in Asia, that indicates that in their eyes, the country's leaders are not doing their best.

Being far-far-away from the powerhouses of the world may have disadvantaged us in the past because these powerhouses were mainly on the other side of the world. But we have the advantage now of our near location to the fast-growing and emerging economies of Asia, which presents Australia with a very different opportunity for the future.

Inward-looking island culture

When your country is not physically connected to another country, there is little need to consider anyone else. This does not originate from a desire to 'go it alone' or 'ignore the needs of others', but it can result in the formation of introspective attitudes and behaviours. I heard from many of the leaders interviewed that there are strains of these behaviours filtering their way through our business and society, which is not helpful.

These elements of an island culture arise out of a lack of close day-to-day contact with people from other cultures. Without neighbourly distractions or the need to consider others, you get used to only having to accommodate those within your own culture, so you have less tolerance for others and develop fewer skills in knowing how to work together for common good.

This can be a challenge for all island cultures, not just Australia, but the arrogance that people talk of above possibly comes from having been very successful throughout the 20th century despite the challenges of the distance and island status. Australia has much to be proud of in terms of its achievements and lifestyle, which attracts immigrants and tourists from every corner of the world. However, the less attractive qualities of the Australian culture outlined in Chapter 5, will not make us many friends.

Another feature of the local culture that people have remarked on is the competitiveness of the people, which is evident in all elements of Australian society – not only on the sports ground but also on the roads and in the workplace. Again this behaviour is both a strength of the culture and a weakness. With regard to the corporate sector one reason offered was that it is a very small market and there wasn't enough room for everyone (which is why returning expats and immigrants are expected to 'wait their turn').

When I came to live in Australia I observed something that I had not seen before, the very unusual behaviour between women in the corporate sector. As I described what I was seeing to others, they told me about a phenomenon that was common here but which I was oblivious to in all my years in New Zealand, Asia and Europe. They confirmed what I had seen was 'Women climbing the corporate ladder and pulling it up after them'. I had seen competition between people before, but I had not observed the lack of willingness to help other women get up there or the deliberate act of blocking the pathway for other women.

I was flabbergasted. How could I be so naïve? Why had I not seen that elsewhere? Was I walking about with my eyes closed in the other countries I had worked in or was this peculiar to Australia's culture?

It never occurred to me that any women after the long journey to get to the top, would not consider that supporting other women to get there too was the right thing to do. I started to wonder what underlying assumption of the Australian culture would have led to the formation of this attitude and behaviour. Why did women in Australia feel the need to protect their patch in this way? I now understood the concept of the Queen Bee.

In Chapter 5 a quote by Ann Sherry referred to Australia as a 'closed society' and in Chapter 7 Paul Waterman asked "Is it a sign of weakness if you are a woman and you lean down and pull other women up?" If the closed nature and competitiveness of our island culture has led us to fight among ourselves, how do we expect to be competitive regionally or on the world stage? How can we expect to achieve gender equality if women are unsupportive of one another?

If you recall Arni Hole's comment in Chapter 7, there is an important message for us there:

Corporate women climb the ladder and it's very competitive. It is okay to compete with men and women, but in Norway we have long-term solidarity between women. You can have solidarity and be an individual at the same time. You need solidarity among women to help each other because that's what men do; they have the old-boy network.

Arni Hole, Director General, Norwegian Royal Ministry for Children, Equity and Social Inclusion, Oslo, Norway

The message is: competition between individuals for jobs is okay, but to not stand by one another in the face of adversity is not too clever. The adversity here being 'male dominated workplaces' and for women not to support one another is a lost opportunity. Worse, for women to climb the ladder to executive and board levels and take on the norms of an exclusive male culture – adopting their male-oriented values and behaviours and not try to influence a more gender-balanced approach to operations at the top – invites the question 'What are they doing there?'

I really was surprised at the common knowledge and acceptance of the Queen Bee and ladder-retracting behaviours; it suggests that these are acceptable features of the Australian culture. The fact that women and men in Australia talk knowingly about these behaviours as if it were normal indicates that perhaps it is. I wondered what assumptions would drive this behaviour. Could they be:

- That people in the 'the old boy network' do not like women among its ranks so, if you manage to get there you need to behave like a male to survive, or at least camouflage yourself?

- That men don't believe women are equal, so don't make a nuisance of yourself or you will confirm their suspicions?
- That women who 'bang on' about women's rights cause problems for men and are excluded entry to positions of power and influence because they could be dangerous with that power?

Some other comments were offered on the subject of island culture:

Being on this island, no one can take it over and we have a 'she'll be right mate' attitude. We have the luxury of a higher standard of living and we cannot be threatened on our soil.

Russell Tipper, Chief Executive Officer, Brockman Resources, Perth, Australia

When we observe the rest of the world in a crisis, we don't necessarily buy into it. We see ourselves as observers not participants. We are aware of our smallness and we remark on it frequently. We are a small critical mass, isolated and distant from others. We are vitally aware of the teeming masses in the North: and we worry about the security issue.

There is one single thing that links the people of Sydney in 1795 and the people who live here today. It's the empty island syndrome. While everything else has changed this one thing connects us and will connect people 200 years from now. Australians are stewards of this empty island at the edge of the universe.

Bernard Salt, Partner, KPMG, Melbourne, Australia

The island mentality is strong here. You can't get people here to tell you what ethnicity they are willingly. When you ask people about their ethnicity, they don't seem to want to tell you. They don't want to be the nail that sticks out, you are either 'just' Australian, and if you are not, you are an outsider.

Paul Waterman, President. BP Australia, Melbourne, Australia

In 1901 Australia was first in the world for its standard of living and New Zealand was second. We slipped in the late 1980s but we are back up to number seven. We have slightly regained our mojo. The cause of the slip was Australia's excessive protectionism and isolation.

Phillip Ruthven, Chairman, IBIS World, Melbourne, Australia

There is a something in our corporate culture that says "if you leave us, it's like a divorce". It means "you turned your back on us... and we got on with our lives while you were away". It is like living in a remote country town and those who leave to pursue careers may find it difficult to get back in. It comes from the natural insularity of the isolation. It will be a great revelation when we are able to say "and you will always be welcome back".

Hugh Mackay, Social Researcher and Writer, Sydney, Australia

In addition to the incredible independence and resilience of the Australian people, they are also resourceful and tenacious and we can use all of these talents to our advantage. That is, we can apply these skills that have arisen out of our isolation and island situation, to address the challenges caused by the isolation and island situation. There is irony in the fact that the strengths, which have contributed to the weaknesses, can to also be used to address them.

Lack of cross-cultural experience

While Australians and New Zealanders alike, are known for their travelling spirit, both tend to either make one big annual trip to some far-far-away place or spend 6–12 months travelling around the world as young adults with a pack on their backs.

In contrast, people who live in Europe, the Middle East, Asia or South America might travel to a neighbouring country for a weekend or longer holiday 5, 10 or 15 times a year, each time going to a different country or region.

Through their more regular exposure to people in these countries they learn more about their cultures, understand their behaviours and become more skilled at working across cultures. For countries that are land-locked or share common borders with other countries there is often a more regular flow of immigrants from one nation to the next and the language and customs travel too.

For example, when you live in southern California you are surrounded by Mexican language, food and customs of the many people who have migrated across the border. In the north of the country, you can see and hear the influence of the neighbouring French Canadian culture. Likewise people in Switzerland are surrounded by four countries and the influences of these on Swiss society results in there being three main cultural regions within the one country – the German, French and Italian regions each have their own accent and slight variations of the language, food, music, art and so on.

Because of Australia's lack of physical neighbours and isolation, its people have less cross-cultural experience. When you live side by side with another country, your culture (assuming relations are amicable) sympathises with that of the other. Your food, art, music and languages are influencing each other and you can even start to take on each other's behaviours. There is a blending, which allows each culture to learn from the other.

The lack of cross-cultural exposure and subsequent appreciation is evident when you arrive in Australia from a more cross-culturally savvy nation. There is an apparent lack of interest by some Australians in visitors, immigrants and foreign workers.

Recently I was chatting with two people who migrated to Australia as a couple in 2002. I talked with them about this point and I asked them what their experiences were. They had both worked in several countries around the world (across North America, Asia and Europe) before settling in Australia. They are now in their 40s and both have university qualifications. They are well informed on matters of the world and are politically astute. Here are a couple of examples they shared with me:

The male partner is a French Canadian entrepreneur, musician, entertainer, recording artist and music teacher – he has his own electric blues band that he tours with internationally every year. We will call him Bernard.

Bernard is charming, extremely eloquent, interested in others and has a humble disposition. He speaks three languages and is highly educated. He speaks with a slight Canadian accent. He writes all his own songs and music, and plays guitar like the best. He has an array of students in his music school from 8 years old to 50. I asked him what his observations were about acceptance of other cultures in Australia. Bernard said "When I do my annual tours through Europe and Asia I find that people are interested in where you come from and what you do; they ask inquiring questions and seek to know more about you. When I tour Australia that doesn't happen; they don't seem interested."

The female partner is a German fashion and interiors designer who has worked for global fashion houses across Europe, Asia and America. We will call her Beatrix.

Beatrix is personally very stylish and has a 25-year career as a professional designer, interior decorator and trend forecaster for European, Japanese and US fashion and retail businesses. She also speaks three languages and is professionally and personally well networked. After 10 years in Australia, a long-time friend of hers (who is Australian) told her "You really don't fit in here, you'd be better off living in America where people would understand you better".

Her friend sought to be helpful but failed miserably. Feeling quite hurt Beatrix asked me what it was that made her so unacceptable and I replied "I can't answer why she made that remark, but I can tell you what I see as being your 'differences', which is what she might be referring to when she says you don't fit in. You have a slight accent, you speak quicker than the average Australian and you are not frightened to speak your mind. Perhaps she thinks you need to perfect the Australian accent, slow down and stop speaking your mind. As odd as it may seem; some people have no patience with others who are different."

So no matter what your skin colour, intolerance and bias exist. Both these Caucasian people are good-looking, stylishly dressed in a creative way, are worldly, educated, skilled, and multilingual, and still they are not fully accepted into Australia's multicultural society.

Their cross-cultural experience and multilingual skills make them well qualified to comment on how accepting Australia is as a multicultural society. I am sorry to tell readers that they, and many other skilled immigrants I have spoken with, think we have a long way to go to join the countries of the world which behave in a more accepting way towards people of different backgrounds and show interest in their journey and what they have to offer.

Anglo-Saxons rule a multicultural nation

Another interesting phenomenon of Australian culture is that despite the arrival of many non-Anglo-Saxon immigrants since the early 1880s and more particularly after WWII, the ruling class is still largely Anglo-Saxon and the English language dominates the affairs of government, business and all main aspects of society.

Let's take a brief look at the flow of immigrants to Australia:

- Australia's first immigrants arrived in 1788 from the UK and parts of Europe where the English language and Anglo-Saxon culture was established;
- The first Chinese immigrants arrived in 1818; more came during the gold rush and in the 1850s 40,000 Chinese arrived to capitalise on the gold rush along with Italians, French, Germans and Americans;
- Large numbers of Irish immigrants arrived in 1840 to escape the famine and between 1845 and WWII the Irish were the second largest group of immigrants after the British;
- Japanese fishermen arrived in the 1890s to work in the pearling industry, although most did not stay permanently, and Pacific Islanders, the majority being short-stay workers, arrived from 1863 to work in the Queensland plantations;
- Since 1945, WWII, nearly 7 million people have arrived and the main arrivals have been from Europe (UK, Italy, Germany, Greece, Yugoslavia, Netherlands, Spain and Austria); Middle East and Africa (Egypt, Malta, Lebanon and Turkey); Asia (India, Vietnam, Hong Kong, Philippines); New Zealand and the USA.

One in four Australians living here today was born overseas and almost another one in four has one parent born overseas. Every decade another 1 million immigrants arrive (average since the 1950s). There is no doubt that Australia is a multicultural society in one sense, yet people of Anglo-Saxon and European heritage still largely hold the majority of power and influence.

People from other ethnic backgrounds have not made their way to the top of corporate Australia, despite the fact that many businesses report that their graduate recruitment intake is 50 per cent native Australians and 50 per cent from a variety of Asian nations. What could be the reasons for their departure? Why are they opting-out?

Executives interviewed indicated that the main reasons were cultural and included:

- that the organisation culture is not tolerant of their ways or accepting of their difference, which makes them feel uncomfortable and unappreciated;
- that Western managers don't feel as comfortable working with or delegating to people of non-Western origin as they feel there are communication barriers to getting a good delegation which impacts on their ability to do a job (so the managers tend to go to employees with cultural backgrounds they better understand);
- that there are no Asian role models at senior management, executive management or on the board;
- that they hit their head on the metaphorical 'bamboo ceiling' finding it difficult to get recognition or meritocratic promotion.

There could be other reasons for their departure. They may have been homesick and returned to their homeland. They may have preferred to change industry sectors or to take a self-employment option. However, the pattern that emerges of the majority of Asians by their mid-career is similar to the profile of females leaving the corporate sector.

How can we call ourselves a multicultural society if we have only one main language and permit only one cultural group to control the power and influence? The effect is that one homogenous group makes all the economic, political and social decisions for people of all races and ethnic backgrounds. Why is it that in 2012 leaders of other ethnic and racial groups are not given equal right to share in the decision-making?

The big question is: do the people in power care about the waste? Do they even see the waste? Is it a cost they are prepared to accept to keep the status quo? If they are producing good results now, then perhaps the waste doesn't matter. But if they are not achieving the required growth and profitability, then perhaps it's time we talked more openly about how to change this situation.

The next decade (and beyond) offers massive growth throughout Asia: in particular, close neighbours China and India are going to take over as the two largest economies in the world. They are predicted to become Australia's largest trading partners and the main source of immigrants, foreign students and growth in inbound investment. With our own mature economy, can we hope to maintain the necessary growth to ensure our standard of living and status in the world without developing our regional connections and global trading operations?

Many of the 100 leaders interviewed think not. In Chapters 4 and 6 they shared their opinions about what needs to change. These changes, and their suggestions, need to be opened up for broader discussion leading to action.

The force field

The *force field* phenomenon – which keeps returning expats, women, skilled foreign workers and immigrants from rising to the top – came up in a number of places in Part Two. It is the unseen and unconscious barrier (or bias) that serves to keep people from reaching the top levels of our organisations: it keeps trespassers out.

Earlier Stephen Roberts of Citi described the parochialism he experienced when he returned to Australia after being away for 17 years. I, too, experienced 'the hand in the face' as I tried to access opportunities in my first few years in Australia. I had to get enough notches on my metaphorical belt and get some local experience as there was little interest in the experience I obtained from my ten years working with global organisations in Asia or Europe.

I recently spoke with two other Australian male executives who returned from overseas postings to Singapore and New Zealand in the past 12 months. Let's call them Dave and Dan. Both men are early 40s, one has a solid career in the food and beverage sector and worked overseas for six years in Singapore and New Zealand. The second man has a blue-chip experience in funds management. He worked in Singapore for almost five years.

When they returned to Australia, Dave and Dan were faced with two things in common. First, that no one was interested in learning about their experience abroad and that it did not add value to the recruitment conversation. They said when they started to talk about their experiences the person listening would display a lack of interest and change the subject. Second, they had to go backwards in their careers to secure employment. Both are now working at a level below their experience, for less money, and feel disappointed in their fellow countrymen.

This parochial behaviour, which I call the *force field* seems to affect most new arrivals to some extent and it seems we have come to accept it as part of the

Australian culture. I know this because I questioned some Australian nationals about the existence of the *force field* and they did recognise the behaviour and either laughed it off or shuddered at the thought of it; but all thought it was poor form.

The *force field* is a mechanism which has been set up, consciously or unconsciously, by those who hold the power to manage who gets into the inner group; the top layers of the organisations. It is not necessarily a behaviour exclusive to Australia, but it does not sit well in a country that promotes egalitarianism, meritocracy and multiculturalism.

The Anglo-Saxon and male domination of politics, business and society combined with the *force field* which protects it must appear so unattractive to people who do not fit the mould. But that is not the greatest cost to our society: the apathy that I hear from people who are resigned to the fact that these limitations exist and who cannot do anything about it is the greatest cost.

If the majority of the people living in Australia believe they can never reach the top or that the battle to push through the barriers of the *force field* to get to the top is too great, then are we suffering as a nation? What greater performance are we missing? What heights could we reach as a nation if the pathways to the top were open to anyone based on merit, no matter the gender, race, colour, age or sexual orientation?

If in Australia we are not embracing the talent as it arrives, by making returning expats wait and blocking immigrants of other cultures to 'the good life' until the second generation, then we are not accessing the skill and knowledge available, which equates to loss of productivity and impacts on growth.

I worry that if corporate Australia's *force field* continues to repel newly arrived skilled foreign workers, returning Australian expats and immigrants, the best people might just stop coming. How do we know that this is not already happening? How do we know that the best skills available don't consider Australia a viable option?

Outside influences on performance

The first thing to remember is that the performance of your organisation culture is influenced by your country culture and the individual culture of the founders and subsequent leaders. The country culture is the dominant culture in the Culture Circuit. The flow is impacted by other cultures that are introduced to your organisation by the people who work there.

Employees' attitudes and behaviours can positively and negatively impact performance

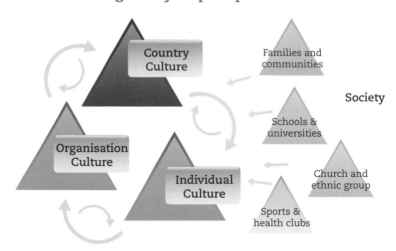

Every new person joining your culture brings with them assumptions, values, beliefs and behaviour that they adopted from their previous cultural experiences. Sometimes you might hire people from a certain background to bring in the values you seek. Other times you might avoid hiring people from certain industry or company backgrounds whose values don't fit yours. Recruiters and hiring managers often use psychometric and other testing to help identify behavioural traits that will fit, or not fit, their organisation.

In addition to the cultural influences (values and behaviours) that your people bring in with them, those in your supply chain also have an impact. From suppliers to industry bodies and customers, all the cultures have an impact. And as all the cultures are primarily influenced by country culture, then country culture is the first place to look for change.

Spot unhelpful behaviours in the value-chain

The diagram below is an example of an organisation in the IT sector servicing clients in the telecommunications industry. Suppliers to both industries and their industry associations all have values, behaviours and business artefacts that impact how business is done.

Let's look at this industry example. The IT and telecoms sectors attract few females. You need to ask what it is about these sectors and the nature of work that lacks appeal to women. Are the things that deter females from entering these careers behavioural (the way women are treated), functional (the roles women are channelled into), technical (the nature of the work) or strategic (the career pathways and demands they make on the individual)? Conversely, these

Industry and client values impact your performance too

sectors attract a large number of Asians by comparison with other industries and they often have a more highly diverse cultural mix of employees.

Problems in sectors considered to be non-traditional or inappropriate for females can be self-perpetuating. IT suppliers wishing to attract telecom clients might use more masculine language and symbols in their sales and marketing than they realise. If so they are appealing to the dominant gender they are presented with – reinforcing beliefs of females. This can alienate the few females present and those outside looking in and leave them feeling undervalued. Male owners and leaders who are used to dealing mainly with males, may have written policies and built organisation systems that favour men – not consciously but in response to the situation at the time. We need to check our old behaviours and question whether they continue to be relevant.

The way in which suppliers and industry associations interact with clients in male-dominated industries can reinforce male values and behaviours – and vice versa. As you know, the flow of influence in the Culture Circuit goes both ways.

Insist on diversity in your value-chain

If you recall in Part Two, Paul Waterman, President, BP Australia, described how he changed the way he briefed his recruiters to force a change in their behaviour. When he started to ask "Why don't we employee females to marketing and sales roles?" he realised part of the responsibility lay with the suppliers: their recruiters seldom presented women as candidates. The recruiters had a preconception about the type of people BP wanted to hire. Once BP insisted on having gender equality in the selection process, the recruiters started to identify women who were skilled and experienced for the job. You will recall Paul said that the woman they appointed to VP Marketing was quieter than the men, she did not beat her chest and go drinking with the boys but she did do an excellent job and delivered results in her own way, which was different from men.

In doing this, Paul initiated the shift of industry assumptions that "Only males were appropriate for sales and marketing roles at BP", and that "Hiring managers would not consider females" and "BP's clients would only buy from males".

It would help if leaders were to think more broadly about the impact their organisation cultures have on minority groups. In a speech given by a female mining engineer at a conference I heard about the challenges she faced when she first joined a mining company. The overalls in the stock room were for large men and even the crotch of the smallest size was down around her knees. The toilets and sleeping arrangements were all for men and when down in the mine site she was aware that men were very uncomfortable with her presence. Mining historically was established for male workers in the days when women stayed at home. The industry has not evolved to accommodate females with engineering degrees who would like a career in the sector. Men and women need to work together to fix this so that they can attract females to this exciting and thriving industry.

Watch for discriminatory habits

Every year major suppliers entertain their clients and other stakeholders by hosting events that involve golf days, horse-racing events, rugby championships and other male-oriented sports. The message this conveys to everyone watching – men and women – is that females have not been considered, are not expected to attend, or that they are less important in the relationship between the two organisations.

What messages do these activities send to Asian, Muslim and other employees who do not drink alcohol or enjoy the Australian style of male entertainment? It seems that these activities are suited only to the local Australian male population who like sports and drinking.

With the increasing number of senior females in management and on boards, and with our increasingly multicultural communities, companies need to rethink the habits they practise and question the habits and practices of suppliers and clients too. As country culture is the common and dominant feature in every organisation's Culture Circuit, we need our country's leaders to rethink the impact that Australia's culture, under their leaderships, is having on our industries and businesses. They have the power and the mandate to lead culture change.

Eliminate economic and opportunity costs

Here are some of the costs that the current situation, as described by the 100 leaders above, place on industries and businesses in our economy:

Business costs of being far-far-away and having an island culture

- Limited ability to attract skills and experience from other countries due to our isolation, costs of travel and lack of connectedness to the world.
- Lack of understanding of the relative problem, due to limited overseas exposure, means we don't look for solutions to the compensating behaviours we have developed.
- Insufficient experience of what cross-cultural management of highly diverse nations or businesses looks like (or what benefits they deliver), so how do we know what we need to build?
- Our independence means we don't need others for much, so we don't appreciate what we could have if we collaborated and shared more with other cultures.
- No burning platform and no vision of what is missing (or what it could be like) so there's no driver for cultural evolution or change.

Business costs of cross-cultural inexperience and Anglo-Saxon dominance

- Tendency to disappoint employees from other cultures – losing them early in their career.
- Confidence in our own capability and happy with our performance, so not open to looking at what others can offer.
- Homogenous decision-making groups may lack insight into the needs of cross-cultural customers and therefore miss opportunities.
- Limited innovation when you have people from the same cultural background looking at complex problems.
- Lack of exposure, learning and growth that comes from working amongst highly diverse teams.
- Limited success when operating your business in other countries.

Business costs of the *force field*

- Lack of diversity on a board or executive team limits problem-solving and decision-making to the experiences of the homogenous group.
- Their decisions are perceived to lack credibility and therefore their decisions are either overtly questioned or passive-aggressively undermined.
- Those who are not permitted beyond the *force field* opt out of their careers early as they see no pathway to the top beyond mid-management.

- Many highly skilled and experienced people and ideas are not getting into senior decision-making roles, which limits Australia's competitiveness in the region and global markets.

How do we evolve Australia's country culture?

First we need to identify the assumptions at the bottom of the culture that drive the top layers.

As we read in Chapter 4, the government's White Paper 'Australia in the Asian Century' detailed 25 objectives to be met by 2025 but they all related to changes at the top of the country culture. To effectively and sustainably implement these 25 developments, leaders in government, business and society need to address assumptions, values and beliefs held by people living in Australia which are *not aligned* to these objectives.

They need to 'jolt' the culture: as we saw with the introduction of the Carbon Tax and as you will see in the three company cases in Chapter 11, a 'jolt' to the culture creates a revolutionary change that facilitates a significant leap forward.

The first step is to identify the elements at each layer of the country's Culture Iceberg.

I have made a start on this below by taking a selection of remarks made by the 100 leaders as recorded in Part Two and matched them to the appropriate layers of Australia's Culture Iceberg. These are indicative only (a comment I have placed as an indicator of an 'assumption' may also be describing a 'value') but they do give you a sense of how things we say are representative of the assumptions we make, the beliefs we hold and the attitudes we express.

As you read through the comments again below, remember that the interviews were made in light of a narrowly focused discussion on cultural and gender diversity, the growth opportunities in Asia and the aspects of Australian society that impact on leadership and social change.

If we were to do the exercise relating to different aspects of Australian business and society we would obtain different information. When you read these tables you'll get a sense of the challenges we face, but remember there is much that is good about Australia's culture which might not have come out whilst exploring the topic of diversity and growth.

Indications of Australian Culture can be found in these remarks made by the 100 leaders:

(We will review the assumptions first – and work from the bottom of the iceberg upwards – as that is how the influences flow)

Assumptions are indicated by these remarks:

- We still teach French and German in schools and we are still focused on London and New York (assumption: our interests are best served by Western allies)
- If we are going to grow the mining sector then some other sector has to shrink (assumption: mining rules Australian industry, or we can't grow the pie)
- We have not learned Asian languages or made a collective effort as a nation to engage with Asian nations (assumption: we don't need Asia)
- Australia is a sexist place; I see men drinking a lot of beers and the ladies gravitate to the kitchen (assumption: men can enjoy mateship while leaving responsibility to women)
- All through school people called me a foreigner, once Australians get to know people from other cultures, it gets better (assumption: immigrants cannot be accepted until they have done their time)
- They say they can't find great women for boards but they are only looking for lawyers and accountants (assumption: only female lawyers and accountants are worthy equals of males on boards)
- Men on boards say they want diversity but they are much more comfortable with what they have got: an all-male team. Typically they select people who will agree with them and won't attempt to challenge their way (assumption: females rock the boat and upset the status quo)
- There is something in the Australian culture that prevents us from being aggressive on targets, people say they won't set targets (assumption: egalitarianism means we can decide for ourselves, not be told what to do)
- I don't think that we will get anywhere without quotas (assumption: men will always resist gender equality and they are in control)

Begin challenging your own assumptions. Your assumptions are your windows on the world. Scrub them off every once in a while, or the light won't come in.

Alan Alda, American actor, director, screenwriter and author

Values are indicated by these remarks:

- Our government maintains stronger relationships with America and the UK than it does with Asia (value: Western allies)
- Australia should be opening its doors to so many more people but we are not willing to do that (value: isolation, lifestyle, exclusivity)
- I think we are good at multiculturalism: you can see people of mixed cultures in sports, the arts and music (value: mixed cultures)
- Multiculturalism is an excuse for indifference. It is still pale, stale and male. We have a very macho culture, therefore it is culturally difficult (value: males are more valued than females)
- Australians excel because they are more competitive and ambitious (value: winning, achievement)
- There are a few less egalitarian places in the world; people ask "What school did you go to?" so that they can categorise you (value: status)
- People in Australia like to work but they want work–life balance, this has become an important value (value: work–life balance)
- The short-term attitude is a hindrance. There are no long-term plans and we are not good at investing in our future (value: immediacy)
- There is still racism in Australia and it is generally directed to the most recent arrivals (value: white Australia)
- When politicians talk about stopping immigrants, it shows a lack of insight into the needs of corporate Australia (value: restricting population growth)
- Mateship almost got constitutionalised. It is a vehicle for the exclusion of women by men (value: gender segregation)
- You can turn 12 pages of the Australian Financial Review before you will see a picture of a woman and it is likely to be an advertisement of an attractive long-legged woman with a big smile carrying shopping bags. All the wrong messages are still going out and it is building up in our children's DNA through what they see and experience every day. (values: men's opinion count more; women are the entertainment)
- Motherhood is a sacred cow. It's taboo. It is precious and wrapped up in political correctness (value: a woman's place is in the home)

Attitudes are indicated by these remarks:

- We are not addressing the Chinese tourist market correctly
- When it comes to Asia it seems like we have been arguing about who to align with for decades
- The UK is becoming less important and Asia is becoming increasingly important to the Australian economy
- Australians who come up to Asia can be a little arrogant. Some almost lecture Asian people on how things are done in Australia as if that is how it should be done here too
- Hiring managers in Australia are generally risk averse so they will seek out people with local experience, others have to wait and prove themselves
- Australia is a good society, but unfortunately there are strains of racism
- There are some people who are passionate about diversity; others are just not interested
- When people come to Australia we like them to appreciate our culture as a mark of respect and dignity. This works both ways
- Most organisations nowadays have women somewhere in their pipeline but for some reason they (the executives) say they are not ready
- It is a closed society and international experience is not well rewarded; skills/talents acquired elsewhere have no value in Australia
- I refused to join women-only groups and I won't speak to women-only audiences because it feels hypocritical to have female-only functions

As you grow older, you will discover that you have two hands, one for helping yourself, the other for helping others.

Audrey Hepburn, (1929-1993) British actress and humanitarian

Behaviours are indicated by these remarks:

- I am struck by the lack of cultural awareness between Australia and its Asian neighbours
- There is increasing demand by corporate Australia for cultural and language training
- We say we are part of Asia and want the best talent, but our behaviour says the opposite. It's the same with women and meritocracy, we say yes but our behaviour says the opposite
- A lot of companies send people overseas, but when they get back there is no space for them to return to
- There is a huge 'can-do' attitude in this country and Australia is very pioneering
- The media are harder on women than men when they stumble
- Socially there is definitely segregation between men and women
- There is a passive-aggressive culture here; people don't challenge the bosses; there's no overt resistance, it's underlying resistance
- The isolation and the delusion that we are special make us self-centred and self-interested
- It's a male dominated society. Women take the line of least resistance. They go off and find a different way to survive: they start their own businesses.
- In Australia we want people to do well, but not too well. You are not to be outstanding. We want people to live in a 'the Goldilocks zone' – not too much and not too little
- Women aren't always the best supporters of each other. Working women are not always supportive of nonworking mothers and vice versa
- I have always found extremely successful businesswomen very scary. They would ignore me at conferences and turn their back on me
- It's a shame there are those women who pull the ladder up behind them when they get to the top. It is because no one helped them and they feel that others shouldn't need help either
- Men are being pressured to share the domestics at home and to be more involved with child-minding by working wives. Some feel that the jobs are now going to women and they feel discriminated against
- Women have to have a toughness to get to the top in a male environment but then they get criticised for it. They get called 'aggressive'

Artefacts are indicated by these remarks:

- Our inadequate child-care systems make it hard for more women to build careers
- There is a hangover from the *Keep Australia White* policy
- The university system is biased towards private school students because the entrance criterion is based solely on grades so immigrants are very unlikely to get in
- Cultural diversity is at a low level in Australia; it gets more 'white' as you go up the ladder
- There is a noticeably different ethnic composition in the under-35 group – Asians join companies but reject the system before mid-level
- Our media has a lot to do with a lack of cultural diversity: they report nationality saying when its an Asian or African (never a Caucasian)
- Having one 'stay at home' parent is such a binary concept…it affects Australia's productivity and the workforce participation rates of women
- We are still predominantly white. There are many cities and towns of Australia with little exposure to non-white people
- If being multicultural means that we need a multicultural parliament, then no, we are not multicultural
- SBS conducted a survey on national attitudes towards asylum seekers. It showed 45 per cent of the population was found in some way to have anti-refugee sentiments
- People say we are a meritocracy. That's simply not true. We need to ask male board members and executives "Why do all the smart people look like you?"
- We know that 60 or more of the top ASX200 still have no women on the board at all
- Women are as well educated as men and ultimately they should get 50 per cent of the roles
- Many of the most successful women in high-level positions don't have children

The above remarks illustrate how we come to form knowledge about cultures. 100 people provided these valuable insights into how things get done – or don't get done – in Australia. The placement about whether something is a value or an attitude is subjective and just as people can debate 'what is a vision' and 'what is a mission' at length, so can people argue where in the Culture Iceberg something best sits.

My advice is don't get hung up on placement – just focus on identifying the assumptions, align them to your future plans and then everything above will fall into place. The opinions shared by the 100 leaders have helped us to uncover some of the challenges of Australian culture and this valuable contribution highlights what we can do to help change it.

How can you contribute to change?

Each and every one of us can help influence a shift in the assumptions and values of Australia. Each of us has the capacity to share the issues identified by this research with people in our own cultural groups. All we need to do is talk with them about the challenges we face and need for change. If everyone just takes one small step each – that's 22.7 million steps towards a better future.

I know it is not always easy to start these conversations, but it is always possible. Here's an example. Towards the end of 2012 I was at my son's school attending a meeting between a dozen parents who assist in school communications and events and the Principal. It was my first time there so I was sitting quietly observing the protocol. On the agenda there was an item called 'Feedback on *Women's Dinner* and *Secret Men's Business Dinner*' – two fund-raising events that had occurred in the month prior.

I had already conveyed my curiosity about the title of these events to the fund-raising executive a few months before. I highlighted that the design and branding of these events (which I understood dated back 5–10 years) were at odds with the current message that the school's working parents from the city were getting from their company leaders and the ASX about gender role modelling and biased behaviour. I explained that marketing executives in the city would be less inclined to run segregated events as they send messages that would be unhelpful to achieving gender diversity.

When we reached this agenda item I had no intention of raising the matter again: I didn't want to spoil the general euphoria the group was sharing about the success of these two fundraising events, or offend the people who had been involved in running them. However, I thought about my appeal to readers of this book to step up and to 'speak up' and decided I needed to take this opportunity to convey information and canvass opinion about the ongoing appropriateness of the events and their branding. I felt a little nervous at the likely reaction, but I felt I couldn't come back to my desk that day to carry on writing this book if I wasn't prepared to speak up.

I asked "Has anyone ever questioned the names of these events and what they convey to the children, or whether we should segregate the genders, or whether this is the right thing to do given that many of the working parents attending these events are responsible for removing gender bias and delivering gender targets to the ASX?"

Many of the mothers present were not working people so I got a mild reaction at first. So I restated the questions and provided a little insight into my research findings, which was news for most there. I explained what was happening in the business community and how stereotyping in schools and society reinforced outdated notions of both gender roles, which impacted on the industries and job types that attracted or repelled females, how long they stayed in careers and the kind of behaviour young males felt they needed to live up to.

I answered the objections and restated the facts and eventually, when presented with the information, about four of the dozen parents expressed an 'aha' moment and I could see a shift began to occur. Others conveyed later that day that a review was probably the right thing to do.

From time to time we need to question the traditions that once served us so well and that we treasure as being an important part of our culture. As circumstances around us change, the traditional way of doing things may no longer be relevant.

Change takes a while when you rely on influencing; but if we all take steps to influence others, that is a very good place to start. I am sure every one of you has these opportunities too. Perhaps you might look for one today.

How can you help influence the Australian culture to evolve?

How can you encourage a shift in behaviours?

To shift assumptions you need to 'jolt' people and groups out of The Comfort Zone and remove the belief that outdated behaviors are acceptable. Here are some examples for you to consider:

- If you are a **political leader** you could legislate change that will stop people from acting in a way that creates inequality and install negative stimulus to penalise those who ignore the new behaviour guidelines.
- If you are a **business owner** you could confirm your commitment to gender and cultural equality by promoting men and women equally. You could also promote only those managers who can deliver diversity targets.
- If you are a **purchasing officer** you could advise suppliers that your company only deals with organisations that match your diversity commitment and can illustrate gender and culture balancing.
- If you are an **entry-level employee** you could request that hiring

Everyone in business and society can influence culture change

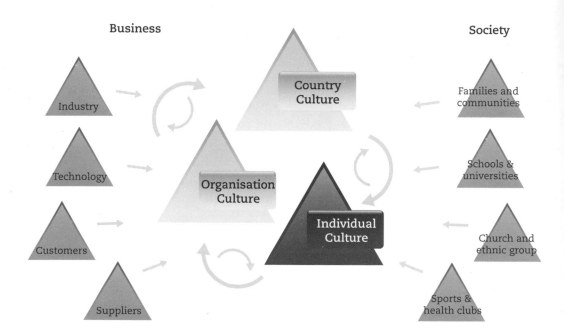

managers demonstrate there is no glass or bamboo ceilings and to outline your career path milestones and timeframes.

- If you are a **working mother** you could stop doing 80 per cent of the household chores and insist that your partner takes up 50 per cent of the admin and chores or helps you to pay for home help.
- If you are a **father** who would like to cut back to 3 or 4 days a week to share the child care with your partner then seek out employers who will offer that and companies that have properly adjusted systems to accommodate part-timers without bias.
- If you are **a lone female board member** and feel constrained from speaking up to champion females then look for a different board that already has women on it so that you can build critical mass and be taken seriously.
- If you are **an Asian manager** seeking a CEO position, look for companies that can demonstrate there is no bias towards non-Anglo-Saxons at top levels, and those companies that have a commitment to doing business in Asia.

- If you are **a school teacher** identify any gender biases and stereotyping teaching methods, and playground activities that force children to take up outdated gender roles. Encourage them to try activities outside their comfort zone.
- If you are **a local mayor** you could influence a shift in perceptions in your community and remove old attitudes and behaviours by putting male receptionists on the front desk and hiring female rangers; and ensure the cultural mix of staff reflects your community.
- If you are **a CEO of a national sports club** be sure that your male teams don't travel business class to sporting events while your female teams fly economy. Ensure the female prize money is equal to the males, that skill development opportunities are equal and remove any barriers that prohibit people of different cultural backgrounds from participating equally.
- If you are **a head of a drama school** actively build in characters into every production that educate audiences about gender and cultural issues and the positive community contributions that everyone can make.

Every one of the culture groups you belong to can influence what happens at work and in society. Examining the players in your Culture Circuit is a good place to start the ball rolling.

Chapter 10

Redirecting your Individual Culture

"I felt so full of gratitude and humility that I clasped my hands in front of me, closed my eyes and said a silent prayer of thanks to God... I had at last achieved something I'd wanted for so long... My insides bubbled with happiness. It was a dream come true. "

Cathy Freeman, indigenous Australian, former 400-metre sprinter and Olympic and Commonwealth Games gold medallist.

Dreams do come true if you *set your mind*. To set *your mind* means to apply dedication, persistence and time. That's what Cathy Freeman did. That's what all Olympians do. They visualise themselves crossing the winning line and they believe it to be true. They can see it. They see themselves in the future having achieved a major accomplishment.

Driving oneself to achieve personal goals is a major challenge and should not be underestimated. But, as a leader, you will need to drive others to achieve a beneficial outcome for a group. That is a different challenge because it requires you to get your followers' attention.

When Martin Luther King, Jr delivered his 'I have a dream' speech on 28 August 1963, he too visualised what the future would look like. He visualised a country where African-Americans could walk freely amongst and equal to white people, where they could sit at the same table and where they would *'not be judged by the colour of their skin but by the content of their character'*. His dream was for a whole nation, an entire cultural group to move to a better place and achieve better things. He dedicated his life to changing the culture of America, by asking for a shift in assumptions, attitudes and behaviours towards coloured people.

The impact of individual culture on the Culture Circuit

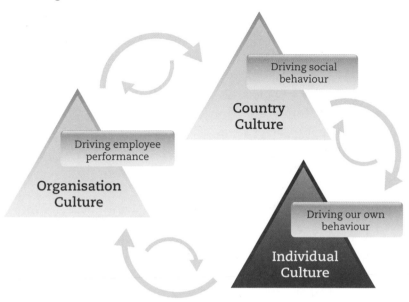

As a leader you get the opportunity every day to convey your vision for a brighter and better future – for Australia, your business, your local town, the cricket club you belong to and the family you are part of. The challenge though, is bringing the people in your cultural group along with you. When we talk about leadership we are actually talking about followship. You are surrounded by people who are looking for guidance and direction; they are looking for you to model for them how things should be done.

The members of a cultural group are sometimes actively looking for their leaders to show them the way, to articulate the future, to know the best way for the group to get where it wants to go. Other times, group members are happy with the way things are and avoid change at all costs. Both appointed and self-selected 'natural' leaders carry a responsibility to think about the future, guide their followers through difficult times and help find new horizons.

Your ability to be the best leader you can be, hinges on your individual culture: the assumptions and beliefs you hold about what you are capable of impacts on your self-belief, the way you behave and ultimately your performance. By understanding your assumptions and values better, you can 'unpick' the ones that don't serve you well and evolve them. Like an Olympic champion, understanding what might limit you from performing at your best is the first step to your next win. Get yourself a coach and start attending to those limitations.

On the following pages I share some stories that will help make that happen for you.

This chapter covers:

- The relevance of a leader's individual culture;
- How to change individual culture: challenging old assumptions and allowing your individual culture to evolve:
  - the story of a leader who found his limitation;
  - my own journey to illustrate how I shifted assumptions;
- Three personal stories by men who have adjusted their individual cultures to support career wives.

Influences on your own culture

In Chapter 8 we looked at the Culture Circuit and discovered that the most influential culture in our individual circuit is the country culture, followed by our personal and unique cultures – family, community, religion and school. Every one of us has an opportunity to grow and evolve our individual cultures. We all evolve at a different pace depending on the number and type of cultures we are exposed to.

A leader's individual culture has many infuences

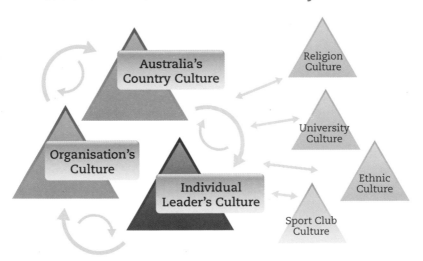

Why would we consciously want to review and evolve our own individual culture? Why would we not just accept what we have been taught by our parents and get on with living day-to-day as best we can? When discussing values with one of the leaders interviewed, he offered me this:

My values came from my home and it's very hard to change the values you get from your home. People grow up with all kinds of prejudices that they get from their parents. It's the schools that can help to change things; that's where it should start.

(Anon – pseudonym Eric) non-executive board director.

I really enjoyed my interview with this board member: he had great examples of gender diversity in his companies and some very interesting stories to share. However, I was perplexed when he conveyed that he was unable to change the prejudices he obtained from his parents and said responsibility to change society should be done in schools. I know many people actually believe there is nothing they can do to change who they are, so in this chapter we will look at how you can change your own assumptions.

Of course I agree that schools have a big role in shaping the values and behaviour that our children adopt, but they cannot alone achieve culture change. Our political leaders supported by leaders in business, sports and communities have to direct that achievement. The education curriculum, budgets, policies and programs are all artefacts at the top of Australian culture – but they alone cannot shift it.

That said, the values, attitudes and behaviours of a school's culture and a teacher's culture will transfer to the children in their charge to some degree. So it is right that schools can help address the challenge, or hinder it. But schools are only part of the solution.

There's another quote I'd like to share with you. This one comes not from one of the 100 leaders interviewed but from one who was invited to interview but was not available. Instead he emailed me his thoughts and said:

The subject you are writing about is very important and I think you are starting to get at the heart of the real issues.

I have moved a long way past the rhetoric and the fad – I remain frustrated at the deeply seated cultural biases in Australia, the business community, my own company, and of course, in my own behaviour … that prevents [us building] an environment based on merit –independent of gender, race, physical ability, creed etc.

However, there are concrete actions we all must take to drive change.

(Anon – pseudonym Charles) CEO, ASX100

He did not say what 'the concrete actions we must all take' are, but I know his company has a diversity council, a dedicated diversity function, people and programs. The big question is – if this CEO feels frustrated that the challenges remain, despite their efforts over many years, what is the cause of his frustration and what can he do about overcoming it?

Both these leaders are challenged – one because he knows he has a problem and is trying to address it (Charles), the other because he doesn't realise that his culture will be drifting and his challenge is yet to present itself (Eric). The difference between these two leaders of Australian business is that one is accepting responsibility for leading cultural change and the other is leaving it to the schools.

These examples illustrate the relevance of a leader's individual culture.

We know that Charles' assumption is that good can come from change and improvement and that he values a better world; his frustration implies he has been actively seeking ways to achieve culture change to deliver diversity. Eric on the other hand has expressed his assumption that prejudices we acquire throughout our childhood are a life sentence. His inaction implies that he values constancy and is prepared to live with the status quo, and that schools should address these issues. This also implies he is prepared to wait for the next generation to make the changes needed.

A leader of any cultural group holds great responsibility to manage the evolution of its Culture Iceberg. These two examples represent two of the most challenging states that a leader of any cultural group can be in:

- The conscious frustrated state – when you are trying to effect cultural change by encouraging the members of your cultural groups to adopt new ways of behaving so that you can realise your ambitions, but the forces of the existing culture are working against you so they are not following your lead;
- The unconscious, oblivious, state – when you are unaware, or unprepared to recognise, that your Culture Iceberg is drifting or that it may end up on a collision course, destined for rough waters and possible disaster.

If you are not conscious of the challenges of your culture or of its drift, your lack of guidance over its direction will be increasing its potential to collide or implode as members become confused and disillusioned about its purpose and destination.

When you are consciously looking for ways to direct your culture, and if your members are slow to respond or don't follow easily, it is more likely that you are suffering from some of the culture blind spots described in

Chapter 8. Identify and address the blind spots as early as you can because your individual efforts will be insufficient to turn around a firmly embedded culture.

As a leader, your individual culture is highly relevant to the culture of the organisations you lead. Your assumptions influence those of the organisation and your attitudes and behaviours are observed and modelled by the group members.

Proving assumptions wrong

Before you address the culture of your organisation, club or community, you'd do well to check your own individual culture to enable your best performance as a leader of change.

Contrary to Eric's view we can, and some people do, change our assumptions, values, beliefs, attitudes and behaviours at any point in our lives. What helps us to do that is to receive data or information that disproves the assumptions (the foundations of our culture) we already hold. Here's a trivial example to show how assumptions can be challenged and changed.

Say you live in a rural town close to the coast. You were raised on the assumption that there were no longer any fish in the local river and for 20 years you watched your parents drive to the ocean to catch the dinner. One day your assumptions are shattered as you walk down to the river and see 10 people standing there hauling in large barramundi on their lines.

Instantly the assumptions held by your family and the local community, that the river was incapable of sustaining life, would be put into question and your beliefs about whether fish lived there would be reversed. You would suddenly value the river's new life source and possibly bring your fishing gear next time you are passing and try your luck (a newly adopted behaviour). Your individual Culture Iceberg would be changed by the old assumptions becoming void, and new assumptions becoming the truth.

When it comes to overturning the prejudices and biases we hold about people from other cultures or gender roles we need two things:

- disconfirming data proving the old assumptions are incorrect or outdated plus a display of new assumptions;
- willingness to accept the new assumptions and preparedness to allow the higher-level elements of the Culture Iceberg to evolve (the threat of losing power, status or wealth as a result of a change can lead to resistance, covert and overt).

Resistance to change is common. Humans are hard-wired to resist change as it upsets the equilibrium, the comfort, the status quo. Change requires work. Sometime it is hard work; always it is different work. Cultures and people that are used to change are generally adaptable and perform well under conditions of change.

Identifying assumptions

Every time you move about the Culture Circuit you have the opportunity to evolve your individual culture a little.

When you get a new job you are exposed to a new organisation culture. The new culture may have been formed on different assumptions than those you have experienced before, so you are put in the position of having to accept them or reject them.

Similarly, every time you move to a new country or city, or join a new university or swimming club, you are exposed to a new culture, formed from different assumptions. Generally speaking, the more new and different cultures you experience, the more adaptable you become – although this assumes you don't go through life with a 'I reject anything that I didn't invent' banner stuck to your forehead.

Also, the more cultures you experience, the more skilled you will become at identifying assumptions. Because assumptions are 'taken-for-granted' and hidden at the bottom of a culture, they are very hard to see and understand. It generally takes an independent, trained eye to search them out; it is often too hard to find the unconscious drivers of your own behaviour.

Running a culture survey, to identify the elements of culture that are above the waterline by asking individuals to share their views, can help. If you seek to identify the values, beliefs, attitudes and behaviours, you can then try to extrapolate the assumptions from these. However this can be a challenge for people living within the culture to do for themselves. Getting help from someone outside your culture who is familiar with how cultures operate will help you to be more objective. And you'll possibly discover the truth more quickly and fully.

When you join new cultures, which are all formed on different assumptions, think through what you are experiencing and find a reference point for it in your own mind. Sometimes you will feel a good fit and you'll unconsciously adapt your culture (e.g. belief or attitude) to accommodate the new learning. This is a positive and happy experience. At other times, you might not find a reference point that fits with your belief system and this may be a less comfortable and less happy experience.

To fit in (stay in the culture) or opt out (leave the cultural group to find another) – that is your choice. If you stay for too long in a country culture or organisation culture that that does not fit your individual culture, your behaviour will become dysfunctional (relative to the rest of the group). Or, if you suppress your feelings of not 'fitting in', you'll not be able to be who you really are and that will begin to fell oppressive. Either way it is not healthy.

Each culture we experience influences our assumptions

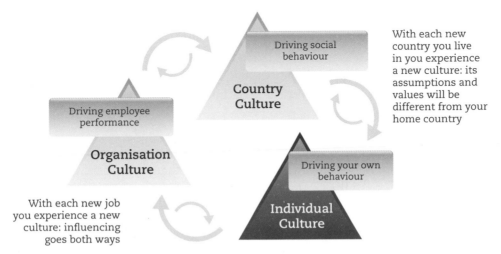

With each new country you live in you experience a new culture: its assumptions and values will be different from your home country

Driving social behaviour

Country Culture

Driving employee performance

Organisation Culture

With each new job you experience a new culture: influencing goes both ways

Driving your own behaviour

Individual Culture

How you can shift assumptions

Here's a story of one of my earliest personal observations of how you can modify your own individual culture by shifting an assumption, which changes your self-belief and enhances your leadership behaviour.

Back in 1990 I had a client in New Zealand named Brett. He was the co-founder of a loss-adjusting practice. In the mid-1980s he and his partner had decided to make a national chain through a series of mergers and acquisitions. Soon after they did this they sold their newly formed national business to an international loss-adjusting company.

In a very short period of time, Brett went from being an owner-operator of a small private partnership to the Managing Director New Zealand of a global business reporting to bosses in Geneva. He was faced with the challenges of systematically integrating the many newly acquired business operations, moulding a single firm culture and learning how to lead this initially disparate group of professionals from many disciplines, industries and trades.

Brett approached me to support him on this journey and specifically to guide him and his executive team to prepare the new company's first-ever strategic plan. One day, as we were planning to roll out the executive team's vision and plans, I detected that he was a little anxious about his leadership speech. I was mystified: here was a man who regularly addressed industry conferences to deliver technical papers, yet for some reason my suggestion that he share his vision, hopes and dreams for the new company in an inspiring and impassioned talk unnerved him.

When I enquired I discovered that there were two issues:

- Firstly he had two styles – one for work and one for his personal life. He had learned from observation as a young accountant that the business of accounting and loss-adjusting was technical, factual and commercial. These were assumptions he had adopted from the industry Culture Iceberg as his own and they influenced the way he behaved at work.
- Secondly he had not previously had to actively 'gain followship'. In his small private practice everyone knew each other and there was an informal personal connection. Leadership went with professional excellence. Now with hundreds of people spread across 18 offices, most of them new, he had to provide something that would capture their attention, earn their respect, get them to follow his vision of the future and obtain their commitment to help.

The second of these was vital because, having just sold the national practice at profit to their new international owners, ongoing results and growth required that he pull that team together quickly.

At that point I remembered that he once told me he was religious and that from time to time he delivered a sermon at his local church. I had also observed that Brett expressed himself freely and with emotion when he talked of his religion, his two beautiful daughters or his talented wife. Then the penny dropped, he had learned that business presentations were factual and to script, yet in his personal life he allowed himself the freedom to express views about his beliefs and family with the feelings they invoked in him.

We talked about the hidden assumption that drove these two very different behaviours and I encouraged him to unleash the vision and passion he had when he made his speech to his followers. He needed to apply the delivery style he used at church in the office, and to do that he had to shift his beliefs about his role. At work he was a professional manager – at church and in the home he allowed his emotions to express themselves.

That was apparently a breakthrough moment for him: over the next few years he grew into an extremely passionate and visionary leader who was recognised by his international owners and plucked out of New Zealand to lead a global unit based in Geneva. This left-brain accountant got in touch with his inner self and put his values and beliefs 'out there' for his followers to see. When he did that, they connected with his vision of the ideal world of loss-adjusting and they followed him. At 65+ he is now back in New Zealand and continues to provide professional excellence to his customers and passion at home and at church.

The assumption that he could not show feelings, passions or emotion at work prohibited him from developing his visioning skills and leadership capabilities. Once he flipped that assumption, the result slowly became evident in his values, beliefs and behaviours and his people latched on and they made the journey together.

Being open to changing assumptions

I am going to briefly refer back to my own journey outlined in Chapter 3 to highlight just a few of the points at which my individual Culture Iceberg changed. As I mentioned earlier, my individual culture was at first influenced by the following cultural groups: New Zealand (country); Wellington (city culture); Catholicism (church culture); St Mary's College (school culture); English, Irish and Lebanese ethnic groups (my parents' ethnic heritage); clubs comprising multicultural friendships (European, Polynesian and Maori cultures); close-up access to the justice system and criminal communities (the industry and social groups my step-father brought into our home).

When I became an adult I moved cities and then countries and each time my assumptions were challenged and my values and behaviours evolved. In addition to these physical moves, there were many other occasions when a personal experience or revelation – an 'aha' moment – caused my assumptions to shift again and again. Over time there have been many major shifts. It is for this reason that I have become comfortable with different cultures and have learned how to manage change.

The table below highlights a few of the occasions when my assumptions changed, impacting my life and career. On each occasion, the assumptions I had taken from my childhood and adolescence, which I had been unconsciously relying on, were challenged by actual experience. Each time this happened I realised that what I had taken-for-granted was incorrect. When this happens a few times you learn not to rely on your assumptions but to be open to, and look for, differences.

As you review the summary below you will probably remember the many times your iceberg has evolved and what you learned from those growing experiences. It's good to review the occasions when we have faced adversity and recognise how we travelled through them – it gives us confidence and courage to allow more changes to occur naturally.

When and how my assumptions altered

Where and when in my journey	Assumptions shifted from/to
Wellington New Zealand, Victoria University, early-20s	From – School is boring and restricting and tertiary education is not valued in our family culture as we live in the ordinary classes. To – Learning is exciting and anyone can get a degree if they apply themselves.
Auckland as a new graduate, late-20s	From - I could never run my own business as accounting is not my best subject. To – I can run my own business because I know people, clients, and markets.
Singapore, early-30s	From – All Asian people are small business owners and traders who run $2 shops and greengrocery stores. To – 'All Asian' people are not just 'one race', they are many different people who live at all levels of society just like us (educated and talented individuals in all roles – professionals, public servants, managers, innovators, entrepreneurs, etc.).
London, England late-30s	From – The English are quite like people from the antipodes, they recognise leaders and allow them to step up when the need arises. To – In England you wait for the group to invite you to lead and even if you have position title you don't presume to lead others or 'suggest how things should be done' until they signal they are prepared to follow you and invite you to step up.
Sydney, Australia early-40s	From - Australia is the same as New Zealand, except for the accent and the weather, and people are welcoming and get along very well there. To – Australia's independence serves to protect the rights of first comers against newly arrived immigrants and others who might seek to influence how things are done there.
Sydney Australia Mid-40s	From – Australia is a modern leading Western society that values women at work and in leadership roles too. To – Australian businesswomen are struggling to gain recognition by businessmen, get a piece of the leadership action and change values and systems that limit their growth and development.

Changes to your individual Culture Icebergs can occur regularly and continuously – it's up to you to take a journey where this can happen. Each change, or evolution, of your individual culture is an opportunity to learn and grow and, if you wish, you can make it an opportunity to influence people around you too.

If you are a traveller or you have a career built across several different countries and cultures then you will have gained learning from these different experiences to offer those who have not. But whether that learning is shared depends on:

- Whether you feel comfortable sharing it and being an influencer of change (I had a conversation with an executive who spent 8 years in other countries, who could see the challenges facing Australia when he returned but it didn't occur to him that he could do anything about it – in the 5 years since his return he had neither shared his learning nor tried to influence others);
- Whether people around you are interested in listening: the research from the 100 interviews has revealed that overseas business experience and cross-cultural experience are not highly valued by people in Australian business or society so there's no natural condition for sharing that knowledge.

Three men adjust their Icebergs

I met dozens of inspiring women leaders during the interview process and I discovered that on many occasions part of their career success was attributed to the balance they had achieved in their lives: balance that came from a true partnership with their spouses. I asked a couple of them if their husbands would mind sharing their perspective of the journey. I figured if they can do it we ought to find out how, so that others might learn from their experience what the future could look like.

Below are three personal stories of men who are married to three highly successful women leaders: Chris Komor married to Diane Grady (chair and non-executive director of a number of boards and former Partner of McKinsey & Company); Peter Gooding married to Julie Coates (Director of Big W with a long-standing career in human resources and operational management roles); and Con Tatlis married to Angela Tatlis, (Managing Director of Invoke Performance with a long-standing career in supply-chain management).

Their stories illustrate how both the men and the women moved away from traditional roles: as the wives built their professional careers, the husbands adjusted their individual Culture Icebergs and balanced their lives and work to make space for their wives to grow too.

Two of these modern families share how they managed dual-careers, describing how they made the dual-career option work effectively. They outline how they shifted their assumptions, values and behaviours as they decided who would work, how much and when; how the house would be managed; how the children would be raised; and how they would both pursue their careers to ensure that each got what they wanted from the partnership.

The third story is by a stay-at-home dad who describes how he and his partner adjusted and balanced their lives to reverse the traditional roles.

These stories illustrate how times are changing and reinforce the need for more rapid cultural change and modernising of our social and economic systems to support dual-working families and house-husbands.

'A sense of humour and no tugging' by Chris Komor

Chris Komor is Principal, Willow Bend Station and is married to Diane Grady (Non-Executive Director of Macquarie Bank and BlueScope Steel and Chair of Ascham Girls School and of the Hunger Project. Diane was also interviewed and her opinions are shared throughout this book.) They live in Sydney.

Having a successful business person as a wife is damaging neither to the male nor to the kids. The caveat is that there needs to be a sense of humour and confidence on the part of the male.

I was born in New York and came here when I was 20 years old. After obtaining a law degree from the Australian National University, I started my career as a lawyer in Sydney and went back to New York in 1980 to pass the New York bar exam and work on Wall Street. When I returned I practised at Allens law firm and I met Diane, who was at McKinsey & Co, an international consulting firm. As our lives and careers progressed we made an early decision to support each other's careers. You need to be decisive about how you want to plan and grow your careers, manage the home and parent the children. You can't be tugging at each other on these things.

After several years as a solicitor in a law firm and then as in-house counsel in industry, I decided I wanted to be more active in business and started a small corporate advisory practice for an international merchant bank. After this I traded futures for a while, co-founded a smartcard start-up and then purchased a sheep property in central New South Wales, which now takes 80 per cent of my time.

Diane had a thriving career at McKinsey and was the leader of the Organisation and Change Management Practice and the first woman outside the USA to be elected to McKinsey's global partnership. During this time I was the 'significant other' at McKinsey partner functions and conferences and I was one of very few males at these events. As a somewhat humorous idea I started a 'spouse action group' to help initiate some activities for spouses that were more gender neutral (massage and shopping days were okay but how many of those does a bloke need?). We had slogans and special waves as part of our tongue-in-cheek campaign to limit our partners' extensive travel for the firm.

After a long and successful career at McKinsey, Diane became a non-executive director. She sits on a number of high-profile boards and is a very active champion of gender equality.

Having a successful businesswoman as a wife allows the male partner much wider career opportunity and flexibility. Because the financial responsibility has been shared, I have been able to make choices to try my hand at a number of different things throughout my career, which I may not have done had one of us been the sole breadwinner.

What are some of the secrets to success as a dual-career couple?

Well, the first thing is that the husband has to have a strong sense of self and be comfortable with who they are. To be the guy married to a successful businesswoman you have to be able to field questions about what you do. My career was so much less structured than Diane's and some people, including my mother-in-law, might have been challenged by that. You might be seen to be 'the handbag' at your wife's corporate events and you need to be able to positively respond to the views of other people.

Secondly, as a successful businesswoman you need to have the ability to bounce back when faced with discrimination. There have been times throughout Diane's career when in a meeting she felt that the female voice was not an equal voice, especially if she was testing a new idea. You have to have the ability to believe in yourself and remain confident when faced with bias.

Because both of our careers at one time or other required extensive travel, it was important that we both felt secure in our relationship. When you are away on business trips for weeks on end, you need to keep the communication lines open and not be concerned about the distance and duration. Our trust in each other meant the travelling did not cause problems.

One of the benefits of dual careers and regular business travel is that our children have experienced so many countries and cultures that otherwise they may not have. They have been trekking after gorillas in southern Uganda, walking with wildlife in Botswana, walking through the desert in Chile, backpacking in southern Japan, getting lost in eastern Hungary, exploring northern Madagascar and western Brazil and travelling to the Vietnam–China border. Both our children, following all the exposure to different cultures, have chosen to complete International Studies at university.

On the less glamorous side, our children have had to step up to take responsibility around the house and have had a more independent life than they would have had their mother been a stay-at-home mum. We had live-in nannies for many years but we still required our children to make their own beds, fold their washing, prepare their lunches and share in the running of the house.

A big lesson for dual working parents to get to grips with early on is to learn to treat the nanny as a partner in the child-rearing relationship and to value their input. On several occasions we invested in our nanny becoming our personal executive assistant as the children got older. With a live-in nanny you have an additional adult in the house and everybody needs to make adjustments to make it work for all members of the household.

Diane has been a wonderful role model for our two daughters. They see women being respected in the workplace and they see both parents supporting one another and neither of them being the 'helicopter parent'. As we are both busy with our careers during the week we both have to do household catch-up at the weekend. I could never find time to take five hours off to play golf with 'the boys'. Our time together as a family is precious and productive and we wouldn't change a thing.

Both our girls are developing their own careers with vision about who they can be and with the belief that anything is possible. We couldn't be more proud of them.

Chris Komor

'Set boundaries, manage expectations' by Peter Gooding

Peter Gooding is Integration Director, People & Change, AMP. He is married to Julie Coates (Director of Big W, whose journey is included in Chapter 11.) Peter outlines his personal values and explains how he and Julie managed their lives and careers together to enable both of them to achieve. They live in Sydney.

Julie and I started thinking about our career pathways before we got married 25 years ago in Melbourne. We both started out in careers as teachers and after a while decided that we would look at alternative careers for future options. We both moved out of teaching and into HR positions.

I knew back then that Julie was really talented and after she worked in several HR roles at Cadbury Schweppes, BHP, Target and then Officeworks, she was offered a role with David Jones in Sydney. About the same time I was in an HR role at Ford and I was offered my next promotion in the USA.

This was the junction for us. I resigned from Ford and we went with Julie's opportunity in Sydney. The kids were aged five and one and we decided this was the best option for them, and to allow Julie's career to go ahead.

I looked at a number of new positions and chose AMP and the financial services sector as the culture there provides greater flexibility than I had been used to at Ford. Julie and I discussed how we would need to adjust our lives a little to support her ongoing development.

In 2002 Julie moved to Woolworths as the Director of Human Resources, then she was promoted to Chief Logistics Officer in 2007 and asked to run Big W in 2008.

We have had a full-time nanny since 1999 when we came to Sydney and that helps us enormously to balance work and life with the children. We have always been prepared to invest in getting the right help to support us. Our view is that if either one of us stayed at home, we would be incomplete humans and would probably drive the children nuts. We both think we can make a difference and there is innate satisfaction from achieving things at work.

To make this work for us, and the kids, we set some boundaries and guidelines. We try not to work at home in the week or the weekends. Work is work and home is home. We are both aware of our responsibilities as parents and we've been lucky – our three kids, Amy, Rose and Tess are fantastic, well-adjusted and capable children.

Living in our house you have to be organised, independent and responsible. These are life skills they have acquired and which benefit them in every aspect of their lives, not just at home. Everyone packs their own bags for school and if they forget their jumper, they have to borrow one.

There is a stereotypical view in society that one of the parents needs to be at home with the kids. It's actually about what you are actively doing with the children when you are at home; it's not about just being present. Of those people who say "you need to be a stay-at-home-mum to be a good mum", I feel that is their conscience speaking and that they are being judgmental or critical of those who are not at home.

I am happy for people to sit back and judge us on our children. They have respect for people around them and those from other cultures, they have respect for each other and they are independent thinkers. I am really proud of them.

What makes it work is about how you run your life and the relationships in your family. It is about the boundaries and expectations that you set and in your consistency in applying them. When you're at home, you must be tuned into the family and not just be there physically. Julie constantly keeps us engaged and focused on the children and each other.

We manage expectations at work too. We tell our bosses and colleagues that we can do anything that is required, so long as we know in advance and can organise things at home. Our PAs talk to each other so that they can coordinate our diaries and avoid us both having to travel away for work at the same time. They sync in the school and sporting activities with the nanny and other parents so we don't miss out on anything that we need to attend.

Women are more circumspect and reflective and I think we need more of this in organisations. Many leaders think the solution to keeping women in careers, is in providing flexible work practices, but that is not the solution. There is a high degree of paternalism and many male leaders see women having babies as a problem and they offer flexible work options as the solution. But the underlying culture hasn't changed. While flexibility is essential, it is not the solution to the attitudes that prevail.

It is an unfortunate coincidence of timing that women are now having children later (early to mid-30s) and that this is also the time when they are most promotable. Organisations have to look through that and see it as a short-term issue to deal with and commit to a long-term view of keeping them, supporting them through maternity leave and promoting them when the time is right. Have conversations with them about their career and make it clear that having children need not stand in the way.

That said, if you want to be a senior person in business it is not a part-time job whether you are a man or a woman. Once you get that reality, then you can start having meaningful career conversations.

In those companies where males are not addressing the loss of women, shareholders should be revolting. Companies that only access part of the labour market are narrow-minded. Women bring a different thought pattern and they moderate male behaviour. We need to be aware of the football mentality. If you get all white Anglo-Saxon males at the top, they all think the same. If they've been to the same schools together and played the same rugby together, then a clubby mentality permeates the organisation. Quite often when you have this old-boy culture, you also find that the senior male executives' wives are rarely career women.

Peter Gooding

'Top Tips' by Con Tatlis

Con is married to Angela Tatlis (Managing Director, Invoke Performance who was also interviewed for this book.) Con explains how their joint decision to have a stay-at-home parent, led him to take on this role and he shares some hot tips for males looking to do the same. He works part-time as finance manager for her business and as administrator for a not-for-profit. They live in Melbourne, Australia.

I started my career with a degree in applied chemistry and worked in an R&D lab for Shell. After Shell, I worked in sales roles for a Mobil-owned company. I met Angela and we both settled down quite young (I was 29 years old).

When we married we realised that we both wanted a stay-at-home parent for our kids. We discussed our careers and decided that Angela's career looked more promising than mine due to the diminishing opportunities in the chemicals industry. Angela's career was growing and it made sense for me to take on the stay-at-home-parent role. I don't think we thought through the implications of it at the time but, now that I've been at it for 10 years, I can share some tips.

I started in 2001 raising one child and I found it easy and very enjoyable. Even in 2003 when our second daughter came along I was managing okay. I had to be organised and I still did a little office work part-time.

But then in 2005 we had twins and that was demanding. We had four kids under the age of four. The twins were premature and in hospital for a while. Three of the children were in nappies at the same time, which meant I was changing about 120 nappies a week. I had not expected this but still managed pretty well under the circumstances, but the sleep deprivation made life really difficult. I had to get by on three hours sleep: I think I was a little irritable and short-tempered for a while.

At first I adopted a kind of siege mentality: I'd just do what I needed to do to get through the day. I'd try to plan and organise things. I learned not to try to do too much. I did whatever it took to get through the day and come out on top.

Once the twins were sleeping through the night we organised 'date night'. It was great. Once a fortnight we would put all the kids to bed, my father would come over to sit with them and Angela and I would go out and do whatever took our fancy – movie, dinner, a swim or sunset walks by the beach. This was a real relief, like someone had opened a pressure release valve. We continue with date night even now, years later.

When I look back now, 10 years on, I realise I was learning as I went along. Being a stay-at-home dad back then was a new phenomenon in Australian culture and it would have been helpful if someone who had done it before me shared their experience. So here are some of my hot tips for males who are thinking of giving it a go.

Top tip number one: Keep involved in something intellectually stimulating, whether it is part-time work or a community or sports club committee. By the time I felt the need for something it was too late. I had let everything go and I realised that I shouldn't have. As much as you love your children and being able to parent them, raising children is often not intellectually demanding and you're talking at the kids' level all day. Ideally men should try to organise other outlets or stay professionally connected in some way.

Top tip number two: Keep close to your mates. Being a stay-at-home dad was isolating and it happened relatively quickly so we didn't have time to think about what we needed to do to adjust. As the job at home got bigger, as we had more children, I saw less of my mates. After a while we ended up living in different neighbourhoods and as a consequence we drifted apart. As time went by I wished I had managed that better and made more of a conscious effort to keep in contact with my friends.

Top tip number three: You need to have patience: your day is repetitive and children often need to be told what to do over and over. It can be frustrating and if you add that to the isolation it takes a special kind of patience. You need to be good at keeping yourself amused and try to plan ahead to do things that leave you feeling like you have achieved something worthwhile.

Top tip number four: You need to be strong enough to feed your own self-esteem. You need to know that you can manage without getting the 'sense of who you are' from your work. I knew I was alone as there were no men's support groups. While I see more men pushing prams now than 10 years ago and there are many more stay-at-home dads, it is not for everybody.

Top tip number five: Take help when it's offered. There's no prize for being macho about this. Raising children 24/7 is intensive and break-free so you need to give yourself time out to distance yourself and revitalise your energy.

Top tip number six: Use child care as relief. By putting the older two children into childcare one day a week it gave them social development and me a break. Use the resources around you: you don't have to do it all.

Angela has been amazing throughout: together we worked through the challenges and we are happy with the path we have taken. The four kids are now in school and I have time to start thinking about retraining to get back into some interesting work. In the meantime I am working part-time for Angela's business and for a not-for-profit organisation while I am looking to build a new career. That said, we have put so much effort into having a stay-at-home parent we don't want to abandon the children now: we want to make sure we are still there for the kids after school.

We were fortunate to have been in a position to have a full-time parent. Not every family can do this. I understand that even those who can afford to take this option choose not to as both parents wish to maintain their careers. We all have to make the best decisions we can under the circumstances we find ourselves in.

The ultimate benefit is that I have a wonderful relationship with all four children that working fathers wouldn't have. This relationship could never have been established if I been the working parent and I am so lucky.

Con Tatlis

Be the leader that will honour you

As they say, life is not a dress rehearsal: this is it. This is your opportunity to do something sensational – to be the leader that will make you proud. You do not have to be a Cathy Freeman to be a champion or a Martin Luther King, Jr to be a visionary leader. Everyone in their own way can contribute to evolving Australian culture – leaders can courageously show the way, followers can support the developments rather than resist them.

My dream is that everyone living in Australia joins the workforce believing that the opportunities are equal, their path to the top meritocratic and the door to positions of power and leadership open.

As the individual in the Culture Circuit, you are the second-most influential element in it, after the country. As a leader you take your individual culture with you everywhere and you can influence people and other cultures to which you belong. Those who observe your attitudes and behaviours are influenced by it. So, as a leader, you have a duty to make sure that the assumptions, values, attitudes and behaviours you convey to the followers in your family, business, clubs and communities are the right ones – those that encourage cooperative behaviour and engender unity. With those things in place nations, companies and communities can grow and prosper. Without them we are divided and weak.

If you have a vision for a more diverse and equal society in Australia to maximise our productivity and gain a stronghold in Asia to secure continued growth and prosperity for all, then check your individual Culture Iceberg. Check to see what it is conveying to onlookers. Make sure it is relevant and that you are evolving with the times. Make sure you don't have any hidden assumptions or unconscious biases undermining progress.

Leaders of any cultural group carry a great responsibility: to manage the group's evolution, to convey their own vision for a brighter and better future and to inspire others to follow them. But their efforts need to begin with an awareness of their own individual culture.

Any one of us can change our individual culture – our assumptions, values, beliefs, attitudes and behaviours – and we can continue to change it throughout our lives. Every new experience, from a new job or a change of location to joining a sports group or community club, can help us evolve our individual culture. And sometimes along the way we need to have our old, long-held assumptions vividly disproved before we can let them go and move on.

Chapter 11

Redirecting your Organisation Culture

'Stand up for what you think is right. That might be very different from what I am saying today, but you are allowed to differ from me just as I am allowed to differ from you.

Dr John Yu, AC, addressing graduates at the University of Sydney, 2008; Australian of the Year 1996, former CEO Royal Alexandra Hospital for Children.

'Living diversely' conjures up notions of freedoms that anyone can enjoy. However, we live with a dilemma in Australia: until the pathway to top jobs in Australia is unencumbered for everyone, those that get up there are, by the limited opportunity and special circumstances, privileged.

While the majority are presumed to have arrived there on merit, some people believe that the channels to promotion are insufficiently transparent, the selection processes exclusive and the significant remuneration available only to a select few. It is these aspects of getting to the top that makes it a privileged class. The dilemma is that this is not behaviour generally consistent with an egalitarian nation; exclusive behaviour ought not to survive, yet it does.

Women and men at the top of Australian organisations – board members and executives alike – are charged with the responsibility of changing their organisation culture to address the poor diversity situation. Therein lies another dilemma: those who benefit from the privileged position are responsible for removing it.

Listed companies have been instructed by the ASX to set targets and deliver diversity and all other organisations across business and society carry a moral duty to deliver diversity for the people of Australia. We have heard from 100 leaders on this and they have explained how the culture of Australia, its organisations and communities suffer from biases and discrimination towards females, immigrants, non-white Australians and returning expats.

The evidence is irrefutable – poor gender and cultural diversity exists across business and society, and the problem escalates as you rise up organisations to top levels.

In this chapter I have prepared three company cases that illustrate how to change assumptions in an organisation. What better way is there to learn than to examine the progress made by others who have trodden the path before you? These three companies' stories illustrate how an early desire for greater gender diversity allowed women to rise to the top, and paved the way for them to move into non-traditional operational roles too.

Each story illustrates how the company's culture, illustrated by its assumptions and the values, attitudes and behaviours of its leaders, was deliberately directed and aligned to help meet the desired outcomes – higher female participation rates at senior levels of the business.

Leaders deliver gender diversity

The third most influential culture in the Culture Circuit is the organisation culture. I suspect that some readers might be wondering why I have left organisation culture to last. Well, the reason is that it is the last of the three main cultures to form: country and individual cultures form first.

The impact of organisation culture on the Culture Circuit

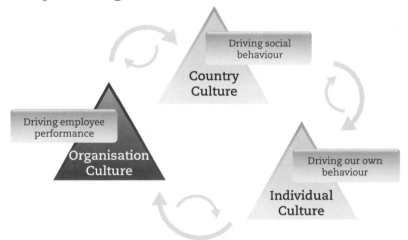

As a leader you create your organisation culture and by outlining the other cultures ahead of this one (in Chapters 9 and 10), I hope that you will appreciate the very real influence you have on your organisation's performance, due to the assumptions and values you bring and those that you allow others to bring.

As I interviewed people from across 26 industries, I found some exceptional examples of gender diversity where courageous and committed leaders made the changes happen. I can't express how excited I was when I found them.

Once I found them, I asked to speak to a handful of women in each to hear their stories. The three organisations are quite different from one another – each from a different industry. What was exceptional about them was not only that they had opened the pathways for large numbers of females to earn high-level executive jobs; there was also a high degree of women in operations and many of the women whom I found running billion- and million-dollar companies, arrived there through a career path that started in functional roles.

It seemed to me that two myths had been shattered by these exceptional organisations:

- that women were best suited to functional roles (HR, marketing, communications);
- that people were unlikely to make a successful transition to operational roles from a functional background.

Both myths are well and truly shattered in these three examples and they also illustrate how they evolved their organisation cultures and addressed some of the blind spots. Many of the features of cultures outlined in Chapter 8 are discussed below.

Each of the cases has three main components:

- they discuss the strategies employed to remove barriers for females rising to the top;
- they provide an example of the organisations' Culture Icebergs for you to review against their story;
- and they outline the careers of 14 executive women, explaining the paths they took, who sponsored them and other factors that influenced their journey.

When I went to interview these companies I expected to write up only the first two of these three points. But the individual stories of the women in these organisations was so interesting that I thought they not only blew the myths away completely but they also provided role models for many aspiring young women who I hope will gain ideas and confidence to set their limits high.

Evolved cultures foster women-in-operations

Evolved organisation cultures – those that have adapted and matured in response to changing economic and social conditions – are generally more aligned with external market trends and are more adaptable to internal organisational issues. As a consequence more evolved cultures typically encourage future thinking and exhibit more progressive attitudes towards the nature of work and how it might look tomorrow.

As I carried out my research I was delighted to find so many women-in-operations and the reason I present them here is because they would not be in these roles if their organisational cultures did not value women in operational roles or believe that they could perform them well.

The first of these is Woolworths which is a story about four female executives who moved from functional roles to operational roles after being sponsored by male executives in the company. This story illustrates how the leadership's long-term commitment to achieving gender equality keeps the top team focused on evolving the culture that elicits the behaviours needed to attract women into senior management roles, then to develop and retain them. Woolworths employs over 190,000 people in Australia.

The second is McDonald's Australia, which is a story about a woman CEO who rose to the top in a highly gender-conscious environment and enjoys the company of many other skilled women in the senior management ranks. This story illustrates that an organisation's cultural heritage travels with it and how the commitment of McDonald's USA to building a diverse workforce, has also delivered benefits to McDonald's Australia too. McDonald's employs over 90,000 people in Australia and over 1.7 million people worldwide.

The third is Ernst & Young Oceania (E&Y) which is a story about four women Office Managing Partners (OMP) who became the majority in a team of six OMPs which included just two males. This occurred with unprecedented speed, shifting the culture's assumptions about the gender of its leaders. In an industry where the partnership group is historically male-dominated this is outstanding progress. This story illustrates how new blood on the executive team brought values and skills from outside the existing organisation culture and positively impacted the firm's Culture Iceberg. E&Y employs over 4600 people in Oceania and 152,000 people globally.

It seems that these three organisations had some things in common:

- they had leaders with the right individual cultures who recognised the business need for gender balancing and greater diversity to address skills shortages and meet growth requirements;
- they allowed their cultures to evolve;
  - they encouraged a change in values (valuing women as well as men);
  - a shift in attitudes towards people and their possibilities developed;
  - the values were reinforced through company artefacts;
  - the right behaviours start to flow and reinforce the cycle.

Let's take a look at Woolworths' story first.

Woolworths: Sponsoring women to grow business

Proudly, this leading ASX100 company, which opened its first store in Pitt Street, Sydney in 1924, has been able to boast great progress on the gender-diversity front in recent years. Changes began in the early 2000s when Roger Corbett was CEO, they escalated during Michael Luscombe's reign between 2006 and 2011 and they continue under Grant O'Brien's leadership today.

Woolworths has committed to be an early adopter of the new ASX Diversity Recommendations and as part of this commitment it aims to have women as 33 per cent of direct reports to the CEO, and 33 per cent of their executive reports at the next three levels, by 2015.

Woolworths is a results-driven culture and as the trading figures in retail are available daily there is no escaping performance feedback. Back in 2003 Roger Corbett and his team looked at the growth targets they had set and discussed where they were going to find the people to meet the growth targets.

They began by looking at their succession planning and talent management programs and reviewed the make-up of their employee profile looking for patterns and intelligence that might provide clues or answers. There it was: they had just 16.7 per cent women in executive management and even less in the store management. Also, retention of women after maternity leave was very low.

Getting serious about change

After much discussion on what the numbers were saying about the organisation's culture and performance, Roger Corbett signalled to the organisation that they were serious about change and making a difference. While he had already established a group-wide HR function he went on to raise the profile, expectations and mandate of that function and the role of the group HR Director to develop and deliver the outcomes, all of which signalled the importance of Woolworths' people.

He had already launched a transformational program called 'Refresh', which was reported as the beginning of Woolworths' commitment to culture change and which was starting to deliver tangible results. He also created a Women in Management Committee to set up programs to help support women to progress to higher levels. To encourage women to come back to work after maternity leave he asked the female HR executives to maintain close relations with female employees while they were away and to look for ways to support them to come back, if not full-time, then in some other capacity.

Diane Grady (currently non-executive director of Macquarie Group and BlueScope Steel and formerly worldwide leader of Organisation and Change

Management practice at McKinsey and Co) was the Chair of the People Committee on the board at that time. She guided Woolworths' executives to seek out their untapped resources and explained how to drive culture change. Her input helped them to realise some early wins: all of the women interviewed from Woolworths talked about the positive influence and support Diane provided to them personally and to the senior management team while on the board. Diane's experience as a change consultant, which is unusual to find on a board, was highly valued and was reported to have delivered much benefit to the business.

By 2006 the number of women in executive management had risen from 16.7 per cent to 20 per cent. The needle had shifted and they knew they were on their way. To keep this going was the challenge.

Valuing and investing in females

Also in 2006 Michael Luscombe was promoted to CEO after a long career within Woolworths. He introduced something that had not been done by any other retailer before – he paid maternity leave. He did this early in his new role and it sent a very clear signal to the Woolworths' community, both internally and externally, that it valued its female employees and wanted to support them to take family breaks and return to continue their careers.

Where appropriate, women were promoted while on maternity leave to further demonstrate the organisation's commitment to them and encourage their timely return. The company also improved its succession planning and reached a point where it rarely had to advertise externally for vacant positions. Two of the women interviewed were beneficiaries of the improved succession planning processes and said it was the rigour of these new processes that ensured women were remembered while away on leave. Woolworths' retention of women post-maternity leave rose to 90–100 per cent, a very satisfying result.

While Woolworths started out with just 16.7 per cent female executives in 2004, the numbers increased to 23 per cent in 2008, 27 per cent in 2010 and to 28.3 per cent in 2012. (The 2012 figure was diluted a little by some new business additions). Woolworths' executives are committed to reaching their 2015 target of 33 per cent female executives in the top four levels.

As I prepared this book, the new CEO, Grant O'Brien, had only been in the seat for 10 months so it is no surprise that the women interviewed referred more frequently to the work of the recently departed CEO. Michael Luscombe was known for his ability to identify female talent and he mentored a number of them through several positions, bringing them to the senior ranks. The senior women, whose stories are outlined below, conveyed their admiration for his support throughout their careers at Woolworths. This leader illustrated great empathy for the people around him and was known for telling people that 'they could do it' as he encouraged them to try operational roles outside the traditional functional pathway.

Woolworths' organisation iceberg

Which layers of the organisation iceberg did Woolworth's leaders modify to achieve the change? Why did they commence the journey? How did they do it?

You may be able to arrive at the answers to these questions yourself, but let's just go through them briefly together.

Why did Woolworths set out to get more women in management?

Organisational culture change is most successful when driven by a business need and led from the top. At Woolworths in the early 2000s there was a need to grow employee numbers to meet the business growth targets. Retailing is very much a people-intensive business and to grow your market share and open more and bigger stores, you need more staff and managers for the stores, possibly a few more at head office and most likely a couple of extras (if not 100s or 1000s) in procurement and logistics. So Woolworths' strategy was to identify the top female talent amongst their 190,000 employees, develop them, promote them and minimise the loss of these trained and skilled people once they were in place.

Which layers of the Iceberg were impacted and how?

Having decided on a strategy to 'access the other half of the talent pool' (females), they needed to prepare the organisation to support their development and retention. It was no small task.

To implement this strategy, they had to make a fundamental change to a firmly embedded and enduring assumption. If the senior management team back in 2003 was 84 per cent male and the percentage of male store managers was even higher than that, the existing assumption must have been something like 'only men could perform these roles effectively' (or else they would have brought women up into these roles before). They had to change this assumption to get sustainable change in behaviour. If you refer back to Chapter 8, you will remember that assumptions are the hidden and unconscious parts of a culture and they form the foundation that all the higher levels are influenced by.

How do I know that they must have shifted this underlying well-embedded assumption? Well, if they had not, their development and succession programs (artefacts) would have acted like Band-Aids. That is, they would have been only a temporary solution to the problem. Artefacts alone won't produce sustainable change: without a change to the underlying assumptions they smother the symptoms and cover up the effects for a while, but sooner or later the underlying forces of the drifting iceberg will turn it back onto its original course and the 'token good behaviour' will revert to type (previous undesirable behaviour).

Remember, icebergs drift in the current and they do not turn against the prevailing flow easily: you need to create sufficient opposing force to steer them in an alternative direction permanently. Cultures don't lie. 'You are what you are' and you can't hide or suppress the beliefs and attitudes that flow from the underlying assumptions.

The fact that Woolworths has had a steady climb in the number of women represented in senior management and store management since 2003, suggests they were able to shift that assumption. There has been sufficient momentum and this can only come from a shift in an underlying assumption.

Briefly this is an example of how it might have looked:

Example of some elements of Woolworths' evolving Iceberg

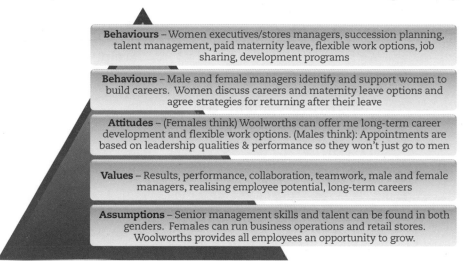

Behaviours – Women executives/stores managers, succession planning, talent management, paid maternity leave, flexible work options, job sharing, development programs

Behaviours – Male and female managers identify and support women to build careers. Women discuss careers and maternity leave options and agree strategies for returning after their leave

Attitudes – (Females think) Woolworths can offer me long-term career development and flexible work options. (Males think): Appointments are based on leadership qualities & performance so they won't just go to men

Values – Results, performance, collaboration, teamwork, male and female managers, realising employee potential, long-term careers

Assumptions – Senior management skills and talent can be found in both genders. Females can run business operations and retail stores. Woolworths provides all employees an opportunity to grow.

- early changes would have sent a shudder up the spine of the organisation iceberg shifting the deeply rooted assumption that 'only males could be managers in this retail business' to 'women can and will be effective managers in retailing too';
- the change in assumption would have created a new value that female talent had to be seriously considered for development and promotion;
- as employees came to believe this to be true, it would have shifted their attitudes about their own careers to 'Woolworths offers opportunity and development for females to build long-term careers' but perhaps not until the succession planning and talent development programs were in place (artefacts) proving the shift in the underlying assumption;

- these changes would also have conveyed to men that their previous assumptions (that only males could manage stores) and beliefs would have to shift to something like 'I'll need to be more conscientious about identifying female talent than before';
- overall these changes would have led to a shift in organisational behaviours as males and females were being asked to perform differently.

Getting 190,000 people then employed at Woolworths to follow you does not happen overnight. These culture changes would not necessary have moved the compass needle of such a large organisation alone. But clear and focused leadership, committed to a vision of a future that included women in senior management, was key to Woolworths continued success in changing culture and its continued upward trend of the numbers of women executives.

Sustainability comes from getting to the bottom of the culture; the hefty, unseen and misunderstood solid infrastructure that lies beneath the waterline. Tinkering with only the top layers will not deliver sustainable change. It will result in Band-Aids and, as we all know, they get wet and dirty and fall off after a while.

Woolworths' women-in-operations

Let's meet four of Woolworths' most senior women-in-operations and hear a little about their journey to the top of the hierarchy in one of the country's largest publicly listed companies. .

Julie Coates

Julie is Director of Big W, a $4 billion business employing 24,000 people. She rose to this position in November 2008 following 5 years as Woolworths' inaugural group HR Director and 18 months as the Chief Logistics Officer.

She commenced her career in Melbourne in 1985 as a teacher working for the Victorian Education Department. She had a mathematics degree and was the Mathematics Faculty Head at the Maribyrnong Secondary School. She moved on in 1988 to try her hand in a corporate career at Cadbury Schweppes as the National Sales Training Coordinator, then she became Corporate Training Officer at BHP, a training and development manager at Target, GM Human Resources at Officeworks, and then she spent five years at David Jones in a variety of roles before joining Woolworths Limited in 2002.

In some of these companies Julie had also had responsibility for logistics, supply chain and property management, which meant she took broad experience to her new post at Woolworths.

When Julie was recruited into the Human Resources Director role at Woolworths it was one of the largest existing HR roles in Australia at that time. Five years on, Michael Luscombe had taken the top job and one day he approached her with an opportunity. He asked Julie if she would help sort out the logistics operation. As the Group HR Director she had led the work to relocate and retrain 4000 of the 6000 people in the logistics area and had illustrated her understanding of the needs of that business.

Julie recalls that she had some doubts about moving into this role but Michael reassured her that the job was less about logistics and more about leadership. He selected her because of her skills with people, process and building relationships. In addition, as a mathematics graduate she was skilled in working with numbers and could read quickly what the financial reports were saying about the business's priorities.

Julie was appointed Chief Logistics Officer in May 2007 to establish and execute strategies that would further improve the operations to meet ongoing growth targets. This meant she was responsible for the storage and distribution of stock to the company's stores nationwide and this involved managing the flow of goods from vendors, wholesalers and distributors through warehousing and transportation to get them onto the shelves for customers in time and in good condition. They say women are good at multi-tasking and this is a wonderful example of how women can perform effectively in roles that were traditionally reserved for men.

By November the following year Michael was on her doorstep once again to offer Julie another challenge. Michael had watched Julie's progress in that short time and clearly had no doubt that she was capable of running an even bigger operation. In November 2008 Julie was appointed General Manager of Big W to lead 20,000 people across 164 stores and to be responsible for delivering $4 billion in revenues (2011).

If the myth were true, that women are best suited to traditional careers and functional roles, this talented and skilled woman would still be a teacher. Julie's progression throughout her career – leapfrogging from teaching, to training and development, to HR Director roles – is obviously due to her own ability to deliver results and to grow into the next job quickly. However, as history has shown, women are rarely given the opportunity to move out of functional roles and into frontline roles running revenue-generating businesses. Thank goodness there were some men at Woolworths who could see the potential and create the opportunity.

Julie is quick to acknowledge Michael Luscombe's foresight of her ability to be effective as an operational leader, as well a functional one. She says it was his sponsorship of her into the roles of Chief Logistics Officer and Director of

Big W that enabled her to make the moves confidently. Knowing that your leader believes in you positively impacts your self-belief to do the job.

Julie explained she has been on maternity leave three times and that she was promoted while away on two of those occasions. She says that having experienced what it's like to come back to a better job and more money, she is fully aware of the power of that strategy and how it has worked for Woolworths as a key lever in getting women to return and stay with the business.

Julie had a champion. She clearly had enormous capability as well, but without the courage of many leaders throughout her career to break away from the long-held view that women are best in traditional roles, this opportunity may not have been realised.

Debra Singh

Debra was GM Dick Smith, a $1.5 billion business employing 4500 people at the time of the interview. She was the first woman to be appointed to run a trading division at Woolworths. Like Julie Coates, she had a long career in both human resources and operations and was able to effectively combine her skills to reach the executive of Woolworths.

Debra joined Woolworths in 2001 in a human resources role after an impressive career with major brands like Freedom and Vox Retail. She joined as the GM for Human Resources Woolworths Supermarkets and was responsible for the people strategy for 130,000 employees. Debra recalls what an exciting challenge that was having been responsible for only up to 5000 employees previously.

Debra enjoyed the role immensely but became aware quite early on that she was missing being involved in the operational side of the business. Six months later she shared this with Michael Luscombe, who was then the Director of Supply Chain. He encouraged her to carry on doing a great job in HR and wait for the right opportunity. He then asked her if she would like a mentor and offered to support her to achieve her ambition. "He was absolutely brilliant", recalls Debra in our interview, "and he's the reason I stayed on to take up other roles".

Michael mentored Debra for 12 months and helped her prepare for her move into an operations role. Soon after he became the CEO he offered her an opportunity in India. Michael wanted to establish Woolworths Wholesale Division, which provides buying, supply chain and operations consulting to the Tata Group's joint venture with Woolworths. He picked Debra Singh to do the job. She had a long-standing association with India where she was married in 1977 and she not only had operational skills and experience but also the cultural understanding to launch Woolworths successfully.

"OMG, will I be up to it?" Debra asked herself. She didn't tell Michael Luscombe that she had concerns about such a big role. Instead she said to him "Michael, I'll do you proud!" Debra admitted that having doubts about her ability was a 'female thing'. She knows that Michael would not have offered her the position if she was not capable of it and feels that businesses could do more to help women recognise their skills and talents rather than let them deny that they exist.

Debra started in India with only one store and by the time she left there in late 2007 (two years later) she had built it to 22 stores. (By the end of 2011 Woolworths had 70 stores and Debra looked after the Indian business until 2011 when they appointed a Head of India).

When Debra returned to Australia she was appointed general manager for Dick Smith Electronics (Australia, New Zealand and India) in February 2008. Debra attributes much of her progress to Michael Luscombe and his intuition about her fit and potential. "He picked up that I was a bit frustrated where I was and he changed my career. Most men wouldn't have picked that up, and frankly they wouldn't have cared. I loved every single minute of it. I like the feeling that I am treated equally and I like the toughness. There were times when things were really challenging and Michael would tell me to 'suck it up' and when I look back now I see that that was the best advice he could have given me. We are very supportive of each other and we are really fortunate to have a great team."

Melinda Smith

Melinda is Chief Operating Officer, Masters, a relatively new Woolworths brand. She started working at Woolworths as a casual in the delicatessen when she was just 14. She started in 1987, the same year as Grant O'Brien, who later became the CEO in 2011. Now 25 years on she is one of Woolworths' top 1000 executives and like Julie Coates and Debra Singh her story is also peppered with references to male mentors. This is a common theme.

Melinda has had many careers at Woolworths and she says that she gained much credibility from pushing trolleys in her teenage years. "It helps if you are able to match the blokes and show them that you can do what they can do."

First she was the deli manager, then the store manager, a trainee buyer, a buyer for Victoria and then she moved to Sydney and took on a national buying role. After that Melinda was a line manager in the transport business.

Melinda worked with Grant O'Brien to investigate the home improvement market, which took them overseas to look at potential partners and together they gave a presentation to the board about the opportunities. This led to the joint venture with Lowes of the USA and the opening of Masters in Australia in 2011.

Melinda says "Launching Masters into the Australian market is changing the game. This is part of the Woolworths culture: you can try anything. It was pleasing to hear the Lowes executives comment on 'the large number of senior women at Woolworths' and 'the high level of performance of these women' and that made us all proud."

She describes her career at Woolworths as akin to being part of a family. "There are characters who support you and those who protect you. Sometimes you might not agree with the family values, but they are there to guide you and Woolworths' leaders communicate the values they want us to follow."

Kathryn McLay

Kathryn is General Manager – Replenishment, but at the time of interview she was Operations Manager North, Woolworths Logistics.

Kathryn is another of Woolworths' outstanding women-in-operations. She started her Woolworths career in 2001 being promoted in 2004 to the Head of Audit reporting to the CEO and Head of the Audit Committee.

During these early days at Woolworths Kathryn was appointed Chairman and President of the Institute of Internal Auditors, and it was publicly noted that she was the first female President. The Australian Financial Review wrote an article on her appointment and its significance and she says it was the publication of this story that brought the issue of gender balancing to the forefront of her mind. She says she did not think about it or notice it before that time.

"I was focused on my contribution, not my gender. At the end of the day it's about the complement of skills that you bring to the job" Kathryn said.

In 2008 Kathryn was appointed to General Manager Business Development and one year later she was appointed to General Manager Cost Focus where she was required to deliver cost savings throughout the Woolworths network. "As GM of Cost Focus I honed my skills in driving results by working collaboratively within the business and this experience, combined with that of the previous role, awakened a desire to try my hand at an operational role with P&L accountability: to be a do-er not a reviewer".

Kathryn's broadened skills were widely recognised and this opened up another opportunity running one of the most 'blokey' jobs in the business – logistics! In 2011 she was appointed to Operations Manager North, Woolworths Logistics and became responsible for managing warehousing and transport services across New South Wales and Queensland. Then her most recent promotion was to General Manager – Replenishment in 2012.

Woolworths provided Kathryn with a number of sponsors throughout her career there, who she says have been very generous with their time and advice including Roger Corbett, Julie Coates and Tom Pockett (Finance Director, Woolworths Ltd). She says they have each provided her with new job opportunities and then continued to support her whilst in these roles.

As mentioned above, logistics is a critical component of running an effective retail operation and it is rare to find females leading this kind of business. Like Julie Coates before her, Kathryn also had the skills and capability to perform effectively in a role that was traditionally reserved for men. I am tempted to say "Who says girls can't drive trucks!", but I suspect that Kathryn rarely gets the opportunity to drive a 36-pallet B-double. If the business fails to get those lofty Woolworths-branded Maxi-Cube trailers to the store on time with produce still fresh and intact, their customers start walking.

Kathryn's story is another example of a female's ability to move from a functional career to one in operations and perform equally as well as a male. The myth that women are more suited to functional roles is just that, a myth.

Leadership and mentoring are key

In the Woolworths' story we can see the influence of the individual culture of Michael Luscombe, its leader between 2006 and 2012. His personal beliefs played a big part in driving the changes to the Woolworths' culture iceberg. During this period many developments occurred at all levels of their iceberg and they were able to shift the underlying assumptions and achieve a sustainable solution.

Woolworths' executives provided consistent leadership and mentoring to talented females to keep them, encourage their return after maternity breaks and provide them with access and support to try challenging new roles. These evolutionary cultural changes led to the adoption of new values and they produced behaviours that permitted women to rise into senior management and operational roles. This occurred time and time again and they have increased the numbers of females on their management team from 16.7 to 28.3 per cent. In doing this they moved their organisation Iceberg towards the Redirection Zone.

All four Woolworths' women talked of having very supportive husbands, the commitment they made together with their partners and how they shared the responsibilities at home early on. All of these women have children and two of the four had their children while building their careers in Woolworths. It is fabulous to see that managing a career at the same time as parenting children is possible if you have systems that support you at the office and a supportive partner at home.

McDonald's: No barriers, no limits

"What a well-kept secret!" I said to Catriona Noble, CEO of McDonald's when we met for the interview in the restaurant of one of her Sydney franchises. I was puzzled. Why was the McDonald's story not known more widely? They have so much to celebrate including: the CEO is female and she has enjoyed a long-term career resulting from continuous mentoring and performance; the McDonald's Australian Board has 4 women and 2 men; the executive team is gender-balanced with 11 females and 15 males; over 50 per cent of the restaurant managers are female; and they have a highly diverse employee base.

McDonald's Australia is not a small business. It started operations in Australia in 1971 and it has enjoyed great progress in that time. It has more than 870 restaurants across the country and almost 90,000 staff of which 400 are in the corporate office providing support services to the restaurants, managers and franchisees. They employ people of all nationalities and they are very focused on reflecting their local community through the staff of each restaurant. For example, at the Punchbowl restaurant, the standard grooming policy has been adapted to be inclusive of employees wearing hijabs. In Townsville there is a focus on employing people with indigenous backgrounds to reflect the local population of the area.

Catriona says that the franchises are largely owned by males, with only 10 per cent females, and this is somewhat due to males having had higher incomes historically (i.e. they have better access to investment funds) and that they had reached more senior roles providing the necessary experience to operate their own business. Despite these challenges Catriona and her team are focused on encouraging more women to take up the opportunity. She says "We are actively seeking to recruit new licensees to the McDonald's system with a focus on diversity in both experience and gender. Already we are seeing success with increasing numbers of female applicants at the review board [with their husbands playing a support role] and they are now either in training or have already opened [and are operating] successful restaurants."

McDonald's Australia has made remarkable progress in adjusting the gender balance between 2007 and 2012. This is summarised in the following table, which shows how the percentage of females at each of the eight levels of their business has moved. There are more females at each of the top three levels and fewer females in the entry level (levels six to eight) which was traditionally over-represented by females. Being able to attract more males at the entry level suggests they have illustrated that McDonald's is a worthwhile career option for men too.

McDonald's Australia: females at all levels 2007–2012

Year	% Female by Level				
	Level 1	Level 2	Level 3	Levels 4&5	Levels 6-8
2007	38%	38%	41%	49%	80%
2012	45%	44%	54%	49%	68%

McDonald's brief history

The story began the USA in 1955 with a man called Ray Kroc who was a milkshake salesman with a passion for things that he believed could be replicated: higher sales meant higher revenues! His passion for fast-food kicked in one day when he saw the McDonald brothers (to whom he supplied milk-shake machines) enjoying a rapidly moving line of customers who were queuing for burgers and fries for lunch and he said to himself "This will go anyplace!" He convinced them to take him on to be their nationwide franchising agent.

He was 52 when he set up McDonald's System Inc and took the brothers' simple formula – *a limited menu, quality food, an assembly-line production system and fast, friendly service* – and spread it across the nation.

Kroc believed that making franchisees buy their supplies from him as a condition of doing business would put them at a long-term disadvantage. He decided that McDonald's Systems Inc would only franchise 'the formula' and nothing else. Their franchisees would have to buy their equipment, food, beverages and packaging from suppliers.

To facilitate this Kroc established the 'three-legged stool' – the relationship between the franchisees, the suppliers and the company – and signed up suppliers based on quality, ability to deliver value and loyalty.

How assumptions drive behaviour

In examining the history we can identify some of the assumptions of the organisation culture that Kroc established back in the mid-1950s. Based on what we know from the company's stories, I would say his main *assumptions* which influenced what he valued and what got done were probably these:

- that '*the formula' was the key to sales and long-term growth* (not ownership of the products) and as a result the company would have valued things that would help to improve *the limited menu, the efficiency of the assembly-line like technology, systems and quality improvement and processes that would support fast, friendly service.*

- that *the 'three-legged stool' concept* – interdependence between the people involved – *was the key to stimulating innovation and* as a result the company would have valued employee, franchisee and supplier relationships and effective communication systems to keep all the parties feeling like one family.
- that *training was critical to being able to replicate the fast, friendly service*, as they opened their first training centre 1956 called Hamburger University in Illinois, which is today delivering worldwide skills training, management education and scholarships. The company would then have *valued* skills and knowledge transfer and as a result it now has programs in 28 languages.

In post-WWII, gender equality was unheard of and Ray only employed men as he believed women would be a distraction. However, before long it became clear to Ray that he needed African-American, Hispanic and Asian entrepreneurs to help sell more hamburgers to the minority communities and the early 1960s staff shortages put pressure on the company to hire women to grow stores across the nation.

Diversity milestones

Since then the McDonald's organisation has had a commitment to building a diverse workforce and it reports many significant milestones over the past 40 or so years. I share some of them below to illustrate why McDonald's Australia is somewhat more advanced in terms of its approach to diversity and its progress in building a diverse workforce. Major achievements that this global company has celebrated, which deliver benefits to McDonald's franchisees and employees the world over, include:

1960: first woman franchisee of a McDonald's restaurant;

1968: first African-American restaurant owner and women were allowed to work as crew-members at company-owned restaurants;

1971: McDonald's Australia opens its first restaurant in the Sydney

1984: first African-American joins the board of Directors;

1986: McDonald's introduces its McMasters program to recruit older workers;

1990: the first woman elected to the McDonald's Board of Directors;

1996: the first Hispanic was elected to the McDonald's Board of Directors;

2004: McDonald's forms a Diversity Advisory Council and Fortune magazine names them as the 'Best Place for Minorities to Work';

2005: McDonald's Gay, Lesbian and Allies Network is established;

2009: McDonald's is named as one of the best companies for Latinas to work for in the United States;

2011: the McDonald's Global Women's Initiative received the prestigious Catalyst Award

2012: McDonald's Australia was named an Employer of Choice for Women.

These are just some of the highlights of McDonald's diversity journey and I include them to dispel the myth that diversity in American organisations is simply about 'black and white'. You can see from these examples that McDonald's has included employees and franchisees of all races, both genders, the aged and those with alternative sexual orientation.

The highlights from McDonald's journey also reinforce how organisation cultures of global companies can be transferred across borders to influence cultures of subsidiaries and franchises in other countries. As we saw in Chapter 8, assumptions of organisation cultures are influenced by the values held by their founders, the country culture, the corporate history, their geographical origin and the processes and systems embedded (artefacts) over time. McDonald's Australia has benefited hugely from the history and values of its US-based parent company and Australian employees, franchisees and suppliers are the beneficiaries of this.

Diversity culture and values go way back

According to Catriona, McDonald's Australia's commitment to diversity goes back to the days when it was run by Guy Russo (CEO 1999–2005) and beyond. She says Guy took time out to involve himself in selecting women and mentoring them into new positions. He also 'took the shackles off' people needing to be seen to be 'doing stuff': he was not concerned about 'presenteeism' and focused more on performance. The trust that this engendered, together with his visible support for women, positively impacted the culture making it a more flexible place to work. Catriona said she benefitted from this flexibility when she took time off for maternity leave on two occasions. Both times she was promoted while she was away.

Then there was Peter Bush (CEO 2005 to 2010). Catriona says "He left a legacy of not only innovation, but also of being truly gender-blind and continuing to drive a culture whereby people were selected for promotion or accelerated development based on their ability and talent, not gender."

When Catriona inherited this business from Guy and Peter it already had a history of recognising that diversity in the workplace helps to deliver better outcomes to multicultural communities of customers. She said "When I took over as CEO in 2010 it was all in place, however my top priorities are to ensure that we continue to be creative and implement innovative ways for people to achieve balance. We are expanding our formal mentoring programs to ensure that all employees have the opportunity to learn from others and ensuring that our policies are not just focused on women, targets or quotas but that they also support males who have child-care responsibilities and people who are caring for parents or siblings."

Catriona says "The culture here is so strong that we have little need for induction, however our values – from quality, service, cleanliness and value, through to giving back to our communities and caring for our people – are conveyed loud and proud in all training programs and touch points."

Catriona says "If you want a high-performing team you need to have diversity. I take my role to let women know that they have choices seriously and regularly remind them that they should aspire to be what they want to be."

Catriona became the first female CEO in McDonald's top 10 global markets, which highlights not only that this female runs a growing and profitable business operation, but also that the Australian subsidiary has been recognised as a market leader. This must surely say something positive about the Australian culture.

But before we review the McDonald's Australia Iceberg, let's take a look at the career opportunities that this organisation culture provided Catriona and four other senior women-in-operations.

McDonald's women-in-operations

Catriona Noble

Catriona is Chief Executive Officer and Managing Director of McDonald's Australia. She started her journey in 1984 as a casual teenage-staffer, whilst at school and university, wearing a polyester pale blue uniform serving customers the well-known Big Mac's and world famous French Fries. As we now know, she was sponsored over many years, during which time she climbed the corporate ladder all the way to the top.

Catriona started as a crew member and in just four years she progressed to Restaurant Manager managing 100 staff and a $4 million turnover. Two years later Catriona was delivering face-to-face training for management courses as the Regional Training Consultant and two more years on she was an Operations Consultant in New South Wales where she delivered significant sales increases and record profits.

Everything seemed to happen for Catriona in two-yearly cycles as she was on the move again two years later. She became the National Training Manager providing strategic expertise to develop training curriculums in the restaurants and she received special recognition for turning the National Training Centre into a Global Centre of Excellence.

From there it was onward and upward again as Catriona climbed through the roles of Franchise Manager in 1999; to Director of Operations (McDonald's Operated Restaurants) NSW in 2001; National Marketing Manager in 2003; Regional Manager, Southern Region in 2004; Senior Vice President, Director Corporate Strategy & Business Planning in 2006; Chief Operating Officer in 2007; Managing Director in 2008; and finally she reach the top job in Australia in 2010 when she became Managing Director and Chief Executive Officer.

I love those stories! They are so inspiring and remove all doubt that females can climb the ladder and get to the top if the organisation culture enables it and the behaviours of people and operating systems (artefacts) support it. Catriona encountered no barriers to progression at McDonald's and told me many stories about being mentored by her bosses, men and women alike, who recognised her potential and consistently and supportively helped her to reach the next step.

Catriona shows us how it is possible to journey from the counter at a McDonald's restaurant as a teenager serving burgers to customers after school, to CEO in rapid succession through 13 positions almost every two years. Every young girl, and boy too, can take from this story that if you get into the right company – one that values its people, diversity and inclusion and has succession, flexibility and retention programs in place (artefacts) – you can get to any level you aspire to reach.

Catriona attributed much of the success of her journey to the positive influence of the two chief executives who held the position before her. Like the women at Woolworths, Catriona had many mentors in the company. There is a common pattern here: organisations that are more evolved not only have more women in operational roles, but they also value mentoring and recognise the benefits of keeping women. To achieve that they promote them on merit.

Helen Nash

Helen is Chief Operating Officer at McDonald's Australia. She came from a marketing career in the media and FMCG sectors of the UK to take up her first role at McDonald's in 2004 as National Marketing Manager. This was her first role in Australia, and in the food and hospitality sector, so she must have made many adjustments to settle into two very new cultures and different work practices.

Clearly these challenges provided no hurdle for Helen as she was made an Officer of the Company in 2005; appointed Director of Consumer and Business Insights in 2006; Senior Vice President Director of Marketing in 2007 and then Chief Operating Officer for McDonald's Australia in 2010.

Helen sits on the board of McDonald's Australia and contributes to the company's direction and development. In just seven years she was recognised four times and offered opportunity to try her hand at something bigger and better.

Helen's story serves to remind hiring managers who feel anxious about people 'who have not had experience in this country', or in a new sector or role, that talented people can and have made the adjustment and performed exceptionally well without having to wait to prove themselves, as we heard in Part Two is too often the case.

Jackie McArthur

Jackie is Vice President Supply Chain Asia Pacific, Middle East and Africa at McDonald's Australia.

If you graduated with a degree in aeronautical engineering, what would you expect your career path to look like? Would you envisage ending up on the executive of McDonald's Australia? Probably not, but Jackie MacArthur did after having joined McDonald's in 2002 as Director of Restaurant Systems following a career with Boeing and Airbus. Her initial job involved the design and supply of restaurant equipment.

Like her colleagues, she too received regular promotions. In 2004 she became Assistant Vice President of Supply Chain. In 2008 she became Senior Vice President, Director of Supply Chain for Australia and New Zealand, in 2010 she also took responsibility for Restaurant Development and in 2012 became Vice President Supply Chain for Asia Pacific, Middle East and Africa.

Jackie's work involves managing the supply of food, beverage and paper products to 870 restaurants across Australia and further afield. You might not expect this of a mother of two young children if you were to meet her socially – you might make the judgment that a woman wouldn't be attracted to, or could be effective at, this kind of job. Well, you'd be wrong.

If you were the hiring manager would you consider someone from the aeronautical sector for a role in the food and hospitality sector? If not, you'd have missed out on the 'diversity of experience and skill' that this person could bring.

Tracey Monaghan

Tracey is Director of Quality Assurance, McDonald's Australia. She is from Ireland and arrived in Australia in 1990 with a degree in Food Science and Technology from Dublin University of Technology. She also brought experience from her early career in Ireland as a food technologist and production manager with General Foods. Once snapped up by McDonald's she has not looked back.

Like the others, she enjoyed regular recognition and promotion. She joined the company as Quality Assurance Manager in 1998, became National Supplier Quality Assurance Manager and then National Quality Assurance Manager. In 2009 she was promoted to Director of Quality Assurance for Australia and New Zealand after she played a lead role in the introduction of the *Heart Foundation Tick* program, and in 2012 Tracey accepted responsibility for Equipment and Workplace Safety.

When you are standing at the counter buying your burger and fries, or cappuccino and cake, you may not be conscious of the talent behind the scenes that makes everything arrive like clockwork. Maintaining the standards relies enormously on these outstanding women and their male peers at the top of the organisation continuously advancing technology and processes.

This last story shows again how resilient and adaptable people can be and it reminds hiring managers not to close their minds to 'difference' and to be especially careful when it is a woman if the old assumption that 'women are more suitable to functional roles' is lingering about. Women have shown that they can do anything, including an operation role.

Keryn Jensen

Keryn is the franchisee of the McDonald's Restaurant in Cremorne, Sydney. While I was in that same McDonald's café enjoying my interview with Catriona Noble, she came over to talk with us.

Keryn also started in McDonald's as a teenager serving burgers to customers after school. When she completed her degree she worked in Human Resources roles including with News Corp and Esprit and at one time between 1992 and 1997 she worked with McDonald's in various roles in HR and Training. While at McDonald's she working on the establishment of McDonald's as an RTO (Registered Training Organisation) of Certificate II through to Diploma.

When she left McDonald's to pursue career options in a different industry she started to feel a rising interest in running a business. She had not run one before but she felt quite sure that her broad experience would be transferable and she wanted to have a go. Having already discovered what a great company McDonald's was to work with she decided to buy a franchise and she now has two sites with nine managers and 150 crew members.

Keryn says "The restaurant business is very different from corporate HR but the skills I learned there are invaluable in running a food-service operation. Running a high-volume, low-price-point operation, which is labour intensive, requires broad skills in every aspect of business, particularly technical, from equipment to IT. It's a great challenge as a business owner."

McDonald's culture embraces diversity

You could not accuse McDonald's of holding women back for fear that 'they are not ready yet' or that 'they might fail' (the argument given repeatedly for why there are so few women on ASX company boards).

To the contrary, on the face of it, it would seem that this organisation moves its people up through the ranks more quickly than most. You would have to ask what is the key to their success? I think Catriona Noble summed it up when she said "The culture here is so strong…".

The story above illustrates that the company has always been very clear about who it is, what its values are and what it needs to build a great company that can attract people from all walks of life to eat in its restaurants. Their definition of diversity includes 'a broad mix of different ideas, opinions, backgrounds and life experiences in addition to the traditional measures like race and gender'.

Example of some elements of McDonald's evolving Iceberg

Artefacts – Policies and programs facilitate career progression of people from diverse backgrounds. Diversity Awards. A Diversity Advisory Council. People of mixed race, gender and experience on board & management teams.

Behaviours – Friendliness at all levels. The family feeling goes behind the front office too. Respect shown to employees and vice versa. Inclusion of people from all races and both genders recognised by industry watchers/magazines.

Attitudes – The 'three-legged stool' is key to our existence – owner/operator, suppliers and employees. Balancing the interests of all three is important to our survival and success.

Values – We value a diverse workforce and the opportunity to leverage the unique talents, strengths and assets of our people. We value results, teamwork, career progression, customers and communities.

Assumptions – The business model works. Diversity among our people is essential to meeting customers needs everywhere. Customers are at the core of all we do. 'Doing the right thing' is important to us.

As we saw in Chapter 8, the assumptions (less visible) at the bottom of the organisation culture drive the behaviour that we see (visible). Catriona described McDonald's Australia culture as "Having a strong family feeling where teens who are both top scholars, the school duxes, and those that don't excel in the school environment, work alongside one another doing their jobs equally well. They share in the responsibility to deliver quality food with fast and friendly service together". She added, "They select friends on the basis of teamwork and it builds the self-esteem of the group". She talked about how often more than one family member is working in a restaurant, how relationships form and some even marry while working there and that it really does feel like a big happy family.

It seems that part of McDonald's success is the atmosphere and family feeling which is not something that can be generated through artefacts. Strong positive feelings of teamwork and family in a culture typically come from it being taken-for-granted and valued, together with having strong leadership, shared vision, pride in the company and its performance and a sense of respect and trust.

I'd hazard a guess that there are two other main assumptions lying at the bottom of McDonald's culture apart from those I assumed Kroc to have instilled, and they are promoted through McDonald's materials:

- 'Diversity among our people is essential to meeting customers' needs everywhere';
- 'Customers are at the core of everything we do'.

These assumptions wholeheartedly support McDonald's business model, the 'three-legged stool' formed back in 1955 by Ray Kroc. They also lie beneath the values and would influence the beliefs, attitudes and behaviours of people working in or with McDonald's today.

If you are in a male-dominated company with few women in operational roles, few women at the top and few younger people at the top of your organisation (suggesting that tenure is more important than meritocracy), then you will have some distance to travel to get where McDonald's has reached. It is very difficult to generate a close-knit family-friendly culture with a preponderance of one gender and especially if that dominance turns to near exclusivity at the top levels – because families are made up of both genders of all ages.

We have in McDonald's Australia a wonderful illustration of how to build a strong and enduring organisation culture that facilitates sustainable diversity and thereby stimulates and fosters long-term careers through which excellence, performance and profitably are realised. This great company is on our doorstep, employing 90,000 Australians, so why is their story not more widely known?

One person said to me 'Diversity is all about black and white in America' suggesting I ought not to waste my time interviewing an American company. But look what I found. Are we turning a blind eye to what is not made in Australia? That would be a shame because there is much to learn from people who come from a different place and in this company, there is much to learn about creating organisational cultures that can sustain diversity.

Ernst & Young: A conscious redirection

Most of you will have some experience with a big-four accounting firm or perhaps the big-eight as they were known in the 1980s and 90s. Whether you are a past or present partner, employee, customer or supplier of one of these firms you will have gained an impression of how evolved the global accounting firms' cultures are relative to other organisations that you have worked with.

They generally stay ahead of the curve by innovating new operating practices and market services in response to changing economic conditions. They do this despite their enormous size and global spread, their restricting professional traditions and their historically male-oriented environments, which affect the tenure of females in these firms. These features of the industry provide significant growth challenges but somehow they do seem to get beyond them. The big-four firms have ample experience and huge success in achieving change of the restructuring kind, but achieving change of the cultural kind continues to be a challenge.

I have consulted to almost every professional sector there is across the world (including law, accounting, engineering, medicine, architecture, education, science, research and more) and no matter what the country culture, organisation history or size, each one that I have experienced first-hand has faced culture change and gender-balancing challenges.

The mere fact that the big-four firms are among the world's best thought leaders on business issues and market leaders in their field, means that their cultures are in many ways a little more evolved than those of other sectors. They are actively embracing diversity, have programs underway and are investing in developing women to support them to climb the ladder to partnership. However they are the first to tell you they have some way to go to get gender equality at the partnership level.

Not surprisingly one firm has shaken the foundations of its culture. I was quite excited the day I walked in to Ernst & Young (E&Y) offices to interview Lynn Kraus, the Office Managing Partner (OMP) of the Sydney Office, and heard about the progress they had made. Not only did they talk the talk, but they walked it too.

When Lynn told me that four out of six OMPs across Australia were female and that it all happened within just 18 months as they moved from having one female OMP in October 2009 to having four female OMPs by February 2011, my jaw dropped as I processed the information, somewhat disbelieving my ears. "That is unheard of in professional-firm-land", I thought. The image of women out-numbering men in the leadership team of most professional service firms around the world is merely a distant mirage. Fascinated, I asked to speak with all four of them and with the leaders who made this possible. They agreed, so I can share their story with you here.

Chicken or egg?

E&Ys advancement was such a massive leap forward that I started to wonder what came first.

As previously discussed, there are several different ways that cultures can evolve; some are gently guided in a particular direction, some are left to drift (consciously or unconsciously) and other cultures are deliberately 'shocked', to unfreeze the embedded assumptions so that new ones can be established to encourage the adoption of new values and behaviours.

When I considered the adjustment of the gender balance at the top of E&Y Australia, I had many questions running through my mind. The foremost was "did the firm culture change first and the four women succeed to the OMP roles second, or did the firm nudge these women into these leadership positions first, so that their presence would impact a shift in the firm's culture second?"

If it was the former, it would take a while to achieve as evolving culture is a slower process. However, if it was the latter then the culture 'shock' could have brought about a culture shift faster than is traditionally possible.

Watching evolutionary change is a satisfying thing and it usually arrives without too much pain, but it can take longer than you are prepared to wait. Sometimes leaders need to respond to internal challenges or market opportunities quickly and initiate more revolutionary culture-change tactics to push through the pain barrier (and the resisters) to get a faster result.

What were the motivators driving E&Y leaders to seek change and which came first, culture change or the appointment of women to these top-level positions? I had to find out.

I obtained insights about E&Y's journey from the four female OMPs first – Lynn Kraus (Sydney), Annette Kimmitt (Melbourne), Lucille Halloran (Canberra), Jenny Parker (Brisbane) – then I met Uschi Schreiber, Deputy CEO Oceania, and finally Rob McLeod, CEO Oceania.

All four women travelled very different pathways to arrive on the E&Y leadership team. I'll outline these briefly as each story illustrates that they came from a different starting place and were selected for quite different reasons at different times.

Jenny Parker

Jenny has been Office Managing Partner (OMP) of the Brisbane office since 2007.

Jenny Parker left Arthur Anderson to join E&Y in 1999 and is the Oceania ITRA & Risk Leader and the OMP for Brisbane. She leads a team of 46 partners and 574 staff. Jenny was the first of the four females to step-up into the role of Office Managing Partner.

Jenny recalls, "When the Deputy CEO at the time, Tim Eddy, asked me to apply for this role back in 2007, he asked me to present my vision and plans for the office. I was given the gig and I was surprised, as there were more senior men than I who had been in the practice a long time. They said I was promoted because 'I had a willingness to have a point of view, but without being on the offensive and that I had demonstrated ability to take people on the journey with me."

She went on to say, "We have been conscious of the cultural change required in E&Y for some time and we know it needs to be a direct intervention. I have a succession plan and when I see people with potential, I actively intervene to make sure both females and males get the opportunity to flourish." It was clear that E&Y's culture-change initiatives were by no means accidental or evolutionary.

"We have hired almost equal numbers of women as men for many years, but we have not been successful at bringing them to the top. We wanted to change that. If you don't do anything about it, you see no change. You need to be open-minded about where you might discover people with potential. If you give people a boost of confidence they often rise up. It is important to say to people "I do see you as a future leader."

She added "We have really grasped onto the importance of having the courage to lead. Success is determined by those around you and we don't allow elitism to occur. We have hired a lot of people laterally (from industry and other firms) and we select people who will fit the culture and embrace our values. We know that people will self-select out if they don't fit, so we are careful about this."

Jenny said the firm had debated gender targets for some time before the ASX changes occurred and she observed "The sky has not fallen in as a consequence of the ASX recommendations being put in place so there must be room for further change". She makes a good point. If we are not getting any major reaction, then perhaps we have not pushed the change far enough. She says "Australia is lagging behind other countries and we are unlikely to get anywhere fast without quotas for women on boards".

Annette Kimmett

Annette has been Office Managing Partner of the Melbourne office since 2009.

She joined E&Y in 2004 and was appointed to the management team as OMP Melbourne in October 2009. She leads a team of 117 partners and 1605 staff. She is also the Victorian Chairman of the Institute of Chartered Accountants in Australia and she sits on the board of the United Nations Principles for Social Investment Secretariat and the Committee for Melbourne, so she is no lightweight amongst business leaders in Australia.

Annette said "The move to change our structure and culture started with James Miller (CEO from July 2005 to June 2009) who introduced profit centres back in 2006 to reduce the impact of the silos. James had adult daughters who were entering the workplace and he used to talk about how they raised his awareness of the need for change not just in business but in society generally. He began to see the opportunity to lead culture change in our firm as his legacy."

Then Gerard Dalbosco (CEO from July 2009 to June 2010) came into the role and Annette says "He was unhappy that there were no women in the executive committee. He saw it as an old boys club. The view that there is 'no room for women to be successful' was challenged by the leadership team and we started to make some initial changes that we thought would address this."

Gerard set up a Diversity and Inclusiveness Council to serve as an advisory team to the firm's leadership, he had his leadership team commit to workshops on diversity including some very personal exploration of unconscious bias and how that manifests itself in the workplace and he had the team spend time understanding and articulating the business case for gender equality at E&Y.

Gender balance and diversity became a topic at each and every leadership meeting across the firm during this time. Annette says "When Rob came in 2010 he shifted the dial: he changed it because he could. He thought there was a lack of diversity around the top table as they were all male and he identified the enormous experience and talent of Uschi Schreiber and promoted her to Deputy CEO almost straight away."

Uschi then appointed Annette to join her and Jenny Parker in the leadership team. Annette said, "It was a really good group to be part of. Throughout my whole career I have been surrounded by males and then all of the sudden I found myself amongst this group of highly talented females. The dynamics of every meeting was different. It was constructive, supportive, and no one was afraid to speak their mind. We do have robust debates from time to time but then we all support each other once a decision is taken and this makes you feel safe to raise issues."

Lucille Halloran

Lucille has been Office Managing Partner of the Canberra office since 2010. Originally from Canada, she arrived in Australia in August 1996 and initially joined Deloitte in Brisbane. She was their inaugural Business Woman of the Year in 2004 and came to join E&Y as OMP, Canberra in 2010. She leads a team of 8 partners and 141 staff.

She says that when she arrived at E&Y she felt that the firm 'lived' its values with regard to diversity and said "I found that it was embedded in the practice". She explained "Formal programs are not always able to address the more complex issues and you must have the basics like 'working flexibly' in place and without those you don't have a starting platform.

"The things that make the difference are the things that touch people every day, like mentoring for females to encourage them to consider a long-term career, and consequences for behaviours that expose unconscious biases that could affect the progress of individuals, teams or the firm at large."

Lucille explained the dilemma many professional firms face with new graduates: they have a different perspective than the bosses on the need for female sponsorship. Young women graduates say there is no gender problem and they don't want to be singled out from their male peers by having special programs and the young males ask "Why are the women getting special attention?" when programs to enhance female careers are established.

As we know from professional service firms' history, what starts out as a 50/50 male/female split in the graduate intake each year, ends up an imbalance 10 years on. The male/female split of partner numbers vary from large to small firms, but there are rarely more than 25–30 per cent females in the new partner promotions and often it can be as low as 15–20 per cent female.

Lucille shares her feelings about her career at E&Y so far, "I feel very valued and supported at E&Y. I feel like I can build my career and that I have a voice. I feel significantly happier since joining this firm. It is about 'the Uschi's' of this world' (outstanding female role models), the behaviours they exhibit and the sense of belonging you get from their leadership. It is about the culture, which values the most basic things like respect. We don't need to talk about diversity programs here because it is just happening.'

Lynn Kraus

Lynn has been Office Managing Partner of the Sydney office since 2011. She leads a team of 168 partners and 2147 staff. She was born in America, studied in South Carolina and became a CPA in the USA and joined Ernst & Young (E&Y) in Atlanta, Georgia at the age of 22 before arriving in Australia in 1996.

Lynn spent six years working in the Australian practice of E&Y before returning to the USA in early 2002. She spent the next few years working on the trading floors of Wachovia Corporation and then later Westpac, upon her return to Australia, so she was no stranger to working in a heavily male-dominated environment.

The partners at E&Y invited her back in 2005 and she became a partner shortly thereafter and became leader of Assurance in the Financial Services team in Sydney. She recalls that those early years were tough as the firm had not yet adopted flexible work arrangements for women with children and she was balancing the demanding career with the lion's share of the housework when she got home each night.

Like most successful women, Lynn progressed quickly. She became a member of the Oceania Advisory Council and was appointed to be one of the first female Client Service Partners (CSP) in 2007. The CSP role is the highest level of client partner in the firm and historically the people who occupied these roles were the long-tenured senior partners who Lynn reminded me were 'almost exclusively older, grey-haired men'. She mused, "They used to call me 'young Lynn' which was a bit patronising although I knew they meant no harm". The CSP team today is now much more gender balanced.

Shortly after that Lynn was appointed to the role of Managing Partner, People for Oceania in 2008. This meant she was now focused internally on managing and developing the firm's people across Australia, NZ, Fiji and Indonesia. She said "When I got into that role I noticed that the pipeline of females was churning and the replacement strategy was unconsciously biased towards males. We identified that women live by their values and if they didn't like what they saw when they looked at the values of our organisation, they would walk. We needed to change things to retain our female talent.

"We were concerned that if we only made HR program changes (like mentoring, training and development) we would only improve fractionally each year. Our actuarial team reviewed our past history of hiring, promotions and retention rates and the statistics were alarming – it would take us 10 years to move the needle for women partners from 13 per cent to 15 per cent. So we agreed 'This is too slow! 10 years is too long to wait to see such a small difference' and we started to look harder at the female talent we had…and that which we didn't have."

Lynn said "In the early days we focused on mentoring and developing women: it was all about 'fixing women'. Now we are looking at how we can better 'value women' not fix them as the organisational culture is what truly needed to be fixed." The firm invested in unconscious bias programs to help senior leaders and partners understand and value difference.

In 2011 the OMP role for Sydney opened up and Uschi Schreiber suggested Lynn should apply for the role. Lynn recalls "I was hesitant as I suspected each of my males peers would probably apply for the role. I'm not sure whether I would have put myself up had I not received a signal that I was a candidate with a chance".

Once appointed, more challenges were illuminated. Lynn said, "After two years in the internal-facing role as MP for People, I was in a market-facing role once again and this gave me an opportunity to refresh my thinking about 'valuing women'. By being back in the market I could see the gender challenge from everyone's perspective: the firms, the clients and the employees. The opportunities that were open to our female employees elsewhere became more apparent and I became more aware of the commercial importance of having gender balanced teams."

As the diversity of teams are now more gender and age balanced, there is just one key area to address: race. "We are adding ethnic diversity to our targets now because our partnership still looks white, even though we have many different country cultures represented there. If you can't get people from different ethnic backgrounds up through the ranks you can't deliver racial diversity in the management team."

Uschi Schreiber

Uschi is Managing Partner, Global Government & Public Sector Centre based in the firm's Hong Kong office. She was the Deputy CEO for Oceania based in Sydney at the time of the interview. She was appointed to this role by Rob McLeod in 2010 just two years after she joined the firm in 2008 to head up, and build, the Government and Public Sector practice.

She was born in Germany and came to Australia as a young adult and has been involved in work with many other countries and cultures throughout her career. As a consequence she has many different references and constructs to draw upon in her role at E&Y.

In July 2010, 23 member countries of the Oceania region were brought together to make one regional firm – all moving to adopt global policies and create one operational centre to service clients in the region and strengthen its ability to participate in the growth occurring across Asia. Uschi's appointment meant that she had oversight of everything that was happening across the whole of the Asia–Pacific region and 1300 partners. If you have met Uschi Schreiber you will know that she is confident in expressing her observations and opinions about 'what is' and 'what should be' without reservation, but with a clarity and intellect that leaves you in no doubt that you should consider her view.

As Uschi reflected on the gender challenges within the regional offices with me, she advised "The USA and Europe have the same challenges: no one in the world has all the answers". She explained that the Australian firm recognised that it was losing females at a certain age (early to mid-30s), that it was highly inefficient and that they needed to make adjustments to keep this talent in the firm.

Uschi was the driver behind many changes within the firm at this time. The leadership team wanted to build the pipeline of females coming up through the ranks and to do this they had to adjust the environment that was turning them away.

They required more senior female role models to guide younger women and they had to build a more gender-balanced culture: and you can't do that with only one gender at the top. So Uschi began by looking more intensively, internally and externally, to identify experienced and skilled females who might not be putting themselves forward.

She also checked the recruitment policies, selection criteria and processes and development programs for any possible biases to ensure that females were getting the same opportunities as men to come forward and get promoted to higher levels. They began to insist that every selection panel comprised a balance of males and females and that every candidate was interviewed by a female partner.

Diversity was now at the top of every management team-meeting agenda: this leadership team knew that achieving gender diversity could be a major business differentiator and they set out to achieve it. Uschi's experience embedded a belief that women with talent added hugely to a business's dynamics and performance and she helped others to see that achieving gender diversity was possible and worth striving for.

When Uschi set out to fill the vacancies for OMP positions for Canberra and New South Wales, she cast the net far and wide. She identified both male and female candidates and asked them to put themselves forward and ran a rigorous interview process to select the best people on merit. Two outstanding female candidates were selected and this took the toll to four female OMPs and two male OMPs for the first time in the firm's history.

The impact that such major changes make to a firm's Culture Iceberg are immense and long-lasting and we will review those after we have met Rob McLeod.

Uschi has publicly supported the move towards quotas for women on boards. She says "The change is too slow and as a society we need to move faster. There is fairly overwhelming agreement in business circles that this kind of systemic change (quotas) is needed and it is no longer acceptable to 'not know' about the debate. It needs to be front of mind and we all need to get into action."

Rob McLeod
Rob McLeod has been CEO Oceania for E&Y since 2010 and is based in Sydney. He was previously New Zealand Country Managing Partner. Everyone I interviewed mentioned Rob's contribution to the redirection and his compelling message about the value that greater diversity could have on the firm's future. They recognised and articulated his values and talked about the changes that had occurred in just 18 months: changes which suggested that he and Uschi together had quite possibly shifted the assumptions of the local firm's culture in that short time.

Rob highlighted how the professional service firms are very people-oriented that he had been concerned for some time that graduate numbers were approximately 50/50 male/female but that within 10 years there was a dramatic fall-off in females in the senior ranks.

Rob said "Our aim is to increase the number of women in the partnership. We have formal plans that contain goals (targets) and we have established counselling and mentoring, and expanded our recruitment efforts. The targets hold leaders to account for their performance in this area. They responded to having these KPIs and you can see the results in the past 18 months: they are more focused on and accountable for meeting the targets so the conversations about outcomes are more challenging. We have a clearer nexus. I believe we are one of the first to embrace the idea of targets and you can clearly see that it works."

He added, "Some men may see quotas as a zero-sum game: that is, if you have 10 positions and you appoint more women, then there are fewer men in the group and that is prejudicial to men. I don't see it like that. When we take on more clients it does not mean that it leaves less space for existing clients. We need to adopt 'abundance thinking': that's where the universe continuously creates unlimited resources for us to take advantage of. By adopting abundance thinking in the firm, we can change our attitude from negative to positive, appreciate how potentially abundant the firm can be if we have both male and female partners and leaders, and look for the good things that can flow from this."

Rob referred to his management style as laissez-faire. He says "When I ask managers to achieve KPIs it's not the setting of targets that is important, it's their ability to achieve them. A liberated manager is always going to find a more effective solution to reaching a target than one who has to work within a controlled environment."

When I enquired how the firm produced four females out of the six OMP roles, he replied, "Jenny and Annette were put in place by my predecessor; they were there when I came to the CEO role. But then Uschi came into the role of Deputy CEO and she appointed Lucille and Lynn. All OMPs report to her and she found that these two women were the best fit for the roles and the most highly skilled to meet the challenges of each location."

He added "When Uschi was looking to fill the two OMP roles she was looking for technical skills – you have to be as good as the tribal members when you work in a professional services firm – and she was looking for people who could coach and mentor others. The need for gender balancing was definitely a priority but meeting that requirement was not enough: the candidate had to pass the other hurdles first. You don't dumb-down the decision so that you can get a female into the seat. Uschi got the organisation moving. She's both conceptual and good at execution. She gets things done.

"I believe in affirmative action, but my advice is that you need to be careful that your people don't think that you are promoting women just because they are female. It's important that your criteria for selection are transparent. Our women leaders were selected because of their relationship skills, technical experience and client servicing ability. They had also demonstrated their leadership capability in previous roles. I personally don't think the problem is about attitude: we just need to be more rigorous about identifying the female talent and appointing them into the roles."

Shifting assumptions delivers sustainable solution

So there you have it. Between 2007 and 2011, five remarkable women were identified and appointed to the leadership team of this global professional services firm.

The rapid succession of the four significant appointments in 2010–2011 would have nudged the firm's organisation Culture Iceberg to take on a whole new direction. The arrival of Rob McLeod from New Zealand as CEO (a cross-cultural appointment); then Uschi Schreiber as Deputy CEO (a new entrant taking the second most senior position over long-term male partners in the firm); and then to the two additional females to the team of six OMPs (making it female-dominated for the first time in history) would have sent a strong message to employees, clients and market watchers that E&Y was making change.

So what came first? The chicken (evolutionary culture change modifying assumptions about gender and increasing the value of women in leadership positions), or the egg (revolutionary multiple appointments of senior females, two of the five being laterally hired, designed to jolt culture change and push through the barriers)?

I think you'll agree that what we see here is a combination of culture-change strategies. We heard that changes were introduced by James Miller and Gerard Dalbosco in the mid-2000s and that Jenny Parker and Annette Kimmitt were appointed during their time. The changes that occurred between 2006 and 2010 included the communication of new values espoused by the leaders about the need for gender balancing, some new behaviours by partners who mentored women and offered development opportunities and adjustments to artefacts that supported recruitment and development of females through the firm. This was steady progress and evolutionary in nature.

The revolutionary measures came when Rob McLeod stepped off the plane in 2010, promoted recent arrival to the firm, Uschi Schreiber, to be Deputy CEO and gave her the mandate, and presumably the KPI's too, to make change. Her message to the partners in the Oceania region that diversity matters was loud: watching women in the pipeline leaving in their mid-30s due to lack of a role model was wasteful; failing to provide a culture that supported the way females manage their careers was passé and needed to change to address the 'churn'; and the firm's growth and performance was reliant upon its ability to attract the talent it needed to remain viable in the ever-changing and competitive market place.

Uschi wanted talented females to come forward for all appointments. She knew she had to set the example. She needed to looking intensively and broadly at women everywhere to find the talent her firm needed to shift the assumption that E&Y 'provided no room for women to be successful' as identified by Annette Kimmitt some years earlier.

Rob McLeod's and Uschi Schreiber's methods were more revolutionary. They were courageous and made changes with conviction and yet the firm did not convulse. Their ability to pull it off must be attributed somewhat to the earlier leaders who made evolutionary changes preparing the organisation for further, more radical change. In a way, the earlier measures would have served to reduce the resistance that Rob and Uschi might otherwise have encountered. By 2010, the benefits of the changes that were made were evident (as were the costs of the changes that were not yet made) making their more radical moves more acceptable.

The key milestones signalling a new era to employees and clients were:

- multiple laterally-hired senior people to the top team;
- senior appointments made on the basis of meritocracy not tenure;
- the appointment of more females than males to the leadership team;
- the cross-cultural mix in the top team (which includes New Zealand, Germany, Canada and USA providing flexible working options to leaders in the top team.

E&Y Australia changed significantly between 2000 and 2006, and even more by 2012. To help us understand the way in which the changes would have affected the E&Y organisation Culture Iceberg I have prepared three illustrations for each of these time frames to show how the changes often start at the top of the iceberg, with the more visible and better understood elements. Remember as you view the iceberg examples that they are indicative only.

NOTE: In the Woolworths and McDonald's cases above, I compiled just one example of the Culture Iceberg at one point in time, although their cultures would have evolved in a similar way as I am about to illustrate in the E&Y case below.

The Comfort Zone: We like it this way

Examples of some elements of Ernst & Young's evolving Culture Iceberg – 2000

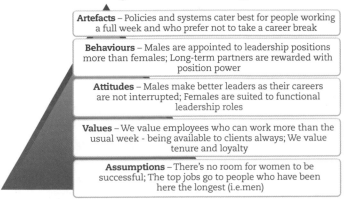

These elements of the 2000 Culture Iceberg illustrates that in days gone by the firm's values were biased towards the careers of males (due to historical reasons explained above). Despite the fact that E&Y leaders had been trying to increase female partner numbers for many years prior to 2000, the underlying assumption that there was no space for women to grow and succeed prevailed. This meant that the attitudes and behaviours were still influenced by this underlying force and even changes in recruitment policy or newly stated values about female partners were not sufficient to 'turn the churn'.

The Band-Aid Zone: The tip of the Iceberg

Examples of some elements of Ernst & Young's evolving Culture Iceberg – 2006

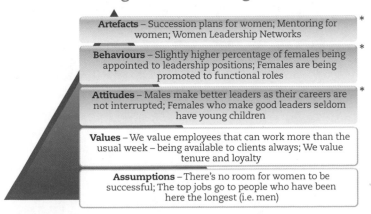

* These layers have been adjusted between 2000 and 2006

By 2006, leaders started to make changes to the visible and better-understood elements of the organisation Culture Iceberg: the ones at the top, above the waterline. Typically diversity initiatives start with HR interventions, which come in the form of artefacts designed to influence a shift in behaviour (e.g. policies, processes, systems, education, training, mentoring, rewards and so on). As we learned in Chapter 8, adjusting your artefacts will not alone lead to a sustainable change in behaviour. You need to get deeper into the culture to impact a lasting change.

That said, most companies typically start at the top of the Culture Iceberg as that is the most obvious way to signal an evolutionary change. But you need to be very careful with 'top down' evolutionary measures: if you don't ever reach the bottom layer you will not achieve sustainable change as old assumptions when left unchanged continue to undermine new values and behaviours. In the 2006 Iceberg we can see that the top three levels have evolved. Following this, more changes were made by successive leaders at E&Y to reach the 2012 Culture Iceberg.

The Redirection Zone: Shifting assumptions

Examples of some elements of Ernst & Young's evolving Culture Iceberg – 2012

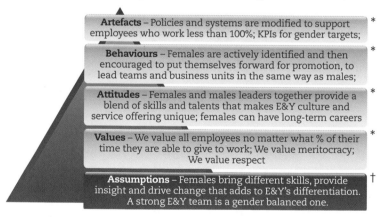

Artefacts – Policies and systems are modified to support employees who work less than 100%; KPIs for gender targets; *

Behaviours – Females are actively identified and then encouraged to put themselves forward for promotion, to lead teams and business units in the same way as males; *

Attitudes – Females and males leaders together provide a blend of skills and talents that makes E&Y culture and service offering unique; females can have long-term careers *

Values – We value all employees no matter what % of their time they are able to give to work; We value meritocracy; We value respect *

Assumptions – Females bring different skills, provide insight and drive change that adds to E&Y's differentiation. A strong E&Y team is a gender balanced one. †

* Evolutionary adjustments 2000–2009
† Revolutionary 'jolting' of the assumptions 2010–2011

As we have heard throughout E&Y's journey, more recent leaders moved things more rapidly. As its people had sufficient warning from earlier leaders of the need for change and some early experience of change, the leaders who took over next could confidently move to discredit the assumptions of the firm's culture that were holding back progress. It just takes one radical change, one revolutionary step, combined with conviction and commitment by a united top team to achieve this.

In the 2012 Culture Iceberg, we can see that the assumption 'There's no room for women to be successful' has been replaced with 'Females bring different skills, provide insight and drive change that adds to E&Y's differentiation' and 'A strong E&Y team is a gender balanced one'. These shifts are expected to lead to new beliefs that 'females can have long-term careers that are not limited by career breaks or working flexibly' and new behaviors that see female partner numbers rise.

Professional service firms' cultures

In addition to Ernst & Young I interviewed a number of leaders of other professional service firms for this book and each of them also shared insights, lessons and advice into Australia's challenges and their own culture change and diversity journeys. Their comments are peppered throughout the book.

The intellectual power held within professional service firms is significant. The people who provide the intellectual property that these firms deliver are clever, passionate and driven. The knowledge these firms contain and the services they perform for business and society locally and globally is progressive, adds huge value and can rarely be trumped.

There is just one thing that all professions struggle with and it has changed little in my 25-year career. That is, the elements of the organisation culture that hold progress back. At the core of the culture lies centuries of tradition, professional values, a partnership economic model, male-dominance, power structures, tenure over meritocracy and 'the chargeable hour', to name just a few. These features are peculiar to the professions and while they are part of the reason for their success, they can also create blockages to their growth.

The challenge of changing culture arises from the challenge of changing the behaviour of people. As professional firms have long histories, embedded ways of doing things and contain large numbers of highly intellectual and strong characters, changing 'the way they have been doing things' is naturally going to receive some resistance. But as we have seen through E&Ys experience, the secret is to get to the bottom of the culture and shift the old, out-dated, assumptions or you will be tip-toeing around the problem for decades.

Hanging on to the past is not the answer to future success. Letting go and allowing your culture to evolve is the smart thing to do to adapt your organisation to the rapid industry and economic changes around us.

Organisations and the Culture Iceberg

None of the three organisations whose cases are outlined above knew of or had seen my models – the Culture Iceberg or the Culture Circuit – prior to me preparing their cases. But as you can see, the models help us to appreciate their stories.

All three of them had recognised the need to be very clear about what could be 'taken-for-granted' and what was not acceptable. The people in their organisations learned from their firm hand that changes were being made and they were not negotiable. They made 'valuing females' visible and changed artefacts and behaviours to support the changes to assumptions and values.

One of the helpful things about case studies is that you can use them as a learning experience with others and the last thing I present in this chapter is a workshop tool that you can use with your managers and other staff. On the next page I have prepared some 'discussion starters' to help you highlight the key 'take-homes' for your people and then contrast these with your own organisations. You can also prepare some of your own too. As you analyse your organisation culture, uncover any blind spots and identify which zone you are in, you can use these three cases and their Culture Icebergs as a guide to map out your journey with your teams.

If you are reading this thinking 'we tried everything they did but we still have females walking out the door in their mid-30s', then you haven't shifted your assumptions, or some other blind spot exists.

Getting to the bottom of your culture is vital. If you don't, any initiatives you are investing in will, as sure as day-turns-to-night, come unstuck. The challenge for you is determining your assumptions, which as outlined above, can be extrapolated from the higher-level elements in your organisation Culture Iceberg.

Any leader can take the journey to change a culture to which they belong. It just takes vision, courage and conviction. Bon voyage.

Not all those who wander are lost

J. R. R Tolkien, CBE, from 'The Fellowship of The Ring': also author of 'The Hobbit' and 'Lord of the Rings'.

Organisation Culture: Contrasting your culture with another

Step One:
Examine the case (state which company case you are analysing)

What stands out as being the most compelling reason for their diversity success?
What were the biggest challenges they faced on their diversity journey?

Identify the highlights of their journey:

- **Exploring their Culture Iceberg:**
  - What challenges do you think they faced as they shifted their assumptions?
  - Which assumption do you think would have been the biggest challenge for this business to change? Why?
  - What assumption do you think they have yet to address?
  - How would these be impacting their diversity and growth?
  - Repeat each of these four questions for each layer above assumptions – values, attitudes, behaviours and artefacts.

- **Exploring blind spots:**
  - What blind spots did they, or could they have, encountered in each zone and how did they, could they have addressed them along the way?
  - How did they/could they have identified them?
  - What blind spots might still exist?
  - What could be the impact of these on their diversity and growth?

- **Exploring the culture zones**
  - How fast did they move through the culture zones?
  - When and where did they start the journey?
  - Could they have gone faster? How?
  - What would be the impact of that?
  - What strategies did they employ to build diversity and grow?

- **Exploring their Culture Circuit**
  - What impact did each of the main cultures in the Culture Circuit have on this organisation's diversity and growth:
    - Country culture? How?
    - Individual cultures? Whose? How?
    - Organisation culture? How?

Step Two:
Contrast their experience with your own organisation culture:

- What does your Culture Iceberg look like?
- How fast is your culture drifting and where is it heading?
- What assumptions exist at the bottom of your Culture Iceberg and how do they aid or inhibit your diversity and growth?
- Are the assumptions of your culture aligned with your strategic intentions and will they help you realise your ambitions and goals?
- What values, attitudes, behaviours and artefacts exist? How well aligned are they to your ambitions and goals?
- What blind spots exist and need addressing?
- How could you begin to address the blind spots?
- Which zone are you in? How fast are you evolving? Is your pace sufficient to keep you from drifting behind?

To test the accuracy of your Culture Iceberg you could repeat the workshop with different groups in your culture.

WHAT
**The power
of diversity**

WHY
**The issues
impacting
growth**

HOW
**Changing
cultures**

WHO
**Leaders
and
society**

PART 1

PART 2

PART 3

PART 4

Taking the Mantle
Chapter 1

Listening
Chapter 2

Discovering Diversity
Chapter 3

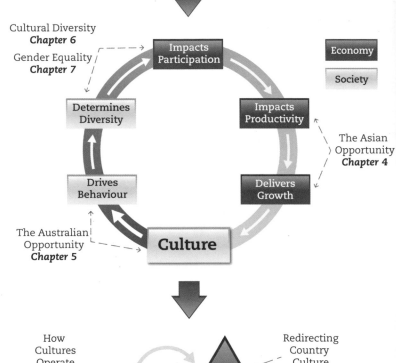

Cultural Diversity
Chapter 6

Gender Equality
Chapter 7

Impacts
Participation

Economy

Society

Determines
Diversity

Impacts
Productivity

The Asian
Opportunity
Chapter 4

Drives
Behaviour

Delivers
Growth

The Australian
Opportunity
Chapter 5

Culture

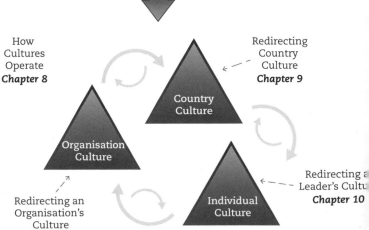

How
Cultures
Operate
Chapter 8

Redirecting
Country
Culture
Chapter 9

Country
Culture

Organisation
Culture

Redirecting a
Leader's Cultu
Chapter 10

Redirecting an
Organisation's
Culture
Chapter 11

Individual
Culture

Stepping Up
Chapter 12

Part Four

Leaders and Society

Part One looked at what greater diversity can do for the growth prospects of business and society, and Part Two explored why the 100 leaders believe that we need to evolve Australia's culture and allow greater participation of both genders and all cultures. Part Three explained how to analyse cultures and direct a change in any of the cultures to which we belong.

Chapter 12 explores who should lead and who would follow. Most of the 100 leaders have said that leadership on achieving diversity has been underdone, and that changing culture to support growth in our businesses and communities is too slow. Now it is time for leaders to step up to lead the social change needed to allow Australia to keep pace with the progressive nations of the world.

Who should lead?

'Great minds discuss ideas,
average minds discuss events,
small minds discuss people.'
Eleanor Roosevelt, advocate for civil rights and women

Many good ideas

So many people have so many good ideas but the challenge is implementing them. Time constraints, priorities and sometimes anxieties get in the way of us acting on them.

We are not short on good ideas. When it comes to ideas for how to achieve diversity or how to stimulate growth across the Asia region, our 100 leaders have shared many and I hope you have gained some further ideas from reading the case studies.

With all these good ideas, all that's left to do is establish who will lead. That is, who will ensure we implement these good ideas? Who will step up to drive the change, provide the vision and redirect the cultures that are slow to adjust to the world around us? I suspect you have formulated some answers in your mind as you have journeyed through this book and it would be good to hear your views if you'd like to share them.

Any good idea needs to be led. As we discussed previously, 'hope is not a method' for getting things done and 'talk does not cook rice' (Chinese proverb presented earlier). So if we can't rely on hope, or stimulating conversation, then we need to look for action.

The last two questions

The last two questions I asked the 100 leaders during the intensive interviews were about how to get the action we need to see change in Australia. I asked:

- If you agree there's a need to work towards achieving diversity to ensure full participation, boost productivity and stimulate growth, then who should we expect to lead?

- How ready do you think Australians are for cultural change, which is essentially social change, and what needs to be done to get them to follow?

These questions are challenging; they require a gear-shift. The answers involved 'big picture' and visionary thinking, which is not what most people focus on in their day-to-day lives. A number of answers to these questions started with statements like 'that's a good question', 'I haven't thought about that' and 'no one has asked me that before'. This is not unusual as they are questions that require careful consideration. One person replied to the leadership question with:

What an interesting question. I have no idea. It should be led politically, but there are no leaders there. Could it be the Governor General? She leads by example. I have no easy answers, but you have to start at the top and you need to communicate your message relentlessly.

(An anonymous 100 leader)

The aim of *Stepping Up* is to encourage more 'big picture' thinking. If we don't think broadly and strategically regularly enough, we can get buried in the business of solving today's problems and meeting short-term goals. When our head is down, we can't see where we are going. Without a clear vision, we are misguided and can drift.

We have been reminded many times throughout this book through the 100 leaders' comments and in the work of Geert Hofstede's in Chapter 9 that Australia, like most Western nations, is very short-term-focused in its orientation.

For Australia to resolve its challenges, it must think 'big picture', in a visionary way and strategically. In this chapter we will explore the things that are necessary to bring about diversity and growth in Australia. Specifically we will look at:

- Who should lead on diversity in society?
- Who should lead on diversity in business?
- Who should follow?
- Is Australia ready for social change?
- Leading culture change.

Before we take a look at the answers that were given to the questions about leadership and social change, let's remind ourselves of the big picture within which the change we seek sits and briefly review the key themes arising from the book.

The big picture

The feedback from the 100 leaders has given us much to think about and their many good ideas were summarised at the end of Chapters 4-7 so all we have left to do is identify who will lead the change we seek.

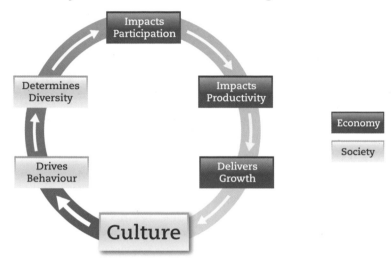

Society Drives Economy... and Diversity Boosts Workforce Participation

Throughout *Stepping Up* we have explored the link between Australia's social maturity and its economic performance. We have discussed the impact that behaviours in society have on the agility and performance of local business and communities. We have also specifically looked at the issues surrounding low levels of diversity at higher levels of our organisations and how this impacts the country's growth.

At the start of the book I proposed that if we could encourage a cultural shift to remove blockages so that both genders and all cultures could fully participate in their chosen careers and in decision-making about the country's future, it would boost national and individual productivity levels. At the same time it would prepare our workforce to be more effective in operating across Asia. That is, greater cultural diversity in senior management of Australian businesses would increase our cross-cultural awareness and understanding, thereby improving our international trade relations.

Relationship between cultures

We also looked at the relationships between a country's culture and those of the organisations that individuals establish and run. The Culture Circuit, like an 'alternating' electrical current, can flow both ways. We know now that to improve either the country's GDP or a company's profit performance the most effective solution is to initiate an evolutionary shift in *both* the country and organisation cultures. If you only shift one culture, the influences of the other will eventually flow back and undermine the changes you have already made.

The flow between any of the cultural groups in the Culture Circuit can help or hinder a group's ability to achieve its ambitions and it is important for our leaders to be mindful of these influencing factors as they embark upon change. The breadth and complexity of the many challenges and opportunities highlighted by the 100 leaders reinforce the critical nature of the connection between all cultural groups.

Assumptions within a culture

One of the most compelling learnings for me throughout my career so far has been how assumptions can trip you up – often they are wrong. Not only have I learned this personally on my own journey, but I have witnessed dozens of organisations embark upon strategic initiatives, mergers, divestments, restructuring and culture-change programs without fully appreciating the power of the underlying assumptions and the effect they can have.

The cases in Chapter 11 have helped us to understand how shifting assumptions can be the key to making a 'step-change' (or revolution change) to the way an organisation operates. Also, this kind of change can be a very successful strategy for signalling that the future is different from the past and that old, out-dated practices are no longer appropriate or tolerated.

Truth begs action

The stories that individuals have shared throughout *Stepping Up* are illuminating. We know that Australia is no longer a society that has a 'White Australia Policy' or prohibits women from having their own bank account or requires them to resign a job when they get married. However, Australia is still the country that tolerates discrimination and bias towards women like Georgia and Rachel's, immigrants like Bernard and Beatrix and returning expats like Dan and Dave.

When you combine the messages from these incidental stories to the highly consistent and clear messages voiced by the 100 leaders about the very real issues that need addressing in our society and across industry, we are left with a problem. The problem now is that we have to make a choice. Do we fix it or ignore it. To fix it we need leadership.

Leadership: Overused and under-delivered

Having worked with many leaders over the years – old and young, experienced and green, appointed and self-nominated, effective and sleepy, inspiring and challenged – I have come to the conclusion that having the title of leader ought not to entitle you to privileges until you have delivered the goods. Those who carry the mantle outstretched for all to see and who use it wisely and fairly to yield returns for all followers are the ones who merit our attention.

To put it another way, there are many leaders, but not enough who lead change. When we are not leading, we are managing. The definition for 'to lead' is 'to go in advance' and if we are not 'ahead' of the people who are supposed to be behind and following, then we are not really leading.

To be a leader of change takes courage and confidence because you have to stand apart from the groundswell of opinion that 'she'll be right' and challenge the status quo. It takes courage to say "No, she'll not be right because our people are not fully productive, our population is not fully integrated and our level of competitiveness in worldwide markets is being challenged by our lack of language skills and inability to get females and non-Anglo-Saxons to executive levels of our business and society."

It requires 'steel' to speak up about something when you know that what you have to say is not the popular view nor generally understood. It involves confidence to hold fast to your good ideas and persevere with trying to illustrate to others that the alternative way forward that you propose ought to be given some consideration.

Cultural impediments to *stepping up*

There are a number of different kinds of constraints limiting the performance of leaders in Australia.

As we have read previously, there are several features of the Australian culture that inhibit people from stepping up to lead. The 100 leaders gave examples of the continued existence of the 'tall poppy' syndrome, the fact that newly arrived immigrants have to wait a decade or two to be accepted and that returning expats have to wait to prove themselves. Then there is also the force field which protects the privileged class and limits who can share the space at the top.

A number of people also commented on the Australian government's lack of leadership, how its focus is short-term and driven by popular vote and how its commitment to matters important to long-term growth – especially with regard to Asia – oscillates, making it difficult for businesses to plan ahead. There has also been criticism about the lack of leadership on the need for gender equality and on the pace of change.

It is a matter of being a bit brave about the changes we need. I don't understand how we can have a woman PM and get no leadership from her party on this.

Professor Julianne Schultz AM FAHA, Non-executive Director, Australian Broadcasting Corporation, Chair Australian Film, Television and Radio School, Sydney, Australia

If you wait for government you might be waiting until hell freezes over.

Phil Ruthven, Chairman, IBIS World, Melbourne, Australia

Then there's the biggest cultural impediment of all – the firmly entrenched assumptions, attitudes and behaviours of some of the existing leaders. As times change we are supposed to change with them, but sometimes the pace of change is so fast that people can't or won't keep up with it. Another reason why change doesn't occur with the times is that the old ways served the incumbents well and they are reluctant to let go of the features that deliver benefits and provide a sense of security.

Perhaps leadership should come from people who are not currently leaders because many of our existing leaders are entrenched in their views. Maybe these are leaders at the middle level management: we could be looking to give them space to step up.

Stephen Roberts, Chief Country Officer, Citi, Sydney, Australia

Who should lead on diversity in society?

As mentioned above, I asked the 100 leaders at the end of the interview who they think we should expect to lead on change to achieve diversity and growth in the Asian Century. Let's review a few of the comments.

A number of people said the leadership challenge rested with the business, government or education sector, and some said all three should help:

Business should lead

The corporate sector should be leading; especially those with the largest workforces. It's not just about gender – it's broader than that. Working parents are falling under the strain – it requires social change.

Ilana Atlas, Non-Executive Director, Coca-Cola Amatil, Sydney, Australia

It has to come from a multitude of directions, it has to come from boards – CEOs must take leadership. I think it is important for women executives to be supportive and encouraging of other women.

Graham Bradley, Chairman, Stockland, Sydney, Australia

Government should lead

Government: they have to do something but everyone has a responsibility. It has to be driven somehow as there is no leadership anywhere yet.

Margaret Dreyer, Partner, Deloitte Touche Tohmatsu, Sydney, Australia

The leadership needs to change at the top. Politicians should be more vocal. Corporate Australia should be leading as they have ability to influence outcomes. They need to get boards to buy into the benefits.

Kim Schmidt, Director People and Culture, Grant Thornton Australia, Sydney, Australia

Government plays a very important role to explain to Australians what we need to do. The PM is very passionate about education and media has a role to emphasise the need for change in education

Uschi Schreiber, Managing Partner – Global Government & Public Sector Industry Centre, Ernst & Young Global, Hong Kong, Australia

There's no doubt that the biggest change is the cultural shift. We hear so often 'I am successful so you should look like me, act like me and be like me'. But success can look like many different things and we need to allow for this to get social change happening across all parts of society. We need bipartisan leadership from government; quotas to force some change; and commitment from big companies to check their notion of success.

Diana Cross, Australasia Human Resources Leader, Arup Group, Melbourne, Australia

It needs political leadership that is engaging for people: they need to say what's in it for Australia. The world is changing. Everyone talks of the 21st century being the Asian Century and we need to get a plan. Is it that we will teach Asian languages? Is it that we will use the Asian students that are here? We have so many opportunities but we are 'the land of plenty' and we are complacent.

Ann Sherry AO, Chief Executive Officer, Carnival Australia, Sydney, Australia

Regarding social change – you can't get too far ahead [of people in society] or it will die. You need a legislative basis for the change you seek and these changes need to be reflected by the society to be sustainable. It might take a generation to achieve social change because cultural change is slow.

Jillian Segal AM, Non-Executive Director, National Australia Bank, Sydney, Australia

Schools and universities should lead

You need to start the change in schools, before university. The challenge is how to motivate people to want to move [to change their ways] rather than stay the way they are. If we got serious we could do it in a third to a half of a generation – say 5–10 years. But it's like the need for sustainability – who is going to start it, who will lead the change?

Dr Robert Care AM, Chair UK, Middle East and Africa Region, Arup Group, London, United Kingdom

If I was queen for a day, I would start by changing our education system. I would make selective schools co-ed. I would not let people into schools or universities based on a single exam mark. I would invest in selection processes that recognise and encourage broader contribution, and I'd want to know what work kids had done, what volunteer work, what leadership initiatives they had been involved in and what aspirations they have. I fear that students from Asian backgrounds are not building the breadth of experience or the connections needed to be successful in Australia. At the same time, students with Aussie backgrounds are not encouraged enough to connect with Asia.

If we are really going to make any big culture change we have to start with education. We need more universities to offer exchange programs and we need them to do exchanges with non-English speaking universities too.

Diane Grady AM, Non-Executive Director, Macquarie Group, Sydney, Australia

Are we ready for it? We should be ready for it! Schools can help. Change is an absolute constant and should be embraced.

Catriona Noble, Chief Executive Officer, McDonalds Australia, Sydney, Australia

Changes need to start at the education system. We can't be open about things we don't know about.

Rosemary Howard, Executive Director AGSM Executive Programs, Australian School of Business, UNSW, Sydney, Australia

A mix of government, business and education

The onus is on us to lead social change. We will all benefit from cultural and gender diversity. There are three key areas: business has to recognise the talent, government has to help with policies that reinforce what we want Australia to become and practical assistance like tax relief to encourage people to make these changes, and we have to use our education system properly to provide what we need to get to our goals.

Mike Smith OBE, Chief Executive Officer, Australian and New Zealand Banking Group, Melbourne, Australia

The principal in the school is an important leader to lead on Asian languages in schools. Teachers are critical too. Parents need to push for Asian languages for their children. It's also important for businesses to support Asian language development and literacy skills.

Sid Myer AM, Chairman, Myer Family Company, Melbourne, Australia

Senior politicians and senior educationalists should lead this. Also, leaders of any institution that can influence public opinion should use it.

Shirley In't Veld, Non-Executive Director, Asciano, Perth, Australia

Australian businesses have to take more of a leadership role in leading change to get diversity and our universities should really be thinking about their role in facilitating this change in a way that they haven't done before.

Diane Grady AM, Non-Executive Director, Macquarie Group, Sydney, Australia

It requires the leadership of government and industry to create that environment and you need commitment from boards and shareholders too. Executives need to establish diversity counsels and policies and then women, immigrant and Aboriginal leaders – the strong ones – need to step up to help.

Russell Tipper, Chief Executive Officer, Brockman Resources, Perth, Australia

It needs to be a collaboration of government and business working together. It needs to be boldly led and it will require them to go out and be audacious. It will require someone who is prepared to challenge and who will push things through. It also needs dollars and time. It needs to be bi-partisan. But people are frightened to speak about it

Dr Jacqui Abbott, Head of Flexibility and Diversity, Allens Arthur Robinson, Sydney, Australia

It needs to come from the broader business leaders and from government. Government see their role as providing policy and legislative changes, but they don't seem to lead on this issue.

Alec Bashinsky, National Partner People & Performance, Deloitte Touche Tohmatsu, Sydney, Australia.

Others said that responsibility rested with all of us – and that everyone needed to share the problem and arrive at a solution together:

Everyone should be involved in the change

I think it has to come from across all spheres of society. Obviously leaders in organisations need to embrace it and the press need to be more even-handed in the way they represent females in Australia.

Jane Owen, Partner, Middletons, Sydney, Australia

We should expect better political leadership. Polarisation of political parties is driving a vacuum in leadership on big issues. Businesses tend to be relatively self-interested: they should lead but are not doing it. Maybe the community voices should be louder.

Ann Sherry AO, Chief Executive Officer, Carnival Australia, Sydney, Australia

It should come from many places. We should look for leadership from our politicians, businesses, people in society, religious leaders, sporting leaders, artistic people and other cultural leaders. Not just political leaders

Jillian Segal AM, Non-Executive Director, National Australia Bank, Sydney, Australia

I look straight at us – women in leadership. Too many get to the position where they can take the top job and then opt out; they are fearful what the next step might do to their families or their career. Too few take that last step. Women need to feel confident to step up. Men need to bring along as many women [as possible] on the journey; that can make a real difference.

Debra Singh, Former General Manager, Dick Smith, Sydney, Australia

Where should it come from? It should come from me; from all of us. Kennedy once said 'Ask not what the world can do for you, but what you can do for the world.'

Dr Robert Care AM, Chair UK, Middle East and Africa Region, Arup Group, London, United Kingdom

It has to come from government and businesses: the simple answer is, it has to come from everybody.

John Harvey AO, Executive Director, IBM Australia, Sydney, Australia

Leadership needs to come from government, academics, church and schools. You need to get all those players to move. Normally you'd say government should take charge but governments are so poll-driven now – you need convergence of leadership from big business. I think [if you had] a convergence of leadership from many sectors and institutions you might start to see some change. The media also has an important part to play.

Katie Lahey, Chief Executive Officer, Korn Ferry, Sydney, Australia

People who have taken on a leadership role have a huge obligation to help. Male and female political leaders – they should step up. Senior executives and community leaders need to recognise this is their opportunity to make this happen.

Catriona Noble, Chief Executive Officer, McDonalds Australia, Sydney, Australia

It's hard to know where it should come from – societal change. Obviously government has to promote change through education and to working with schools. There is a need to transform the education agenda, to challenge stereotypes and discuss the nature of work in the future. Parents and teachers would all have to have a responsibility to help with this. Business leaders are working hard to create opportunities for women and not lose them in the mid-levels. Everyone has to play a part in this – including women.

Peter Bailey, Chief Executive Officer, Arup Group, Sydney, Australia

Leadership should come from everywhere: not just the top – it must come from the factory floor too.

Nigel Garrard, Managing Director, Amcor , Melbourne, Australia

It is not just government – it crosses all aspects of the community, schools, boardrooms and sports playing fields. It's a broad problem and we need a very holistic solution. We need to find a catalyst – it should be a combination of government and private sector, then involve everyone in the community.

Joanne Wood, Chairman, Capital Eight, Shanghai, China

In Asia it would be government who would take responsibility on this – but that's because their government takes a paternalistic view on society. In Australia it's a democracy therefore it should be a community issue.

Dharma Chandran, Chief Human Resources Officer, Leighton Holdings, Sydney, Australia

Finally there were those who offered an alternative view:

Smart people should lead

It would make a difference if we could find a group of smart people that ask tough questions. It starts at the top with the leaders; if they don't hold it as a core value, how do you lead? People watch what we do more than what we say so we need to live those values.

Paul Waterman, President. BP Australia, Melbourne, Australia

We need the media to help

The media have helped to keep the discussion alive in the public forum...that is the appropriate forum for the public debate. But it doesn't substitute the debate.

Uschi Schreiber, Managing Partner - Global Government & Public Sector Industry Centre, Ernst & Young Global, Hong Kong, Australia

It's not clear who: no one is stepping up

Business passes it off to government. It should be the universities but they don't have the money. We lack the right think tank and body and we are scratching around.

Kevin McCann, Chairman, Macquarie Group, Sydney, Australia

We need to start at home

We need to start on the street that we live in.

John Denton, Chief Executive Officer, Corrs Chambers Westgarth, Melbourne, Australia

We need a hero

Everyone wants a role model – a church leader, a political leader a great boss. Everyone in life has a hero: those people who influence what they think. But in Australia we seem to be missing vision and values. Where is our hero?

Nigel Garrard, Managing Director, Amcor , Melbourne, Australia

We need leaders to lead

We need to look at men and women that are already there [at the top] for leadership – they need to take on the mantle.

Marie Malaxos, GM Production and Development, Buru Energy, Perth, Australia

We can't wait for government

Our political structure needs to reflect social reality: if you behaved like politicians do in a business you'd be dismissed. Government is less and less relevant to people. Change in society would need to happen without government.

Melinda Smith, Chief Operating Office – Masters Home Improvement, Sydney, Australia

When you read through these suggestions it is clear there is no single front runner in the leadership stakes, which highlights the dilemma that we have in Australia in driving social change. Government is thought to be too busy with meeting short-term goals and chasing votes and the corporate sector is unable to turn the tide on underlying assumptions of Australia's culture alone.

The education sector was well recognised as having a big role in meeting this challenge, which reinforces the notion that our values are set early in life and our schools and universities need to do a better job at preparing Australians for the 21st century.

A large number of people thought of the challenge as being one in which everyone should participate; that we should all be involved in doing whatever we could to help move things forward, collectively and individually. Nigel Garrad's suggestion about the need for a hero is fitting: history is full of heroes who change the world around them and all cultures have heroes who are revered for their greatness and contributions. Australia's cultural impediments mentioned above could be one of the reasons why heroes are thin on the ground.

So what is the answer? I think Australia needs *someone* couragous to 'kick off' and *everyone* else who is holding a mantle to lock arms and drive forward.

If someone, or some group of courageous, visionary and inspiring leaders doesn't step up soon to lead the social changes we need in Australia and to provide direction for the followers, Australia will undoubtedly slip further behind other nations. We can't evolve our culture and improve our position by willing it. Action needs to be taken.

In order for my dream to come true, *that everyone living in Australia joins the workforce believing that the opportunities are equal, their path to the top meritocratic and the door to positions of power and leadership open*, it is going to require leadership and significant change. What is your dream? What will it take for your children to live in the world you dream of?

Who should lead on diversity in business?

The answer to this question depends entirely on how evolved the organisation culture and country culture are and how diverse your organisation is. In Australia, neither the country nor its businesses are yet enjoying full diversity at all levels and until this is achieved the CEO should be leading the culture change.

In a business that has a completely diverse population, representing all elements of its society and existing within an evolved country culture where diversity is also highly valued and displayed, working to 'build diversity' is not necessarily going to be a strategic advantage. In this case it is less likely to need a CEO's direction, sponsorship or control. Once 'being diverse' is embedded in the culture's assumptions and it has become 'the way we do things around here' then it will just happen instinctively and the CEO can pass the reins to line managers and the human resources department to ensure balance perpetuates.

However, in organisations where poor diversity exists – as in the ASX2000 and many non-listed companies that lack gender and cultural diversity at the top – there is an enormous opportunity and competitive advantage to be gained from making the attainment of diversity a core strategy. In these cases,

Leading change for diversity: The evolutionary (inductive) method

		Phase 1	Phase 2	Phase 3
		Diversity is driven by human resources : starting with Band-Aids to shift attitudes & behaviours to encourage diversity	Business managers getting involved: KPIs attached to performance	CEO appreciating diversity can provide strategic advantage: Top team taking ownership of 'the way we do things around here'
Level of involvement	CEO and Leadership			Sponsors and champions Driving culture change Leading by example Unfreeze the culture with a 'jolt'
	Line Managers		Building KPIs and business process changes	Using diverse teams to gain business advantage: diversity lead business wins
	HR Department	Changing artefacts and shifting behaviours and attitudes	Supporting business change – valuing led diversity outcomes	Reinforcing new assumptions at all levels of the organisation's Culture Iceberg

the strategy needs the backing and visibility of the CEO from the start. Waiting for your organisation to 'get in the game' to become aware of the issues, then to 'get serious' about identifying barriers and installing Band-Aids can cost you a decade or two. You need your leaders to take up the mantle immediately.

The tables below show the difference between evolutionary culture change that has been practised over the past 20 years (inductive), and a more revolutionary method that some organisations are now adopting (deductive). Organisations that already have experience with change are more open to a deductive method: it is led by the CEO, it's faster and it recognises diversity as a strategic imperative that can produce tangible business advantages.

You need a more revolutionary method to leading culture change if you want to get to the Redirection Zone of your culture's journey faster and start enjoying the benefits sooner: increased participation and productivity, lower costs of acculturating hundreds or even thousands of new employees annually, more informed decision-making and more creative and innovative solutions to problems and take-up of opportunities.

When there is low diversity in the country culture too, as is the case in Australia (evidenced by the fact that we are 20–30 years behind others in

Leading change for diversity:
The revolutionary (deductive) method

		Phase 1	Phase 2	Phase 3
		CEO appreciating diversity can provide strategic advantage: Top team taking ownership of 'the way we do things around here'	Business managers driving diversity	Diversity is supported by human resources: business as usual
Level of involvement	CEO and Leadership	Sponsors and champions Driving culture change Lead by example Unfreeze the culture with a jolt		
	Line Managers	Introducing KPIs and business change processes	Using diverse teams to gain business advantage: diversity lead business wins	
	HR Department	Reinforcing new assumptions at all levels of the organisation's Culture Iceberg	Supporting business change – valuing diversity led outcomes	Reinforcing new assumptions at all levels of the Culture Iceberg Maintaining diversity profile

allowing a female to lead the country and our status on the WEFGGG report) CEOs can also use their influence outside their organisations. They can work to shift the other cultural groups to which they belong, which are impacting on the values and behaviours of people in society who are employees of industry.

Organisational leaders in the 1980s and 1990s could be excused for not knowing the importance of culture to the bottom line. But in 2013 and beyond, not aligning your culture to delivering diversity, full participation and productivity will become increasingly inexcusable.

In the 21st century, leaders at the top of organisations need to lead culture change to achieve diversity and growth because it is 'the hard stuff'. They need to lead with courage and confidence, to drive culture change strategically. If we fail to develop these leadership capabilities in our people and create the cultural environment that allows this kind of leadership style to flourish (eliminating the tall poppy effect, Queen Bee and the *force field*), we will continue to be challenged as a nation, and in our businesses, for a long while to come.

Experienced leaders use more advanced methods

It was identified at the start of *Stepping Up* that the knowledge base for organisational culture and change, and its use as a strategic tool for improving profit performance and growth, has only been developing since the late 1980s, so we can be forgiven for taking the evolutionary road to changing culture until now. For the past 20-plus years we have been developing know-how, learning how cultures operate, practising culture change methods and measuring the outcomes and impact on business performance.

This process has allowed us to evolve the practice of 'leading culture change' and to prepare our societies and institutions for change. We are now aware that change is a constant and we know that the countries, organisations and individuals who are most adaptable will survive.

But times have changed. Smart organisations and skilled leaders are moving to the deductive method for leading culture change outlined in the table on the previous page. Based on their experience of the past 20 years, they are now confidently adopting this faster method for leading change. As a result, greater diversity progress and growth are achieved faster. These leaders are moving their organisations to the Redirection Zone faster and jolting their cultures to adopt 'a new way to do things around here'. They are able to move with courage and confidence, their organisations are used to change and their employees are learning how to respond to change initiatives. It has become part of the daily routine.

As we have seen throughout *Stepping Up*, achieving diversity in Australia is an emotionally charged affair. By that I mean it is linked to many very sensitive issues relating to how people in society treat one another. Words such as racism, bigotry, sexism, discrimination and bias are being used to describe the behaviours of people in Australia and many of these words were used to reflect the frustrations expressed by the 100 interviewees.

When you are in a leadership role you carry responsibility to provide an example for others. You are supposed to be – as another leadership definition says – 'the initiative in the action'. Your followers are looking to you for guidance. Are you satisfied that you are being the best leader you can be?

Who should follow?

Leadership is really about followship and it is those who have voluntary followers who are the most powerful. Their followers are loyal and there is an emotional connection not just an economic one. When people tell you 'that was so inspiring' after you talk, you know you are onto the truth.

We rarely talk about followship. Yet if we were to talk about followship as much as we do about leadership I think we would have many better leaders. When you talk about followship you have to put yourself in the shoes of the followers and there's no better place to be when you are trying to appreciate what it is that will inspire them to take the path you want them to go down. The focus is on them, the followers, not you, the leaders – and that makes a whole different conversation.

So who should we expect to follow and what does followship look like? Let's consider what followship means to two of our 100 leaders whose views are dissimilar. Chris Komor expressed his view that people of Australia would follow a charismatic or enlightened leader if we could find one:

People are at the poles on many issues but they will follow a charismatic leader more than they will an institution, they seem to lack trust in institutions. People follow women too – look at the female Premiers. I think we need someone who is strong and enlightened; we would follow a good leader if we had one.

Chris Komor, Principal, Willow Bend Station, Central NSW, Australia

Natalie Filatoff took a long time to consider my question 'Who should lead?' and after silence and contemplation she replied with an answer that was quite unexpected.

I don't think we like to follow anyone. I think Australians are unlikely to say 'I'll follow your lead'. I don't know who we would look to for leadership on diversity: no one is standing up saying 'Come on, I'll lead it'.

Natalie Filatoff, Principal, Filatoff Editorial and Writing, Sydney, Australia

I have since wondered, is this lack of willingness or need to follow others a result of our island culture, isolation and independence? Does the notion that you might 'follow others', in an Australian sense, suggest that you are in some way inadequate or feeble or needy? I'd hope not as this is not the meaning of followship. To follow the leader in an organisation setting means to work in harmony, in unity, as a team – to achieve a common goal.

If, as we have heard from the 100 leaders, people in Australian society hold disparate views (attitudes) on most important issues, then perhaps it makes sense that they are also disparate in their behaviour too and don't wish to follow – preferring to remain independent.

If this is true, then we are facing a more serious problem than lack of leadership – we could also be facing lack of followship. The challenge then magnifies and we have much more work to do, making the leadership job colossal. The longer we leave this unattended, the more difficult the problem becomes.

I did not ask the 100 leaders 'Who should follow?' but it is a question that would benefit from some discussion. As a leader of a business you have an expectation that your people will align their thinking and behaviour to your organisation goals and act in a team-like and cooperative way to produce agreed outcomes. The same goes for people in society. Australians are possibly ready for a discussion about direction, vision and goals to help get people aligned and pulling together.

Is Australia ready for change?

The final question I asked the 100 leaders was about Australia's readiness for change. Specifically I asked:

- whether people were ready for a national campaign to drive social change to achieve greater diversity across the nation (country culture change);
- whether leaders and organisations were taking the need for change seriously or were they paying lip service to it (organisation culture change);
- whether the leader being interviewed was up for being more actively involved in leading change (individual culture change).

Instinctively I think we all want to believe and say 'Yes of course we are mature enough to talk about what we could do better' and in most cases people did respond with something along these lines.

God help us if we can't have a dialogue to openly challenge, discuss and debate the impediments and roadblocks to diversity. If we can't, then this country will wither. Change is going to come through shame and transparency or we will be struggling for generations to come.

Stephen Roberts, Chief Executive Officer, Citi, Australia and New Zealand, Sydney, Australia

I also detected a level of nervousness or anxiety about starting a conversation to discuss these sensitive topics. I could only surmise that some people were not sure where it might lead or how it would be received. Perhaps the tall poppy syndrome is impacting on our ability step up and lead on this. One person told me that 'A national program to drive social change' is akin to social-engineering, yet no one complains when we have government-sponsored advertising about the adverse effects of smoking, drinking, or diabetes in children.

I think of this remark every time I see the advertisement by ancestry.com where the actor proudly says 'I looked on ancestry.com and discovered that my family used to own a pub!'. If this advertising, which perpetuates the highly-cherished drinking culture, gets prime time on national television without an uproar, then what is the concern about some national advertising to promoting more equitable careers for females, greater integration of immigrants and the need to learn Asian languages?

There were a few comments that raised doubt about the willingness of Australians to try new things:

Australians are change-resistant. If they don't know things well, if they lack the knowledge, they are hesitant. So getting change can be difficult.

Robert Milliner, Former Chief Executive Partner, Mallesons Stephen Jaques (now King & Wood Mallesons), Sydney, Australia

There were some people who thought we had been enjoying the good life for too long and were complacent:

We need to create the burning platform, and to do that our leaders need to create a vision for this country.

Rosemary Howard, Executive Director AGSM Executive Programs, Australian School of Business, UNSW, Sydney, Australia

There were some who thought that Australians were open to discussion but that if push-comes-to-shove, we might need to use coercive means to get change:

I think society is open to the debate and we are mature enough to have the conversation – we just get busy. Sometimes it does take regulation to force change and there probably should be strong disincentives for bias. The media could help but maybe it is bored with the subject as it sells more papers with a new topic.

Russell Tipper, Chief Executive Officer, Brockman Resources, Perth, Australia

Ultimately, our interest in following someone else's lead on change comes down to having inspiring leadership:

We need an inspired leader and we should have a strategy for Australia. What we have are politicians who worry about the three-year cycle and this is not creating the legacy. We need enlightened leadership to get social change

> Mike Smith OBE, Chief Executive Officer, Australian and New Zealand Banking Group, Melbourne, Australia

And a vision for what has to be done and how we are going to get there…

It is all about culture and beliefs and we can't change beliefs unless you have people to follow who you admire. I'd like to be part of something that has a clear way of dealing with this. It is a matter of building a 'groundswell' of support. Whenever I have the opportunity I talk with people about the need for change, but I could do more….yes, I could do more….

> Ilana Atlas, Non-Executive Director, Coca-Cola Amatil, Sydney, Australia

And then there was a view that 'the change is done' by a leader whose sees women in roles around him.

'Are we ready for change?' That question would come over as yesterday's conversation. We have women in all roles…so the debate is over. The biggest challenge is getting the skills. I think the gender discussion was yesterday's discussion. I know the mining companies are looking for skills of any gender. I don't see the issue in society.

> Graham Bradley, Chairman, Stockland, Sydney, Australia

My sense from the 100 interviewed is that change is needed and leaders need to be found, now. Many of the leaders interviewed are actively involved in initiatives to lead change in their companies and communities and it was encouraging.

However, my sense from hundreds of others I have spoken with informally on these topics over the past 18 months – in the city, at school, in the community, on the sports field, at social functions and beyond – is that people are occasionally resigned to the fact that political leadership on this is not forthcoming so we may as well get used to things being the way they are.

People were also polarised. At one end of the spectrum those who think everything works just fine are fewer in numbers, comfortable in their lives and are not themselves affected by the lack of diversity. At the other end are those who can see the issues, and agree that someone should lead on this, but who are not actively seeking to lead the change themselves.

Leading culture change

There is opportunity for everyone to contribute to evolving Australia's culture and thereby impacting social change. For example, you could help others who you see harbouring old assumptions and values by demonstrating there is a different way 'to be', which can help us to progress in society and in the world.

We know that we are each influenced by and can influence other cultures in our Culture Circuit. Leading change does not require you to be in a leadership position or to have a degree in change management; you simply need to want things to be different and better and be prepared to step up, get up, and make it happen.

Stepping up: permission not required

I want to share a couple of stories with you to illustrate how others have made this happen.

The first story is about shifting your *individual culture* to lead change. It is about an individual who took up the mantle in 1958 aged 26 and how she changed the face of her local Queensland town forever. Her story is very inspiring and shows just how practical Australians can be.

The second story is about shifting your *organisation culture* to lead change. It is about how you can find amazing leadership capabilities in people at *all* levels of an organisation who can help to drive culture change. It illustrates what happens when you tap into budding young leaders (who are waiting for permission to step up): it shows you can discover and ignite energy and ideas that may not be found in a homogenous group of older leaders. I have observed many successes when people of all ages and different levels of experience have been engaged in leading change and I'd like to illustrate how a broader approach to sourcing leaders for change teams can be very effective.

The third story is about encouraging a shift in *country culture* and achieving social change. It involves a discussion about the 'chicken and the egg' and it explores how to get a collaborative effort to involve everyone in the community.

Individuals: Taking up the mantle

Sometimes people are driven internally to do things they believe in without having any special mandate to do it. Sometimes they just step forward and before they know it they have achieved amazing things. Here is a short story about a young woman who, in 1958, wanted change in her local community and how she stepped up to make it happen. It's a delightful story and illustrates how abundantly skilled Australians can be.

Dellys Kelly and 'a good idea' that she acted on

In November 2011 I ran a series of workshops for female employees of the University of Southern Queensland (USQ) in Toowoomba and for women from non-traditional industries from regional Queensland. In the same week, USQ was holding its Annual Go WEST Awards, which is for women and girls from the university and local and rural communities in these non-traditional areas of study and careers.

At the Awards evening the Chancellor welcomed dignitaries in the front row including Mrs Dellys Kelly who was announced as 'the founder of the University of Southern Queensland'. I looked at the woman who nodded an appreciation and thought she looked more like a grandmother rather than a founder of the University with 25,000 students. Well, it turned out that she was both, and she was about to turn 80. I felt the need to hear her story.

It was Easter of 1958 and Dellys Kelly and her husband had recently bought the Tourist Hotel in a small town called East Greenmount, 18 kilometres outside Toowoomba, in southern Queensland. One day she was watching her two sons Michael (4) and Gregory (1) playing and she thought about their lives and where they might go to university when they grew up. She did not want them to go out of the area: she decided she wanted a university in Toowoomba.

After spending some time talking to the Mayor and Councillors of Toowoomba about the possibility of establishing a University, she felt she top'. So she asked her parents to come and run the hotel and mind the children so that she could go to where the top man lived.

When her parents arrived the following day she packed an overnight bag, fuelled up her new FJ Holden, bought a map to navigate her way and headed south to Canberra. Thirteen hours later she arrived there and found a hotel for the night. The next morning she drove up to old Parliament House, parked outside the main doors, walked into the reception and asked to see the Prime Minister, Robert Menzies, briefly outlining what she came for. The receptionist looked amazed that someone would arrive without appointment and ask to see the Prime Minister, but she excused herself and came back a few moments later and asked Dellys to take a seat and wait.

Prime Minister Robert Menzies, accompanied by Treasurer Harold Holt, came out to greet her. Dellys says "After shaking my hand and simultaneously patting me on the shoulder (as you did to young women in those days) he showed me to a meeting room where he indicated that he would take a few moments to listen to me as I had driven so far to see him."

Dellys explained what she wanted: "I would like a university in Toowoomba please, that's all". After a short discussion about the reasons behind her request the Prime Minister suggested that they think about it over lunch and they took her to a Parliament House restaurant. After lunch Robert Menzies said "If you can raise £30,000 come back and see us then". She left feeling elated…but she was sure they really did not expect to see her again.

She had never had to raise money before so she wasn't sure how to go about it. She slept on it overnight and woke up thinking "why can't I just ask for it?" She prepared a list of the people to ask and put her own name at the top of the list with £500 alongside. After adding the other names to the list she realised they were mostly men so she raised her contribution to £1000 assuming they would want to better 'the little lady's offer'.

In just 11 weeks Dellys raised £30,000. She approached farmers and business people from around the South West region. She spent the 11 weeks driving from town to town seeking support and collecting contributions from as little as five pounds (a week's wages for some) and up to £10,000.

When Dellys phoned Robert Menzies to tell him that she had the £30,000 she could hear his surprise. He set her a second challenge. "You need to get yourself an executive committee and when you have one, call me back again".

It took two years for Dellys to establish a committee. She found that while people were prepared to give up cash, they were somewhat reluctant to step forward and take responsibility for such a project. She eventually persuaded enough people to form a committee, which was initially chaired by Mr Heathwood, a businessman from Toowoomba.

Finally the Menzies government came to the party and The Darling Downs University Establishment Association (DDUEA) was formed in December 1960. It took six years to buy the land, develop the buildings and grounds, recruit the staff and establish the necessary university infrastructure. In 1967 the University was opened with its first 54 students. The following year the University's intake went up to 400 students and Dellys was back on the campaign trail fundraising for student housing. Her favourite fundraising tool was the art union lottery, which she used again and again as a mechanism for building the University year on year.

Dellys remained on the committee until 1991. All her work for all of these years was voluntary. When I asked her if she ever sought to be paid for her work she replied "What's the point of that? I'd just have to raise more money to pay for my wages".

Her two sons completed degrees at University of Southern Queensland (USQ) and three of her 10 grandchildren have completed degrees there too in business studies, journalism and education so far (there are more to come).

Today USQ has 25,000 students and more than 1,500 academic and support staff. It is a vital part of the Toowoomba economy and is the centre of innovation and thought leadership in the region.

By now you might have conjured up an image of this woman, Dellys Kelly of Queensland, as a woman of significant stature and presence who could command the attention of the Prime Minister and the businessmen who supported her back in 1958. She is in fact just 148 centimetres tall but has an enormous capacity to engage with people around her. When you talk to Dellys Kelly, and hear not just this story but many others that make up her life journey, you are left in no doubt that she could achieve anything she put her mind to.

It is fitting that this amazing story of this motivated, confident and visionary young woman be shared with the people of Australia as a role model. The 26-year-old hotelier and mother of two toddlers travelled 13 hours in her FJ Holden to obtain a promise from 'the top man' so that her children and the children of Southern Queensland communities would have the opportunity to go to university.

She had a good idea, she believed it was possible, and the next day she acted on it. If Dellys Kelly can get in to see the Prime Minister and get his commitment and funding to establish such an institution in 1958, what is possible today? If you have a good idea about something that needs to be changed in your community, how would you go about achieving it?

This story highlights the benefits of tenacity, courage, commitment, self-belief and getting things done. You don't need to be a business leader, or a city leader, or a community club leader to lead change. You don't need to be male or of senior age. You just have to have what Dellys Kelly had; vision to see what is possible, confidence to enable you and passion to drive you.

Organisations: Allow leaders at all levels to help

Organisations are by their very nature hierarchical and that means people generally start at the bottom and work their way up through a series of promotions to the top – except of course when you move between organisations laterally. This method of succession signals to people that they have to earn the right to be involved in important matters and meetings.

With each new job description that you get as you rise up, you are afforded a little more responsibility and authority and when you eventually get into management you are given more freedom and latitude to make decisions. You 'learn' to wait your turn. You observe that you have to have tenure to get taken seriously. But if you are a budding young leader with vision and passion you will probably be a little frustrated that you can't get involved in leading change or realising your good ideas earlier.

I have on many occasions identified budding young leaders around me and given them the opportunity to step up. Having watched them move up and excel in the new space given to them, I formed the belief that without the need for tenure – where you have to wait behind older people to be granted rights and privileges – younger leaders could perform at similar and in some cases, the same levels as older and more experienced people.

Not all achievement is based on experience, being from a later generation with different perspectives and advanced understanding of technology can make a world of difference. In addition, younger leaders tend to have more courage and enthusiasm as they are not yet moulded to conform and this spirit can lead to greater innovations.

Using leaders at all levels

Identifying people at all levels and inviting them to step up, is an extremely effective method of accessing available talent, building leadership capacity and driving change through your business virally.

If you continue to make people 'wait' to show their leadership capability, you continue to frustrate talent lying undiscovered in the bowels of your organisation.

There is an ageist element to many countries' cultures that limits their progress. The cultural norm that says grey-haired older people with greater experience are 'wiser' and have insight and answers, so they should be the ones to make the rules and whom we will permit to lead the rest of us. The 'wiser' part might often be correct, but the 'insight and answers' is not necessarily so.

Generational differences are important in this rapidly changing, technologically driven, globalising world. Younger people have vastly more comfort with, and foresight of, our current and future workplace environment. Leaders can be found under 40, even under 30 and they also have different values and expectations about how we should live our lives and what we should plan to have and be in the future. As they will be the inheritors of this great nation it would be naïve and very limiting to seek to build a more diverse workforce and to debate gender roles and education without their input.

The minders of this great country, the baby-boomers, have a responsibility to hand over a strong and prosperous nation. The chances of that happening will be increased if leaders of all ages participate in the journey.

An example of 'tomorrow's leaders' *stepping up*

A few years ago, I was leading a transformation change program for a global firm that had nine businesses across 80 countries. Every two years they brought the Top 100 most senior people together for a conference to formulate strategy and plan forward. We were several months into the 'review and analysis' phase of the program identifying issues.

When they were ready to engage a wider group of leaders to agree the change strategies, they decided to bring their Top 100 together again for that purpose and produced the list of names. The people on the list had tenure, position power, status – and grey hair. They were also predominantly operations people with few functional leaders present. When I asked them to review the list against the leadership criteria and level of commitment needed to drive the transformation, it became evident that only about half of the Top 100 people were the most appropriate for the task.

So we asked the CEOs of the nine businesses to produce a second list of people from each of their companies who matched the criteria to lead change. When they did this the list took on a very different profile. Many of the people now on the list were previously nowhere in sight.

From the combined lists we selected 120 people from across the 9 businesses and dozens of countries and arrived at a multi-talented highly diverse group of people from all levels of the organisation and from every functional and business unit. The CEO had a challenging task explaining to the usual Top 100 why different criteria were used and why some of them were not being invited to attend this special strategic event to discuss change.

His unprecedented action sent a strong message to the business and at the same time it *shifted a long-held assumption* of that firm's culture. The old assumption that 'People with tenure and position power were automatically given first rights to be involved in strategic initiatives' to 'People who exhibited great leadership would be given rights to be involved in strategic initiatives.'

By shifting an assumption that had reigned for about 30 years he 'jolted' the company's culture and moved it to a different place. Every one of the top layers of the organisation's Culture Iceberg adjusted according to the shift in assumption at the bottom. The shifts were recognisable in many ways but included:

- the investment to gather 120 people from around the world for 4 days signalled that those selected (all ages and cultures, both genders and people of short and long tenure) had the required leadership capabilities and were highly valued;
- the 120 believed they had been called for a reason and that was to help lead change;
- supportive behaviours were observed far and wide as the 120 started rolling out the programs in their home countries and championing the way forward.

The younger leaders of this group of 120 leaders were remarkable. Many were in their 20s and 30s and when given the opportunity to be involved, and provided with a forum to step up to lead, they blossomed. It was an amazing four days watching leaders of all ages working together, energising one another, respecting each other's views (and challenging them) and growing together as a new virtual team. These connections, which they would otherwise not have made, generated outcomes that were not previously imagined.

The diversity in that conference room over four days stimulated innovative thinking that is unlikely to have come from the original group of Top 100. Following the four days of strategising, planning and bonding, the 120 leaders formed 7 project teams to drive and implement agreed changes across the global business. The younger and older leaders, of both genders and many races, together led the changes and energised people around them to fix things that were broken and find new ways to meet the changing market conditions.

Here are some of the things those 120 leaders of all ages from many different countries said as they left on the last day of the first-ever mixed-level leaders conference:

- 'When I arrived at the conference I met 120 delegates...what is now leaving after 4 days are 120 believers' (senior male manager from Australia)
- 'The revelation for me is that I am part of something that is actually global: we have to start thinking big...it's so obvious to me now (mid-career male manager from the UK)

- 'I see the way clearer...I have more knowledge and I can take back the message and tell them 'this is it' and we will challenge the way forward together (mid-career female professional from Ghana)
- At the start of this conference I was 'one of them'...now I am 'one of us' and fully engaged in this program (male Board member)
- 'Energised, overwhelmed and excited. I have learned that we are all 'one', we really are all one company, we haven't been before, but we are now '(first level female manager from Australia)
- 'I am more confident in my company now and I want to be part of it, I am excited to be involved in making the future happen (younger male professional from Philippines)
- 'I'm invigorated: this company is headed to where I am aligned to, so it's great that I'm here to participate (new male employee, mid-career professional from Australia)
- I'm feeling challenged, excited, with some trepidation, not totally confident that I can achieve all this but hey, I am going to give it a go (junior level female from Australia)

It was apparent at the end of the four days that the people who arrived wide-eyed wondering 'how did I get selected' left knowing that they were now connected with like-minded leaders from all levels, all business areas and from across *all* countries. They also knew that this 'anointed' group shared the vision, understood what had to be done and would work supportively across all internal boundaries to deliver the change plan. Because these leaders who were part of the program design team were at all levels of the organisation they were equipped to influence people at all levels. This was neither a top-down nor a bottom-up approach, it was penetrating at all levels.

A few final tips
Organisations don't much like radicals who push the boundaries. However young people with leadership potential often need to push a little to be recognised. So when you see a young person pushing, resist the urge to label them a troublemaker. Take the time to assess their potential and mentor and sponsor them to allow the budding leader to blossom. Flatter organisation structures, meritocracy, free-flowing two way communication and an open door to the executive suite are elements that you want to have in your organisation culture to entice younger leaders to step up.

Avoid Band-Aids at all costs. Band-Aids are alluring and do help in the very short-term but if you don't get beneath them fast enough your initiatives can come unstuck and you have to restart your culture change program or launch a new one. Restarts, or serial change initiatives, can create unhelpful behaviours. With every effort you create expectation and that elicits certain behaviours. When your Band-Aids fail there is a further behavioural response – which can either be a reversion to previous behaviour, which you were trying to get rid of, or it can generate resistance to the next change effort.

Finally, a word about Diversity Councils. The first cautionary word is about how councils and committees are fraught with danger as they can become talk-fests and lead to little action. To get action you need proper responsibility, authority and measurement attached to a role or person. In my experience the creation of a Diversity Council is often used to signal to employees that you are serious about diversity and to provide a discussion forum to identify the issues. You need to ensure that your Council is not only a decision-making body but that members are also accountable for action.

Another challenge with Councils is that it's very difficult for people 'living within' a culture to be objective about the elements in its Culture Iceberg. Effective Councils have people from outside the culture providing objective assessment and transparency to the issues: by being outside the culture they are not influenced by the assumptions and behaviours and have no stake in the changes or outcomes recommended. Having a coach sit alongside you as you journey through your culture-change program is as important as having a coach sit alongside the football field as you play in the Grand Final.

Country: Leading a change in country culture

To ignite social change to achieve greater diversity and growth in Australia requires a leader or group of leaders to step up and make this happen. Perhaps that is you. Or maybe you are an opinion leader or influencer who can help persuade others to step up to lead this. What is your role in this?

The 100 leaders were almost unanimous in their view that we are lacking leadership on diversity and the culture change to achieve it. Lethargy is a really unhelpful state to be in. Our government and leaders in business and society need to be action orientated when it comes to achieving diversity, boosting productivity and building relations across the Asian region. What will it take to motivate them into action?

When leaders are not leading, sometimes they are replaced by more skilled or enthusiastic people. But in this case there seems to be no obvious contenders for replacement. Perhaps the job appears so enormous that no single person feels confident to give it a go.

Is complaining about it helping? No. Will asking them to step up make it occur? It hasn't helped so far. Will a further decline in Australia's rating on the World Economic Forum Global Gender Gap report make a difference? Unlikely. Would it help if we were to march on the street with banners? Probably not.

Everyone seems too busy and too preoccupied with short-term goals and no one seems to be willing to put themselves forward to step up and try to lead on such a challenging and complex situation. Yet it clearly needs addressing.

Suggestions from the 100 leaders above about 'who should lead' indicated that more than one party is responsible and the main players mentioned were government, business, education and 'everyone'. It would make sense therefore for the three main players in the Culture Circuit to collaborate – that is, our country leaders (which includes education under governments control) our organisational leaders and individual leaders (who are at the same time the country leaders).

The main influencers in the Culture Circuit are these three leadership groups and a partnership between them to take up the mantle seems like the most effective solution.

Private-public partnership for social change

A private–public partnership of a social kind, if united in its vision, could drive a shift in the nation's assumptions and values and thereby influence a change in our attitudes and behaviours. This may sound visionary but it is not an unrealistic notion. The challenge is getting a bunch of people to form a think-tank and organise things to make it happen.

Just for a moment, think of Australia as if it were a global partnership requiring consultation across all divisions and levels. If we identified leaders from all levels of government, business and society and ensured representation of all cultures that have made Australia their home, we could initiate a national consultation and communications process to engage in a change program similar to one that would be employed to drive change across a global business. In doing so we could touch every sector and get a culture change process underway.

What kinds of organisations could reach every sector of our society? Well, they could include those that have geographical spread across the country and large employers who deliver products and services that affect the daily lives of everyone living in Australian cities and country towns. For example, on the government side it could include the departments of Education, Health, Police and Australia Post; on the business side it could include one of the four big banks, a leading telecommunications company, a national food chain, a major retailer and a transport business; and finally organisations to contribute from broader society could include national sports and community service organisations and those representing the major ethnic groups that live here.

A think-tank and directorate, comprising leaders from these sectors and with bipartisan political support, could drive the change we need. A group of leaders that shared a vision for a more diverse, Asia-ready and globally-inspired Australia, and who were prepared to commit themselves and their organisations to a long-term plan, could make it happen if they were to a step forward and agree on a strategy and pathways. We are not asking them to close the hole in the ozone layer, but to request that the people of Australia follow their lead to advance our national values to encourage broad diversity and make full participation in the workforce possible. The benefits to local businesses and communities would flow almost immediately and there would be no looking back.

The first step to changing any culture is recognition of the elements of the Culture Iceberg that no longer serve the group's current needs and future ambitions. In any population, there are always enough supporters who take up the mantle to drive the change – the champions – and there is also a majority prepared to follow their lead, as long as their vision and commitment is transparent and believable. Based on a sample of 100, which is statistically sound, there is general consensus from the people that change is needed to help the country address its challenges and maintain its standing in the world.

The final group, those who need convincing and may resist change, are generally a minority. The proposal that Australia evolve its culture, update its education systems and free itself up from bias and discrimination to allow both genders and all cultures to participate fully in the country's future does not seem like something that most Australians would disagree with. Maybe the 'how' will meet with some serious debate, but the 'what' and the 'why' parts of this proposal would seem to have majority support.

A private-public partnership of a social kind could reach across the country and engage in national and local discussions utilising the internal resources of the bodies concerned. Taking ownership of the problem is best addressed by using your own people. It would connect leaders of government organisations with public and private sector company leaders and community organisations of all kinds. This leadership group would then work in cooperation to engage groups across business and society to shift cultural assumptions and values that stand in the way of economic progress and social development. They would also facilitate changes to ensure both genders and all cultures get a fair go in Australia's future.

By adopting a cascading approach to touching people at all levels (depth) across all of society (breadth), we can ensure that 'everyone' is involved in the discussion about what Australia's ambitions are, where it is heading and what elements need to be in its Culture Iceberg to be a thriving and progressive society in 2025.

We must have leadership on this. We can all get involved. Let's take up the mantle and take a step forward now.

Australia in the Asian Century

Creating a vision for the future is not so difficult. Imagine it is 2025. Where are you? Which city? Which country? Who are you with? What are you doing? What have you achieved between now and then? What have you succeeded in and what have you failed at? How? Why?

Where is everyone else you know? Why are they there? What have they achieved? Are they happy? Are they successful? Why, or why not?

What does Australia look like, relative to other countries? How many people will live here? What industries will be thriving? What exports will we be known for? What reputation will we have in the world? What will our children be doing in the future? Who will be the leaders? Was our journey an easy one or did we have to work hard to get to 2025? When we get to 2025, what will we be most proud of?

Are you happy with this vision of the future? Are you happy to be living in the place you have visualised for yourself in 2025? Will your children have opportunity? Will they be free to choose careers, where they live and what they do? Really free, unencumbered from assumptions of others about who they are and what they should be? Are you satisfied that you have contributed your best as a citizen and leader in your community, business and family?

Stepping Up has been written to provide people with meaning, motivation and the mettle with some good ideas to consider as they contemplate the challenges Australia faces in the Asian Century, and the challenges they face personally in their lives, careers and communities. We could wait for others to do the leading for us, or we could get involved. Using that well-praised Australian spirit of mucking-in-to-help-others when the going gets tough, we could start the conversation.

The conversation would include:

- *Leadership*: who can we encourage to step up to guide the social development of our nation in a world that is fast changing and demands a response if we are to keep up?
- *Culture*: what assumptions, values, beliefs, attitudes and behaviours would be helpful for Australian's to adopt, to ensure everyone who lives here has equal access to opportunity at home and abroad?

- *Change*: are we prepared to give up a little of the past to adjust 'the way we do things around here' to continue building a future that we can be proud of? Are we prepared to follow the lead of others who are prepared to take up the mantle?
- *Diversity*: what can we each do to facilitate greater diversity at all levels of our business and society and what checks and balances can we put in place to eliminate bias and discrimination from our culture?
- *Growth*: as there are many avenues to achieving growth, which ones are we prepared to invest in nationally and locally and what can we do to keep a longer-term view of how to achieve the desired outcomes?
- *Australia-Asia*: of all the opportunities available to Australians that arise from our close relationship and proximity to Asian nations, which ones are we interested in taking up?
- *Commitment*: What level of commitment are we prepared to make to the culture change necessary to achieve diversity and stimulate growth both internally and across Asia?

A conversation on these topics might have appeared challenging 18 months ago when I started my research for *Stepping Up*, but after so many hours of listening I can say that people are ready to talk and they do want change. It is difficult to raise these sensitive topics sometimes and it takes tenacity to push through the resistance and the barriers, but when you do arrive on the other side, it doesn't seem that hard.

Similarly, while the issues are many and may seem uncontainable at first, it doesn't take too long to filter through the emotion and get to the causes to find solutions. The causes are quietly hiding beneath our Culture Iceberg; out-dated assumptions that need our attention.

I have a dream that everyone living in Australia joins the workforce believing that the opportunities are equal, their path to the top meritocratic and the door to positions of power and leadership open. My belief is that our future prosperity rests on our ability to embrace being part of Asia and being more connected with the rest of the world.

Stepping Up is a contribution to achieving this and to inspiring leaders to initiate the action.

> *Everyone here has the sense that right now is one of those moments when we are influencing the future.*
> Steve Jobs (1955–2011) co-founder and former Chairman & CEO of Apple Inc

Join Australians on

www.steppingupaustralia.com

Stepping Up is not just a book. It is also a vehicle for change and a companion to help you take action. *www.steppingupaustralia.com* is a resource available to all. It provides a forum for people who are stepping up to lead change, to share solutions to the issues and challenges they are facing. And if you like, you can register your change projects and provide regular updates to participate in our sponsors' quarterly change Awards.

Share your ideas for social change

Join others and discuss what could be done to 'advance Australia' so the changes can be considered by our national, state, community and industry leaders who are prepared to take action to evolve our culture. Connect with people in different states across Australia on *www.steppingupaustralia.com* to achieve common goals for the good of everyone.

Share your ideas about organisation change

Evolving organisational culture to build greater diversity and improve productivity is a strategic issue, a business imperative and a social challenge. You can connect with other business leaders and change agents through *www.steppingupaustralia.com* and engage with other executives, managers or employees to exchange your ideas and solutions.

Share your ideas about individual change

Chat with individuals in Australia who want to shape the country culture to ensure Australia keeps up with the progressive nations of the world. You can contribute to evolving the nation's culture and values and removing blockages to full participation and opportunity by connecting with people from across the country and all walks of life who want to share suggestions and initiate action.

Go to *www.steppingupaustralia.com* to get involved in leading change.

Cascading your change

The most effective way to get fast change happening in your organisation is, as outlined in Chapter 12, to identify leaders 'at all levels' who can be your 'change champions' and get them involved in your program.

Start by asking them to read *Stepping Up*, to understand the issues, learn how cultures operate and commence a dialogue across, up and down your organisation about its Culture Icebcrg. Ask them to detail the helpful and not-so-helpful features of all layers of the Iceberg and assess which ones need to change.

Most importantly, you need to identify your assumptions. It's a good idea to seek outside independent views on this, perhaps from board members, suppliers, customers or specialist culture-change consultants.

After you have identified the elements of your Culture Iceberg that are limiting your performance and progress, categorise them into themes and set up a culture-change project team for each, sponsored by the CEO and led by an executive.

Your 'themed' project teams are then ready to start cascading the findings up and down the organisation to further the dialogue, seek feedback and get engagement from employees to contribute to the changes required. By having people from all levels of your organisation leading your change effort, you are increasing the probability that employees at all levels are going to follow.

Tools and discounts

If you go to the TOOLS menu on www.steppingupaustralia.com you will find materials there to support you to cascade your culture-change programs.

If you go to the SHOP menu you will find options to buy multiple copies of the book for members of your organisation at a discount.

100 leader biographies

The 100 leaders who contributed to *Stepping Up* are:

Alec Bashinsky, National Partner, People & Performance, Deloitte, Sydney, Australia
Alec has been with Deloitte since 2005 and is responsible for around 6000 employees. Prior to this he was Senior Director Human Resources – Japan & Asia Pacific for Peoplesoft; Group Manager – Human Resources for Cisco Systems Australia/New Zealand; and Asia Pacific Human Resources Manager for 3Com. Alec is on the Board of Diversity Council Australia. He is Australian-born, has Ukrainian heritage and speaks fluent Russian. He has lived and worked in the United Kingdom, Ireland, Japan, Korea, China, Singapore, Hong Kong, the United States and Canada.

Professor Alec Cameron, Deputy Vice-Chancellor (Education), University of Western Australia, Sydney, Australia
Alec is Deputy Vice-Chancellor (Education) at the University of Western Australia. Prior to this he was Dean of the Australian School of Business at UNSW from 2006 to 2012, and Deputy Vice-Chancellor (Resources and Infrastructure) at UNSW from September 2003 to 2006. He is a Fellow of the Australian Institute of Company Directors and has served as a Director for the Centre for International Finance and Regulation; the Society for Knowledge Economics (SKE); Capital Markets CRC; the Australia India Institute; Uniseed; and NewSouth Innovations. Alec is Australian-born and has lived and worked in the United Kingdom and United States.

Amanda Mostyn, Executive General Manager, People & Development, ASX Group, Sydney, Australia
Amanda has been EGM People & Development for ASX since 2006. Prior to this she was General Manager, Human Resources at the Sydney Futures Exchange from 1991 to 2005. She is a member of the Australian Human Resources Institute and Australian Institute of Company Directors. Amanda is Australian-born.

Andrew Macintosh, Chief Executive Officer, Hanhong Private Equity, Hong Kong, China
Andrew is the CEO of Hanhong Private Equity and Adjunct Faculty at the Macquarie Graduate School of Management. Prior to this he was the General Manager of National Australia Bank Hong Kong and Head of Private Bank for Westpac Hong Kong. He is a Director of the Australian Chamber of Commerce Hong Kong and a Fellow of the Financial Services Institute of Australia. Andrew is Australian-born and has lived or worked in the United States, Japan, Hong Kong, China, Taiwan, Philippines, Indonesia, Singapore and Thailand.

Angela Tatlis, Managing Director, Invoke Performance, Melbourne, Australia
Angela is the Managing Director at Invoke Performance. Prior to this she was the Executive Director at Melbourne Forum, Director of Regional Supply Services at Treasury Wine Estates and Director of Global Supply Best Practice and Performance at Fosters Group Ltd. Angela is Chair of the National Association for Women in Operations and founder of the new Chief Supply Officers ANZ forum. She is Australian-born.

Ann Sherry AO, Chief Executive Officer, Carnival Australia, Sydney, Australia
Ann is the CEO of Carnival Australia, a Non-Executive Director at Australian Rugby Union, and a Non-Executive Director at ING Australia and The Myer Family Company Ltd. Prior to this she was the CEO of Westpac NZ, a Group Executive at Westpac and CEO at Bank of Melbourne. Ann was made an Officer of the Order of Australia in 2004. She is Australian-born, speaks fluent French, and has lived and worked in the United Kingdom and New Zealand

Annette Kimmitt, Office Managing Partner, Ernst & Young Global, Victoria, Australia
Annette has been the Melbourne Managing Partner for Ernst & Young since 2009. She is a member of the Australian Institute of Company Directors, a Fellow of the Institute of Chartered Accountants in Australia, on the Board of Airservices Australia and Chair of its Board Audit and Risk Committee. Annette is a Director of the Committee for Melbourne, the Melbourne Business School and the Victoria University Foundation. She is also a former Councillor and Victorian Chair of the Institute of Chartered Accountants in Australia. Annette is Australian-born, has Maltese heritage and has lived and worked in the United Kingdom.

Arni Hole, Director General, Norwegian Royal Ministry for Children, Equity and Social Inclusion, Oslo, Norway
Arni is Director General in the Royal Ministry of Children, Equality and Social Inclusion; and heads the Department of Family and Equality. Prior to this she war Director General of the Royal Ministry of Food and Agriculture, Managing Director of the Norwegian Sports University, and Deputy Director General of the Royal Ministry of Research and Education. Arni was born in Norway, speaks Norwegian, Swedish, Danish, French and German and has worked and lived in the United States, United Kingdom and France.

Bernard Salt, Partner, KPMG, Melbourne, Australia
Bernard is a Partner at KPMG, Social Editor at The Australian Newspaper, a bestselling author and adjunct professor at Curtin University Business School. Bernard is currently Chairman of Tourism Forecasting Committee, a Fellow of the Australian Institute of Company Directors, a member of Australian Institute of Management, an Affiliate of Chartered Accountants and a Director of MLC Girls School. He is Australian-born.

Carol Schwartz AM, Non-executive Director, Stockland, Melbourne, Australia
Carol is currently the Chairman of Our Community and Founding Chair of the Women's Leadership Institute Australia. She is also Director, Yarra Capital Partners, Director, Stockland, Director, Bank of Melbourne, Director, Qualitas Property Partners, board member St James Ethics Foundation, board member National Australia Day Council, Executive in Residence at Melbourne Business School, council member of the Australian Innovation Research Centre, University of Tasmania, board member Centre for Advanced Journalism, University of Melbourne, member of the Enterprise Melbourne Advisory Board, member the Milken Global Advisory Council, member Harvard Kennedy Women's Leadership Board and she is also the Co-Chair in Australia for Women Corporate Directors.

Catherine Livingston AO, Chairman, Telstra, Sydney, Australia
Catherine is the Chairman of Telstra Corporation Ltd, a Director of Macquarie Group Ltd, WorleyParsons Ltd and The George Institute for Global Health. She is a member of the New South Wales Innovation and Productivity Council and is President of the Australian Museum Trust. Prior to this she served on the Boards of Goodman Fielder Ltd and Rural Press Ltd, and was the Chairman of CSIRO and the President of Chief Executive Women. Catherine is a Chartered Accountant and became an Officer of the Order of Australia in 2008. Catherine is Australian-born.

Catriona Noble, Chief Executive Officer, McDonald's Australia, Sydney, Australia
Catriona has been the CEO of McDonald's Australia since 2010. Prior to this she had spent her entire career with McDonald's and held various positions including Managing Director, Chief Operating Officer and Director Corporate Strategy & Business Planning. Catriona is also a Member of the Business Council of Australia. She is Australian-born.

Dr Charlie Teo AM, Director, The Centre for Minimally Invasive Neurosurgery, Sydney, Australia
Charlie is the Director of the Centre for Minimally Invasive Neurosurgery at Prince of Wales Hospital, the Founder of Cure For Life Foundation and the Chairman of the Scientific Advisory Board. In 2003 he was NSW State finalist for the prestigious Australian of the Year award and in 2005 he was awarded the Vocational Service Award by the Rotary Club. In 2007 he was given the Paul Harris Fellowship for his contribution to International Health and Welfare and became a Member of the Order of Australia in 2012. Charlie is Australian-born, has Chinese and Singaporean heritage, and has also lived and worked in the United States.

Chris Komor, Principal, Willow Bend Station, Central NSW, Australia
Chris is the Principal of Willow Bend Station. Prior to this he was the Head of Mergers and Acquisitions at Amro Bank N.V. (Sydney) and Group Head of Mergers and Acquisitions at Tricontinental Ltd. Chris was also a solicitor with Allen Allen & Hemsley (now Allens Arthur Robinson). He was born in the United States and has lived and worked in Australia.

Christopher Lim, Senior Manager, Ernst & Young Global, Kuala Lumpur, Malaysia
Christopher is a Senior Manager in the Human Capital practice of Ernst & Young's Kuala Lumpur office. Christopher was born in the United Kingdom, has Chinese heritage and speaks fluent Malay. He has lived and worked in the United Kingdom, Malaysia and Australia.

Con Tatlis, Finance Director, Invoke Performance, Melbourne, Australia
Con is the Financial Director of Invoke Performance. Prior to this he received a degree in applied chemistry and worked for Shell in research and development, then later held a sales role in a Mobil owned company. Con was born in Greece, speaks fluent Greek, and has lived and worked in Australia.

Craig Drummond, Chief Executive Officer, Bank of America Merrill Lynch, Sydney, Australia
Craig has been the CEO of Bank of America Merrill Lynch since 2009. Prior to this he held various roles with Goldman Sachs JB Were including Chief Operating Officer, Executive Chairman and Co-Chief Executive Officer. Craig is a Senior Fellow of FINSIA and is a Chartered Accountant. Craig is a Director of Scotch College, Florey Institute of Neuroscience and Mental Health, the Australian Financial Markets Association and the Geelong Football Club. He is a Member of the Business Council of Australia and a Member of the University of New South Wales' Australian School of Business Advisory Council. Craig is Australian-born.

David Gonski AC, Chairman, Future Fund of Australia, Sydney, Australia
David is Chairman of Investec Bank (Australia) Ltd, ASX Ltd, Coca-Cola Amatil Ltd and Ingeus Ltd. He is Chancellor of the University of New South Wales and Chairman of the National E Health Transition Authority Ltd. Prior to this David was a member of the Takeovers Panel, President of the Art Gallery of New South Wales, Director of ANZ Bank Ltd, Director of the Westfield Group, Chairman of the Australia Council for the Arts and Chairman of the Board of Trustees of Sydney Grammar School. He was born in South Africa and now lives and works in Australia.

David Kelly, Research Director, China Policy, Beijing, China
David is Research Director at China Policy, a Beijing-based research and advisory company, and a Visiting Professor at Peking University. Prior to this he was Professor of China Studies at UTS, Sydney. He has held senior positions at the National University of Singapore, the University of New South Wales and the Australian National University. He held a Fulbright Fellowship at the University of Chicago. David was born in Australia, has lived and worked in China and Singapore, and speaks fluent Chinese.

David Olsson, Partner, King & Wood Mallesons, Beijing, China
David is a Partner of King & Wood Mallesons based in Beijing and leads the firm's banking and finance practice in China. Prior to this he headed the firm's Melbourne and Hong Kong office as well as working in London and the Middle East. David is the Chairman of the Board of Directors of China-Australia Chamber of Commerce and the founder of its Financial Services Working Group.

Debra Singh, Former General Manager, Dick Smith, Sydney, Australia
Debra is the Former General Manager of Dick Smith Australia, New Zealand and India. Prior to this she was the Managing Director of Woolworths Wholesale India, and General Manager of Human Resources Woolworths Supermarkets, leading the people strategy for 130,000 employees. She is a Member of Chief Executive Women and on the Advisory Counsel of Executive Women's Business. Debra was born in New Zealand and has lived and worked in Australia and India.

Dellys Kelly, Founder, University of Southern Queensland, Toowoomba, Australia
Dellys was Founder of the University of Southern Queensland in 1958 and was awarded a Fellowship of the University in 2009. She was Chair of the Toowoomba Women's Council of the Liberal Party for 27 years and has been an active fundraiser for her entire adult life. At 81 she is still actively involved in event management and fund-raising for the Liberal Party. She has 14 great-grand-children. Dellys was born in 1932 in Toowoomba, Southern Queensland.

Dharma Chandran, Chief Human Resources Officer, Leighton Holdings, Sydney, Australia
Dharma is the Chief Human Resources Officer at Leighton Holdings. Prior to this he was Ernst & Young's Far East Area Leader of the Performance and Reward Practice during which he completed a secondment with Suncorp as Interim Group Executive, Human Resources. Dharma spent a number of years with Westpac Banking Corporation where he was initially Group General Manager of Employee Relations, Performance and Rewards and later, General Manager of Strategy and Human Resources for the Consumer Banking division. He is Malaysian-born, is of Sri Lankan-Tamil ethnicity and speaks fluent Bahasa Malay/Indonesian. He has lived and worked in Australia, Malaysia, Singapore, Thailand, Indonesia, South Korea and Hong Kong.

Diana Cross, Australasia Human Resources Leader, Arup Group, Melbourne, Australia
Diana is currently Head of Human Resources for Arup in Australasia and has been with the company since 2004. Diana is also an Officer of the Board for the Australasian region. Prior to this she worked in senior Human Resources roles within Spherion Group, Nortel and Honeywell. She is Australian-born.

Diane Grady AM, Non-Executive Director, Macquarie Group, Sydney, Australia
Diane is a Non-Executive Director of Macquarie Group and Bluescope Steel. She is also a member of the McKinsey Advisory Board, Chair of Ascham School and Chair of the Hunger Project Australia. Previously Diane was a Director of Woolworths Ltd, Lend Lease Ltd, a Trustee of the Sydney Opera House and President of Chief Executive Women. Before becoming a director, Diane was a partner of McKinsey & Co leading the Retailing and Consumer Goods practice in Australia and the firm's Change Management practice

globally. She was made a Member of the Order of Australia in 2009 for services to business and promoting women leaders. Diane has an MBA from Harvard, a Masters in Chinese Studies from the East West Centre at the University of Hawaii, and a Bachelor of Arts in European History from Mills College.

Doug Buckley, VP Commercial, Shell Australia, Perth, Australia

Doug has been the Vice President Commercial at Shell Australia since 2009. Prior to this he was General Manager of Optimisation at Shell Energy Europe and General Manager of Sakhalin LNG Marketing Services BV. He is also a Director of Shell Energy Holdings Australia Limited and its subsidiary companies.

Edyta Torpy, Oceania Diversity & Inclusiveness Leader, Ernst & Young Global, Sydney, Australia

Edyta is the Oceania Diversity and Inclusiveness Leader at Ernst & Young. Prior to this she was the Human Resources Relationship Senior Manager at Ernst & Young Australia, Human Resources Manager at Arthur Andersen and Human Resources Specialist at Caltex. Edyta was born in Poland, speaks fluent Polish and now lives and works in Australia.

Professor Fred Hilmer AO, President & Vice-Chancellor, University of New South Wales, Sydney, Australia

Fred has been the President and Vice-Chancellor of UNSW since 2006 and is also a Director of Westfield Holdings Limited. Prior to this he was the CEO of media company John Fairfax Holdings Ltd and had been Dean and Director of the Australian Graduate School of Management (AGSM) at UNSW. He has served as a director of a number of Australian companies including Port Jackson Partners Ltd and McKinsey & Company. He was made an Officer of the Order of Australia in 1998. Fred was born in Australia, speaks conversational German and now lives and works in Australia.

Gabriel Yam, Associate, Arup, Hong Kong, China

Gabriel is an Associate of Arup, Hong Kong, China. He received his secondary school education in Brisbane and graduated from the University of Queensland in 1995. Upon his return to Hong Kong he joined an Australian engineering consulting company Meinhardt (C&S) Ltd and worked on many large scale infrastructure projects like the new Hong Kong International Airport at Chek Lap Kok, Hong Kong Disneyland and extension line for the Mass Transit Railway. He was the project manager for construction of the Australian International School in Hong Kong with Leighton Asia as the contractor. He is married to an Australian-Chinese, has two children and currently works for Arup on many challenging engineering projects.

Dr Geoff Raby, Chief Executive Officer, Geoff Raby & Associates (former Australian Ambassador to China), Beijing, China

Geoff is Chairman and CEO of Geoff Raby & Associates and an independent, Non-Executive Director on the boards of Fortescue Mining Group, OceanaGold, and SmartTrans. Prior to this he was the Australian Ambassador to China and Deputy Secretary of the Department of Foreign Affairs and Trade. He has recently been appointed as Vice Chancellor's Professorial Fellow at Monash University and was appointed by the Minister of Education, Employment and Workplace Relations to the International Education Advisory Council. Geoff is Australian-born and has lived and worked in China, Switzerland, France and the United Kingdom.

Georgia (Anon), Vice President, Investment Banking, Sydney, Australia

Georgia is highly qualified and skilled banker with a 15-year career in global and Australian investment banks. Georgia's true identity will not be revealed as she shares her story anonymously in the book about why she recently opted out of this career. She is Australian born.

Giam Swiegers, Chief Executive Officer, Deloitte Touche Tohmatsu, Sydney, Australia
Giam is the CEO of Deloitte Touche Tohmatsu Australia and is a member of Deloitte's Global Board and the Global Board of Governance Committee. He began his career as an auditor for Deloitte in South Africa and currently serves on the UTS Vice-Chancellor's Industry Advisory Board. Giam was born in South Africa, speaks fluent Afrikaans, and has lived and worked in the United States. He now lives and works in Australia.

Graham Bradley AM, Chairman, Stockland, Sydney, Australia
Graham is the Chairman of Stockland Corporation, HSBC Bank Australia, Energy/ Australia and Anglo American Australia. Graham is a director of Hongkong and Shanghai Banking Corporation and is a former director of Singapore Telecommunications. Prior to this he was President of the Business Council from 2009 to 2011 of Australia and Managing Director of Perpetual Ltd. He is a Director of the European Australian Business Council and a Member of the Order of Australia. Graham was born in Australia.

Greg Couttas, Partner, Deloitte Touche Tohmatsu, Sydney, Australia
Greg has been a Partner in Deloitte since 1988, during which time he served as Lead Client Service Partner for AGL Energy, APA Group, Centennial Coal, CSR, Rinker Group and Woolworths. Greg is a member of the Board of Partners of Deloitte Australia and Chairman of the firm's Audit Committee. He is a Fellow of the Institute of Chartered Accountants in Australia and a member of the Audit Committee for the University of New South Wales. He is Australian-born and has Greek heritage.

Greg Stanmore, Managing Director, Spencer Stuart, Sydney, Australia
Greg is the Managing Director at Spencer Stuart. Prior to this he was the General Manager at James Hardie Building Products and Manager at LEK Consulting. He was also a Project Manager at CRI Ltd and Site Engineer at Bovis Lend Lease. He has an MBA from the Macquarie Graduate School of Management.

Hayden Flinn, Partner, King & Wood Mallesons, Hong Kong, China
Hayden is a Partner in the King & Wood Mallesons Hong Kong office. His work includes negotiating joint ventures and mergers and acquisitions in the Asia region. His experience spans the Asia Pacific region including Hong Kong, India, Philippines, China and Singapore. Hayden was born in Melbourne and has lived and worked in Hong Kong since 2001.

Hugh Mackay, Social Researcher and Writer, Sydney, Australia
Australia's leading social researcher, Hugh is the author of fourteen books, including five novels. In recognition of his pioneering work in social research, he has been awarded honorary doctorates by Charles Sturt, Macquarie, NSW and Western Sydney universities. He is a Fellow of the Australian Psychological Society and a recipient of the University of Sydney's alumni award for community service. A newspaper columnist for over 25 years, Hugh is currently an honorary professor of social science at the University of Wollongong. Previous appointments have included deputy chairman of the Australia Council, chairman of the board of trustees of Sydney Grammar School and the inaugural chairman of the ACT government's Community Inclusion Board. Hugh is Australian-born.

Ilana Atlas, Non-Executive Director, Coca-Cola Amatil, Sydney, Australia
Ilana Atlas is a Non-Executive Director of Coca-Cola Amati Ltd, Suncorp Group Ltd and Westfield Holdings Ltd. She is the Chairman of Bell Shakespeare Company and a Councillor of the Australian National University. Her last executive role was as Group Executive, People at Westpac. Prior to this she was a Partner in the law firm Mallesons Stephen Jaques where she also held a number of management roles including Executive Partner, People and Information and Managing Partner. Ilana is Australian-born and has lived and worked in the United States.

Dr Jacqui Abbott, Head of Flexibility and Diversity, Allens Arthur Robinson, Sydney, Australia

Jacqui has been with Allens Arthur Robinson since 2008 and has subsequently launched the flexibility program, refreshed the gender program and expanded the understanding and awareness of the broader diversity agenda within the firm. Prior to this Jacqui has worked as Workplace Diversity and Flexibility Manager at Orica, Workplace Culture Manager at Shell Australia and People Strategy Manager at Ernst & Young/Arthur Andersen. Jacqui is a board member of Diversity Council Australia. Her PhD explored the latest thinking related to management and employee perspectives of work/life benefits in large multinationals. Jacqui is Australian-born.

James MacKenzie, Chairman, Mirvac, Melbourne, Australia

James is the Chairman of Mirvac, Non-Executive Director at Pacific Brands, Director of Melco Entertainment Ltd and Co-Vice Chairman of Yancoal Australia Ltd. Prior to this he was a Partner in both the Melbourne and Hong Kong offices of an international accounting firm now part of Deloitte. James lived in Hong Kong from 1984 to 1994 and was responsible for the establishment of the firm's China desk in 1984. Subsequently, James led the transformation of the Victorian Government's Personal Injury Schemes initially as Chief Executive Officer of the Transport Accident Commission (TAC) and later as Chairman of TAC and the Victorian WorkCover Authority (WorkSafe Victoria). James is a Fellow of both the Institute of Chartered Accountants in Australia and the Australian Institute of Company Directors and in 2003 was awarded the Centenary Medal for services to Public Administration.

Jane Hemstritch, Non-Executive Director, Commonwealth Bank of Australia, Melbourne, Australia

Jane is a Non-Executive Director of the Commonwealth Bank of Australia Ltd, Santos, Tabcorp Holdings, Lend Lease Corporation, and the Victorian Opera Company. She is Deputy Chairman of The Global Foundation and a Member of the Research and Policy Council Committee for Economic Development of Australia. Prior to this she was Managing Director, Asia Pacific at Accenture as well as Managing Director Resources Operating Group for Asia Pacific. Jane is a Fellow of the Institute of Chartered Accountants in Australia, England and Wales, a Fellow of the Australian Institute of Company Directors and a member of Chief Executive Women. Jane was born in Kenya and has lived and worked in the United Kingdom.

Jane Owen, Partner, Middletons, Sydney, Australia

Jane is a partner in Middletons' Innovations Group and is a member of the IP Society of Australia and New Zealand, the Copyright Society of Australia, the International Trademark Association and Law Society of NSW. She is also a director of UNSW Press. Prior to this Jane was a Partner at Griffith Hack. She is Australian-born and has lived and worked in the United States and the United Kingdom.

Cmdr Jennifer Wittwer FAHRI, Royal Australian Navy, Canberra, Australia

Jennifer is currently serving as a Gender Advisor for the NATO International Security Assistance Force Afghanistan. Prior to this she was the Navy Women's Strategic Adviser in Navy Strategic Command. In the past ten years Jennifer has also served as the Director Navy Organisational Culture, the Senior Military Investigator for serving member's complaints, and Deputy Director Culture Program, New Generation Navy. Jennifer was awarded a Fellowship to the Australian Human Resources Institute in 2010, was the 3rd place winner of the inaugural 2010 Centre for Leadership for Women national Advancement of Women in the Workplace Award, and was a finalist for the 2011 Telstra Business Woman of the Year. She is Australian-born.

Jenny Parker, Office Managing Partner, Ernst & Young Global, Queensland, Australia
Jenny is the Managing Partner, Queensland at Ernst & Young and has been a Partner with the company since 1999. Jenny is the Independent member on the Queensland Department of Public Works Audit Committee, a Member of the National Education Board for the Institute of Chartered Accountants in Australia, and a Fellow of the Institute of Chartered Accountants in Australia. Prior to this she was an Independent Member of the Brisbane City Council Audit Committee and an Independent Member of the Department of Main Roads Audit Committee. Jenny is Australian-born.

Jillian Segal AM, Non-Executive Director, National Australia Bank, Sydney, Australia
Jillian is a Non-Executive Director of ASX Ltd, National Australia Bank and The Garvan Institute of Medical Research. She is also a Member of the Federal Government's Remuneration Tribunal, Chairman of the John Monash Foundation and Deputy Chancellor of the University of NSW as well as a Member of the Sydney Advisory Council of the Centre for Social Impact. Prior to this she was a Commissioner, then Deputy Chair, of the Australian Securities and Investments Commission and a partner at Allen Allen & Hemsley (now Allens Arthur Robinson). Jillian is also a member of Chief Executive Women, Co-Chair of the Australian Chapter of WomenCorporateDirectors and a Fellow of the Australian Institute of Company Directors. She was awarded the Centenary Medal in 2003 and appointed a Member of the Order of Australia in 2005. Jillian was born in South Africa and has lived and worked in the United States. She now lives and works in Australia.

Joanne Wood, Chairman, Capital Eight, Shanghai, China
Joanne is the Founder, Managing Partner and Chairman of the investment bank Capital Eight. Prior to this she worked at UBS, Jardine Fleming and GE Capital in corporate finance positions. She has an MBA from London Business School. Joanne is currently a Vice Chair of the British Chamber's Financial Services Group, previously held a Vice Chair position in the EU Chamber of Commerce and recently stepped down as the inaugural Chairman of the Australian Chamber of Commerce, Greater China. She is Australian, speaks fluent Mandarin, and has lived and worked in the United States, United Kingdom, Switzerland, Hong Kong, China, Brazil and Singapore.

John Daley, Chief Executive Officer, Grattan Institute, Melbourne, Australia
John has been the CEO of Grattan Institute since 2009. Prior to this he was the Managing Director of ANZ's online stockbroker E*TRADE Australia, Group General Manager of Strategy for ANZ, and an Engagement Manager at McKinsey & Company. He is a member of the Board of the Malthouse Theatre, and chaired the Steering Group for the Journey to Social Inclusion Project at the Sacred Heart Mission. John was born in the United Kingdom, grew up in Australia, and completed a doctorate in the United Kingdom. He now lives and works in Australia.

John Denton, Chief Executive Officer, Corrs Chambers Westgarth, Melbourne, Australia
John is a Partner and CEO of the law firm Corrs Chambers Westgarth. He is a Prime Ministerial representative on the APEC Business Advisory Council, Board Member of the Business Council of Australia, and Chair of its Global Engagement Taskforce. John is Chairman of the United Nations High Commission for Refugees Australia and Deputy Chair of the Australia Council for the Arts. He is Australian-born and speaks Russian.

John Godfrey, Senior Commissioning Editor Documentaries, SBS Television, Sydney, Australia
John has been the Commissioning Editor for Documentaries at SBS since 2008, and Senior Commissioning Editor for Documentaries since 2011. Prior to this he was Head of Development/Executive Producer for Becker Entertainment, and worked in UK broadcasting for 10 years. John was born in the United Kingdom and has lived and worked in Ghana and Kenya. He now lives and works in Australia.

John Harvey AO, Executive Director, IBM Australia, Sydney, Australia
John is an Executive Director of IBM Australia and sits on a number of Boards including IBM Global Finance Australia, IBM Australia and New Zealand Holdings and IBM Australia. In 2010 he was made an Officer of the Order of Australia. John holds a Doctorate of Business Leadership from Charles Sturt University and is an Adjunct Professor at the University of Ballarat. He is Australian-born and has lived and worked in the United States and Japan.

Professor Julianne Schultz AM FAHA, Non-executive Director, Australian Broadcasting Corporation, Chair Australian Film, Television and Radio School, Sydney, Australia
Julianne is the founding editor of Griffith REVIEW and has been a Non-Executive Director of ABC since 2009 and was appointed chair of the Australian Film Television and Radio School in 2012. She is a professor at Griffith University's Centre for Cultural Research and is Chair of the Queensland Design Council and Arts Minister Crean's reference group for the National Cultural Policy. She is a Director of the Grattan Institute, the Centre for Advanced Journalism and the Editorial Board of the Companion of Australian Media. Julianne was made a Member of the Order of Australia in 2009 and an honorary fellow of the Academy of Humanities in 2010. She was born in New Zealand and has lived and worked in the United States and the United Kingdom.

Julie Coates, Director, BIG W, Sydney, Australia
Julie has been the Director of Big W since 2008 and is a Member of Woolworths Management Board. Prior to this she was Chief Logistics Officer and Human Resources Director at Woolworths Ltd. She also held the positions of Operations Director, Human Resources Director and General Manager Supply Chain at David Jones Ltd. Before that she held various roles at Officeworks, Target, BHP Billiton and Cadbury Schweppes. She is a CEW Council Member & Co-Chair of Marketing & Communications Committee. Julie is Australian-born.

Kathryn Fagg, Former President Corporate Development, Linfox Australia, Melbourne, Australia
Kathryn is currently the Chair of the Thought Leadership Council for Chief Executive Women and Chairman of the Melbourne Recital Centre. Prior to Linfox, Kathryn was President of BlueScope Steel Asia and was previously Managing Director of Global Transaction Services for ANZ. She is Australian-born and has lived and worked in New Zealand and Singapore.

Kathryn McLay, General Manager Replenishment, Woolworths, Sydney, Australia
Kathryn has been the General Manager Replenishment for Woolworths since October 2012. Prior to this she held other roles in Woolworths including Logistics Operations Manager (North), General Manager of Cost Focus, General Manager of Business Development and Head of Group Audit. Kathryn was President and Chairman of the Institute of Internal Auditors and a National Director for the Institute of Internal Auditors Australia. She was born in Australia and has lived and worked in New Zealand.

Kathy Matsui, Managing Director & Chief Japan Strategist, Goldman Sachs, Tokyo, Japan
Kathy is Chief Japan Equity Strategist and Co-Director of Pan Asian Investment Research for Goldman Sachs Ltd Japan. Prior to this she was Chief Japan Strategist for Barclays de Zoete Wedd Securities and Export-Import Bank of Japan in Washington, D.C. Kathy is a board member of the Asian University for Women Support Foundation, a trustee of the American School in Japan, and a member of Keizai Doyukai. Kathy was born in the United States, has lived and worked in Japan, and is fluent in Japanese and German.

Katie Lahey, Managing Director Australasia, Korn Ferry, Sydney, Australia
Katie has been Managing Director Australasia for Korn Ferry International since 2011. Prior to this she was Chief Executive of the State Chamber of Commerce and later Chief Executive of The Business Council of Australia. Katie is a Director of David Jones, Chairman of Carnival Australia and an Ambassador for the Australian Indigenous Education Foundation. In 2003 she was awarded a Centenary Medal and has an MBA from the University of Melbourne.

Katy McDonald, Director of Human Resources, Minter Ellison, Sydney, Australia
Katy has been the National Director of Human Resources at Minter Ellison since 2010. Prior to this she was the Head of Employee Relations Legal at Westpac Banking Corporation and later appointed Head of Employee Relations, Policy and Diversity at the company. Katy was also the Director of Diversity at the University of Sydney. She is Australian-born.

Kerry Jukes, Consultant, Chief Executive Women, Sydney, Australia
Kerry has been a Business Research Consultant for the Chief Executive Women since 2011. Prior to this she was Manager of Human Capital Consulting at Deloitte Australia and Organisational Development Associate at Aequus Partners. She was also the Finance and Human Resources Manager for British Airways and is a Chartered Accountant. Kerry was born in Australia and has lived and worked in the United Kingdom.

Kevin McCann, Chairman, Macquarie Group, Sydney, Australia
Kevin is the Chairman of Macquarie Group, Chairman of Origin Energy Ltd, and a Director of BlueScope Steel Ltd, NSW President and a member of the Board of the Australian Institute of Company Directors. Prior to this he was a Partner and Chairman of Partners at Allens Arthur Robinson, Chairman of Healthscope Ltd and Chairman of ING Management Ltd. He is also a Fellow of the Senate of the University of Sydney and a member of the Order of Australia.

Kim Schmidt, Director People & Culture, Grant Thornton Australia, Sydney, Australia
Kim is the former Director of People and Culture at Grant Thornton Australia and former Director of Human Resources for Woolworths Australia and New Zealand. Prior to this Kim was the National Human Resources Manager at Big W then Human Resources Manager at Woolworths South Africa. Kim is a member of the Chief Executive Women and sits on the Smith Family People & Culture Sub Committee in an advisory capacity. Kim was born in South Africa and now lives and works in Australia.

Laura Wong, General Manager Specialities, Amcor, Sydney, Australia
Laura has been the Regional General Manager NSW and Qld at Amcor Cartons since 2006. Prior to this she was an assistant accountant with the company. She was born in Vietnam and arrived in Australia at age six as a refugee resulting from the Vietnam War. Laura can speak fluent Vietnamese.

Lisa Eccleston, Group General Manager Human Resources, Amcor, Melbourne, Australia
Lisa was appointed Group General Manager of Human Resources for Amcor Australasia in 2008. Prior to this, she was Director of People and Change with Price Waterhouse Coopers, Head of Workforce Planning and Organisation Design with Australia Post, Human Resources Strategy Advisor with National Australia Bank, Human Resources Business Partner with ANZ and Human Resources Manager with Henderson's Automotive. Lisa is Australian-born.

Lucille Halloran, Office Managing Partner, Ernst & Young Global, Canberra, Australia
Lucille has been the Office Managing Partner for Ernst & Young in Canberra since 2010. Prior to this she was a Partner at Deloitte where she was the firm's inaugural Business Woman of the Year in 2004. Lucille has a unique blend of Australian and Canadian public and private sector experience across the education, employment, human services and health sectors. She was born in Canada, speaks fluent French and has lived and worked in Australia.

Lynley Corcoran, General Manager Human Resources Beverage Division, Amcor, Melbourne, Australia
Lynley is the General Manager of Human Resources Beverage Division and has been at Amcor since 2010. Previously she was the Asia Pacific Human Resources Director for Global Business Services at Delphi Automotive. Prior to this she was the Human Resources Manager for General Electric Plastics Australia and New Zealand and also held the role of Senior Human Resources Advisor at BHP Billiton. Lynley is Australia-born.

Lynn Kraus, Managing Partner Sydney, Ernst & Young Global, Sydney, Australia
Lynn has been the Office Managing Partner of Ernst & Young's Sydney office since 2011. Prior to this she was Managing Partner, People for Ernst & Young and a member of the Oceania Advisory Council. She is a US CPA and an affiliate member of the Australian Institute of Chartered Accountants. Lynn is the Chairman of the Ernst & Young's Diversity & Inclusiveness Council and a Council Member and Treasurer of Kidsafe NSW. She was born in the United States and now lives and works in Australia.

Margaret Dreyer, Partner, Deloitte Touche Tohmatsu , Sydney, Australia
Margaret Dreyer is a senior Partner in the Deloitte Sydney practice and has been with the firm since 1986. In addition to these roles, Margaret is a member of the Board of Deloitte Touche Tohmatsu Australia and the Global Steering Committee for Inspiring Women. She was born in South Africa, Margaret speaks Zulu and Afrikaans and now lives and works in Australia.

Marie Malaxos, Chief Operating Officer, Buru Energy, Perth, Australia
Marie is the Chief Operating Officer of Buru Energy Ltd. She is also a Board Member of the Petroleum Club of Western Australia and Ready to Work. Prior to this she served as Chief Operating Officer of Arc Energy Ltd and served on the Board of Fremantle Ports and the Australian Pipeline Industry Association. Marie was born in Australia and has Greek heritage.

Matt Tomaszewski, Director-Writer, Triton Media, Sydney, Australia
Matt is a director, writer and producer for Triton Media. Prior to this he was an international science and remote adventure reporter for National Geographic and Discovery Channels. He has won a number of awards for his work including People's Choice Award 2010 Sydney Film Festival and Inside Film Independent Spirit Award 2010. Matt is Australian-born.

Megan Dalla-Camina, Director of Strategy, IBM Australia and New Zealand, Sydney, Australia
Megan is the Director of Strategy for IBM in Australia and New Zealand, where she is also responsible for Organisational Culture and Change, and Gender Diversity. Prior to this, Megan held international roles at PricewaterhouseCoopers and GE, working across Asia and the United States. Megan holds Masters degrees in both Business Management and Wellness (Positive Psychology). She is the author of the book, *Getting Real About Having It All* (Hay House/Penguin). Megan is Australian-born and has spent time living and working in Hong Kong.

Melinda Smith, Chief Operating Officer – Masters Home Improvement, Woolworths, Sydney, Australia
Melinda is the Chief Operating Officer for Masters Home Improvement at Woolworths. She began her career with Woolworths as a casual deli assistant at the age of 14. Prior to her current position she held various Senior Business Manager roles within Supermarket Buying, Marketing and Logistics.

Mike Smith OBE, Chief Executive Officer, Australian and New Zealand Banking Group, Melbourne, Australia
Mike has been the CEO of ANZ since 2007. Prior to this he was the CEO of Hongkong and Shanghai Banking Corporation, Chairman of Hang Seng Bank, Global Head of Commercial Banking for the HSBC Group and Chairman of HSBC Argentina. He is Chairman of the Australian Bankers' Association; a Member of the Business Council of Australia; and a member of the Asia Business Council. Mike was born in the United Kingdom, speaks fluent Spanish and French and has lived and worked in Argentina, Hong Kong and the Solomon Islands. He now lives and works in Australia.

Natalie Filatoff, Principal, Filatoff Editorial and Writing, Sydney, Australia
Natalie Filatoff is the principal of Filatoff Editorial and Writing and has worked in consumer magazines for the past 30 years. She has written on a broad range of topics, from the arts to health, and has been on the launch teams of several magazines, including award-winning fashion title *In Style* and the women's healthy-lifestyle magazine, *Prevention*. She now works as a freelance journalist, editor and writing coach, with clients such as the *The Global Mail* independent news website, several titles in the Pacific Magazines stable, and the National Prescribing Service. Natalie is Australian-born.

Neil Cockroft, Head of Diversity and Culture, King & Wood Mallesons, Sydney, Australia
Neil is the Head of Diversity and Culture at the law firm King & Wood Mallesons. Prior to this he held roles in Human Resources and Diversity in National Australia Bank worldwide, UBS, Citigroup, Lend Lease and Babcock & Brown. He was born in the United Kingdom and has lived and worked in Germany. He is now living and working in Australia.

Nicola Evans, Deputy Company Secretary, BHP Billiton, Melbourne, Australia
Nicola was appointed the Deputy Company Secretary of BHP Billiton in 2012. Prior to this she was Vice President Human Resources Group Functions, Talent & Organisation Development Manager-Marketing Singapore, and Human Resources Manager Australian Operated Assets.

Nigel Garrard, Managing Director, Amcor, Melbourne, Australia
Nigel has been the Managing Director of Amcor Australasia since 2009 and also had the equivalent role in Amcor's Packaging and Distribution business in the United States and Mexico. Prior to this he was Managing Director of SPC Ardmona and Managing Director of Coca Cola Amatil's Food & Service Division following SPC's acquisition. He is a Chartered Accountant, former Chairman of National Food Industry Strategy Ltd and former Director of Australian Food & Grocery Council and Victorian Relief Foodbank Ltd. Born in Australia, Nigel has also lived and worked in Papua New Guinea and New Zealand.

Partner (Anon), Ernst & Young, China
Contributions were made by a Managing Partner at Ernst & Young's Greater China practice based in Hong Kong who was born in China and speaks fluent Chinese. He has worked in Western countries and shared his views and perspectives adding great insight to the book's knowledge base about Australians working in Asia and vice versa and about adjusting to working across different cultures.

Paul Waterman, President. BP Australia, Melbourne, Australia
Paul is President of BP Australasia and Chairman of the BP group of companies in Australia. Prior to this he was Vice President of Consumer Marketing at Castrol North America, and later Vice President of Castrol Lubricants Aviation, Industrial, Marine and Energy. He is a Board Member of the Australian Institute of Petroleum and holds an MBA in Finance/International Business from the Stern School of Business. Paul was born in the United States and has lived and worked in the United Kingdom. He now lives and works in Australia.

Peter Bailey, Chief Executive Officer, Arup Group, Sydney, Australia
Peter Bailey is the CEO and Chair of Arup in Australasia. A senior member of Arup in Australia since 1985, Peter has worked as a structural engineer and project manager in Sydney, London, New York and Frankfurt. Now based in Sydney, Peter sits on the Arup Group Global Board and has acted as the Australasia Board member responsible for sustainability and diversity, key areas of continual focus and improvement for him and the firm.

Peter Gooding Integration Director, People & Change AMP Sydney Australia
Peter has been the Integration Director, People and Change at AMP since 2011. Prior to this he was Human Resources Director of Financial Services Australia and New Zealand for AMP Ltd, and Director of Human Resources and Operations with AMP Capital Investors. Before that Peter was Head of Education, Training and Organisation Development at Ford Australia where he was also a member of the Human Resources leadership team and the Ford Asia regional L&D team. Peter is Australian-born.

Phil Ruthven, Chairman, IBISWorld, Melbourne, Australia.
Phil Ruthven is the founder and chairman of IBISWorld, Australia, he is also a Director, Open Family Australia, a Director, Institute of Applied Economics & Social Research (Melbourne University), Fellow, Australian Institute of Company Directors and Fellow, Australian Marketing Institute. Phil contributes regularly to radio, TV, newspapers, magazines and documentaries on business, economic and social issues and addresses over 75 congresses, seminars and conferences each year. Before establishing IBISWorld in 1971 he spent over 10 years in the food industry, including executive positions in research, production and marketing.

Philip Iskandar, Engineer, Arup Group, Singapore
Philip has been a Civil Engineer with Arup Group since 2001 and has recently been working in the Hong Kong office on a rail project. He was born in Indonesia and comes from Chinese decent. Philip has lived and worked in Australia, Singapore and Hong Kong and speaks fluent Indonesian.

Philippa Jones, Managing Director, China Policy, Beijing, China
Philippa is Managing Director at China Policy, a Beijing-based research and advisory company. Prior to this she was Senior Advisor at the EU-ChinaTrade Project, Beijing, responsible for EU trade policy issues across a range of sectors. She held an economic post at the Australian Embassy, Beijing from 1999 until 2003. Philippa was born in the UK and speaks fluent Chinese. She first studied in China in 1975 and has again lived and worked there for the past 14 years.

Pradeep Khanna, Executive Director of Integrating Australia with Asia & CEO of GLOBAL MINDSET, Sydney, Australia
Pradeep is Executive Director of Integrating Australia with Asia, CEO of GLOBAL MINDSET, Director at Mindfields Consulting, and Chairman at Royal Star Owners Corporation. Prior to this he was the Australia and New Zealand Global Delivery Leader at IBM Global Business Services. He has also work with Austrade and number of international companies. He has an MBA from the Australian Graduate School of Management, M.Sc in Computer Science from UTS, and a B.Tech from IIT Delhi. Pradeep was born in India and speaks fluent Hindi.

Rachel (Anon), Former Lawyer, Banking and Legal industries, Sydney, Australia
Rachel has worked in Australia's leading law firms and investment banks until 2011 when she moved into the consulting sector. More recently she took on a role as commercial manager in industry. Rachel's true identity will not be revealed as she shares a very personal story in the book. Rachel is a triple-degree qualified lawyer. She is Australian-born and has German heritage.

Rachel Slade, General Manager, Westpac Group, Sydney, Australia
Rachel is the General Manager of Multi-brand & Business Optimisation, Australian Financial Services at the Westpac Group. Prior to this she held a number of positions within Westpac including Head of Group Strategy, General Manager of Mergers & Acquisitions, Head of International Trade and Payments and Head of Diversity and Flexibility for the Westpac Group. Rachel is a graduate of the Australian Institute of Company Directors, a graduate of the Harvard Business School's Women's Leadership Program, and a former executive committee member of Women in Banking and Finance. Rachel is currently the Treasurer of the Global Banking Alliance for Women and a non-executive director of Australian Network on Disability. She is Australian-born.

Richard Mazzochi, Partner, King & Wood Mallesons, Hong Kong, China
Richard is a Partner in King & Wood Mallesons and leads the Banking and Finance practice in Hong Kong. He has extensive experience in capital markets financing in the European, American and Asian markets; securitisation, repackagings and other structured finance; structured products; derivatives; and market regulation. Richard is Australian-born and has lived and worked in the United Kingdom, Singapore and Hong Kong.

Richard Padfield, Electrical Engineer, Arup Group, Ho Chi Minh, Vietnam
Richard is an Electrical Engineer with Arup Group based in Vietnam. Prior to this he was a Commissioning and Support Engineer at Siemens and at Satchwell Control Systems. Richard was born in the United Kingdom and has lived and worked in China, Australia, the United Arab Emirates and Vietnam.

Rob McLeod, Chief Executive Officer, Ernst & Young Global, Sydney, Australia
Rob has been Ernst & Young's Oceania Managing Partner and CEO since 2010. Prior to this he was the New Zealand Country Managing Partner, Chairman of the New Zealand Business Roundtable, and appointed to the government-sponsored Tax Working Group and the Capital Markets Development Taskforce. He also chaired the NZ Institute of Chartered Accountants Tax Committee and was Chairman of the Government's Tax Review 2001. Rob was born in New Zealand.

Dr Robert Care AM, Chair UK, Middle East and Africa Region, Arup Group, London, United Kingdom
Robert is the Chair of Arup's UK, Middle East and African Regions. He is a Visiting Fellow at the School of Civil and Environmental Engineering at UNSW; Fellow of Engineers Australia; Fellow of the Australian Academy of Technological Sciences & Engineering; Associate Fellow of the Australian Institute of Management and formerly Chair of RedR Australia. Robert is Australian-born and has lived and worked in Australia, the United Kingdom, Hong Kong, Papua New Guinea and Japan.

Robert Milliner, Former Chief Executive Partner, Mallesons Stephen Jaques (now King & Wood Mallesons), Sydney, Australia
Robert was the Chief Executive Partner at Mallesons Stephen Jaques until 2011. Robert is director of Asialink, a member of the International Legal Services Advisory Council, Deputy Chairman of the firm's 'Mallesons in the Community' Board and a director of Australian Business and Community Network and the Australian Charities Fund. Prior to this Robert was Managing Partner, International for Mallesons based in Hong Kong. He is Australian-born and has lived and worked in Hong Kong.

Robert Orth, Director Human Resources ANZ, IBM Australia, Sydney, Australia
Robert has been the Director of Human Resources at IBM Australia and New Zealand since 2002. Prior to this he was the Director of Talent for IBM Asia Pacific and a serving officer

(Flight Lieutenant) in the Royal Australian Air Force. He is a Fellow of the Australian Human Resources Institute, and on the Boards of IBM Australia Ltd, Diversity Council Australia and The Leadership Consortium. Robert is Australian-born.

Rosemary Howard, Executive Director AGSM Executive Programs, Australian School of Business, UNSW, Sydney, Australia

Rosemary is the Executive Director and Conjoint Professor of the AGSM Executive Program at the Australian School of Business, UNSW. Prior to this she was CEO at TelstraClear, the inaugural Managing Director Telstra Wholesale, and Executive Director for the NSW Department of State Government. In 2003, she was awarded an Australian Government Centenary Medal for 'Service to Australian Society in Business Leadership'. Rosemary was born in the United Kingdom and has lived and worked in Australia, the United States and New Zealand.

Russell Tipper, Chief Executive Officer, Brockman Resources, Perth, Australia

Russell was appointed the CEO of Brockman Resources in 2012. Prior to this he was the General Manager of Iron Ore for Aquila and Group Treasurer for North Ltd. A mining engineer, Russell has worked in senior management and operational roles for both Robe River and BHPB. Russell is currently on the Board of Directors for Asenjo Energy and has an MBA from the University of Melbourne.

Ruth Medd, Chair, Women on Boards, Sydney, Australia

Ruth is the Executive Chairman of Women on Boards, Past President of the National Foundation for Australian Women Ltd, and Independent Chairman of the Australian Ethical Investments Superannuation Ltd. Prior to this she was Executive Director at the Association of National Advertisers, General Manager of Australian Broadcasting Tribunal and Director of the NSW Casino Control Authority and Infants Home Ashfield. Ruth has inspired and supported many hundreds of women to achieve and succeed at taking board roles from ASX-listed companies through to community organisations. This contributed to her being named as a Top 100 Women of Influence in the Australian Financial Review and Westpac awards in 2012. Ruth was born in the United Kingdom and now lives and works in Australia.

Sally Wong, Structural Engineer, Arup Group, Hong Kong, China

Sally Wong studied at the University of Western Australia and graduated in 2009 with a BE (Honours) and Commerce, majoring in civil engineering, investment finance, and corporate finance. Upon graduation, Sally started a full-time structural engineer position in the Arup Perth office. She was predominantly involved in energy-related infrastructure projects. In 2011, Sally transferred to Hong Kong on a two-year assignment and is currently enjoying working on the conservation and revitalisation of heritage buildings in Hong Kong.

Shirley In't Veld, Non-Executive Director, Asciano, Perth, Australia

Shirley was the CEO of Verve Energy until 2012. Prior to this she was the Vice President of Primary Business Development with Alcoa and the Managing Director of Alcoa Australia Rolled Products. She is an Independent Non-Executive Director of Asciano Ltd and Board Member with the Co-operative Research Centre for Landscape Evolution in Mineral Exploration (CSIRO) and the Association of Mining and Exploration Companies in WA (AMEC). Shirley is Chairperson of the Sustainability Committee of Asciano, and is a Council member of the Australian Institute of Company Directors (WA). She began her career as a commercial lawyer with King & Wood Mallesons. Shirley was born in New Zealand and lives and works in Australia.

Sid Myer AM, Chairman, Myer Family Company, Melbourne, Australia
Sid is Director of The Myer Family Company Holdings and Chairman of Asialink and Asia Society AustralAsia Centre. He is also the CEO of the Yulgibar Group of Companies and Director of OC Funds Management. Sid is a Trustee of the Sidney Myer Fund and Chairman of the Beyond Australia Taskforce. He was appointed a Member of the Order of Australia in 2011. Sid is Australian-born and has lived and worked in the United Sates, Malaysia and Switzerland.

Stephen Roberts, Chief Country Officer, Citi, Sydney, Australia
Stephen is the CEO and Chief Country Officer of Citi in Australia and New Zealand and Citi Country Officer, Australia. Prior to this he was head of Citi's Asia Pacific Markets business in Hong Kong, Director of European Capital Markets for Salomon Brothers and Regional Head of Capital Markets for Lehman Brothers. Stephen is a member of the US Studies Centre Council of Advisors and is the Deputy Chairman of the Australian Bankers Association. He is Australian-born and has lived and worked in the United States, United Kingdom and Hong Kong.

Tristan Landers, Executive General Manager, Corporate Sustainability, Commonwealth Bank of Australia, Sydney, Australia
Tristan is the Executive General Manager of Corporate Sustainability for the Commonwealth Bank of Australia. She is a Director of The Humour Foundation, an Ambassador for the Australian Indigenous Education Foundation, and Director at YWCA NSW. Prior to this she was the General Manager of Culture, Group Strategy at Commonwealth Bank of Australia and a Management Consultant at KPMG. Tristan is Australian-born.

Uschi Schreiber, Managing Partner Global Government & Public Sector Industry Centre, Ernst & Young Global, Hong Kong, Australia
Uschi is the Deputy CEO of Ernst & Young's Oceania branch and the leader of the company's Government and Public Sector practice across Asia Pacific. Prior to this she held a number of positions such as Director-General and Deputy Director General of significant Government departments in Australia. Uschi was born in Germany, speaks fluent German, and lives and works in Australia.

References

Growth and Asia

ASIALINK 'Developing an Asia Capable Workforce' report September 2012
http://www.asialink.unimelb.edu.au/our_work/business/asialink_taskforce

Australian Government 'Australia in the Asian Century White Paper' October 2012
http://asiancentury.dpmc.gov.au/white-paper

China versus USA GDP projections
http://www.economist.com/blogs/dailychart/2010/12/save_date

Gender Diversity

Goldman Sachs JBWere Australia's Hidden Resource report
http://www.asxgroup.com.au/media/PDFs/gsjbw_economic_case_for_increasing_female_participation.pdf

2012 Australian Census 'Women in Leadership' report
http://www.eowa.gov.au/Information_Centres/Resource_Centre/EOWA_Publications/EOWA_Census.asp

Women on Boards *Board Director Index* (percentage of women on Australian Boards)
http://www.womenonboards.org.au/pubs/bdi/2012/index.htm

Women on Boards shares Norwegian story told by Arni Hole
http://www.womenonboards.org.au/pubs/articles/norway.htm

World Economic Forum *Global Gender Gap Report* (participation level of Australian women at work relative to 135 other countries)
http://reports.weforum.org/global-gender-gap-2011/

Culture Diversity

Diversity Council of Australia (diversity resources, advice and tools)
http://www.dca.org.au/

The Australian Multicultural Council (launched August 2011)
http://www.amc.gov.au/index.htm

The British Council's English Next report, 2006 (why English-speaking children should learn Chinese)
http://www.britishcouncil.org/learning-research-englishnext.htm

Geert Hofstede's National Cultural Dimensions
http://geert-hofstede.com/australia.html

Everett Rogers Diffusion of Innovation
http://www.stanford.edu/class/symbsys205/Diffusion%20of%20Innovations.htm

Understanding Behaviour

Byrne, Eric. (1964), *Games People Play*, New York: Ballantine Books

Index

Pamela Young

Globally experienced executive and consultant:
Visionary and strategic thinker, business driver and change agent, leader and motivator

Pamela has an extensive global career in both consulting and executive management.

She has lived and worked in many cultures including Australia, New Zealand, Singapore, the UK, continental Europe and the USA. Her cross-cultural and international experience with global businesses adds richness to her insights and vision for the future of business and society.

She generously shares her experience with people wanting to become inspirational leaders and change agents. She is passionate about helping others to improve their organisations and lives to achieve business growth and personal development as well as delivering diversity.

Pamela was the founder and Managing Director of Cording Young Ltd consultancy in New Zealand delivering strategy and change consultancy to clients in New Zealand, Australia and Singapore. Following this she was Executive Director for a Singapore-based law firm, Shook Lin and Bok, then joined Kinsley Lord Towers Perrin in London, England, a specialist strategy and organisation change consultancy as a member of the executive team. After returning to Australia she established Growthcurv Pty Ltd to consult on discrete transformation projects, provide strategy and change advisory services and deliver board, CEO and top-team mentoring and coaching.

While in London she worked across Europe with leading global institutions including Barclays Bank, Lloyds Bank, Prudential Bache, Winterthur Life, Zurich Financial Services, KPMG Europe and Freshfield Bruckhaus Derringer. She has also worked down-under with Fletcher Challenge, Sun Alliance, Macquarie Bank, AGSM, Fairfax Media, ACP Magazines, Russell McVeagh, Mallesons Stephen Jaques, Beca Group, Coffey International and PriceWaterhouse. Pamela also has extensive experience working with a range of government organisations including health, medical, education and research sectors, plus a wide range of SMEs.

Pamela is an enthusiastic life-long learner, who keeps actively involved in the community and is interested in contributing to making the world a better place.